New Research in Children with Neurodevelopmental Disorders

New Research in Children with Neurodevelopmental Disorders

Editor

Dulce María Romero-Ayuso

MDPI • Basel • Beijing • Wuhan • Barcelona • Belgrade • Manchester • Tokyo • Cluj • Tianjin

Editor
Dulce María Romero-Ayuso
Physical Therapy
Occupational Therapy
Division
University of Granada
Granada
Spain

Editorial Office
MDPI
St. Alban-Anlage 66
4052 Basel, Switzerland

This is a reprint of articles from the Special Issue published online in the open access journal *Children* (ISSN 2227-9067) (available at: www.mdpi.com/journal/children/special_issues/New_Research_in_Children_with_Neurodevelopmental_Disorders).

For citation purposes, cite each article independently as indicated on the article page online and as indicated below:

LastName, A.A.; LastName, B.B.; LastName, C.C. Article Title. *Journal Name* **Year**, *Volume Number*, Page Range.

ISBN 978-3-0365-4392-5 (Hbk)
ISBN 978-3-0365-4391-8 (PDF)

Contents

About the Editor

Dulce María Romero-Ayuso

Dulce Romero Ayuso completed her doctoral thesis for her PhD degree on neuropsychological and neuromagnetic profiles in children with ADHD. She received the Extraordinary Doctorate Award from the Faculty of Psychology at the Complutense University of Madrid. She has been intensely active in research on neurodevelopmental disorders. She is a researcher and member of the Cognitive Neuroscience Group of the Brain, Mind and Behavior Research Center (CIMCYC) at the University of Granada. She has recently joined the Granada Ibs Research Group TECe2'-Rehabilita-T.

Among her lines of research is the study of cognitive processes that underlie the performance of activities of daily living, occupational therapy and the application of new high- and low-cost technologies for evaluation and neurorehabilitation in childhood. She has directed different research projects, mainly focused on attention-deficit/hyperactivity disorders. She is currently the coordinator of the Degree in Occupational Therapy and is the Director of the Master's Degree in Occupational Therapy in Functional Diversity in Childhood at the University of Granada.

children

MDPI

Editorial

Future Challenges in Research in Children with Neurodevelopmental Disorders

Dulce Romero-Ayuso

Department of Physical Therapy, Occupational Therapy Division, Faculty of Health Sciences, University of Granada, 18016 Granada, Spain; dulceromero@ugr.es

The prevalence of neurodevelopmental disorders exceeds 15% worldwide, and often they are associated with other neurological disorders [1]. Neurodevelopmental disorders are characterized by showing different patterns in the acquisition of motor, cognitive, linguistic and socio-emotional skills, which affect the functioning in the different contexts relevant to children. They are, therefore, a relevant topic for clinicians engaged in evaluation and intervention in children. The aims of this Special Issue are to present new approaches and results on evaluation and intervention, emphasizing the importance of the full active participation of the child in the different environments, personal, family and/or academic, that are part of their daily life. In this way, the studies included in this monograph allow us to cross the barrier of the clinical context, changing the focus of evaluation and intervention to other spaces where the main significant activities of children occur, such as play, educational learning, activities of daily life and self-care, rest and social participation. A section has also been dedicated to studies that provide more evidence on new therapies, such as the use of hypnotherapy or virtual reality systems.

Several evaluation tools are presented in this Special Issue. The first of them is a new tool developed from Angel Riviére's autism spectrum inventory [2] of these children, including the response to sensory stimuli [3]. According to the last diagnostic classification of DSM-5, the importance of sensorial hypersensitivity in autism spectrum disorder [4], which may result from a sensory processing disorder, has been recognized [5]. The second tool is a cross-cultural adaptation to the Spanish population of an instrument called My Child's Play [6] that allows the evaluation of the play of children between 3 and 9 years old. This instrument, through the play, provides a cut score that helps to differentiate children with typical development and with neurodevelopmental disorders [7]. Additionally, this study enabled us to determine what factors of the play can be weaknesses or strengths: cognitive flexibility and executive attention, communication and social interaction, the preferences and characteristics of the play or the opportunities of the context. On the other hand, Sewani and Kashef [8] show an innovative proposal with a study that allows us to approach the diagnosis of autism spectrum disorders using a machine encoder based on the learning of neural networks. Finally, within the evaluation tools, a new approach is presented with the aim to develop children's understanding of death, through the EsCoMu scale [9]. This instrument is an important contribution given the lack of research that addresses bereavement in the child. The authors provide a useful tool, with good psychometric properties and four factors underlying children's understanding of death: universality, irreversibility, nonfunctionality and causality.

Regarding interventions, the effects of low-intensity modified Constraint-Induced Movement Therapy on upper limb functionality in eight children with hemiplegia aged 4–8 years are presented. The results of this study show an increase in the spontaneous use of the affected upper limb in bimanual tasks and dissociated and propensity movements [10]. Likewise, the study of Riquelme, Sabater-Gárriz and Montoya [11] delves into the impact on the family of chronic pain in children with cerebral palsy (CP) and its relationship to the quality of life of these children and their ability to communicate. This volume also

Citation: Romero-Ayuso, D. Future Challenges in Research in Children with Neurodevelopmental Disorders. *Children* **2021**, *8*, 328. https://doi.org/10.3390/children8050328

Received: 20 March 2021
Accepted: 22 April 2021
Published: 23 April 2021

addresses the effectiveness of two types of emerging therapies: hypnotherapy in children with CP [12] and the use of virtual reality in children with attention-deficit hyperactivity disorder (ADHD) [13]. Both studies allow us to advance the available evidence. Thus, it is concluded that hypnotherapy, for 8–12 weeks, stimulates proprioceptive and balance reactions, reducing muscle spasticity, through rhythmic and symmetrical movement, leading to an improvement in the gross motor function in children with CP, such as lying down, roll, sitting and walking [12]. The meta-analysis of Virtual Reality-Based Interventions for Children and Adolescents with ADHD highlights the need to design randomized controlled trials with virtual reality and concludes that virtual reality may be effective in improving performance in sustained attention tasks in children with ADHD [13].

Three studies address the impact of neurodevelopmental disorders on personal, educational and social functioning. In the first of these, Blanco-Martínez et al. [14] present a cross-sectional study on participation in different everyday contexts, finding differences between children with and without neurodevelopmental disorders and their possible impact on daily life. Among the significant activities in children between the age of 6 and 12 are school activities. In this way, Maciver et al. [15] approach Scotland's experience in developing strategies and models that promote the participation and inclusion of children with support needs at schools, through the involvement and training of teachers, in order to reduce inequalities. The proposed model, CIRCLE, incorporates the concepts of the model of human occupation, with the aim to broaden our perspective beyond deficits, including the strengths, motivation, routines of the child in a comfortable, flexible school, able to innovate, that train teachers, professionals and include families. Likewise, the concern about the care of children with autism at school is also reflected in the study of Taresh et al. [16] conducted in Yemen.

We hope the studies presented in this Special Issue will be useful and of value to the different professionals and researchers in the fields of occupational therapy, physiotherapy, psychology and education and, above all, to help improve the opportunities in the everyday contexts of children with neurodevelopmental disorders. Research along with clinical experience and clinical reasoning will enable the development of practices based on the best available evidence. Additionally, we hope that this volume serves its intended purpose: an advance in two of the challenges of the H2031 Strategy and the 2030 agenda for sustainable development, related to Goal 3 "Good health and well-being" and Goal 10 referring to "reducing inequalities": (1) promoting the dissemination of research on factors that can provide safe, nonviolent, inclusive, and effective learning environments for all and (2) presenting interventions that reduce inequality to enhance or promote social inclusion and the improvement of the self-regulation processes of children with neurodevelopmental disorders. The challenges of the future are stimulating, and we want this Special Issue to be an initial approach to continue advancing and creating the best opportunities for the development, health and well-being of all children.

Funding: This research received no external funding.

Conflicts of Interest: The author declares no conflict of interest.

References

1. Fejerman, N.; Grañana, N. *Neuropsicología Infantil*; Buenos Aires: Paidós, Mexico, 2017.
2. Riviere, A. Tratamiento y definición del epectro autista. In *El tratamiento del autismo. Nuevas, Perspectivas*; Rivière, A., Martos, J., Eds.; Ministerio de Trabajo y Asuntos Sociales-IMSERSO: Madrid, Spain, 1997.
3. Barrios-Fernández, S.; Gozalo, M.; Díaz-González, B.; García-Gómez, A. A Complementary Sensory Tool for Children with Autism Spectrum Disorders. *Children* **2020**, *7*, 244. [CrossRef] [PubMed]
4. American Psychiatric Association. *Diagnostic and Statistical Manual of Mental Disorders*, 5th ed.; American Psychiatric Publishing: Washington, DC, USA, 2014.
5. Miller, L.J.; Anzalone, M.E.; Lane, S.J.; Cermak, S.A.; Osten, E.T. Concept Evolution in Sensory Integration: A Proposed Nosology for Diagnosis. *Am. J. Occup. Ther.* **2007**, *61*, 135–140. [CrossRef] [PubMed]
6. Schneider, E.; Rosenblum, S. Development, Reliability, and Validity of the My Child's Play (MCP) Questionnaire. *Am. J. Occup. Ther.* **2014**, *68*, 277–285. [CrossRef] [PubMed]

7. Romero-Ayuso, D.; Ruiz-Salcedo, M.; Barrios-Fernández, S.; Triviño-Juárez, J.M.; Maciver, D.; Richmond, J.; Muñoz, M.A. Play in Children with Neurodevelopmental Disorders: Psychometric Properties of a Parent Report Measure 'My Child's Play'. *Children* **2021**, *8*, 25. [CrossRef] [PubMed]
8. Sewani, H.; Kashef, R. An Autoencoder-Based Deep Learning Classifier for Efficient Diagnosis of Autism. *Children* **2020**, *7*, 182. [CrossRef] [PubMed]
9. Fernández-Alcántara, M.; Santos-Roig, M.D.L.; Pérez-Marfil, M.; Cruz-Quintana, F.; Vázquez-Sánchez, J.; Montoya-Juárez, R. A New Instrument to Assess Children's Understanding of Death: Psychometrical Properties of the EsCoMu Scale in a Sample of Spanish Children. *Children* **2021**, *8*, 125. [CrossRef]
10. Palomo-Carrión, R.; Romero-Galisteo, R.-P.; Pinero-Pinto, E.; López-Muñoz, P.; Romay-Barrero, H.; José, F.G.-M.S. Application of Low-Intensity Modified Constraint-Induced Movement Therapy to Improve the Affected Upper Limb Functionality in Infantile Hemiplegia with Moderate Manual Ability: Case Series. *Children* **2020**, *7*, 127. [CrossRef]
11. Riquelme, I.; Sabater-Gárriz, Á.; Montoya, P. Pain and Communication in Children with Cerebral Palsy: Influence on Parents' Perception of Family Impact and Healthcare Satisfaction. *Children* **2021**, *8*, 87. [CrossRef]
12. De Guindos-Sanchez, L.; Lucena-Anton, D.; Moral-Munoz, J.A.; Salazar, A.; Carmona-Barrientos, I. The Effectiveness of Hippotherapy to Recover Gross Motor Function in Children with Cerebral Palsy: A Systematic Review and Meta-Analysis. *Children* **2020**, *7*, 106. [CrossRef]
13. Romero-Ayuso, D.; Toledano-González, A.; Rodríguez-Martínez, M.; Arroyo-Castillo, P.; Triviño-Juárez, J.; González, P.; Ariza-Vega, P.; González, A.; Segura-Fragoso, A. Effectiveness of Virtual Reality-Based Interventions for Children and Adolescents with ADHD: A Systematic Review and Meta-Analysis. *Children* **2021**, *8*, 70. [CrossRef] [PubMed]
14. Blanco-Martínez, N.; Delgado-Lobete, L.; Montes-Montes, R.; Ruiz-Pérez, N.; Ruiz-Pérez, M.; Santos-Del-Riego, S. Participation in Everyday Activities of Children with and without Neurodevelopmental Disorders: A Cross-Sectional Study in Spain. *Children* **2020**, *7*, 157. [CrossRef] [PubMed]
15. Maciver, D.; Hunter, C.; Johnston, L.; Forsyth, K. Using Stakeholder Involvement, Expert Knowledge and Naturalistic Implementation to Co-Design a Complex Intervention to Support Children's Inclusion and Participation in Schools: The CIRCLE Framework. *Children* **2021**, *8*, 217. [CrossRef] [PubMed]
16. Taresh, S.M.; Ahmad, N.A.; Roslan, S.; Ma'Rof, A.M. Preschool Teachers' Beliefs towards Children with Autism Spectrum Disorder (ASD) in Yemen. *Children* **2020**, *7*, 170. [CrossRef] [PubMed]

children

MDPI

Article

Preschool Teachers' Beliefs towards Children with Autism Spectrum Disorder (ASD) in Yemen

Sahar Mohammed Taresh [1,2], Nor Aniza Ahmad [1,*], Samsilah Roslan [1] and Aini Marina Ma'rof [1]

1 Department of Foundation of Education, Faculty of Educational Studies, Universiti Putra Malaysia (UPM), Serdang 43400, Malaysia; sahartaresh30@gmail.com (S.M.T.); samsilah@upm.edu.my (S.R.); ainimarina@upm.edu.my (A.M.M.)

2 Department of Kindergarten, Faculty of Education, Taiz University, Taiz, Yemen

* Correspondence: nor_aniza@upm.edu.my

Received: 6 July 2020; Accepted: 8 September 2020; Published: 6 October 2020

check for updates

Abstract: It is perplexing that some preschool teachers not only advise parents who have children with autism spectrum disorder (ASD) to go to religious healers, but also attribute such neurological disorders to The curse of The "evil eye" or vaccines. Although it is now The twentieth century, this behavior simply reflects The concerns of over-protective teachers and The cultural misperceptions about The actual definition of ASD. In Yemen, The term "ASD", with its wide range of symptoms, is still ambiguous among preschool teachers. Thus, in a rather insightful piece for The education community, this study has attempted to look beneath The surface of The beliefs (religious belief–social belief–personal belief) of Yemeni preschool teachers regarding ASD. Based on The data collected from 213 teachers (20–30\31–40-~≥40 age) in The Taiz district, this study found that misconceptions specific to autism spectrum disorder were strongly evidenced among teachers who taught preschoolers. Due to personal ignorance and growing superstitions, these teachers tend to believe The society's perceptions of ASD, thus resulting in The ignorance of scientific views. However, The mass media can increase this group's awareness of ASD by continually assessing The inaccurate views on ASD, and correcting them. And by influencing The teachers to take a more conceptual scientific approach in serving their special needs students, furthermore, by informing preschool teachers of children's rights in normal life in The future through providing children with an optimal chance of development by early intervention.

Keywords: autism spectrum disorder (ASD); preschool teachers; religious belief; social beliefs; personal beliefs; Yemen

1. Introduction

The Republic of Yemen's decision in 1991 was The first legislation for The care and rehabilitation of children with disabilities in Yemen. In 1999, The Higher Committee for The Care of Handicapped Rehabilitation was established, which launched The Handicapped Care and Rehabilitation Fund. Unfortunately, The Handicapped Care and Rehabilitation Fund considered autism spectrum disorder (ASD) as one of The disability categories. In their strategy for The years 2004–2018, The first goal was to change society's view towards children with disabilities by raising The level of awareness of their rights and capabilities. During that period, Yemen was rapidly improving towards urbanization, while suffering a deteriorating economy. According to The United Nations Human Development Report ranked in 2007, Yemen was estimated to be one of The poorest countries in The world. Specifically, it was rated number 140 out of 182 (United Nations Development Program-Human Development Report 2009). Low admission to education became an essential poverty-related issue in Yemen. According to The World Bank, 87% of The poor in Yemen are illiterate or have not completed primary school. All of this was reflected in The individuals' beliefs and attitudes towards children with disabilities in general and children with developmental disorders, as is The case with children with ASD. Thus, these beliefs can be used to explain any strange phenomenon, including ASD. Due to a lack of visible symptoms in children with ASD, many may attribute ASD with stigma and misconception. For example, uninformed people may perceive a child with ASD to be someone who looks "normal" but acts voluntarily in ways that violate social norms [1,2]. In a longitudinal study of families with children diagnosed with autism, it was confirmed that autism spectrum disorder is often characterized by pervasive impairments in social interactions, communication skills, and restricted patterns of behaviors and interests [1]. The severity of The symptoms varied significantly; children with ASD often have intellectual abilities within normal borders [3]. Despite their ordinary intelligent abilities, preschoolers with ASD show a prorate weakness in language, social skills, and executive performance, thereby making it tough for them to learn and to forge relationships with their peers. Consequently, these limited capabilities contribute to an increased misunderstanding regarding this disorder, and such misunderstanding is associated with different positive and negative beliefs [4,5].

In recent years, families and communities have been reported to be The primary cause of ASD misunderstanding [6]. Armstrong and Fitzgerald [5] also confirmed that different cultures often use explanations and observations with significant differences in descriptions and classifications to describe The disability. To depict cultural differences, The Multicultural Disability Advocacy Association (MDAA) of NSW, Australia, suggested that while The disability is often explained as a medical concept in Western cultures, other cultures view it as a punishment or gift from a higher power [7].

The above perceptions strongly affect The behavior of disabled children as well as their guardians [8]. Considering The misconception that The disability is related to specific actions, there is a high risk that families and communities deny children diagnosed with autism their rights to receive adequate help [6]. When explanations for The disability are placed outside appropriate interventions, there is also a high risk that The incapacity of The disabled children will be kept private [9].

Previous studies have found that knowledge of ASD is associated with a lower rate of stigma [10–12]. However, this is not always The case because most ASD information that The public receives comes from The media, which is made up of stereotypical beliefs or convictions that people see as truth [13]. However, these beliefs are not backed by sufficient proof [14]. There are many beliefs about autism spectrum disorder that originate from extreme superstition and cultural views. Hence, several investigations have been carried out to get an in-depth explanation regarding The root of The problem. The results of such investigations point toward a pattern of negative opinions towards autism spectrum disorder, whether as a punishment for The family's previous sins, The mother's negligence, or The work of wicked ghosts [15,16]. Similar to an investigation into South Korean society, The psychiatrists were more likely to deduce that "bad" mothers and pregnant mothers who were depressed and introverted caused their child to become autistic [17]. On The other hand, another study determined how five Muslim parents who had children diagnosed with autism interpreted their religious beliefs to empower them to seek an understanding of their children's special needs [18]. Other published studies support The above works, proving that The beliefs that The family is at fault for causing a children's mental disorder are extremely spiritual and religious [10].

The effect of spirituality is amazingly profound among some believing families. Parents or guardians were able to self-heal by accepting that Allah, The Creator of The Universe, had chosen them to be The caretakers of children diagnosed with autism due to their piety, diligence, nobility, and capacity to support. This notion of Allah's involvement does play a role in enabling The affected families to reach a more profound acceptance of family members with disabilities. In other words, a child with ASD brings them closer to their religion and The Creator. It was also found that Pakistani and Bangladeshi Muslim believers learned that not only did Allah put an autistic child in their care as a result of destiny, but also because Allah wished to test their family and to see if they would continue to be excellent or unkind to The child. Beyond this, however, it seems that teachers, in general, are still plagued by misconceptions. For instance, one previous study on various cultural groups examined The role of culture in influencing teachers' beliefs within an ecological framework—discussing The nature and causes of childhood disability and The teachers' ideas about treatment. Another study revealed that The teachers held both biomedical and socio-cultural views that reflect duality in their beliefs [19]. The view of both parents and teachers is a relevant factor in The above relationship. With their consent, some researchers sought to determine The cognitive, emotional, and developmental characteristics of children with The disorder by assessing The parents' and teachers' beliefs and knowledge about specific areas of The disorder. The views of The parents and teachers were not interrelated nor accurate, which made cooperation between The two parties difficult [20].

People with less experience and knowledge of ASD often hold inaccurate beliefs about The disorder [21]. Based on The discussion above, a lack of knowledge regarding autism spectrum disorder creates a wide avenue for social stigma, which means that children diagnosed with autism and their families may be more stigmatized than other children with disabilities. In a study in which adults and teens with ASD were asked about their challenges, The respondents reported feelings of being evaluated and rejected by their families and friends. Some even stated that they were victims of bullying at social events [22]. Besides, another study evaluated The knowledge of 15 early childhood preservation teachers about ASD adaptation as an entry questionnaire to autism spectrum disorder. Of The 15 elements with true/false reaction options, The results illustrated that pre-service child teachers did not know The subject matter.

Furthermore, they had some misunderstanding about ASD etiology and The behaviors of children with ASD. Regarding etiology, it was found that 93% of preschool teachers did not identify ASD as a developmental disorder, while 60% of them believed that The children could "overcome" their situation. Only 53.3% of them recognized The genetic contribution to The disorder, and 20% of them wrongly indicated The effect of trauma as a cause for The visible behaviors of ASD.

Moreover, 73.3% of pre-service teachers thought that behavioral treatment was not an effective intervention, and 66.7% of them affirmed that children with ASD were entirely similar to others. The results also indicated that 46.7% of them did not identify with The justification for early interventions to help children with ASD, and 26.7% of The participants considered it an erroneous behavioral intervention for a child with ASD. This finding is similar to The results of Barned et al. [23], which indicated that The pre-service preparation for ASD in preschool is inadequate [24].

Another noteworthy study reviewed The beliefs regarding ASD among The general public, including teachers in The United States and Canada (n = 823), as well as people dealing with childcare services in The State of Idaho. The results showed that nearly all participants properly understood The genetic and neurological cause of ASD (not parenting, drugs, or a recent diet) that can be recognized early on in a child's life for prompt intervention. The study also emphasized The correct community knowledge of ASD to facilitate early identification and effective intervention. The results suggest professional development courses for childcare providers as well as effective channels for transmitting accurate information such as broadcast and online media from which The general public, especially followers of ethnic minority groups, are most likely to learn about ASD [25].

Theoretically, through The health belief model (HBM), it can explain The preschool teacher's beliefs based on this theory, as this theory describes health-related behaviors and medical decision-making. The HBM was developed initially in The 1950s to explain why people did not participate in preventive disease programs [26,27]. Preschool teachers' beliefs can be a barrier to healthy behavior toward their children, and preschool teachers' belief in their actions can protect their children in The class and estimate when to take action [28].

Interestingly, this data presented a whole collection of findings that differed from those reported in The Eastern world, specifically The Arab world. Hence, it is critical to correct such misunderstanding and stigma surrounding ASD, mostly in countries where ASD services are scarce. ASD in Arab countries such as Yemen has received relatively little attention from The research community so far.

Preschool teachers' judgments of The perceived barriers and The perceived benefits of action define The course of action taken; these two components together form The dimension outcome expectations [28]. This includes preschool teachers' "perceived costs involved in seeking a diagnosis (e.g., time, don't have evidence, social stigma, how to voice their concern to parents, not knowing who to contact, refuse The parents, etc.).

A current analysis of ASD research in Arab countries revealed a total of 75 articles being published between 1992 and 2012 [29]. In contrast, The United States has been producing international ASD research articles for years, including 1040 publications in 2010 alone [30]. Thus, there is an urgent need for further research, as in The case of The current study, to assess teachers' beliefs about ASD in Yemen.

1.1. Religious Belief

Beliefs and behavioral health are rooted in religion and spirituality. Many religious and spiritual traditions observed in cultures around The world are associated with health practices [31]. Aside from having a profound influence on The views of health and diseases in many cultures, these two elements can also have implications for The field of health communication [32]. In essence, religion affects various social, cultural, and personal aspects, such as traditional norms, values, and customs [33]. Consequently, traditional cultural perspectives inevitably influence ASD treatment recommendations. One important aspect to consider when discussing ASD from a cultural perspective is that there could be many weird explanations. While ASD is clearly defined by its visible features in all cultures, The systems of cultural and religious belief vary drastically and, therefore, create a different experience of illness with different religious perspectives.

Among Muslim families, it is generally recognized that Allah puts an autistic child under their care not only because of fate or reincarnation, but also because Allah wants to test that particular family to see if they can care for The child. This concept, quite simply, prohibits any inhumane treatment or immoral behavior towards children with ASD [10]. Some families, on The other hand, embrace The child's disabilities as qadar/kismat (fate) [34], a situation which is similar to that reported by other Muslim families in other studies, especially because religious considerations have long been taken at The family level. For example, Muslim mothers in Turkey mentioned Allah, fate, spells, and evil spirits as The causes for having disabled children, while strong traditional beliefs exist concerning The possibility of a child's restoration, which in turn determines their actions relating to help or treatment [35]. In a small part of The Indian subcontinent, various cultural and ritual superstitions surround The disabled. Some Punjabi Muslims believe that treating people who are either called defective or crazy, will ensure their direct admission to heaven when they die. Some also blame evil crimes for The health deterioration of children [4].

Besides, Pakistani and Bangladeshi Muslims believe that Allah wants The parents of children diagnosed with autism to play a pivotal role in improving their children's life skills through various forms of therapy. The Muslim community here trusts that a suitable therapy is one that improves both The health and The soul [36]. However, some traditional families become angry at The Western point of view on ASD treatments and exclude their children diagnosed with autism from a proper diagnosis [10]. For instance, parents would refuse to work with certified professionals, focusing on The child's weaknesses instead of highlighting The child's potential [10]. This calls for a form of willingness to find religious healers who ignore The negative side and focus on The positive side of ASD instead [10]. As part of their spiritual belief system [4], Pakistani and Bangladeshi Muslims have also resorted to prayers and pilgrimage to seek guidance in helping their children diagnosed with autism reach their maximum potential and mission in life [17].

Religious implications on beliefs concerning children with developmental problems are not only limited to Muslims believers [10] but also include other religious groups. As reported in a previous study, 55% of Latina mothers believe that their autistic child is a sign of Allah's existence [37], while other Latina mothers believe them to be blessings or gifts from Allah that would give them The chance to do good and to surrender parts of their lives to serve others [38]. Furthermore, it was found that

Latin Americans have The option of opting for non-traditional treatments, such as The use of folk healers [39].

Meanwhile, numerous Hindu parents of children with "mental disorders" in The United States believe that Allah has given them The child as a response to sins committed in their previous lives [40]. While white Americans use traditional treatments and professional services [39], many African-Americans would seek advice from friends, families or church members before going to professionals. Asians, on The other hand, are often hesitant to seek professional assistance; they are more likely to "go alone" and get help if they cannot manage their child [38,39].

In contrast, it was found that ultra-orthodox Jewish families often change community dynamics by receiving medical advice from a Rabbi [41]. If a given treatment modality is contradictory, then The advice of The Rabbi is followed [10,42] regardless of whether insights into The disability are deemed as pessimistic or a celebration of life. The underlying concept, however, rests on The fact that religion often plays an important role in understanding The ASD experience [10,43,44], and therefore, families who believe that ASD can be cured tend to follow The mandate of The treatment designed to cure, while unbelieving families are less likely to challenge The course of The disorder [45].

The above discussion highlights The importance of religion. Based on The available knowledge on culture, religion can help families emotionally and socially, while playing an important role in boosting The capacities of parents to care for their child. However, religion may be misinterpreted, thus affecting The way families make decisions about further treatment and help.

1.2. Social Belief

Culture affects an individual's common belief system and serves as an explanatory model for disorders such as ASD [31]. In spite of The contrasting interests with which ASD has to contend, multiculturalists assessed The pressures of ASD differently, and these evaluations offer both negative and positive reviews [31]. On The negative side, culture makes people believe that ASD is a stigma. A stigma is known as The manifestation of a diverse form [46]. It is discriminating in nature and does not correspond to The normative expectations of society, and therefore results in a deteriorating social identity for affected individuals or even groups. Stereotyping against those with disabilities often occurs because of The negative perception of ASD [47]. The stigma surrounding ASD has resulted in discrimination against not only children diagnosed with autism but also their families [48]. It is often negatively perceived that children with ASD would find it hard to achieve success in life. Some parents go to The devastating extent of hiding their children diagnosed with autism from The community to prevent The family from losing respect [31].

In other communities, The disabled group is pushed to social exclusion and often their quality of life is put at risk [31]. Discrimination against children with ASD has been broadly described in The United States and around The globe to acknowledge The burden that stigma can bring to both parents and children with ASD [49].

Because The reason for ASD is still unknown, numerous multicultural groups have propped up their own belief about The reasons for developmental disorders. When people's beliefs about ASD etiology were reviewed, it was found that people, including preschool teachers, believed that genetic, environmental factors, and birth-related events were The contributing factors. Despite having been debunked in multiple extensive studies, anecdotes from parents support The suggestion that vaccines can cause developmental disorders in children. Millions of parents firmly believe that genetics, birth trauma, illness, inheritance, perinatal damage, The environment, or some combination of these disorders could cause children to become autistic [50,51]. However, many parents also believe that genetic factors are The main cause of these disorders [52,53]. Given The vast storehouse of myths and half-truths, more scientific inquiries on various cultural groups and their genetic and biological make-up will help confirm The causes of ASD. Cultures have often perpetuated false beliefs in The field of ASD because different groups may have a specific way of explaining atypical behaviors and beliefs [54].

1.3. Personal Belief

Beliefs inevitably take on a more influential role than knowledge in determining how people organize and identify tasks and problems. Moreover, beliefs are The strongest indicators of people's behavior [55]. Preschool teachers often stigmatize children with ASD, highlighting individual perceptions that may be incorrectly ascribed to people with disabilities. For some people, The regularity of The education system may be The most important factor in determining their beliefs [33].

In a study among special administrative region university students living in Macau, most of The participating students confirmed that The ASD etiology stemmed from negligent and emotional parents. However, only about one third of The students believed in genetic etiology. There was also a significant difference in The strength of each belief. On average, The participants expressed mild-to-moderate agreement with statements describing paternity as The etiology for ASD. Instead, they responded with a slightly neutral opinion or reaction to statements regarding genetic factors as The etiology of ASD [54]. Furthermore, a study by Hoekstra et al. proved that The personal beliefs of preschool teachers influences The transference of information to The parents of an ASD child [56].

In Arab countries, Hasnain et al. (2011) highlighted The commonly used Arabic word for ASD (التوحد), as individuals with a behavioral, mental, physical, and/or emotional disability. However, for many, The word itself is commonly interpreted as "to introvert" or "withdraw". Therefore, many individuals may have incorrectly interpreted The nature of ASD as introversion [31]. In China, a lack of ASD knowledge has been confirmed among preschool teachers. Similarly, this lack of knowledge has been reported due to The literal translation of both Chinese terms for autism spectrum disorder —zibizheng Gūdān—as "loneliness" or "introvert disease", which implies a more misunderstand form of psychological etiology [54].

The aforementioned findings provide support for The positive belief that children with ASD are talented in art, music, language, and computing [21]. However, figuratively, it is believed that children with or without ASD may possess extraordinary abilities. Moreover, their sophisticated skills may have been confused with general interests in public, social, and scientific discourses. Thus, having in-depth knowledge about ASD is equally important for members of The society, including preschool teachers. Countering misconceptions is best done through professional training that focuses on equipping teachers with The skills they need to improve The experience of children with ASD [33].

Needless to say, researchers have pointed out The importance of conventional directions—what preschool teachers have traditionally believed, their religious, social, and personal views on ASD, as well The relationship between several independent variables such as their education level and teaching experience and one dependent variable, which is a preschool teacher's belief about autism spectrum disorder. Therefore this study aims to answer The following two questions:

- What are The beliefs of preschool teachers concerning children with autism spectrum disorder?
- What are The potential differences in The beliefs of preschool teachers towards ASD according to their age, education level, and teaching experience?

2. Methodology

2.1. Research Design

A quantitative descriptive survey research design was utilized in this study to assess The different forms of beliefs of preschool teachers in general education towards ASD in Yemen. This design has been used in some previous studies such those of Qi et al. and Chirico et al. [54,57] to assess belief about ASD among teachers and parents as well.

2.2. Instrument

Overall, The instrument used in this study, specifically The ASD Beliefs Questionnaire (ABQ), consisted of two sections. The items in The developed instrument were adapted from questionnaires by Harrison et al. [58] and Al-Sharbati et al. [59], with their permission. The first section focused on The demographic information of The respondents (i.e., gender, age, marital status, education level, and teaching experience). The second section consisted of 20 ABQ items to assess The religious (five items), social (seven items), and personal (eight items) beliefs of preschool teachers towards ASD. For this section, The respondents were required to provide their responses according to a five-point Likert scale with The endpoints of " from strongly disagree" (1) to "strongly agree" (5). In addition, a "less agree" option was included in The response scale, instead of "neither agree nor disagree," in order to avoid respondents trying to guess their responses.

Firstly, The religious belief, in this case, represented one's belief on how ASD and behavioral health disorders are rooted in religion and spirituality. Examples of religious belief include "ASD is likely a result of a curse or evil eye put upon or inflicted on The family" or 'I think it is possible to treat ASD by consulting with religious therapists". Secondly, The social belief, in this case, represented one's common belief based on The cultural effect as an explanatory model system for ASD. Examples of social beliefs include "My society thinks that vaccination causes ASD" or "ASD holds a social stigma in some communities, such as Yemen society". Lastly, The personal belief, in this case, represented one's perception (maybe correct or incorrect) on children with ASD. Examples of personal beliefs include, "I think The majority of children with ASD suffer from mental retardation" or "I believe ASD can develop due to child maltreatment".

For this study, The developed instrument was back-to-back translated carefully. The equivalence of The translation was first reviewed by a panel of five experts (special educational needs teachers). Meanwhile, The face validity of The instrument was initially verified by four education specialists (two psychologists and two psychiatrists) who were professionally trained in The field of special education. This group of professors rated The clarity and appropriateness of The Likert scale statements. Necessary adjustments, including The rewording of certain phrases, were made according to The group's observations and suggestions. Following The adjustments, The percentage of The agreement from The group achieved 0.94. The face validity of The Yemeni version of The Likert scale statements was subsequently confirmed during The pilot study that involved 45 preschool teachers. All items were revealed to be easily understood, and no changes in wording were needed. The responses during The pilot study were not included in The actual study. Besides, The internal consistency of The instrument recorded Cronbach's alpha coefficient of more than 0.83, which reaffirmed The reliability of the items.

2.3. Procedure

The school administrators in one of The biggest cities in Yemen, specifically The Taiz district, were contacted to obtain their permission to conduct this study that involved their preschool teachers. After obtaining The permission of school administrators to conduct this study, preschool teachers were randomly selected to complete a self-administered ABQ on their beliefs towards ASD. The data collection was conducted during The summer of 2018. A total of 250 preschool teachers were randomly selected to complete a questionnaire on their beliefs towards ASD. All questionnaire sets were then returned to The researcher. However, 37 returned questionnaire sets had missing information. The exclusion of these incomplete questionnaire sets resulted in a final sample of 213 preschool teachers.

2.4. Data Analysis

The categorization of scores in this study represented The different levels of beliefs of preschool teachers, specifically religious, social, and personal beliefs, towards ASD. The recorded scores were interpreted according to three distinct levels: (1) low level of accurate beliefs (mean value $\geq$ 3.34); (2) moderate level of accurate beliefs (mean value of between 1.67 and 3.33); (3) high level of accurate beliefs (mean value $\leq$ 1.66) [60]. In other words, a low level of accurate belief implies that The preschool teacher displays disbelief towards ASD; a moderate level of accurate belief implies that The preschool teacher displays some misbelief towards ASD; a high level of accurate belief implies that The preschool teacher displays an accurate belief towards ASD.

Accordingly, The obtained survey responses were analyzed using IBM SPSS (version 19). First, The demographic information of The participating preschool teachers as survey respondents was descriptively analyzed. Second, The reliability and validity of ABQ were determined based on The results of Cronbach's alpha coefficient. Third, after ensuring that The obtained data were normally distributed, multilinear regression was carried out to see The differences among dependent variables (religious, social, and personal). Two-way ANOVA was carried out to assess The relationship between independent variables (i.e., age, education level, and teaching experience) and The dependent variable (personal belief). Besides this, post-hoc analysis (Scheffé post-hoc criterion for significance) was also performed.

On The other hand, data for The other dependent variables (religious belief and social belief) reported non-normal distribution. Moreover, The homogeneity equality of variance was less than 0.05 ($p = 0.042$). Therefore, The non-parametric test—The Kruskal–Wallis test (K–W test)—was valid and used instead of The ANOVA test. Thus, it was concluded that assumptions for The two-way ANOVA had been violated. The transformation was rather difficult because The specimens were small and difficult to interpret, especially in The two-way ANOVA. Therefore, The non-parametric test (K–W test) was valid and applied for religious belief and social belief [60].

3. Results

The respondents of this study were preschool teachers in normal schools in Taiz. Only 5% of The participants have reported that they have had previous contact with children with ASD, which was expressed through The (Yes, No) open question "Have you ever contacted a child with autism?". Table 1 presents The sample distribution according to gender, age, education level, and teaching experience.

Table 1. Sample characteristics.

	n	%
Gender		
Female	213	100
Age		
20–30	57	26.8
31–40	113	53.1
~≥40	43	20.2
Teaching Experience		
From 5 and below	54	25.4
Between 5–10	111	52.1
~≥10	48	22.5
Education		
High school	24	11.3
Diploma	55	25.8
Bachelor	134	62.9

3.1. *Preschool Teacher's Belief Regarding Autism Spectrum Disorder*

The first research question focused on determining The beliefs of preschool teachers towards ASD. With respect to this research question, The descriptive statistics (i.e., mean, standard deviation, and weight mean) of The categorical data in this study were acquired. And multilinear regression to see The differences lie between dependent variables (religious, social, and personal).

3.1.1. Descriptive Analysis

Table 2 shows The weight means for each belief among The preschool teachers according to three distinct levels for interpretation. In particular, The religious belief regarding preschool teachers' belief towards ASD was found to be at a moderate level, whereas their social and personal belief of preschool teacher's belief towards ASD was located at a low level. In other words, preschool teachers display inaccurate beliefs towards ASD resulting from The religious, social, and personal beliefs of The preschool teachers.

Table 2. Preschool teachers' beliefs regarding autism spectrum disorder.

	Items	Mean	Std	Rank
	Religion Belief			
1	item1	2.15	0.804	3.00
2	item 2	2.96	0.773	4.00
3	item 3	3.30	1.038	4.00
4	item 4	3.33	0.955	4.00
5	item 5	3.34	0.957	4.00
	Weighted mean	3.024		Moderate
	Std deviation		0.514	
	Social belief	Mean	Std	Rank
6	item 1	3.34	1.054	4.00
7	item 2	3.69	1.135	4.00
8	item 3	3.79	1.273	4.00
9	item 4	3.71	1.295	4.00
10	item 5	3.73	1.373	4.00
11	item 6	3.41	1.456	4.00
12	item 7	3.48	1.503	4.00
13		3.51	1.365	
	Weighted mean	3.64		Low
	Std deviation		0.643	
	Personal belief	Mean	Std	Rank
14	item 1	3.24	1.392	4.00
15	item 2	3.17	1.570	4.00
16	item 3	3.29	1.508	3.00
17	item 4	3.82	1.274	4.00
18	item 5	3.98	1.308	4.00
19	item 6	3.78	1.370	4.00
20	item 7	3.83	1.285	4.00
21	item 8	3.24	1.392	4.00
	Weighted mean	3.62		Low
	Std deviation		0.591	

std: standard deviation.

3.1.2. Results of Multi Linear Regression

Multiple Linear Regression analysis is an appropriate statistical method that allows us to examine and understand how The relationship among The independent variables are related to The dependent variable and to explore The forms of these relationships (between two or more variables of interest). Regression analysis is also used to understand which among The independent variables are related to The dependent variable, and to explore The forms of these relationships.

One-way ANOVA was employed to determine The effects of The dependent factor on The two independent factors as shown in Table 3. The F statistic was 9.880, indicating that The independent's variables (social belief, personal belief) are statistically significant. The results showed that The two independent factors (social belief, personal belief) have an effect on The dependent factor (religious belief) (p-values < 0.000) as illustrated in The same Table 3. This reflects that The alternative hypothesis of 3 variables are accepted, and that both social and personal beliefs were associated with religious belief.

Table 3. ANOVA test between religious belief (DV) and both social and personal belief (IV).

	Model	Sum of Squares	df	Mean Square	F	Sig.
	Regression	120.413	2	60.207	9.880	0.000
1	Residual	1279.652	210	6.094		
	Total	1400.066	212			

df: degrees of freedom.

The structural model assessment, as shown in Table 4, provides an indication of The hypotheses tests or question research of this current study. If hypothesis H1 (β = 0.142, t = 4.234, p = 0.000) and H2 (β = 0.089, t = 2.121, p = 0.035) are accepted, these could be The correlation relationships between Social Belief and Personal Belief empathy which significantly predicts that The Religion Belief dependent variable holds a strongly positive correlation relationship which is highly significant at The 0.01 level (2-tailed).

Table 4. Coefficients of The structural model assessment.

	Model	Unstandardized Coefficients		Standardized Coefficients	t	Sig.
		B	Std. Error	Beta		
	(Constant)	17.016	1.309		13.001	0.000
1	Social	0.142	0.034	284	4.234	0.000
	Personal	0.089	0.042	0.142	2.121	0.035

std: standard deviation.

The second research question was to assess The potential differences in The beliefs of preschool teachers towards ASD according to their age, education level, and teaching experience as shown below.

3.2. The Interactiont of Age, Education Levels, and Teaching Experience on Religious Believe

Based on Table 5; The Kruskal–Wallis Test (K–W test) interaction effect results indicated that there was a significant difference in religious belief between age (20–30 and 31–40 and above 40 years) and education levels (Diploma and Bachelor) (p = 0.023; p = 0.017). Moreover, there was not a significant difference in preschool teachers' belief regarding religious belief between age and education level (high school) (p = 0.115). The mean score for The age between 20–30 was less than The mean score for The age between 31–40 years. Thus, it was concluded that The age between 20–30 years and above 40 years had lesser inaccurate beliefs than The age between 31–40 years.

Moreover, The results indicated that there was a significant difference in preschool teachers' beliefs based on religious belief between ages (above 40 years) and teaching experience (above 10 years) (p = 0.001). There was not a significant difference in preschool teachers' belief regarding religious belief towards ASD between age and teaching experience (from 5 years and below and between 5–10 years) (p = 0.238; p = 0.226). This is shown in Table 6 below.

Table 5. Kruskal–Wallis Test (K–W) test for religious belief (age with education levels).

Education Levels	Age	*N*	df	Chi-Square	*p*-Value
High school	20–30	6	2	4.328	0.115
	31–40	1			
	>40	10			
diploma	20–30	17	2	7.536	0.023
	31–40	34			
	>40	11			
Bachelor	20–30	34	2	8.173	0.017
	31–40	78			
	>40	22			
		213			

df: degrees of freedom.

Table 6. Kruskal–Wallis Test for religious belief (age with teaching experience).

Teaching Experience	Age	*N*	df	Chi-Square	*p*-Value
From 5 years and below	20–30	12	2	2.875	0.238
	31–40	31			
	>40	11			
Between 5–10 years	20–30	38	2	2.651	0.266
	31–40	56			
	>40	17			
Above 10 years	20–30	7	2	14.367	0.001
	31–40	26			
	>40	15			
		213			

df: degrees of freedom.

Based on The K–W test, there is a significant difference between The mean scoring of teaching experiences (from 5 and below and between 5–10 years) and education levels (p = 0.023; p = 0.000) on preschool teachers' beliefs based on religious belief. However, there is no significantly different between teaching experiences (above 10 years) and education levels (p = 0.920) on preschool teachers' beliefs based on religious belief towards ASD, as it follows in Table 7.

Table 7. Kruskal–Wallis Test for religious belief (teaching experiences and education levels).

Teaching Experience	Education Levels	N	df	Chi-Square	p-Value
From 5 years and below	High school	1	2	7.541	0.023
	Diploma	12			
	Bachelor	41			
Between 5–10 years	High School	5	2	16.259	0.000
	Diploma	48			
	Bachelor	58			
Above 10 years	High School	11	2	0.167	0.920
	Diploma	2			
	Bachelor	35			
		213			

df: degrees of freedom.

3.3. The Interaction Effect of Age, Education Levels, and Teaching Experiences on Social Belief

The K–W test interaction effect results indicated that there was a significant difference in preschool teachers' beliefs regarding social belief between ages and education levels (diploma) ($p = 0.006$). Moreover, there was not a significant difference in preschool teachers' beliefs regarding social belief between age and education levels (high school and Bachelor) ($p = 0.130$; $p = 0.116$). The mean score for The age between 20–30 was less than The mean score for The age between 31–40 years. Thus, it was concluded that The age between 20–30 years and above 40 years had a lesser effect on preschool teachers' beliefs based on social belief than The age between 31–40 years, as is shown in Table 8 below.

Table 8. Kruskal-Wallis Test for social belief (age with education levels).

Education Levels	Age	N	df	Chi-Square	p-Value
High School	20–30	6	2	4.077	0.130
	31–40	1			
	>40	10			
Diploma	20–30	17	2	10.340	0.006
	31–40	34			
	>40	11			
Bachelor	20–30	34	2	4.315	0.116
	31–40	78			
	>40	22			
		213			

df: degrees of freedom.

The results also indicated that there was a significant effect of social belief on preschool teachers' belief between age and teaching experience (between 5–10 years and above 10 years) ($p = 0.002$; $p = 0.002$). There was not a significant effect of social belief on preschool teachers' beliefs between age and teaching experiences (from 5 years) ($p = 0.542$). See Table 9

Table 9. Kruskal–Wallis Test for social belief (age with teaching experience).

Teaching Experience	Age	N	df	Chi-Square	p-Value
From 5 years and below	20–30	12	2	1.226	0.542
	31–40	31			
	>40	11			
Between 5–10 years	20–30	38	2	12.242	0.002
	31–40	56			
	>40	17			
Above 10 years	20–30	7	2	12.514	0.002
	31–40	26			
	>40	15			
		213			

df: degrees of freedom.

According to The K–W test, there is a significant difference between The mean soring of teaching experiences (between 5–10 years above 10 years) and education levels ($p = 0.000$; $p = 0.006$) on preschool teachers' beliefs based on social belief. However, there is no significant difference between teaching experience (from 5 years and below) and education levels ($p = 0.237$) or preschool teachers' beliefs based on social beliefs. See Table 10

Table 10. Kruskal–Wallis Test for social belief (teaching experiences and education levels).

Teaching Experience	Education Levels	N	df	Chi-Square	p-Value
From 5 years and below	High school	1	2	2.880	0.237
	Diploma	12			
	Bachelor	41			
Between 5–10 years	High School	5	2	28.786	0.000
	Diploma	48			
	Bachelor	58			
Above 10 years	High School	11	2	10.280	0.006
	Diploma	2			
	Bachelor	35			
		213			

df: degrees of freedom.

3.4. The Interaction Effect of Age, Education Levels, and Teaching Experiences on Personal Belief

Two-way ANOVA was employed to determine The effects of age, education levels, and teaching experience on personal beliefs. An assumption of two-way ANOVA was checked, and The normality test was also checked for each factor. Each factor showed either that it was normally distributed or slightly skewed positively, which was in The accepted range of skewness. Homogeneity equality of variance was checked using Levene's test and it was found that The equality of variance assumption was met ($p = 0.215$). Thus, it can be concluded that it had not violated The homogeneity of variance assumption for 2-way ANOVA.

As seen in Table 11, The age effect (age between 20–30, age between 31–40, and age above 40 years) and working experience have no significant effect on preschool teachers' beliefs based on personal belief ($p = 0.192$; $p = 0.859$). Only The effect of education levels has a significant effect on The scores of personal belief ($p = 0.002$).

Table 11. Two-way ANOVA for personal belief.

Source	Type III Sum of Squares	df	Mean Square	F	Sig.
age	42.629	2	21.314	1.665	0.192
educational	160.430	2	80.215	6.264	0.002 *
Teaching experience	3.899	2	1.949	0.152	0.859
age * educational	113.789	3	37.930	2.962	0.033 *
age * experience	156.448	4	39.112	3.054	0.018 *
educational * experience	21.816	3	7.272	0.568	0.637

df: degrees of freedom. F = variation between sample means / variation within The samplest. * Means it is significant. R Squared = 0.312 (Adjusted R Squared = 0.252).

However, when a two-way interaction effect between each study factor was checked, it was found that there was a significant interaction effect between age factors with education levels and teaching experience on The scores relating to personal belief ($p = 0.033$; $p = 0.018$). It indicated that The effect of The age effect on personal beliefs may differ between education levels and teaching experiences. The results also found that there is no significant effect between education levels and teaching experience ($p = 0.637$).

Regarding The result of The post-hoc Scheffe's test, and based on The personal beliefs of preschool teachers (aged 31–40), there is a significant effect (mean = 2.57; $p = 0.002$) on preschool teachers' beliefs towards ASD. In addition, The personal beliefs of preschool teachers with a high school degree have significant differences (mean = 6.39; $p = 0.000$) on preschool teachers' beliefs towards ASD. Furthermore, The personal beliefs of preschool teachers who have teaching experience below 5 years have a significant effect on (mean = 2.02; $p = 0.021$) preschool teachers' belief towards children with ASD.

4. Discussion

The current study aimed to gain a better understanding of The impact of religious, social, and personal beliefs on one's perception of etiology, symptoms, signs, and socio-demography correlating to ASD. Overall, The survey conducted in this study revealed that many preschool teachers had misconceptions about ASD. They also repeatedly associated ASD with religion and believed that religious healers could treat children with an autism spectrum disorder. Some also believed that traditional therapy might be useful, as ASD was an atonement for previous sins [61]. Family members or relatives have sought help from traditional healers and shamans, including Rabbis [62], in part due to The lack of a known cure for ASD. Another reason why most parents struggle with finding The right help for ASD is that they believe that ASD is a scourge from Allah and that The disorder is a result of The curse of The evil eye. Neni et al. [63] validated this in their research which demonstrated that 18.2% from their sample of members of The public still believed that evil spirits caused The disability. These findings indicate that religion in many types of culture and practices is known to serve as an explanatory system to provide a reason for The causes or treatment of ASD.

Religious beliefs of preschool teachers aged above 40 years with teaching experience above 10 years have a significant effect on preschool teachers' beliefs towards ASD. In other words, The religious beliefs of those aged above 40 with teaching experience above 10 years were The most significant. Their religious beliefs caused inaccurate beliefs toward children with ASD. The reason for that is that older generations (who have more education and more teaching experience) were raised in an era that had strong religious/traditional interpretations of health. These findings indicate that in Yemen, religion plays a major role in identifying The causes and treatment of ASD. Yemen is among The Muslim countries that belief traditional therapy to be useful for treating cases such as ASD. The most common traditional therapy applied is Quran therapy.

On The other hand, The religious beliefs of preschool teachers with an (high school) education level and teaching experiences (below 5 years and between 5–10 years) have no significant effect on their belief toward children with ASD. Based on their religious beliefs, these preschool teachers had accurate beliefs about ASD. This result could be explained by The fact that preschool teachers with low levels of education attempt to seek more knowledge through attending workshops and training programs that can help them deal with children who have problematic behavior instead of relying only on their religious interpretations.

This study revealed many common social assumptions on ASD among preschool teachers. Their contradicting views are debatable. Some teachers with many years of experience had more accurate beliefs on ASD than those with fewer years of teaching. In addition, more experienced teachers did not consider or view vaccination as a cause of ASD when compared to less-experienced teachers. Many of them believed that ASD was a genetic disorder. Mitchell et al. [25] found that most preschool teachers stayed up-to-date through social media, and yet, they still had inaccurate information about ASD; for instance, The assumption that ASD might be linked to vaccines. Most preschool teachers with less than five years of teaching experience claimed that children with ASD are indeed geniuses with distinguished skills, confirming The results reported by Khanna et al. [64] The preschool teachers in The study also believed that children with ASD were susceptible to negative social consequences and general stigma. Similarly, Al Sharbati et al. [59] pointed out that children with disability challenges in Oman were once hidden within The familial household and had limited access to educational or remedial services.

The social beliefs of preschool teachers aged 31–40 with an educational level (diploma) as well as teaching experience (between 5–10 years and above 10 years) have a significant effect on The accurate belief of preschool teachers towards children with ASD. In other words, The social beliefs of preschool teachers aged 31–40 with educational levels (diploma) as well as teaching experience (between 5–10 years and above 10 years) were The most significant. Their social beliefs caused inaccurate beliefs toward children with ASD. This might be due to preschool teachers with more than 10 years of teaching experience being uninterested in updating their knowledge compared to those who have less than 5 years of teaching experience. Moreover, low-experienced preschool teachers tend to update their knowledge to improve their careers by attending more training programs [2]. Furthermore, The Yemeni culture has social restrictions that are reflected in The preschool teachers' interpretations of any phenomenon such as ASD. For instance, some preschool teachers consider ASD to be a stigma, which is very common in Yemeni society [59]. These inaccurate beliefs held by many Yemeni people might shape The preschool teachers' cultural beliefs affecting their career.

On The contrary, based on social beliefs, The Age effect (20–30; 31–40; >40) with The education levels (high school–Bachelor) as well as teaching experience (below 5 years) have no effect on The accurate belief of preschool teachers towards children with ASD. This may be due to those preschool teachers with less than 5 years of teaching experience, and a high school education being more concerned about gaining basic teaching and behavior modification skills [23]. It may be The case that preschool teachers who have a high education level (Bachelor) may have received university courses in special education needs.

The preschool teachers had personal assumptions or perceptions on ASD that they had formed through thoughts and experiences. This study found that some teachers thought cell phones were a reason for The emergence of ASD and that most children with ASD were introverts. Such findings confirm The results of John et al. [21] in that those preschool teachers with less experience might find it difficult to distinguish between ASD and introversion, thus thinking that they are similar. Another common personal belief was that an autistic child is suffering from "loneliness"—an error also prevalent among preschool teachers in China [33]. The Chinese teachers' inaccurate response to ASD may partially stem from The Chinese terms for ASD that translates to "loneliness disease" or "isolation disease'", implying a more psychological etiology. Some Arabic terms like ((التوحد translated as "loneliness", explains why some of The preschool teachers in this study equated this disorder with The feeling of being lonely. However, The response rates indicate that this disorder could be cured, so training in early childhood development would be adequate to provide teachers with a knowledge base in neurodevelopmental disorders, as recommended by Liu et al. [33]

The personal beliefs of preschool teachers aged (31–40) with an educational level (high school) as well as teaching experience (below 5 years) have a significant effect on The accurate belief of preschool teachers towards children with ASD. In other words, The personal beliefs of preschool teachers aged (31–40) with an educational level (high school) as well as teaching experience (below 5 years) were The most significant. Their personal beliefs caused inaccurate beliefs toward children with ASD. This means that preschool teachers with high teaching experience can change their thinking towards ASD better than preschool teachers with teaching experiences for less than 5 years. On The other hand, The personal beliefs of preschool teachers aged 20–30 (>40) with an education level (Diploma and Bachelor) have no significant effect on their belief towards children with ASD. This indicates that they have accurate beliefs towards ASD based on their personal beliefs. This might be due to personal beliefs being a reflection of individual perceptions gained from life experiences and training programs, which may lead to logical thinking toward any phenomena.

5. Limitations

Despite The importance of The above findings, there some limitations to this study that should be highlighted for future research. The preschool teachers in this study were mostly from normal schools, which might affect The generalizability of The findings of this study. Indeed, The index of beliefs expressed in this study was subjectively informed. There was little evidence to suggest that The beliefs were translated into actions. Therefore, it is difficult to know whether The teachers' beliefs or attitudes would translate into actual behavior. To avoid giving a rather low overall impression of their belief system, The teachers might have responded with what they perceived as favorable answers. A joint effort to rule out such confounding factors is necessary, with a need for large-scale future studies equipped with standardized training techniques that reach a broader demographic of teachers. Furthermore, The respondents were asked to state their choices in The comment section of The questionnaire. This method might have encouraged them to respond positively, even if they were not sure about a particular item, as explained in other studies [65]. It might have been better to use another method, such as a qualitative approach, by asking The respondents to explain their beliefs concerning The different issues surrounding ASD. Finally, only 5% of The preschool teachers of The sample had had contact with children diagnosed with autism, which erodes negative views. Similar to The interaction hypothesis by Brown et al. [66], several works also proposed that having previous interpersonal contacts with a disabled person would likely reduce negative views. This situation is based on The assumption that one side of The personality is uncovered to The other side, while new understanding emerges as prejudice weakens. Thus, if preschool teachers have had more contact, their understanding would have been more positively affected. Future studies could explore The contact versus non-contact factor, which may have a bearing on The teachers' understanding of The condition that is unique to ASD children.

6. Conclusions

The prevalence of children with ASD now exceeds that of Down's syndrome, diabetes, or cancer [67]. Hence, preschool teachers should widen their knowledge on ASD to help parents guide their special-needs children. Educated preschool teachers can help parents obtain proper interventions to ensure that their children reach their full potential. To accomplish this end, preschool teachers need to be correctly educated on this disorder, and any inaccurate information among them in particular and in society generally must be discarded. Perhaps a pre-service training among teachers could address these misconceptions and allow easier access for teachers to obtain such important information. Additionally, special-needs education via lectures, workshops, and courses are urgently needed to improve The mindfulness of people working in schools. Mass media can contribute actively by raising awareness regarding ASD knowledge and on how educators can play their roles effectively.

For The first time, this study has highlighted one of The main educational concerns in Yemen. One conclusion that can be drawn is that incorrect beliefs or misunderstandings of The condition that is unique to children with ASD are social problems that transcend specific culture, geography, or society. It concedes to individual countries The right to work hand-in-hand with others to make ASD education compulsory and jointly face The ever-rising ASD misconceptions and in addition, to give these kinds of children complete rights for social justice in education and jobs.

Author Contributions: N.A.A. is The chair person and main supervisor, S.R. and A.M.M. is The committee member of The project. They contribute to The conception and design of The study, gives a critical revision of The article and give final approval of The version to be published. Writing an article, data collection, data analysis and findings interpretation contributed by S.M.T. and N.A.A. All authors have read and agreed to The published version of the manuscript.

Funding: This research received no external funding.

Acknowledgments: The authors would like to thank all The preschool teachers who participated in this project. Nor Aniza Ahmad and Sahar Taresh are The joint first-authors of this article.

Conflicts of Interest: The authors declare no conflict of interest.

References

1. Gray, D.E. 'Everybody just freezes. Everybody is just embarrassed': Felt and enacted stigma among parents of children with high functioning autism. *Sociol. Health Illn.* **2002**, *24*, 734–749. [CrossRef]
2. dawd Ahlam adeeb, D.A.A. The problems of working in preschools from The teachers and administrators. *J. Fac. Educ. Res.* **2007**, *1*, 105–127.
3. Newschaffer, C.J.; Croen, L.A.; Daniels, J.; Giarelli, E.; Grether, J.K.; Levy, S.E.; Mandell, D.S.; Miller, L.A.; Pinto-Martin, J.; Reaven, J. The epidemiology of autism spectrum disorders. *Annu. Rev. Public Health* **2007**, *28*, 235–258. [CrossRef] [PubMed]
4. Gilligan, P. The Challenge of Cultural Explanations and Religious Requirements for Children with Autistic Spectrum Conditions: South Asian Muslim Parents in Bradford, England. *J. Relig. Disabil. Health* **2013**, *17*, 393–408. [CrossRef]
5. Armstrong, M.J.; Fitzgerald, M.H. Culture and disability studies: An anthropological perspective. *Rehabil. Educ. N. Y. Pergamon Press* **1996**, *10*, 247–304.
6. Harris, P. Culturally competent disability support: Putting it into practice. *Multicult. Disabil. Advocacy Assoc. NSW* **2004**, *11*, 14–17.
7. Multicultural Disability Advocacy Association of New South Wales. *Ethnicity and Disability Factbook*; The Association: London, UK, 2000.
8. Fitzpatrick, M. MMR and Autism: What Parents Need to Know; 2004. Available online: https://books.google.com.my/books?hl=en&lr=&id=XMWuvsJ1WY4C&oi=fnd&pg=FT5&dq=.+MMR+and+Autism:+What+Parents+Need+to+Know&ots=JB7cSsWz05&sig=2WVRTB6O8cFKGmQe6Yl7w98TO0w&redir_esc=y#v=onepage&q=.%20MM (accessed on 7 July 2020).
9. Harrington, J.W.; Patrick, P.A.; Edwards, K.S.; Brand, D.A. Parental beliefs about autism: Implications for The treating physician. *Autism Int. J. Res. Pract.* **2006**, *10*, 452–462. [CrossRef] [PubMed]
10. Jegatheesan, B.; Miller, P.J.; Fowler, S.A. Autism from a Religious Perspective: A Study of Parental Beliefs in South Asian Muslim Immigrant Families. *Focus Autism Other Dev. Disabil.* **2010**, *25*, 98–109. [CrossRef]
11. Mahoney, D. *College Students' Attitudes toward Individuals with Autism*; The University of North Carolina at Chapel Hill: Chapel Hill, NC, USA, 2007. [CrossRef]
12. Ling, C.Y.; Mak, W.W.; Cheng, J.N. Attribution model of stigma towards children with autism in Hong Kong. *J. Appl. Res. Intellect. Disabil.* **2010**, *23*, 237–249. [CrossRef]
13. Butler, R.C.; Gillis, J.M. The impact of labels and behaviors on The stigmatization of adults with Asperger's disorder. *J. Autism Dev. Disord.* **2011**, *41*, 741–749. [CrossRef]
14. Draaisma, D. Stereotypes of autism. *Philos. Trans. R. Soc. Lond. B Biol. Sci.* **2009**, *364*, 1475–1480. [CrossRef] [PubMed]
15. Huws, J.C.; Jones, R.S. Missing voices: Representations of autism in British newspapers, 1999–2008. *Br. J. Learn. Disabil.* **2011**, *39*, 98–104. [CrossRef]
16. Hwang, S.K.; Charnley, H. Making The familiar strange and making The strange familiar: Understanding Korean children's experiences of living with an autistic sibling. *Disabil. Soc.* **2010**, *25*, 579–592. [CrossRef]

17. Grinker, R.R.; Kang-Yi, C.D.; Ahmann, C.; Beidas, R.S.; Lagman, A.; Mandell, D.S. Cultural Adaptation and Translation of Outreach Materials on Autism Spectrum Disorder. *J. Autism Dev. Disord.* **2015**, *45*, 2329–2336. [CrossRef] [PubMed]
18. Hersinta. How Religious Beliefs Influence Understanding on Disability: A Study of Muslim Family's Perception on Autism; STIKOM The London School of Public Relations Jakarta. In Proceedings of The Jogja International Conference on Communication, Jakarta, Indonesia, November 2012.
19. Danseco, E.R. Parental Beliefs on Childhood Disability: Insights on culture, child development and intervention. *Int. J. Disabil. Dev. Educ.* **1997**, *44*, 41–52. [CrossRef]
20. Stone, W.L.; Rosenbaum, J.L. A comparison of teacher and parent views of autism. *J. Autism Dev. Disord.* **1988**, *18*, 403–414. [CrossRef]
21. John, R.P.; Knott, F.J.; Harvey, K.N. Myths about autism: An exploratory study using focus groups. *Autism Int. J. Res. Pract.* **2018**, *22*, 845–854. [CrossRef]
22. Broady, T.R.; Stoyles, G.J.; Morse, C. Understanding carers' lived experience of stigma: The voice of families with a child on The autism spectrum. *Health Soc. Care Community* **2017**, *25*, 224–233. [CrossRef]
23. Barned, N.E.; Knapp, N.F.; Neuharth-Pritchett, S. Knowledge and Attitudes of Early Childhood Preservice Teachers Regarding The Inclusion of Children With Autism Spectrum Disorder. *J. Early Child. Teach. Educ.* **2011**, *32*, 302–321. [CrossRef]
24. Segall, M.J. Inclusion of Students with Autism Spectrum Disorder: Educator Experience, Knowledge, and Attitudes. Master's Thesis, University of Georgia, Athens, GA, USA, 2008. Available online: https://getd.libs.uga.edu/pdfs/segall_matthew_j_200805_ma.pdf (accessed on 7 July 2020).
25. Mitchell, G.E.; Locke, K.D. Lay beliefs about autism spectrum disorder among The general public and childcare providers. *Autism Int. J. Res. Pract.* **2015**, *19*, 553–561. [CrossRef]
26. Janz, N.K.; Becker, M.H. The Health Belief Model: A decade later. *Health Educ. Q.* **1984**, *11*, 1–47. [CrossRef] [PubMed]
27. Rosenstock, I.M. The health belief model and preventive health behavior. *Health Educ. Monogr.* **1974**, *2*, 354–386. [CrossRef]
28. Rosenstock, I.M. The Health Belief Model: Explaining health behavior through experiences. *Health Behav. Health Educ. Theory Res. Pract.* **1990**, 39–63. [CrossRef]
29. Hussein, H.; Taha, G.R.A. Autism spectrum disorders. *Middle East Curr. Psychiatry* **2013**, *20*, 106–116. [CrossRef]
30. Office of Autism Research Coordination N.I.O.M.H.; Thomson Reuters I.O.B.O.T.I.A.C.C. *IACC/OARC Autism Spectrum Disorder Research Publications Analysis Report: The Global Landscape of Autism Research*; US Department of Health and Human Services: Washington, DC, USA, 2012.
31. Gobrial, E. The Lived Experiences of Mothers of Children with The Autism Spectrum Disorders in Egypt. *Soc. Sci.* **2018**, *7*, 133. [CrossRef]
32. Wright, K.B.; Sparks, L.; O'hair, H.D. *Health Communication in The 21st Century*; John Wiley & Sons: Hoboken, NJ, USA, 2012; Available online: https://books.google.com.my/books?hl=en&lr=&id=iAt6qnS0Hp0C&oi=fnd&pg=PA14&dq=Health+Communication+in+the+21st+Century&ots=7y7EEjm7IA&sig=jy09xH8pDr_xPUZsK9wIqUxVsUU&redir_esc=y#v=onepage&q=Health%20Communication%20in%20the%2021st%20Century&f=false (accessed on 7 July 2020).
33. Liu, Y.; Li, J.; Zheng, Q.; Zaroff, C.M.; Hall, B.J.; Li, X.; Hao, Y. Knowledge, attitudes, and perceptions of autism spectrum disorder in a stratified sampling of preschool teachers in China. *BMC Psychiatry* **2016**, *16*, 142. [CrossRef]
34. Hasnain, R.; Shaikh, L.C.; Shanawani, H. Disability and The Muslim Perspective: An Introduction for Rehabilitation and Health Care Providers. 2008. Available online: http://digitalcommons.ilr.cornell.edu/gladnetcollect/460 (accessed on 7 July 2020).
35. Diken, I.H. Turkish Mothers' Interpretations of The Disability of Their Children with Mental Retardation. *Int. J. Spec. Educ.* **2006**, *21*, 8–17.
36. Morad, M.; Nasri, Y.; Merrick, J. Islam and The person with intellectual disability. *J. Relig. Disabil. Health* **2001**, *5*, 65–71. [CrossRef]
37. Skinner, D.G.; Correa, V.; Skinner, M.; Bailey, D.B., Jr. Role of religion in The lives of Latino families of young children with developmental delays. *Am. J. Ment. Retard.* **2001**, *106*, 297–313. [CrossRef]

38. Dyches, T.T.; Wilder, L.K.; Sudweeks, R.R.; Obiakor, F.E.; Algozzine, B. Multicultural issues in autism. *J. Autism Dev. Disord.* **2004**, *34*, 211–222. [CrossRef]
39. Wing Sue, D.; Sue, D. *Counseling The Culturally Diverse: Theory and Practice*. 2008. Available online: https://books.google.com.my/books?hl=en&lr=&id=9aKMDwAAQBAJ&oi=fnd&pg=PA19&dq=Counseling+the+Culturally+Diverse:+Theory+and+Practice&ots=ttG94gstUL&sig=Qo6To2oKquz29uiCQG7S6ddYsec&redir_esc=y#v=onepage&q=Counseling%20the%20Culturally%20Diverse%3A%20Theory%20and%20Practice&f=false (accessed on 7 July 2020).
40. Gabel, S. South Asian Indian cultural orientations toward mental retardation. *Ment. Retard.* **2004**, *42*, 12–25. [CrossRef]
41. Pitten, K. How cultural values influence diagnosis, treatment and The welfare of families with an autistic child. *Rev. Acad. J.* **2008**, *4*, 1–3.
42. Shaked, M.; Bilu, Y. Grappling with affliction: Autism in The Jewish ultraorthodox community in Israel. *Cult. Med. Psychiatry* **2006**, *30*, 1–27. [CrossRef] [PubMed]
43. Katbamna, S.; Bhakta, P.; Parker, G. Perceptions of disability and care-giving relationships in South Asian communities. *Ethn. Disabil. Chronic Ill'n.* **2000**, 12–27. Available online: https://www.semanticscholar.org/paper/Perceptions-of-disability-and-caregiving-in-South-Katbamna-Bhakta/738afe515fe522718d20a99d6476a4c44c281336 (accessed on 7 July 2020).
44. Katbamna, S.; Bhakta, P.; Ahmad, W.; Baker, R.; Parker, G. Supporting South Asian carers and those they care for: The role of The primary health care team. *Br. J. Gen. Pract.* **2002**, *52*, 300–305. [PubMed]
45. Mandell, D.S.; Novak, M.M.; Zubritsky, C.D. Factors associated with age of diagnosis among children with autism spectrum disorders. *Pediatrics* **2005**, *116*, 1480–1486. [CrossRef] [PubMed]
46. Goffman, E. *Stigma: Notes on The Management of Spoiled Identity*; Simon & Schuster, Inc.: New York, NY, USA, 2009. Available online: https://books.google.com.my/books?hl=en&lr=&id=zuMFXuTMAqAC&oi=fnd&pg=PA1&dq=Stigma:+Notes+on+the+Management+of+Spoiled+Identity&ots=R93tIu8IKg&sig=83tQDavmdxu7dPC7QrI37rD9QOM&redir_esc=y#v=onepage&q=Stigma%3A%20Notes%20on%20the%20Management%20of%20Spoiled%20Identity&f=false (accessed on 7 July 2020).
47. Ohan, J.L.; Visser, T.A.; Moss, R.G.; Allen, N.B. Parents' stigmatizing attitudes toward psychiatric labels for ADHD and depression. *Psychiatr. Serv.* **2013**, *64*, 1270–1273. [CrossRef] [PubMed]
48. Cassidy, A.; McConkey, R.; Truesdale-Kennedy, M.; Slevin, E. Preschoolers with autism spectrum disorders: The impact on families and The supports available to them. *Early Child Dev. Care* **2008**, *178*, 115–128. [CrossRef]
49. Dehnavi, S.R.; Malekpour, M.; Faramarz, S.; Talebi, H. The share of internalized stigma and autism quotient in predicting The mental health of mothers with autism children in Iran. *Int. J. Bus. Soc. Sci.* **2011**, *2*, 251–259.
50. Gourdine, R.M.; Baffour, T.D.; Teasley, M. Autism and The African American community. *Soc. Work Public Health* **2011**, *26*, 454–470. [CrossRef]
51. Hughes, J.R. A review of recent reports on autism: 1000 studies published in 2007. *Epilepsy Behav.* **2008**, *13*, 425–437. [CrossRef]
52. Mercer, L.; Creighton, S.; Holden, J.; Lewis, M. Parental perspectives on The causes of an autism spectrum disorder in their children. *J. Genet. Couns.* **2006**, *15*, 41–50. [CrossRef] [PubMed]
53. Selkirk, C.G.; Veach, P.M.; Lian, F.; Schimmenti, L.; LeRoy, B.S. Parents' perceptions of autism spectrum disorder etiology and recurrence risk and effects of their perceptions on family planning: Recommendations for genetic counselors. *J. Genet. Couns.* **2009**, *18*, 507–519. [CrossRef] [PubMed]
54. Qi, X.; Zaroff, C.M.; Bernardo, A.B. Autism spectrum disorder etiology: Lay beliefs and The role of cultural values and social axioms. *Autism Int. J. Res. Pract.* **2016**, *20*, 673–686. [CrossRef] [PubMed]
55. Pajares, M.F. Teachers' beliefs and educational research: Cleaning up a messy construct. *Rev. Educ. Res.* **1992**, *62*, 307–332. [CrossRef]
56. Hoekstra, R.; Happé, F.; de Leeuw, A. A conceptual framework for understanding The cultural and contextual factors on autism across The globe. *Autism Res.* **2019**. [CrossRef]
57. Chirico, F. Religious Belief and Mental Health in Lay and Consecrated Italian Teachers. *J. Relig. Health* **2017**, *56*, 839–851. [CrossRef]
58. Harrison, A.J.; Bradshaw, L.P.; Naqvi, N.C.; Paff, M.L.; Campbell, J.M. Development and Psychometric Evaluation of The Autism Stigma and Knowledge Questionnaire (ASK-Q). *J. Autism Dev. Disord.* **2017**, *47*, 3281–3295. [CrossRef]

59. Al-Sharbati, M.M.; Al-Farsi, Y.M.; Ouhtit, A.; Waly, M.I.; Al-Shafaee, M.; Al-Farsi, O.; Al-Khaduri, M.; Al-Said, M.F.; Al-Adawi, S. Awareness about autism among school teachers in Oman: A cross-sectional study. *Autism Int. J. Res. Pract.* **2015**, *19*, 6–13. [CrossRef]
60. Hair, J.F., Jr.; Sarstedt, M.; Ringle, C.M.; Gudergan, S.P. *Advanced Issues in Partial Least Squares Structural Equation Modeling*; Sage Publications: Los Angeles, CA, USA, 2017; Available online: https://books.google.com.my/books?hl=en&lr=&id=-f1rDgAAQBAJ&oi=fnd&pg=PP1&dq=Advanced+Issues+in+Partial+Least+Squares+Structural+Equation+Modeling&ots=vX46lqK05Z&sig=JcfEwrCbJ8fKOh6IzGkhMYaADCk&redir_esc=y#v=onepage&q=Advanced%20Issues%20in%20Partial%20Least%20Squares%20Structural%20Equation%20Modeling&f=false (accessed on 7 July 2020).
61. Carlsson, E.; Miniscalco, C.; Kadesjö, B.; Laakso, K. Negotiating knowledge: Parents' experience of The neuropsychiatric diagnostic process for children with autism. *Int. J. Lang. Commun. Disord.* **2016**, *51*, 328–338. [CrossRef]
62. Igwe, M.N.; Ahanotu, A.C.; Bakare, M.O.; Achor, J.U.; Igwe, C. Assessment of knowledge about childhood autism among paediatric and psychiatric nurses in Ebonyi state, Nigeria. *Child Adolesc. Psychiatry Ment. Health* **2011**, *5*, 1. [CrossRef]
63. Neni, S.W.; Latif, A.Z.; Wong, S.Y.; Lua, P.L. Awareness, knowledge and attitudes towards epilepsy among rural populations in East Coast Peninsular Malaysia: A preliminary exploration. *Seizure* **2010**, *19*, 280–290. [CrossRef] [PubMed]
64. Khanna, R.; Jariwala, K.; Holmes, E.R.; Ramachandran, S. Autism familiarity and knowledge among pharmacy students. *Curr. Pharm. Teach. Learn.* **2014**, *6*, 150–157. [CrossRef]
65. Groves, R.M.; Fowler, F.J., Jr.; Couper, M.P.; Lepkowski, J.M.; Singer, E.; Tourangeau, R. *Survey Methodology*; John Wiley & Sons: Hoboken, NJ, USA, 2011; Volume 561, Available online: https://books.google.com.my/books?hl=en&lr=&id=ctow8zWdyFgC&oi=fnd&pg=PR15&dq=.+Survey+Methodology&ots=fflN9G2lYc&sig=lrn_gFV45uuOZASJrY5kPLTkqSQ&redir_esc=y#v=onepage&q=.%20Survey%20Methodology&f=false (accessed on 7 July 2020).
66. Brown, R.; Hewstone, M. An integrative theory of intergroup contact. *Adv. Exp. Soc. Psychol.* **2005**, *37*, 255–343.
67. Filipek, P.A.; Accardo, P.J.; Baranek, G.T.; Cook, E.H.; Dawson, G.; Gordon, B.; Gravel, J.S.; Johnson, C.P.; Kallen, R.J.; Levy, S.E. The screening and diagnosis of autistic spectrum disorders. *J. Autism Dev. Disord.* **1999**, *29*, 439–484. [CrossRef]

children

MDPI

Article

Development of a Pathway for Multidisciplinary Neurodevelopmental Assessment and Diagnosis in Children and Young People

Marion Rutherford [1], Donald Maciver [1,*], Lorna Johnston [1,2], Susan Prior [1] and Kirsty Forsyth [1]

1 School of Health Sciences, Queen Margaret University, Edinburgh EH21 6UU, UK; mrutherford@qmu.ac.uk (M.R.); LJohnston2@qmu.ac.uk (L.J.); sprior@qmu.ac.uk (S.P.); kforsyth@qmu.ac.uk (K.F.)
2 Additional Support for Learning Service, Communities and Families, City of Edinburgh Council, Edinburgh EH8 8BG, UK
* Correspondence: dmaciver@qmu.ac.uk

Abstract: There is a variable standard of access to quality neurodevelopmental assessment and diagnosis. People may have negative experiences, encountering lengthy waiting times, and inconsistent practices. Practitioners need guidance on standards and practices for assessment and diagnosis matched to new ways of working. In this paper, we present a new pathway and recommendations for multidisciplinary neurodevelopmental assessment and diagnosis for children and young people (<19 years), developed by the Scottish Government funded National Autism Implementation Team (NAIT). Our research used the Medical Research Council guidance for the development of complex interventions and included several iterative stages. Stage 1: $n = 44$ stakeholders attended an event on developing new practices for diagnosis and assessment. Stage 2: a literature synthesis was completed by the research team of clinical guidelines and diagnosis and assessment tools. Stage 3: an event with $n = 127$ stakeholders included discussion and debate of the data from stages 1 and 2. Recommendations and a draft pathway were written. Stage 4: successive drafts of recommendations and the pathway documentation were circulated among an advisory group, including multidisciplinary clinical experts and people with lived experience, until the final pathway was agreed upon. The finalised pathway includes guidance on terminology, assessment, diagnosis, triage, time standards and engagement of people with lived experience. The new pathway has been adopted by the Scottish Government. The pathway and associated documentation are freely available online for use by others.

Keywords: guideline; autism; neurodevelopmental; pathway; assessment; diagnosis

Citation: Rutherford, M.; Maciver, D.; Johnston, L.; Prior, S.; Forsyth, K. Development of a Pathway for Multidisciplinary Neurodevelopmental Assessment and Diagnosis in Children and Young People. *Children* **2021**, *8*, 1033. https://doi.org/10.3390/children8111033

Academic Editor: Sari A. Acra

Received: 29 September 2021
Accepted: 8 November 2021
Published: 11 November 2021

1. Introduction

People with neurodevelopmental differences present with variations in one or more neurocognitive functions towards the extreme or otherwise out of the 'normal' range [1,2]. Common diagnoses include autism, developmental coordination disorder (DCD), developmental language disorder (DLD), intellectual disability (ID), foetal alcohol spectrum disorder (FASD), and attention deficit hyperactivity disorder (ADHD) (American Psychological Association (APA), 2013). These categories frequently overlap, and most individuals present with interrelated needs and requirements for support [3].

Accessing timely assessment and diagnosis is a known area of difficulty for people with neurodevelopmental differences, and there are few guidelines available to support practice. Delayed or missed diagnosis reduces access to help, and has a negative impact on wellbeing, participation and quality of life [4–8]. An overly deficit-focused approach is also unhelpful. Diagnostic assessment should include an understanding of the individual in context, and their strengths and goals [9]. An approach which considers 'difference not deficit' is important [10].

There has been a tradition of single condition guidelines and pathways [6,11,12]. The focus has been on the presence or absence of a single diagnosis, leading to communities of practice with knowledge, skill and capacity in relation to these areas (e.g., autism). As a consequence, services have become overspecialised, drastically underestimating the true degree of overlap across neurodevelopmental differences [13]. A singular focus on one presenting issue leads to the potential omission of other diagnoses (and supports). People may experience repetitive and lengthy assessment, a process which individuals and families find distressing and burdensome [4,14].

Movement from single condition pathways toward neurodevelopmental pathways is desirable. Although there are strong advocates for this, for example the 'ESSENCE' framework [3], bridging the gap into practice remains challenging [15]. There was no neurodevelopmental guideline for assessment and diagnosis in Scotland. In this research, commissioned by the Scottish Government, we present our work to address this gap.

1.1. Objective

With this paper, we present recommendations to guide multidisciplinary practice from pre-referral to diagnosis for children and young people aged 0–18 years. We focus on the 0–18 age range as we wish to develop future materials for post-18-year-old individuals, which will have a greater focus on employment, while this current guidance includes a greater focus on childhood years, covering the periods of primary and secondary education. In this research we have built on the United Kingdom Medical Research Council (MRC) guidance on the development of complex interventions [16] and engaged with stakeholders, professionals and people with lived experience. Recommendations were primarily derived from consultation in Scotland; however, they may be transferability to other countries with similar characteristics or issues.

1.2. The Scottish Context

In Scotland, services report increasing numbers of children and young people meeting the criteria for one or more neurodevelopmental diagnosis. The current prevalence of autism is 1.035% in Scotland [17]. The estimated prevalence of neurodevelopmental disorders (internationally) is around 10% [3]. Other Scottish neurodevelopmental prevalence data is not known; however, an analysis of 2019 school census data found that 15% of primary aged children and 20% of secondary aged children had an additional support need indicative of neurodevelopmental needs, including learning disabilities, learning difficulties, language or communication disorders, autism, social, emotional and behavioural difficulties, and mental health problems [18]. In Scotland, there are defined pathways for autism [19,20] and largely separate pathways for ADHD and other neurodevelopmental differences. Prior to the COVID-19 pandemic, services had begun implementing neurodevelopmental pathways, and others were considering this shift, but little synthesised guidance existed to support this important change in practice.

2. Methods

2.1. Team

This research was completed by the National Autism Implementation Team (NAIT). This team forms part of the 10-year Scottish Government autism strategy [21,22]. NAIT have a leadership role in this strategy, and have a remit to improve autism and neurodevelopmental diagnostic pathways across the lifespan through integration with education (in children) and with the employment sector in adults. The team includes clinical expertise in autism, occupational therapy, speech and language therapy, education, psychiatry, as well as researchers with expertise in complex interventions development and health systems research. The team has completed previous research on autism pathways, diagnosis, wait times, interventions and guidelines [6,7,19,20,23–26].

2.2. Medical Research Council Complex Interventions Development Framework

Intervention development methods were modernised through the publication of the MRC complex interventions development framework [16]. The MRC framework provided a systematic and cyclical approach to the development of new interventions [16]. Whilst quantitative statistical techniques, including the controlled trial or statistical meta-analysis, are important, such methodologies may not always be feasible. Qualitative methods are an important alternative [27,28]. A key aspect of such approaches is stakeholder involvement, which can be used to understand problems, identify priorities, and collaborate to develop solutions [29,30]. The MRC guidance provides a robust standard for intervention development and includes four phases: development, feasibility/piloting, evaluation and implementation [16]. The development phase, as recommended by the MRC framework, focusses on building partnerships, specifying the population, completing a literature review, collaborating with stakeholders, and developing and consulting on materials to support implementation [30].

In following the development phase of the MRC framework, an iterative multi-stage process was undertaken 2019–2021. This began with stakeholder engagement, followed by a literature review, further stakeholder engagement, and recruitment of an advisory group. We attempted to find and synthesise data focused on the research questions as listed below:

1. How should people with neurodevelopmental differences be identified for diagnostic assessment?
2. Which documents and guidelines are relevant to implementing a neurodevelopmental pathway?
3. Which assessment tools are applicable 'pre-referral' to identify a need for neurodevelopmental assessment, relevant to all diagnoses?
4. What are the key considerations for assessment and triage?
5. Which 'disorder specific' assessment tools should be considered?
6. What are the key considerations for making a diagnosis, and reporting this to individuals and their families?
7. What time standards should be applied to a neurodevelopmental pathway?
8. How can we involve lived experience in the development of pathways?

2.3. Literature Review Methods and Analysis

The research team completed a rapid review of clinical guidelines and available diagnosis and assessment tools. We began searches in December 2019 of Cochrane, Medline, CINAHL, PubMed and Google for pre-existing clinical guidelines and diagnosis and assessment tools for neurodevelopmental diagnoses: autism, developmental coordination disorder (DCD), developmental language disorder (DLD), intellectual disability (ID), foetal alcohol spectrum disorder (FASD) and attention deficit hyperactivity disorder (ADHD). Search terms included ICD-10 and DSM-5 definitions, acronyms and other terminology alternatives for each neurodevelopmental diagnosis, as well as terms for clinical guidelines. The list of assessments for inclusion was developed by consultation with clinicians about local, national and international practice, and consultation with experts, as well as the reviewing of papers to identify commonly used tools in research. Based on these criteria, we identified assessments most commonly studied, most used in research and most used in practice. The focus was therefore on widely used and studied measures, rather than on providing a systematic overview. We revisited the literature throughout the development of the pathway. We set up automatic alerts to monitor the relevant literature for updates.

Summary tables were developed using content analysis and narrative summary methods [31]. Recommendations and guidance were synthesised across the available clinical guidance/guidelines in relation to the key questions of the study. Summaries of assessment tools were prepared, with overview of each tool, users, population, and constructs. A matrix was constructed to indicate which tools were relevant to which neurodevelopmental diagnosis. Tables of diagnostic factors for clinicians were derived. The tables contained descriptions and likely indicators associated with the DSM-5 criteria for autism, ADHD, ID, DLD, DCD and FASD. A matrix was developed to display the complex set of observations and information required in relation to diagnostic criteria. The information developed was used to facilitate stakeholder discussion, and eventually formed a key part of the pathway documentation.

2.4. Stakeholder Engagement Methods and Analysis

Stakeholders were identified for involvement through professional and user networks, and represented every health-board area of Scotland. Senior professionals and people with lived experience were included throughout. Stakeholders included people with lived experience, families and local autism advocacy groups. Professionals included psychiatrists, psychologists, teachers, occupational therapists, speech and language therapists, paediatricians, and academics. Stakeholders also included members who were involved in government and regulatory bodies.

We used group-work, workshops, discussion and debate with stakeholders, applying interactive and participatory methods [32,33] over a series of face-to-face events with follow up review, phone calls, emails, individual meetings, small group discussion and videoconferencing. The first group of stakeholders (n = 44) were invited to attend an initial event. Initial priorities and directions were identified. The key problem under discussion was improvement of diagnosis and assessment, having identified the service and personal costs of missed or delayed diagnosis. There were initial ideas about improvements which could be implemented, and the format or delivery of the proposed pathway. Knowledge about the scope and nature of the problem and possibilities for improvement were discussed, including personal experiences, the work of practitioners, policymakers, and researchers [29,30]. The research team-maintained notes of the discussions, synthesising key themes and main points as discussion documents, which were further shared with the group via email and videoconference. During this period, the review of evidence was undertaken, and draft pathway documentation produced. Next, a larger group of stakeholders (n = 127) attended a face-to-face event. This event included review of the draft pathway, review of the literature review outputs, and identification of themes and feedback. This event helped us to understand issues and generate new ideas concerning the pathway. Additionally, "buy-in" was required from the community, with understanding gained on the feasibility, acceptability and potential future engagement of people with the pathway. Each stage included the careful review of collected information and frequent return to primary documents and stakeholders as necessary. Summaries were derived and synthesised using content and thematic analysis [34]. As the analysis progressed, more refined descriptions and recommendations were created, and detailed prototype pathway documentation and content was written.

2.5. Advisory Group

An advisory group (n = 25) was recruited to consult on and finalise the pathway, representing an expert multi-disciplinary group comprising occupational therapy, clinical psychology, psychiatry, child and adolescent mental health services, paediatric medicine, general practice (family medicine), teaching, speech and language therapy, government representatives, and people with lived experience. Most individuals in the advisory group had participated in one or both of the previous stakeholder events. This was a coproduction team, with stakeholders participating extensively with researchers to finalise the content and documentation of the pathway. As a team, we regularly communicated to discuss and agree upon content. Debate and review were completed and supported by email and videoconferencing. Three cycles of detailed review of draft documentation were completed with the advisory group (December 2020, February 2021 and May 2021). As stakeholders had stressed the need for high quality documentation, a graphics design process was undertaken when the content had been finalized. The pathway was then made freely available online [35].

2.6. Ethics

All stakeholders were volunteers, and were free to withdraw at any time for any reason. Stakeholders were provided with information about the project and consented to participate in consultation events and activities. People with lived experience were volunteers who self-identified as having neurodevelopmental differences, they self-selected to participate, and were identified through pre-existing health and social care programmes for public and patient involvement and government engagement. This work was carried out in accordance with the relevant ethical standards of institutional and national practice in Scotland, and in-line with the Declaration of Helsinki.

3. Results

The final neurodevelopmental pathway was designed to cross professional boundaries and facilitate collaboration between medical professionals, mental health professionals, education professionals, allied health professionals, service users and families. Supplementary File S1 contains an overview of the full pathway. The content of the guidance is detailed more fully in the sections that follow.

3.1. How Should People with Neurodevelopmental Differences Be Identified for Diagnostic Assessment?

There was consensus that neurodevelopmental assessment and diagnosis should be supported by a multi-disciplinary team (MDT), with suitable training and mix of skills and professional groups. Clinical views, assessment and observations are mapped to ICD 11 or DSM 5 criteria. Most commonly, assessments are likely to result in more than one diagnosis, including autism, ID, DLD, ADHD, DCD and FASD. It was noted that classification systems focus on those who have a specific aetiology and/or extreme impairment. These perspectives were contrasted with a neurodiversity paradigm which rejects the idea of 'normal' neurocognition. There was strong debate, leading to a consensus that it was also helpful to consider that children may require a neurodevelopmental assessment when presenting with a need as below:

- Communication and social interaction,
- Emotional regulation,
- Co-ordination and/or movement,
- Developmental delay or difficulties across a range of skills,
- Intellectual development or a need for adaptation to support learning,
- Reduced independence in daily routines and activities.

It was noted that referrers, parents or other family members may see the situation differently and describe what they 'see,' and not necessarily in terms of specific diagnoses. The following were agreed upon as indicators in need of need of further assessment:

- Behaviour changes,
- Distress,
- Obsessions and compulsions,
- Changes in patterns of eating, sleeping, activity levels or passivity.

Rather than seeing an 'in-person problem' the position taken within the pathway (taking account of the views of people with lived experience), supports the right to access diagnostic assessment, even if the individual is relatively unaffected [36]. Whilst this may suggest that the right adjustments are already in place, it may also suggest that the individual is masking or camouflaging [37]. There is a need to balance between efficiency and comprehensiveness [38], and diagnostic assessment should also aim to create a detailed profile of strengths and concerns to inform planning. A lifespan perspective is therefore important. Neurodevelopmental differences are enduring, and understanding which anticipatory adaptations might be helpful at different stages is enhanced when diagnosis is clear.

3.2. Which Documents and Guidelines Are Relevant to Implementing a Neurodevelopmental Pathway?

There was no single Scottish neurodevelopmental guideline. Assessment may result in overlapping diagnoses, and Some, but not all, had a guideline. We identified and summarised the available documentation, and drew on these for the pathway (Table 1).

Table 1. Clinical guidelines used to develop the pathway.

	Scotland	International
Attention Deficit Hyperactivity Disorder	Guideline no longer applies and is superseded by NICE (UK) 2018 [39]	NICE (UK) (2018) [39]
Autism	SIGN (2016) [26]	New Zealand Ministries of Health and Education (2016) [40] NICE (UK) (2011) [12] Penner (2018) [41] Whitehouse (2018) [42]
Developmental Co-ordination Disorder	No Guideline	Blank (2019) [43]
Developmental Language Disorder	No Guideline	Bishop (2016) [44] Bishop (2017) [45] The Association for Child and Adolescent Mental Health (2021) [46]
Foetal Alcohol Spectrum Disorder	SIGN (2019) [47] SIGN (2019) [48]	
Intellectual Disability	No Guideline	British Psychological Society (2000) [49] British Psychological Society (2015) [50] MacKay (2009) [51] Tassé (2019) [52]
Neurodevelopental	No Guideline	Gillberg (2010) [13] Gillberg (2021) [3]

3.3. Which Assessment Tools Are Applicable 'Pre-Referral' to Identify a Need for Neurodevelopmental Assessment, Relevant to All Diagnoses?

Information gathered at the pre-referral stage supports timely and proportionate professional involvement [23]. Avoidance of duplication is desirable. Before commencing a neurodevelopmental assessment, we identified the following suggestions for professionals:

- Review available reports from professionals.
- Indicators for concern can be identified through screening, through the parent/carer or family, and from interviews and observations of the person in their typical environments (e.g., school, home, community).
- Gain the persons consent to include others as necessary, and communicate the likely process (e.g., through a 'leaflet').
- Develop a document containing the referral indicators; this could include the person's current needs, wishes, and environments, as well as the views of the parent/carer or family.
- Gather key information on early development, including alcohol exposure and other relevant family history as required.

In line with the available clinical guidelines, we recommend that pre-referral information can be gathered through:

- Interview (remote or face to face),
- naturalistic observation in typical environments,
- standardised or non-standardised questionnaires or tools,
- contextual assessment approaches,

- locally-used approaches/tools (these are not diagnostic but provide qualitative information—local teams should agree on tools which are used for all individuals, and tools which are used in specific circumstances).

We reviewed and summarised key tools that are commonly used and recommended either in published clinical guidelines or by expert stakeholders, and were applicable to all diagnoses in the pre-referral stage (Table 2).

Table 2. Pre-Referral Tools Applicable to all Diagnoses. Adapted from published NAIT pathway [35].

Tool Summary and Reference	Respondent	Stage/Age
The ESSENCE-Q [53] is a one-page list of yes/no questions to identify areas of concern, with room for brief elaboration. A useful screening questionnaire to gather pre-referral information.	Professional Parent/Carer	Early years, Primary, and Secondary (0–18 years)
The Social Communication, Emotional Regulation Transactional Supports (SCERTS) Tools [54] offer a structured format, adapted to developmental stage (from non-verbal to conversational level) based on observation in naturally occurring environments. Particular focus on social communication, emotional regulation and transactional supports.	Professional with training	All ages and stages
Fife Neurodevelopmental Questionnaire [55] is a developmental history gathering form for use with parents, developed in Scotland, based on the ESSENCE-Q.	Professional	0–18 years
Strengths and Difficulties Questionnaire (SDQ) [56] is a brief emotional and behavioural questionnaire, completed by parents/professionals and older young people.	Professional Parent/Carer Young person (>11 years)	2–17 years
The Developmental and Well-Being Assessment (DAWBA) [57] comprises a set of interviews and questionnaires that can be done on a computer or face to face. Designed to gather information relevant to a range of DSM-5 diagnoses.	Professional Parent/Carer Young person (>11 years)	2–17 years
The Griffiths Assessment [58] is a standardised, observational, play-oriented measure for assessing the rate of development of neurodevelopmental skills.	Pediatrician Professional with training	0–6 years
The CIRCLE Early Years Stages Tool (0–5 years) [59] or the CIRCLE Participation Scale (5–18 years) [18] identify factors that support or interfere with participation in school life for children with additional support needs.	Education professional	Early years, Primary, and Secondary (0–18 years)
The School Participation Questionnaire (SPQ) [60] is a measure to support understanding of participation related factors, involvement and engagement of children with additional support needs in the school context.	Education professional	Primary (5–12 years)
The Child and Adolescent Intellectual Disability Screening Questionnaire (CAIDS-Q) [61] is a quick, easy and accurate way of identifying children/young people who are likely to have an intellectual disability.	Professional Parent/Carer	6–17 years
The Dimensions Tool [62] is an online tool providing personalised information to support a person's well-being and mental health.	A parent/carer, an individual, GP or other professional can use the rating against dimensions related to health and wellbeing	>13 years
The Five to Fifteen Tool (FTF) The FTF 2–5 years and FTF 5–17 years [63] are standardized and validated questionnaires to gather clinical history relevant to the entire range of neurodevelopmental presentations and can be used aid in early detection, enabling further examination and intervention.	Parent/carer Education professional	2–17 years

3.4. What Are the Key Considerations for Assessment and Triage?

Standards for formal neurodevelopmental assessment agreed with stakeholders are presented in Table 3. Recommendations focus on early identification of 'core' and 'complex' cases, presented in Table 4. This categorisation was proposed to support proportionate intervention and avoid duplication. In short, if a team are confident of a straightforward conclusion towards diagnosis (i.e., a 'core' case), there is no need for appointments with several sets of professionals. Where there is less complexity, multi-stage assessment may not be required, and assessments are completed locally by a smaller team. Diagnosis can be completed rapidly in most cases. If there is greater complexity, identification of such is completed promptly. More appointments may be necessary, and enhanced staff skill required, with time allocated for additional standardised diagnostic tools and formulation.

Table 3. Standards for Neurodevelopmental Assessment. Adapted from the published NAIT pathway [35].

1. Neurodevelopmental assessment should (ideally) be conducted by an MDT and always by more than one person
2. Assessment should follow a clinical guideline if available
3. Those undertaking assessment should have the relevant level of training and experience
4. Assessment should be identified as early as possible as 'core' or 'complex'
    a. 'Core'–which can be completed by the team currently involved or other local team
    b. 'Complex'–which should be completed by a team identified at triage, who have skills required and time allocated or training in additional standardised diagnostic tools and formulation across different diagnoses
5. Core assessments should be completed in 1–2 appointments with as much information as possible gathered in advance of the 1st MDT appointment
6. Complex assessments should be carried out by an MDT with expertise in the presenting of differential diagnoses or co-occurring presentations
7. Local teams should consider sending relevant useful information to individuals and families prior to assessment, for example:
    a. 'Information for you while waiting for your appointment'
    b. 'Neurodevelopmental information leaflets and website links'
    c. 'What to expect in an online or face to face appointment'
8. Reports should be written on the day of an appointment and shared as agreed within two weeks for:
    a. each assessment appointment *
    b. diagnostic outcome report
9. Formulation and diagnosis should be made with explicit reference to diagnostic criteria (DSM5 or ICD-11)
10. Time from acceptance of referral to first appointment should be no longer than 12 weeks
11. Local areas should consider including time standards in local pathways

* It is noted that in some circumstances a single assessment may be carried out over more than one appointment.

Table 4. Complexity factors which may be used to identify 'core' and 'complex' cases. Adapted from published NAIT pathway [35].

Complexity Factors	Examples
Medical history	More than one co-occurring diagnosis Genetic or chromosomal abnormalities Other neurodevelopmental disorders Intellectual disability Attachment disorder Mental health condition Sensory impairment Poor regulation in one or more environments Adverse childhood experiences
Individuals who belong to groups where diagnosis is commonly delayed or overlooked	Females Individuals who are or have been looked after and accommodated Black and minority ethnic individuals Individuals who internalise, mask or camouflage or present with 'mild' symptoms
Family factors	Discrepant observations of needs across contexts (e.g., family and school) Different views within the family or between the individual, family members Neurodevelopmental disorders within the wider family Family literacy issues, communication or learning difficulties Lack of access to a person who can give a good quality history (e.g., where parent has a learning difficulty) Cultural differences Family languages other than English or other dominant local language
Clinical team	Lack of access to skills, experience and resources Recruitment and retention of necessary staff Rural and remote areas—the smaller team may be more prepared to meet most needs arising, but may be less able to respond to unusual situations Threshold for complexity will depend on experience of the team
Other environmental factors	Individuals who have needs well met by those around them may present with less obvious signs (this could add or reduce complexity) Difficulty in accessibility and travel to clinics
COVID-19	Potential to add significant complexity

The most 'severe' presentation is not the most complex and nor is the 'milder' presentation the most straightforward. The number of complexity factors may or may not add up to a complex case. In different contexts a particular presentation may or may not be complex depending on the clinical team.

It is desirable, both for those referred and in order to deploy resources, that only those for whom it is relevant undergo diagnostic assessment. Triage is commonly used in healthcare for this reason [6]. See Table 5 for triage outcomes and actions. The triage team should include expert practitioners across the age range of different diagnoses and available local services (e.g., paediatrician, psychologist, OT). Frequency and length of meetings to process referrals depends on referral rate. To support the provision of high quality information prior to referral, a standardised information gathering approach is important, ensuring consistent understanding and documentation. It may be necessary for the team completing triage to complete more information gathering before to the first formal appointment (recommended tools are summarised in Table 6).

Table 5. Triage outcomes and actions. Adapted from published NAIT pathway [35].

Triage Outcomes	
Outcome	**Actions**
Not accepted: adequate information shared and effective conversations with person raising concern	Continue to collaborate in the planning process for this individual as required (support according to needs identified) Communication with person making request explaining the decision Signposting and advice for presenting concerns
Not accepted: not enough information	Communication with person making request explaining the decision, requesting specific further information or assessment Signposting and advice for presenting concerns
Accepted: core pathway	Make initial formulation of possible differential diagnoses to trigger appropriate assessment and enlist the right professionals Request further assessments prior to next appointment Allocate appointments to complete assessment with professionals currently known to individual referred or local team, following receipt of recommended assessments Link family with relevant supports and provide information on processes Inform person making request of outcome
Accepted: complex pathway	Make initial formulation of possible differential diagnoses to trigger appropriate assessment. Enlist the right professional team Request any further assessments required prior to next appointment On receipt of requested further assessments, allocate appointments and identify relevant teams to take assessment forward with named clinician(s) identified. Link family with relevant supports and provide information on processes Inform person making request of outcome

Before triage, check that the following are available: (1) consent for referral, (2) referral form(s), (3) ESSENCE-Q or similar screener, (4) reports on: professional views, reasons for referral; early development and family history (including prenatal alcohol history); parent/carer views about strengths, concerns, expectations; young person's views; Relevant reports/assessments (e.g., occupational therapy).

Table 6. Post-triage further information gathering tools, prior to the face-to-face appointment. Adapted from published NAIT pathway [35].

Details	Respondent	Age/Stage
A Neurodevelopmental-informed school or nursery observation can be used to gather information in a natural setting, especially when there have been discrepant contextual reports from home and school. Any age, when the observation can be made without the child/young person being aware or uncomfortable. May not be suitable for older children. Should be considered but is not essential.	A professional with enhanced or expert skills in diagnosis	All ages and stages
The Social Responsiveness Scale (SRS) [64] is standardised tool, and useful where social communication differences are highlighted, to provide contextual information and clarity over whether or not there are discrepancies between home and school.	Parent/carer Education professional Scored by health professional	Pre-school (0–5 years) School (5–18 years)

Table 6. *Cont.*

Details	Respondent	Age/Stage
The Conners Scale [65] is a questionnaire that is used as a screening tool to understand whether the child or young person may benefit from further detailed ADHD assessment.	Parent/carer School Scored by health professional	6–18 years
Behavior Rating Inventory of Executive Function (BRIEF) [66] is a short questionnaire designed to assess executive function in different contexts. May be used with those with intellectual disabilities and attention disorders, traumatic brain injuries, neurodevelopmental, psychiatric, and medical conditions.	Parent/carer Education professional Scored by health professional	5–18 years

3.5. Which 'Disorder Specific' Assessment Tools Should Be Considered?

We identified that a neurodevelopmental assessment should include:

- medical and developmental history;
- presentation at current time-point;
- reports from the person/self-report/informant report;
- assessments from people in the environment of the person (e.g., home);
- clinical observation in different natural environments (e.g., home, school);
- assessment and skills;
- assessment of function and participation activities/interactions that are developmentally appropriate/relevant;
- the environment, including social and physical features around the child and family.

Several tools can be applied depending on presenting concerns (see Supplementary File S2 for a full list of tools, commonly used and recommended either in published clinical guidelines or by expert stakeholders). Clinical expertise and consultation across relevant teams can be used to identify the necessary assessments. The assessments can be completed together or separately. Assessments do not need to be completed in sequence, and may not be targeted to a specific presentation or diagnosis.

3.6. What Are the Key Considerations for Making a Diagnosis and Reporting This to Individuals and Their Families?

Information should be brought together and considered in a procedure termed 'formulation' [67]. This was a term familiar to some of our stakeholders, but not all. One benefit of a multi-disciplinary approach is the spread of shared language and practices. Formulation ideally takes account of ideas, thoughts and experiences of the individual and their family members in relation to diagnosis. Diagnoses are then made with regard to international criteria. The research team developed tables of evidence (see Supplementary File S3 for full tables of evidence for each diagnosis) to support clinicians in reviewing assessment evidence and reaching a diagnosis. The tables contain DSM-5 criteria for autism, ADHD, ID, DLD, DCD and FASD. Criteria for each are located in a matrix designed to allow clinicians to view and compare information gathered from different elements in one location. The tables were designed to facilitate a decision as to whether enough information was present to support making a diagnosis. If diagnosis is not possible, the tables may indicate aspects requiring further information/review.

Stakeholders identified that qualitative and experiential aspects of diagnostic processes were extremely important. People respond to diagnosis in a multitude of ways, and an approach that is personalised is recommended. Several opportunities for discussion should be provided in order that discussion can be completed adequately and clarifications can be made if required. However, people and their families maintain the option of both accepting and/or disclosing a diagnosis to others. Any issues, idiosyncrasies or behaviours might not necessarily be seen as troublesome to people and their families. There are also important factors related to time, and potential changes in people (and families) view of diagnosis over a lifetime. There are therefore instances where it is necessary to review a diagnosis. Relatedly, there is a need to have a process to seek out, access or improve new or existing supports across the lifespan, including anticipatory support in advance of major transitions.

See Table 7 for agreed standards for diagnosis and follow up.

Table 7. Standards for diagnosis and follow up. Adapted from published NAIT pathway [35].

1. Write report on day diagnostic decision is made and share report with family promptly
2. Follow local protocols for information sharing with the wider team
3. Share a report with the wider team and family according to preferences and consent
4. Provide training and support to all health professionals involved in the pathway in relation to 'sharing difficult news'
5. Share locally agreed upon information on the day of diagnosis, relevant to the child and family attending
6. Offer a 'follow up' appointment soon after the diagnosis to give the family an opportunity to ask further questions and hear more about local planning processes and sources of support [within eight weeks of diagnosis]
7. Make training and information available for school staff and the wider team
8. Staff should follow clear guidelines about recommended sources of national and local support and advocacy for children and young people with a range of needs
9. Staff should follow clear local protocols about linking parents in with parent mediated interventions and information sessions
10. Parent information sessions support and interventions should be offered before, during and after diagnosis. They should be adapted for:
    a. the age and stage of their child
    b. children with neurodevelopmental differences
11. Families report they particularly value:
    a. Face to face meetings with health and education professionals with expertise in the 'diagnosed' presentations at this age and stage, and with professionals with up to date experience and understanding of the local planning process
    b. The opportunity to ask questions
    c. Information relevant to their family, including support to apply for benefits (where appropriate)
    d. Local support groups, parent information/education sessions and parent mediated interventions
    e. Access to recommended supports

3.7. What Time Standards Should Be Applied to a Neurodevelopmental Pathway?

We developed time standards as a benchmark to report against (summarised in Table 8). Waiting for diagnosis is commonly raised as a major concern for those seeking support. We identified few published or formal time standards for diagnostic assessment. Time standards were therefore developed through consideration of the similar standards for autism e.g., [38,41,68] and consensus views gained from stakeholders.

Table 8. Time Standards. Adapted from published NAIT pathway [35].

Stage in Pathway	Time Standard
1. Pre-referral (initial information gathering) *	First appointment should be as soon as possible and no later than four weeks (establish consent to refer/ request assistance and consent to share information)
2. Request for neurodevelopmental assessment (time from request for neurodevelopmental assessment accepted to first appointment after triage)	No more than 12 weeks
3. Diagnostic assessment (first appointment to last appointment)	Up to six weeks (core cases) Up to 22 weeks (complex cases)
4. Diagnosis (last appointment to diagnosis made; may include consensus that no diagnosis is made or individual does not meet criteria)	Less than one week
5. Diagnostic outcome (decision made to diagnostic assessment outcome shared)	Less than one week
6. Total time (from request/referral accepted to diagnosis shared)	No more than 19 weeks (core cases) No more than 36 weeks (complex cases)
7. Follow up (meeting after diagnosis)	Within eight weeks of diagnosis shared

* Offer a first appointment to those who have been identified (e.g., by family doctor) as in need of a neurodevelopmental assessment. Each service or local area will have pre-existing standards for responding to initial or safeguarding concerns.

3.8. How Can We Involve Lived Experience in the Development of Pathways?

There is a need for the co-production and involvement of users of services, experts by experience or 'patient-voices' at all stages [9,69] based on the principle of 'nothing about us without us' [70]. When a diagnosis is made, a new, potentially supportive community of people with similar experiences is opened up. Diagnosis matters to people seeking and receiving assessment. However, the process is experienced differently, and sometimes it is positive, while at other times it may be challenging [14,71]. Based on our consultation with representatives of people with recent experience in diagnostic assessment, key points for reflection are summarised in Table 9 (and Supplementary File S4 for further detail).

Table 9. Lived experience themes and reflections for professionals. Adapted from published NAIT pathway [35].

Theme	Reflections for Professionals
No supports should be diagnosis dependent	Does your service limit access to supports before diagnosis and if so how can this be addressed? Are supports offered before, during and after diagnosis developmentally relevant and individualised to meet particular needs? How well are health, education and other services working together? Are families potentially wasting time on attending programmes that are not right for them?
Quality and timing of information provided is more important than quantity	What information is shared? How is information shared with families? Is information accessible? Are there opportunities both on the day of diagnosis and after, for the individual and family to have conversations with professionals with suitable experience about the diagnosis and financial, health, educational or other supports?

Table 9. *Cont.*

Theme	Reflections for Professionals
Keep families and individuals informed at every stage	How clear and accessible is the information about diagnosis? How predictable is the assessment process? Do things happen at the time and in the way expected? Do different professionals give consistent information? How can the process be made more positive?
Make the request for assessment and support process clear, especially when the decision is made not to proceed	Are individuals/families clear about how to request assessment and are they supported to do so? Do they know why the assessment is proceeding or not? Have they been made aware that a further request can be made if circumstances change or they disagree with the decision? Is information provided and support in place to address concerns raised by individuals/families?
Parents don't know what they don't know	How can professionals support families to ask the right questions and focus on key information?
Help set expectations about waiting times and provide a point of contact	How well are shared expectations communicated with and understood by families? Do families feel informed? Are families signposted to relevant support and made aware of their rights? Do professionals have access to relevant, accurate information about waiting times and sources of support?
At assessment appointments	Reflect on feedback from those who attend appointments. Ask people about what worked well/could be better in advance of the appointment, at the appointment and after it. Ask about the quality of the environment in the 'clinic' setting. Ask about the quality of communication of professionals.

4. Discussion

In this paper, we shared the process and outcomes in the development of a new pathway for neurodevelopmental assessment and diagnosis. Stakeholder engagement, along with review of current guidelines and assessment tools, allowed the development of recommendations that are feasible and evidence informed. In this article, we have outlined the reasons why a neurodevelopmental approach is desirable, together with the presentation of solutions and recommendations for practitioners and services undertaking this change.

The role of diagnosis may be controversial; however, a preference for timely diagnosis is well-supported in the literature [72–74]. We strongly advocate the perspective that people's needs should be addressed irrespective of diagnosis or 'label'. However, it is often the case that a diagnosis can help with accessing needed supports. In particular, when people are at key points in their lives, when they are accessing new environments, situations or changing circumstances, a diagnosis is helpful in clarifying how neurodevelopmental differences may be impacting an individual, and therefore, the interventions, supports or adaptations required. The need for evidence-informed intervention, particularly non-pharmacological interventions and environmental adaptations, could be made more explicit by a recognised diagnosis [3].

4.1. *Implications for Practice*

Key points identified from evidence and consensus are summarised below.

- Our research highlights the need for a neurodevelopmental understanding, rather than focusing on single conditions, in clinical assessment and diagnosis.
- Most individuals will have signs of more than one diagnosis; a co-occurring neurodevelopmental presentation is the norm.

- Diagnostic assessment has historically focused on individual presentations. In Scotland, many areas had a children's autism or ADHD pathway/service. Based on these models, children and young people could wait on one list after another.
- Individual professionals may be highly knowledgeable or experienced in one 'diagnosis' but only have an 'informed' or 'skilled' level for others.
- Assessment and diagnosis services should be multi-disciplinary, people receiving help should be directed to the relevant professionals as required.
- As well as a diagnostic 'label', formulation should encompass the needs, wishes, strengths and goals of the individual, and focus on their day-to-day life and typical environments.
- Neurodevelopmental differences are lifelong, but need not be framed as 'deficits'. Outcomes for individuals are strongly influenced by the environment, demands of activities, available resources and supports, and the individual's own strengths and motivations (i.e., a social model of disability).
- Review and provision of pharmacological and non-pharmacological supports is required for interventions in relation to associated needs including sleep, anxiety, and mood.
- While accurate diagnosis can enhance intervention, assessments and planning, support should never be purely diagnosis-dependent.

4.2. Limitations

Our recommendations are based primarily on expert consensus, although evidence from guidelines has been utilised where possible, and a review of assessment tools undertaken. Recommendations are aimed at children and young people. Adults may share similar features, but their day to day contexts and roles are different. Although this study was completed in Scotland, the demographic and cultural similarities of Scotland to other countries means recommendations are likely to be transferable. There is an ongoing need for service configuration data, and an understanding of ratio and skill mix of staff recommended for a given population. Work is ongoing in Scotland via NAIT to develop this.

4.3. Conclusions

We have developed a practical resource for neurodevelopmental assessment and diagnosis. The recommendations reported here are supported by the Scottish Government. All materials are freely available and recommended for use by those with relevant skills and experience in undertaking neurodevelopmental assessment in children and young people aged 0–18 years.

Supplementary Materials: The following are available online at https://www.mdpi.com/article/10.3390/children8111033/s1, Supplementary File S1: Pathway; Supplementary File S2: Standardised Assessment Tools Recommended for Particular Presentations; Supplementary File S3: Summary Tables of Evidence for Each NDD Diagnosis; Supplementary File S4: Views from People with Lived Experience.

Author Contributions: M.R.: Conceptualization, Methodology, Writing—Original draft preparation, Writing—Reviewing and Editing. D.M.: Conceptualization, Methodology, Writing—Original draft preparation, Writing—Reviewing and Editing. L.J.: Conceptualization, Methodology, Writing—Original draft preparation, Writing—Reviewing and Editing. S.P.: Conceptualization, Methodology; Writing—Reviewing and Editing. K.F.: Conceptualization, Supervision, Funding acquisition. All authors have read and agreed to the published version of the manuscript.

Funding: This research was funded by the Scottish Government.

Institutional Review Board Statement: This work was carried out in accordance with the relevant ethical standards of institutional and national practice in Scotland, and following the declaration of Helsinki. Ethical approval was not required for this study as it was a collecting service improvement information from patients, carers and clinicians; no identifiable information was collected from respondents.

Informed Consent Statement: All stakeholders were volunteers, and were free to withdraw at any time for any reason. Stakeholders were provided with information about the project and consented to participate in consultation events and activities. People with lived experience were volunteers who self-identified as having neurodevelopmental differences, they self-selected to participate, and were identified through pre-existing health and social care programmes for public and patient involvement and government engagement.

Data Availability Statement: Please contact the corresponding author for study data.

Acknowledgments: We wish to give thanks and acknowledge the contributions of stakeholders, the Scottish Government, people who are experts by experience of neurodevelopmental difference and their families, health and education professionals from across Allied Health Professions, Community Child Health, CAMHS and Education in the development of this resource for all those involved in, delivering or receiving neurodevelopmental assessments. All materials are available freely online https://www.thirdspace.scot/nait/diagnosis-resources/ (accessed on 11 October 2021).

Conflicts of Interest: The authors declare no conflict of interest. The funders had no role in the design of the study; in the collection, analyses, or interpretation of data; in the writing of the manuscript, or in the decision to publish the results.

References

1. American Psychiatric Association. *Diagnostic and Statistical Manual of Mental Disorders*, 5th ed.; American Psychiatric Publishing: Arlington, VA, USA, 2013; Available online: https://dsm.psychiatryonline.org/doi/full/10.1176/appi.books.9780890425596.dsm05 (accessed on 22 June 2021).
2. World Health Organization. *International Classification of Diseases for Mortality and MORBIDITY Statistics (11th Revision)*; World Health Organization: Geneva, Switzerland, 2018; Available online: https://icd.who.int/browse11/l-m/en (accessed on 22 June 2021).
3. Gillberg, C. *The ESSENCE of Autism and Other Neurodevelopmental Conditions: Rethinking Co-Morbidities, Assessment, and Intervention*; Jessica Kingsley Publishers: London, UK, 2021.
4. Chamberlain, K.; Reid, N.; Warner, J.; Shelton, D.; Dawe, S. A qualitative evaluation of caregivers' experiences, understanding and outcomes following diagnosis of FASD. *Res. Dev. Disabil.* **2017**, *63*, 99–106. [CrossRef] [PubMed]
5. Kentrou, V.; De Veld, D.M.; Mataw, K.J.; Begeer, S. Delayed autism spectrum disorder recognition in children and adolescents previously diagnosed with attention-deficit/hyperactivity disorder. *Autism* **2018**, *23*, 1065–1072. [CrossRef] [PubMed]
6. Rutherford, M.; Burns, M.; Gray, D.; Bremner, L.; Clegg, S.; Russell, L.; Smith, C.; O'Hare, A. Improving Efficiency and Quality of the Children's ASD Diagnostic Pathway: Lessons Learned from Practice. *J. Autism Dev. Disord.* **2017**, *48*, 1579–1595. [CrossRef] [PubMed]
7. Rutherford, M.; Forsyth, K.; McKenzie, K.; McClure, I.; Murray, A.; McCartney, D.; Irvine, L.; O'Hare, A. Implementation of a Practice Development Model to Reduce the Wait for Autism Spectrum Diagnosis in Adults. *J. Autism Dev. Disord.* **2018**, *48*, 2677–2691. [CrossRef]
8. Winstanley, M.; Webb, R.T.; Conti-Ramsden, G. More or less likely to offend? Young adults with a history of identified developmental language disorders. *Int. J. Lang. Commun. Disord.* **2018**, *53*, 256–270. [CrossRef]
9. Dorsey, R.; Crow, H.; Gaddy, C. Putting Autistic Voices at the Forefront of Care. Leader Live. 2020. Available online: https://leader.pubs.asha.org/do/10.1044/leader.FMP.25102020.8/full/ (accessed on 11 October 2021).
10. Urbanowicz, A.; Nicolaidis, C.; Houting, J.D.; Shore, S.M.; Gaudion, K.; Girdler, S.; Savarese, R.J. An Expert Discussion on Strengths-Based Approaches in Autism. *Autism Adulthood* **2019**, *1*, 82–89. [CrossRef]
11. Hayes, J.; Ford, T.; Rafeeque, H.; Russell, G. Clinical practice guidelines for diagnosis of autism spectrum disorder in adults and children in the UK: A narrative review. *BMC Psychiatry* **2018**, *18*, 222. [CrossRef]
12. NICE. Autism Spectrum Disorder in under 19s: Recognition, REFERRAL and Diagnosis. 2011. Available online: https://www.nice.org.uk/guidance/cg128/resources/autismspectrum-disorder-in-under-19s-recognition-referral-and-diagnosis-pdf35109456621253 (accessed on 14 May 2021).
13. Gillberg, C. The ESSENCE in child psychiatry: Early Symptomatic Syndromes Eliciting Neurodevelopmental Clinical Examinations. *Res. Dev. Disabil.* **2010**, *31*, 1543–1551. [CrossRef]
14. Appleton, R.; Elahi, F.; Tuomainen, H.; Canaway, A.; Singh, S.P. "I'm just a long history of people rejecting referrals" experiences of young people who fell through the gap between child and adult mental health services. *Eur. Child Adolesc. Psychiatry* **2021**, *30*, 401–413. [CrossRef]
15. Thapar, A.; Cooper, M.; Rutter, M. Neurodevelopmental disorders. *Lancet Psychiatry* **2017**, *4*, 339–346. [CrossRef]
16. Craig, P.; Dieppe, P.; Macintyre, S.; Michie, S.; Nazareth, I.; Petticrew, M. Developing and evaluating complex interventions: An introduction to the new Medical Research Council guidance. *Evid. Based Public Health Eff. Effic.* **2010**, *1*, 185–203.
17. MacKay, T.; Knapp, M.; Boyle, J.M.; Iemmi, V.; Connolly, M.; Rehill, A. *The Microsegmentation of the Autism Spectrum: Economic and Research Implications for Scotland*; The Scottish Government: Edinburgh, UK, 2017.

18. Maciver, D.; Hunter, C.; Johnston, L.; Forsyth, K. Using Stakeholder Involvement, Expert Knowledge and Naturalistic Implementation to Co-Design a Complex Intervention to Support Children's Inclusion and Participation in Schools: The CIRCLE Framework. *Children* **2021**, *8*, 217. [CrossRef]
19. Scottish Government. *The Scottish Strategy for Autism*; The Scottish Government: Edinburgh, UK, 2011.
20. Scottish Government. *Scottish Strategy for Autism: Outcomes and Priorities 2018–2021*; The Scottish Government: Edinburgh, UK, 2018. Available online: https://www.gov.scot/publications/scottish-strategy-autism-outcomes-priorities-2018-2021/ (accessed on 22 June 2021).
21. McKenzie, K.; Forsyth, K.; O'Hare, A.; McClure, I.; Rutherford, M.; Murray, A.; Irvine, L. The relationship between waiting times and 'adherence' to the Scottish Intercollegiate Guidelines Network 98 guideline in autism spectrum disorder diagnostic services in Scotland. *Autism* **2016**, *20*, 395–401. [CrossRef]
22. McKenzie, K.; Rutherford, M.; Forsyth, K.; O'Hare, A.; McClure, I.; Murray, A.L.; Irvine, L. The relation between practice that is consistent with NICE guideline 142 recommendations and waiting times within Autism Spectrum Disorder diagnostic services. *Res. Autism Spectr. Disord.* **2016**, *26*, 10–15. [CrossRef]
23. McKenzie, K.; Forsyth, K.; O'Hare, A.; McClure, I.; Rutherford, M.; Murray, A.; Irvine L. Factors influencing waiting times for diagnosis of Autism Spectrum Disorder in children and adults. *Res. Dev. Disabil.* **2015**, *45*, 300–306. [CrossRef]
24. Rutherford, M.; McKenzie, K.; Forsyth, K.; McCartney, D.; O'Hare, A.; McClure, I.; Irvine, L. Why are they waiting? Exploring professional perspectives and developing solutions to delayed diagnosis of autism spectrum disorder in adults and children. *Res. Autism Spectr. Disord.* **2016**, *31*, 53–65. [CrossRef]
25. Rutherford, M.; McKenzie, K.; McClure, I.; Forsyth, K.; O'Hare, A.; McCartney, D.; Finlayson, I. A national study to investigate the clinical use of standardised instruments in autism spectrum disorder assessment of children and adults in Scotland. *Res. Autism Spectr. Disord.* **2016**, *29*, 93–100. [CrossRef]
26. Scottish Intercollegiate Guidelines Network (SIGN) 145. Assessment, Diagnosis and Interventions for Autism Spectrum Disorder. 2016. Available online: https://www.sign.ac.uk/media/1444/neurodevelopmental_areas_of_assessment_criteria.pdf (accessed on 14 May 2021).
27. Mannell, J.; Davis, K. Evaluating complex health interventions with randomized controlled trials: How do we improve the use of qualitative methods? *Qual. Health Res.* **2019**, *29*, 623–631. [CrossRef]
28. Wigginton, B.; Thomson, Z.O.; Sandler, C.X.; Reeves, M.M. Reflexive intervention development: Using qualitative research to inform the development of an intervention for women with metastatic breast cancer. *Qual. Health Res.* **2020**, *30*, 666–678. [CrossRef]
29. Lewin, S.; Glenton, C.; Oxman, A.D. Use of qualitative methods alongside randomised controlled trials of complex healthcare interventions: Methodological study. *Br. Med. J.* **2009**, *10*, b3496. [CrossRef]
30. O'Cathain, A.; Croot, L.; Duncan, E.; Rousseau, N.; Sworn, K.; Turner, K.M.; Yardley, L.; Hoddinott, P. Guidance on how to develop complex interventions to improve health and healthcare. *BMJ Open* **2019**, *9*, e029954. [CrossRef]
31. Mohamed Shaffril, H.A.; Samsuddin, S.F.; Abu Samah, A. The ABC of systematic literature review: The basic methodological guidance for beginners. *Qual. Quant.* **2021**, *55*, 1319–1346. [CrossRef]
32. Langley, J.; Wolstenholme, D.; Cooke, J. 'Collective making' as knowledge mobilisation: The contribution of participatory design in the co-creation of knowledge in healthcare. *BMC Health Serv. Res.* **2018**, *18*, 585. [CrossRef]
33. Gibson, A.; Welsman, J.; Britten, N. Evaluating patient and public involvement in health research: From theoretical model to practical workshop. *Health Expect.* **2017**, *20*, 826–835. [CrossRef]
34. Ritchie, J.; Spencer, L. Qualitative data analysis for applied policy research. In *The Qualitative Researcher's Companion*; Huberman, A.M., Miles, M.B., Eds.; Sage: Thousand Oaks, CA, USA, 2002; pp. 305–331.
35. Rutherford, M.; Johnston, L.; Prior, S.; Forsyth, K. Children's Neurodevelopmental Pathway Practice Framework: A Workbook for Assessment, Diagnosis and Planning, National Autism Implementation Team. 2021. Available online: https://www.thirdspace.scot/wp-content/uploads/2021/05/Childrens-Neurodevelopmental-Pathway-and-Guidance-2021.pdf (accessed on 14 May 2021).
36. Jellett, R.; Muggleton, J. Implications of Applying "Clinically Significant Impairment" to Autism Assessment: Commentary on Six Problems Encountered in Clinical Practice. *J. Autism Dev. Disord.* **2021**, 1–10. [CrossRef]
37. Fombonne, E. Camouflage and autism. *J. Child Psychol. Psychiatry* **2020**, *61*, 735–738. [CrossRef]
38. Penner, M.; Anagnostou, E.; Ungar, W.J. Practice patterns and determinants of wait time for autism spectrum disorder diagnosis in Canada. *Mol. Autism* **2018**, *9*, 16. [CrossRef]
39. NICE. Attention Deficit Hyperactivity Disorder: Diagnosis and Management [NG87]. Published: 14 March 2018. Available online: https://www.nice.org.uk/guidance/ng87 (accessed on 14 May 2021).
40. Ministries of Health and Education. *New Zealand Autism Spectrum Disorder Guideline*, 2nd ed.; Ministry of Health: Wellington, New Zealand, 2016. Available online: https://www.health.govt.nz/publication/new-zealandautism-spectrum-disorder-guideline (accessed on 27 May 2021).
41. Penner, M.; Anagnostou, E.; Andoni, L.Y.; Ungar, W.J. Systematic review of clinical guidance documents for autism spectrum disorder diagnostic assessment in select regions. *Autism* **2018**, *22*, 517–527. [CrossRef
42. Whitehouse, A.J.O.; Evans, K.; Eapen, V.; Wray, J. *A National Guideline for the Assessment and Diagnosis of Autism Spectrum Disorders in Australia*; Autism Cooperative Research Centre (CRC): Brisbane, Australia, 2018.

43. Blank, R.; Barnett, A.L.; Cairney, J.; Green, D.; Kirby, A.; Polatajko, H.; Rosenblum, S.; Smits-Engelsman, B.; Sugden, D.; Wilson, P.; et al. International clinical practice recommendations on the definition, diagnosis, assessment, intervention, and psychosocial aspects of developmental coordination disorder. *Dev. Med. Child Neurol.* **2019**, *61*, 242–285. [CrossRef]
44. Bishop, D.V.; Snowling, M.J.; Thompson, P.A.; Greenhalgh, T.; Catalise Consortium. CATALISE: A Multinational and Multidisciplinary Delphi Consensus Study. Identifying Language Impairments in Children. *PLoS ONE* **2016**, *11*, e0158753. [CrossRef]
45. Bishop, D.V.; Snowling, M.J.; Thompson, P.A.; Greenhalgh, T.; Catalise-2 Consortium. Phase 2 of CATALISE: A multinational and multidisciplinary Delphi consensus study of problems with language development: Terminology. *J. Child Psychol. Psychiatry* **2017**, *58*, 1068–1080. [CrossRef] [PubMed]
46. The Association for Child and Adolescent Mental Health. Developmental Language Disorder. 2021. Available online: https://www.acamh.org/topic/developmental-language-disorder/ (accessed on 22 June 2021).
47. Scottish Intercollegiate Guidelines Network (SIGN) 156. Children and Young People Exposed Prenatally to Alcohol. 2019. Available online: https://www.sign.ac.uk/media/1092/sign156.pdf (accessed on 14 May 2021).
48. Scottish Intercollegiate Guidelines Network (SIGN). Neurodevelopmental Areas of Assessment: Criteria for Severe Impairment. 2019. Available online: https://www.sign.ac.uk/assets/neurodevelopmental_areas_of_assessment_criteria.pdf (accessed on 14 May 2021).
49. British Psychological Society. Learning Disability: Definitions and Contexts. 2000. Available online: https://www.bps.org.uk/sites/www.bps.org.uk/files/Member%20Networks/Faculties/Intellectual%20Disabilities/Learning%20Disability%20Definitions%20and%20Contexts%20%282000%29.pdf (accessed on 27 May 2021).
50. British Psychological Society. *Guidance on the Assessment and Diagnosis of Intellectual Disabilities in Adulthood*; British Psychological Society: Leicester, UK, 2015.
51. MacKay, T. Severe and complex learning difficulties: Issues of definition, classification and prevalence. *Educ. Child Psychol.* **2009**, *26*, 9.
52. Tassé, M.J.; Balboni, G.; Navas, P.; Luckasson, R.; Nygren, M.A.; Belacchi, C.; Bonichini, S.; Reed, G.M.; Kogan, C.S. Developing behavioural indicators for intellectual functioning and adaptive behaviour for ICD-11 disorders of intellectual development. *J. Intellect. Disabil. Res.* **2019**, *63*, 386–407. [CrossRef] [PubMed]
53. Gillberg, C. Essence-Q-REV. 2012. Available online: https://www.gu.se/en/gnc/gncs-resources/screening-questionnaires/essence-q-screening-questionnaire#Download-ESENCE-Q (accessed on 21 June 2021).
54. Prizant, B.M.; Wetherby, A.M.; Rubin, E.; Laurent, A.C. The SCERTS model: A transactional, family-centered approach to enhancing communication and socioemotional abilities of children with autism spectrum disorder. *Infants Young Child.* **2003**, *16*, 296–316. [CrossRef]
55. NHS Fife. The Fife-Neurodevelopmental Questionnaire (F-Neurodevelopmental Disorders Q). 2020. Unpublished. Available online: https://www.scottishautism.org/sites/default/files/nhs_participant_information_leaflet_v3.docx (accessed on 11 October 2021).
56. Goodman, R. Strengths and Difficulties Questionnaire (SDQ). 2005. Available online: https://www.sdqinfo.org/py/sdqinfo/b3.py?language=Englishqz(UK) (accessed on 21 June 2021).
57. Goodman, R.; Ford, T.; Richards, H.; Gatward, R.; Meltzer, H. The Development and Well-Being Assessment: Description and initial validation of an integrated assessment of child and adolescent psychopathology. *J. Child Psychol. Psychiatry* **2000**, *41*, 645–655. [CrossRef]
58. Huntley, M. *The Griffiths Mental Developmental Scales Manual from Birth to Two Years*; The Test Agency: Oxford, UK, 1996.
59. CIRCLE Collaboration. Up up and away Inclusive Learning and Collaborative Working—(Ages 0–5) International Version. 2017. Available online: https://www.thirdspace.scot/circle/education-resources (accessed on 21 June 2021).
60. Maciver, D.; Tyagi, V.; Kramer, J.M.; Richmond, J.; Todorova, L.; Romero-Ayuso, D.; Nakamura-Thomas, H.; van Hartingsveldt, M.; Johnston, L.; O'Hare, A.; et al. Development, psychometrics and feasibility of the School Participation Questionnaire: A teacher measure of participation related constructs. *Res. Dev. Disabil.* **2020**, *106*, 103766. [CrossRef]
61. McKenzie, K.; Murray, G.; Murray, A.; Delahunty, L.; Hutton, L.; Murray, K.; O'Hare, A. Child and Adolescent Intellectual Disability Screening Questionnaire to identify children with intellectual disability. *Dev. Med. Child Neurol.* **2018**, *61*, 444–450. [CrossRef]
62. Coventry and Warwickshire Partnership NHS Trust. The Dimensions Tool. Available online: https://dimensions.covwarkpt.nhs.uk/Default.aspx (accessed on 21 June 2021).
63. Kadesjö, B.; Janols, L.-O.; Korkman, M.; Mickelsson, K.; Strand, G.; Trillingsgaard, A.; Lambek, R.; Øgrim, G.; Bredesen, A.M.; Gillberg, C. Five-To-Fifteen-Revised (5-15R). Available online: www.5-15.org (accessed on 21 June 2021).
64. Constantino, J.N.; Gruber, C.P. *Social Responsiveness Scale: SRS-2*; Western Psychological Services: Torrance, CA, USA, 2012.
65. Conners, C.K. *Conners Third Edition (Conners 3)*; Western Psychological Services: Los Angeles, CA, USA, 2008.
66. Gioia, G.A.; Isquith, P.K.; Guy, S.C.; Kenworthy, L. *BRIEF: Behavior Rating Inventory of Executive Function*; Psychological Assessment Resources: Lutz, FL, USA, 2015.
67. Johnstone, L. Using Formulation in Teams. In *Formulation in Psychology and Psychotherapy*; Routledge: London, UK, 2013; pp. 236–262.

68. Le Couteur, A. *National Autism Plan for Children (NAPC): Plan for the Identification, Assessment, Diagnosis and Access to Early Interventions for Pre-School and Primary School Aged Children with Autsim Spectrum Disorders*; National Autistic Society: London, UK, 2003.
69. Pelleboer-Gunnink, H.A.; Van Oorsouw, W.M.W.J.; Van Weeghel, J.; Embregts, P.J.C.M. Mainstream health professionals' stigmatising attitudes towards people with intellectual disabilities: A systematic review. *J. Intellect. Disabil. Res.* **2017**, *61*, 411–434. [CrossRef]
70. Isom, J.; Balasuriya, L. Nothing About Us Without Us in Policy Creation and Implementation. *Psychiatr. Serv.* **2021**, *72*, 121. [CrossRef]
71. Fusar-Poli, L.; Brondino, N.; Politi, P.; Aguglia, E. Missed diagnoses and misdiagnoses of adults with autism spectrum disorder. *Eur. Arch. Psychiatry Clin. Neurosci.* **2020**, 1–12. [CrossRef]
72. Crane, L.; Chester, J.W.; Goddard, L.; Henry, L.A.; Hill, E. Experiences of autism diagnosis: A survey of over 1000 parents in the United Kingdom. *Autism* **2016**, *20*, 153–162. [CrossRef]
73. Crane, L.; Batty, R.; Adeyinka, H.; Goddard, L.; Henry, L.A.; Hill, E. Autism Diagnosis in the United Kingdom: Perspectives of Autistic Adults, Parents and Professionals. *J. Autism Dev. Disord.* **2018**, *48*, 3761–3772. [CrossRef]
74. McGonnell, M.; Corkum, P.; McKinnon, M.; MacPherson, M.; Williams, T.; Davidson, C.; Jones, D.B.; Stephenson, D. Doing it Right: An Interdisciplinary Model for the Diagnosis of ADHD. *J. Can. Acad. Child Adolesc. Psychiatry* **2009**, *18*, 283.

children

MDPI

Article

A Novel Tool to Assess Basic Activities of Daily Living in Spanish Preschoolers

Sabina Barrios-Fernandez [1,*], Margarita Gozalo [2,*], Andres Garcia-Gomez [3], Jorge Carlos-Vivas [4] and Dulce Romero-Ayuso [5]

1 Medical-Surgical Therapeutics Department, University of Extremadura, 10003 Cáceres, Spain
2 Psychology and Anthropology Department, University of Extremadura, 10003 Cáceres, Spain
3 Education Sciences Department, University of Extremadura, 10003 Cáceres, Spain; agarcil9@unex.es
4 Health, Economy, Motricity and Education Research Group (HEME), Faculty of Sport Sciences, University of Extremadura, 10003 Cáceres, Spain; jorge.carlosvivas@gmail.com
5 Physiotherapy Department, University of Granada, 18071 Granada, Spain; dulceromero@ugr.es
* Correspondence: sabinabarrios@unex.es (S.B.-F.); mgozalo@unex.es (M.G.)

Abstract: Background: Basic activities of daily living (BADLs) are those related to self-care. Their performance depends on the development of sensorimotor and cognitive skills, as well as social and environmental aspects. A good performance in BADLs is required for independence and social participation, so they play an important role in early education and early care. We aim to create a tool for BADLs assessment for Spanish preschoolers. Methods: The tool was administered to 303 participants (48.5% boys and 51.5% girls) between three and six years of age. Analyses to find out the factorial structure and internal consistency was carried out. Results: The instrument was composed of 84 items in four scales (eating, personal hygiene, dressing, and daily functioning) with nine factors (oral sensitivity, good manners, manual dexterity, brushing teeth, toilet management, hygiene and grooming, dressing, higher-order and core executive function). Reliability values were from acceptable to preferred (0.74–0.94). Conclusions: The instrument could be useful and shows preliminary good indicators in construct validity and reliability.

Keywords: activities of daily living; executive function; child; evaluation; assessment

Citation: Barrios-Fernandez, S.; Gozalo, M.; Garcia-Gomez, A.; Carlos-Vivas, J.; Romero-Ayuso, D. A Novel Tool to Assess Basic Activities of Daily Living in Spanish Preschoolers. *Children* **2021**, *8*, 496. https://doi.org/10.3390/children8060496

Academic Editor: Laura Simons

Received: 12 May 2021
Accepted: 8 June 2021
Published: 10 June 2021

1. Introduction

1.1. Activities of Daily Living Conceptualization and Development

Activities of daily living (ADLs) refers to a group of tasks that every person carries out to be independent. Concretely, basic activities of daily living (BADLs) refer to the ones oriented toward taking care of one's own body including mobility, feeding, personal hygiene and dressing. Instrumental activities of daily living (IADLs) are activities to support daily life in home and community, often more complex than BADLs, including home management, taking care of others or community mobility [1,2]. BADLs are gradually acquired during childhood, and through practice they become almost automatic, while IADLs are developed through education and practice, with a greater influence on the individual's life roles [3]. The inability to accomplish ADLs may lead to unsafe conditions, lower participation, caregiver overload and poorer quality of life [4].

ADLs development is related to motor, physical, cognitive and emotional areas [5], but also to practical experience and contextual factors. Thus, their outcomes result from the dynamic intersection of the individual, task/activity and context/environment characteristics [6].

Preschool age is a period of huge growth in ADLs development. Initially, infants are completely dependent on their caregivers in terms of care, even talking of co-occupations. Around 2–4 years, they begin to manage their cutlery, as well as simple clothes. Then, about 5–6 years, most typically developing children perform the most essential tasks/activities included in BADLs, although they usually need assistance from their caregivers for safety reasons or to initiate them, according to their parenting styles and socio-cultural factors. Setting milestones by age about BADLs acquisition is complex, due to the numerous factors that influence them. Table 1 displays some reference examples [7,8].

Table 1. Examples of activities of basic daily living milestones in typical children [7,9,10].

Age	Feeding	Personal Hygiene	Getting Dressed
3 years	Uses spoon and fork. Drinks safely.	Turns taps. Handles clothes before the toilet.	Takes off his shoes. Takes off his shirt.
4 years	Uses the napkin. Mature spoon and fork grip.	Washes hands and face. Soaps his body.	Puts on top clothes. Buttons up.
5 years	Cuts with the knife. Eats by himself.	Brushes his teeth. Cleans himself in the toilet.	Puts shoes on the right foot. Dresses unsupervised.
6 years	Spreads with a knife. All skills are improved.	Blows his nose. Washes hands before eating.	Laces shoes. Handles zippers.

However, children with neurodevelopmental disorders [11] are often unable to reach these milestones, showing significant challenges, poorer outcomes, delays, and impairments compared to their typical development peers [12–15].

1.2. Underlying Factors in Activities of Daily Living

Several factors are important for proper ADLs performance. On the one hand, brain maturation-associated internal factors, especially to the prefrontal lobe, include processes such as perception, memory, or executive function (EF) [16,17]. EF are a set of cognitive skills necessary for goal-oriented behavior. There is some agreement on considering inhibition and interference control, working memory, and cognitive flexibility as core sub-processes [18–20]. Inhibition means being able to control one's attention, thoughts, emotions, or behaviour, suppressing other stimuli. Working memory let us to briefly maintain information while performing other operations. Cognitive flexibility refers to being able to switch between thoughts or actions depending on the demands of the context [21–23]. From core EFs, higher-order EFs are built, including planning (choosing steps to reach a goal), reasoning, and problem-solving [22,24]. Regarding its development, a first phase happens during the first three years of life, where basic skills emerge, and a second one between the third and the fifth years, when different sub-processes begin to coordinate achieving adaptive goals [20,25]. Thus, EF is essential for all ADLs and to succeed in any daily task [26–30].

On the other hand, social and contextual factors are also essentials for ADLs development, including family and school. During childhood, caregivers must provide opportunities for children to practice ADLs in their communities, encouraging their social participation. This repeated practice promotes the establishment of occupational roles and routines, transmitting cultural values to the child [3,31]. Parenting styles are also relevant, considering that democratic styles are associated with greater independence, while overprotection, overcontrol, persistence in performance, or excessive permissiveness negatively affect children's mental health and sense of competence [32].

1.3. Activities of Daily Living in Early Education and Early Intervention Services

In addition to home and community settings, there are two other contexts in which monitoring ADLs development is essential: at school and, when signs of dysfunction are detected in early intervention services. Regarding school, in Spain, preschool education is divided into two stages: 0–3 years, and 3–6 years. Every stage has its own goals, contents, and evaluation criteria. Both stages are structured in three main areas: environment knowledge, languages, and self-knowledge and functional independence [33,34].

Table 2 shows some of the closest contents related to ADLs, including aspects related to EF required for successful performance.

Table 2. Activities of daily living related contents in the early education Spanish curriculum [33].

Preschool—First Stage	Preschool—Second Stage
Area 1. Awakening of personal identity: • Exploration and identification of the parts of the body, pointing and naming them in activities of daily living such as dressing or personal hygiene. Area 2. Personal well-being and daily life: • Progressive adaptation of one's biological rhythms to socially established routines. • Identification of basic needs such as thirst, hygiene, sleep, satisfying them independently or asking for help. • Acquisition of basic habits and rules regarding food, cleanliness, resting or clothing, identifying utensils and spaces and using them properly. • Satisfaction from participating in activities of daily living, progressively assuming responsibility. • Confidence in one's possibilities to solve tasks and overcoming difficulties with help.	Area 1. The body and the image itself: • Identification, regulation, and control of the basic needs of the body. Area 3. Activities of daily living: • Performing activities of daily living with progressive independence and the creation of habits. • Initiative, organization, planning, attention, constancy, and regulation skills while performing activities of daily living. Area 4. Personal care and health: • Actions to improve health and well-being for oneself and others. • Healthy habits: body hygiene, food and resting. • Appropriate use of spaces and utensils. • Preference for a well-groomed appearance. • Collaboration in the maintenance of clean and tidy environments. • Respect for the social rules during meals, resting and hygiene, with progressive initiative in their fulfilment.

Monitoring children's development is critical so that appropriate actions can be undertaken as early as possible; either through educational adjustments or referring to early care services [35,36]. These services aim to respond to temporary or permanent needs presented by children with developmental disorders or at risk [37], and in planning and carrying out interdisciplinary interventions.

In early education, ADLs performance is assessed by teachers, mainly through students' behaviours observation. Families play an unquestionable role in children's education [38], so teachers must obtain information about ADLs performance of their students in natural environments through their caregivers [34]. Therefore, observational tools or questionnaires completed by caregivers seem to be an interesting tool [39]. They can also be useful for early care therapists since, although therapists commonly work in clinical settings, they also need to collect information about children's performance in their natural environments [10,40–43].

1.4. Assessment of Activities of Daily Living in Preschoolers

Several observational tools can be considered to assess ADLs in children from three to six years: The Vineland Adaptive Behavior Scales [44,45], The Adaptive Behavior Assessment System [46,47], The Checklist of Adaptive Living Skills [48], The Inventory for Client and Agency Planning [49], The Pediatric Evaluation of Disability Inventory-Computer Adaptive Test [50], The Battelle Developmental Inventory [51], or the Merrill-Palmer-Revised Scales of Development [52]. However, these instruments present limitations to be applied during the ADL's evaluation process: (1) some of them are not focused on ADLs construct, but on the concept of adaptive behaviour. It can be problematic as adaptive behaviour is not synonymous with ADL, including different domains and giving more or less weight to ADLs according to authors' points of view [53]; (2) some of them do not cover the full range of BADLs; while (3) others are translated into Spanish but, to our best knowledge, without performing a cultural adaptation process.

1.5. Aim

This study aims to present the psychometric properties (construct validity and reliability) of a tool to measure BADLs performance in typically developing Spanish preschoolers aged 3–6 years. We hope this tool will (1) help to characterize the BADLs performance of typically developing children serving as a screening instrument and (2) will be useful to detect deviations from normality in the BADLs development of children with neurodevelopmental disorder diagnoses, helping professionals in early education and early care services.

2. Materials and Methods

2.1. Study Design

Participants were recruited through schools and social events in Extremadura (Spain). Furthermore, a convenience clinical sample of 11 participants with autism spectrum disorders (ASD) aged 3–6 years was included to analyze the classification ability of the questionnaire.

2.2. Participants

Three-hundred and three preschoolers with typical development, aged from 3 to 6 years (3 years = 13.2%; 4 years = 26.1%; 5 years = 32%; and 6 years = 28.7%), participated in the study. The sample was composed of 147 boys (48.5%) and 157 girls (51.5%). All participants provided written informed consent before starting data collection. To be included in the study, participants need to meet the following eligibility criteria: (1) age between 3 and 6 years, (2) attend to ordinary schools, (3) no present disorders according to the Diagnostic and Statistical Manual of Mental Disorders (DSM-5) [11], and (4) provide informed consent.

2.3. Instruments and Procedure

2.3.1. Creation of the Basic Activities of Daily Living Assessment in Preschoolers

A group of five experts from the clinical field (occupational therapists, and specialists in developmental psychology and neurodevelopmental disorders), selected for their experience in childcare (clinical and educational) and development of psychological tests, were recruited. Initially, an exhaustive review of the available instruments assessing children development, sensory integration, cognitive assessments, and ADLs was carried out. A rational criterion was followed for the selection of behaviours represented in most of the instruments (achieved or in process). The selected items were classified, developing a pool of 250 items. An operational proposal for the different dimensions was submitted to the experts' judgement. Thus, the experimental version consisted of 113 items. Subsequently, a pilot study was carried out with the participation of 15 families who were asked to answer the questionnaire, assessing the clarity of each item and allowing them to make proposals about wording. They were also informed about the time required to complete the test. Finally, the relationships between the proposed dimensions were explored and the items that did not fit in the model were removed. Thus, the final version of the tool includes 84 items. Figure 1 shows the steps followed for developing the instrument.

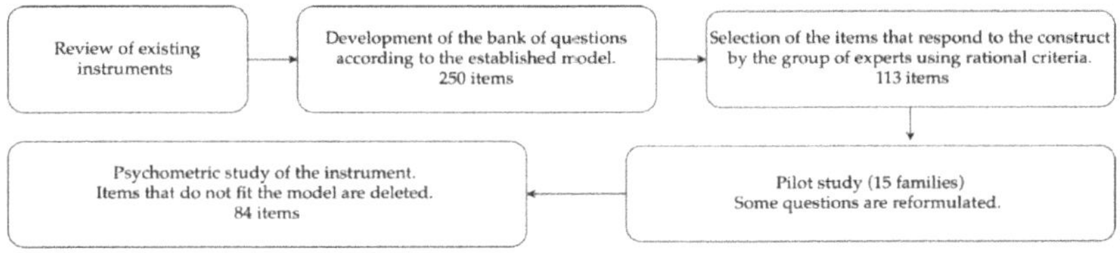

Figure 1. The Basic Activities of Daily Living Assessment in Preschoolers (BADL-P) creation process.

2.3.2. Description of the Basic Activities of Daily Living Assessment in Preschoolers Tool

The Basic Activities of Daily Living Evaluation in Preschoolers (BADL-P), a novel questionnaire created for Spanish preschoolers during this study, was used. The BADL-P included 84 items, distributed in 4 scales with 9 factors that provide a theoretical model to support the instrument. Eating, personal hygiene and dressing are BADLs themselves, as explained, while the daily functioning scale includes information about cognitive skills critical for good BADLs performance (Figure 2).

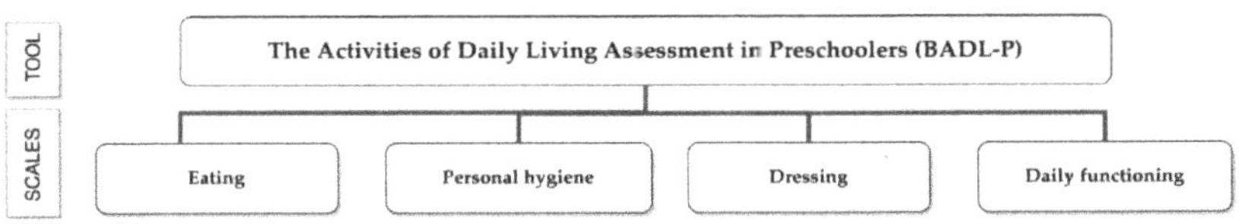

Figure 2. The Basic Activities of Daily Living Assessment in Preschoolers (BADL-P) basic structure.

Most of the items are written in positive form, and those in negative were recoded. This instrument must be completed by interviewing main caregivers. Response options for every item are always, sometimes, never or not known/no opportunity. Therapists or educators must obtain evidence that caregivers' answers are as close to reality as possible.

2.4. Ethical Approval

The protocol followed in this study adhered to the updates of the Declaration of Helsinki [54], and it was approved by the Committee on Biomedical Ethics of the University of Extremadura (198/2019).

2.5. Statistics

Microsoft Office^{TM} Excel v.16 (Redmond, WA, USA: Microsoft Corporation), FACTOR v.10.10.02 (Tarragona, Spain, ESP: Rovira i Virgili University) and IBM^{TM} SPSS v.25 (IBM Corporation, Armonk, NY, USA) were used for data analysis. A semiconfirmatory factor analysis (SCFA) was carried out, that is considered appropriate to prevent errors included in the "Little Jiffy" approach [55,56]. FACTOR performs at the same time an exploratory analysis offering goodness-of-fit indicators, so an additional confirmatory factor analysis is not necessary [57–60].

Considering the ordinal nature of the data, polychoric correlations using the robust unweighted least squares method with oblique rotation were employed. The Kaiser-Meyer-Olkin (KMO) and Bartlett's sphericity tests were used as indices of sampling adequacy [61,62]. Due to the comprehensive nature of the tool, which is intended to be used as a developmental scale to monitor BADLs acquisition and in the absence of cross-loadings, some items with loadings above 0.30 have been included [63].

To assess the goodness-of-fit, we used the chi-squared probability setting as appropriate non-significant values ($p > 0.05$); the comparative fit index (CFI) and the non-normed fit index (NNFI); the root mean square error of approximation (RMSEA); and the root mean square of residuals (RMSR) [62,64].

Ordinal alpha was used to find out the internal consistency of the tool. It represents an alternative to Cronbach's Alpha for ordinal items, being >0.70 values considered as acceptable and >0.80 preferred [65,66].

As external validity criteria, descriptive and contrast results are provided according to sociodemographic characteristics of the sample. Additionally, preliminary data on the classification ability of the questionnaire are presented through the analysis of the receiver operating characteristic (ROC curves), comparing with a sample of 11 subjects with ASD in addition to the sample of 303 typically developing participants.

3. Results

3.1. *Item Analysis and Internal Structure of the Questionnaire*

The BADL-P study version was initially composed of 113 items. After performing the analysis, 29 items were deleted, so the final version was finally formed by 84 items distributed in four scales with nine factors (Figure 3). The instrument is created in Spanish (Supplementary Material), but items are provided in English to facilitate the reading of the paper.

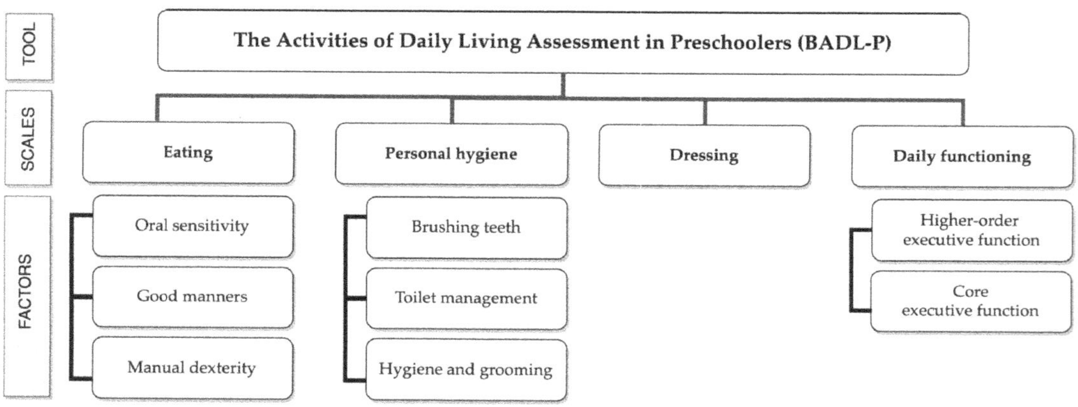

Figure 3. The Basic Activities of Daily Living Assessment in Preschoolers (BADL-P) complete structure.

The factor structure of the resulting dimensions and the factor loading of each item are presented below.

3.1.1. Eating Scale

A KMO value of 0.68, and Bartlett's test, $p < 0.001$ were both good enough to carry out the SCFA. However, 12 items did not reach <0.30 so 16 items formed the final version of the scale.

Eating refers to all the tasks or activities that help in manipulating, keeping food or fluids in the mouth and swallowing [2]. We found an interpretable solution with three factors which explores: (1) items related to sensory integration, (2) items associated with social, educational, and cultural behaviours that must be learnt to be considered nicely behaved during mealtime, and (3) items about hand skills with food, fluids, cutlery, or containers to perform self-feeding (Table 3).

Table 3. Factorial solution of the Eating scale.

Item	Factorial Weight		
Factor 1: Oral sensitivity.			
The child is reluctant to try new foods.	0.820		
The child is unwilling to eat food with some textures.	0.843		
The child shows disgust when certain foods are within his mouth.	0.500		
Factor 2: Good manners.			
The child tests the food carefully to check its temperature.		0.394	
The child chews with his mouth closed.		0.508	
The child chews food until crushed before swallowing.		0.343	
The child maintains a proper posture during mealtime.		0.685	
The child keeps seated at the table during mealtime.		0.774	
The child uses napkins properly.		0.417	
The child tries to maintain good manners during mealtime.		0.676	
Factor 3: Manual dexterity while eating.			
The child can open wrappers.			0.380
The child uses tools to open containers.			0.450
The child uses a knife to spread.			0.747
The child uses a knife to cut food.			0.884
The child uses several cutleries in a coordinated way.			0.792
The child can serve food from a bowl or tray.			0.652

3.1.2. Personal Hygiene Scale

A KMO value of 0.903 and a $p < 0.001$ for Bartlett's test were found. Initially, 36 items formed the scale, but six items were deleted. Thus, 30 items were maintained.

Personal hygiene refers to obtain and use toileting supplies to get or keep clean, including toileting needs, brushing, washing up, bathing and grooming [2]. We got an interpretable solution with three factors: (1) all the items related to brushing teeth, (2) the ones related to toileting needs, and (3) the rest of personal hygiene and grooming activities (Table 4).

3.1.3. Dressing Scale

A KMO value of 0.952 and a $p < 0.001$ for Bartlett's test were obtained. The scale had 30 items, but nine items were deleted, so 21 items form this scale.

Dressing refers to being able to select clothes, shoes, and accessories, putting them on and taking them off, and getting dressed and undressed in the right way [2]. This scale is formed only by one factor, as presented in Table 5.

3.1.4. Daily Functioning Scale

A KMO value of 0.737 and a $p < 0.001$ for Bartlett's test were found. Only 2 items were deleted, so the final version got 17 items on this scale.

This scale joins cognitive aspects that influence BADLs performance, and it is composed of two factors (Table 6): higher-order EF (eight items) and core EF (nine items).

Table 4. Factorial solution of the Personal hygiene scale.

Item	Factorial Weight		
Factor 1: Brushing teeth.			
The child brushes his teeth after eating without being told by an adult.	0.545		
The child brushes for at least one minute.	0.839		
The child brushes most or all areas of his mouth.	0.836		
The child spits into the wash when brushing his teeth.	0.808		
The child checks there are no traces of paste left in his mouth or face.	0.493		
The child leaves the sink clean and picks up everything after brushing.	0.453		
Factor 2: Toilet management.			
The child stays poopless at night.		0.688	
The child stays dry at night, without peeing.		0.510	
The child keeps clean during the day, without pooping himself.		0.726	
The child keeps dry during the day, without peeing himself.		0.746	
The child communicates his need to go to the bathroom.		0.713	
The child acceptably gets clean with toilet paper.		0.384	
The child can lower or raise his clothes to use the toilet.		0.449	
The child lowers the lid and pulls the chain.		0.431	
The child cares about his privacy.		0.313	
Factor 3: Hygiene and grooming.			
The child collaborates using cologne or moisturizer.			0.359
The child keeps his nails clean.			0.408
The child brushes his hair.			0.579
The child checks his appearance before leaving home.			0.479
The child is aware when he needs to wipe his nose.			0.540
The child blows his nose.			0.468
The child checks and adjusts the water temperature			0.575
The child when washing his hands, spreads soap and water in his hands.			0.540
The child when washing his hands, uses an adequate amount of soap.			0.519
The child when washing his hands, wipes himself completely dry.			0.467
The child washes his face.			0.677
In the shower, soaps up all over the body.			0.848
In the shower, rinses until all foam is removed.			0.835
In the shower, uses the towel until is relatively dry.			0.714
In the shower, lathers his hair in an acceptable way.			0.635

Table 5. Factorial solution of the Dressing scale.

Item	Factorial Weight
The child makes sure that the label of the clothes is in the right place.	0.566
The child put. his socks properly.	0.736
The child puts footwear on his feet.	0.699
The child places a shoe on the right foot.	0.657
The child removes shoes with fasteners.	0.320
The child removes simple garments without closures.	0.538
The child undresses completely, including using zippers on garments.	0.717
The child takes off his clothes, leaving them on the right side.	0.523
The child puts on a coat or an open garment.	0.624
The child puts on stretching pants.	0.733
The child puts on a T-shirt or an upper garment.	0.738
The child gets dressed without help (not including closures).	0.838
The child puts on accessories.	0.518
The child clasps snap buttons.	0.691
The child zips up and down.	0.648
The child zips clothes up.	0.693
The child can unbutton.	0.756
The child opens buttons.	0.775
The child undoes his shoes' lacing.	0.542
The child ties a knot in his shoes.	0.499
The child gets dressed without help (closures and accessories).	0.817

Table 6. Factorial solution of the Daily functioning scale.

Item	Factorial Weight	
Factor 1: Higher-order executive function.		
The child begins his activities of daily living in a reasonable time from the adult's direction.	0.517	
The child can perform his activities of daily living without the help of an adult.	0.554	
The child persists in their activities of daily living although he finds difficulties.	0.306	
The child finishes his activities of daily living at an appropriate time.	0.521	
The child becomes aware of the mistakes he makes in his activities.	0.559	
The child tries to solve problems while performing an activity.	0.732	
The child performs his daily activities without unnecessary stops.	0.642	
The child performs his daily activities in a logical order.	0.649	
Factor 2: Core executive function.		
The child gets frustrated quickly when cannot perform an activity.		0.428
The child has more tantrums than expected for his age.		0.459
The child has difficulties to get adapted to changes in the environment.		0.533
The child has difficulties to adapt changes in his routine.		0.622
The child has difficulties moving from one activity to move on to another.		0.506
The child often leaves his activities of daily living unfinished.		0.344
The child loses his attention performing his activities if there is some noise.		0.555
The child spins or rocks excessively, making it difficult to do his activities.		0.654
The child does not perform his activities properly due to excessive movement.		0.546

3.2. Correlations between Factors

Table 7 provides correlations between the different factors of every scale. All BADLs factors are related to each other. Likewise, EF is related to all BADLs except oral sensitivity. Thus, oral sensitivity seems to function independently, and it is only weakly and negatively related to core EF.

Table 7. Correlations between the BADL-P factors.

	Eating Scale			Personal Hygiene Scale			Dressing Scale	Daily Functioning
	Oral Sensitivity	Good Manners	Manual Dexterity	Brushing Teeth	Toilet Management	Hygiene	Dressing	Higher-Order EF
Good Manners	−0.07							
Manual Dexterity	−0.00	0.18 **						
Brushing teeth	−0.03	0.28 **	0.40 **					
Toilet management	−0.01	0.23 **	0.30 **	0.42 **				
General hygiene	−0.01	0.39 **	0.46 **	0.48 **	0.49 **			
Dressing	−0.04	0.30 **	0.50 **	0.42 **	0.43 **	0.53 **		
Higher-order EF	−0.02	0.49 **	0.32 **	0.39 **	0.35 **	0.44 **	0.47 **	
Core EF	−0.14 *	0.25 **	−0.05 **	0.06	0.09 **	0.05	0.07	0.19 **

* Significant correlation for $p < 0.05$ ** Significant correlation for $p < 0.01$.

3.3. Goodness-of-Fit Indices

Table 8 shows that all the indices, calculated with FACTOR software, are acceptable.

Table 8. BADL-P goodness-of-fit indices.

Indices	Cut-off	Eating Scale	Personal Hygiene Scale	Dressing Scale	Daily Functioning Scale
Chi-squared probability p (χ^2)	>0.05	0.000	0.000	0.000	0.009
CFI	>0.90	0.982	0.982	0.987	0.975
NNFI	>0.90	0.972	0.986	0.988	0.981
RMSEA	<0.06	0.039	0.039	0.050	0.034
RMSR	<0.08	0.060	0.073	0.083	0.069

CFI = Comparative fit index; NNFI = non-normed fit index; RMSEA = Root mean square error of approximation; RMSR = Root mean square of residuals.

3.4. Reliability

Ordinal alpha (Table 9) was used to find out the internal consistency of the BADL-P. Results are acceptable (>0.70) or preferred (>0.80).

Table 9. BADL-P Internal consistency.

Eating Scale			Personal Hygiene Scale			Dressing Scale	Daily Functioning Scale	
Manual Dexterity Factor	Good Manners Factor	Oral Sensitivity Factor	Toilet Management Factor	Brushing Factor	Grooming Factor	Dressing	Higher-Order EF Factor	Core EF Factor
0.81	0.74	0.76	0.80	0.82	0.88	0.94	0.78	0.76

3.5. Results According to Sociometric Variables and Questionnaire Structure

Table 10 shows descriptive and contrast statistics referring to the participants' scores considering sex (boys and girls). Significant differences of moderate magnitude according to sex in the toilet management dimension ($p < 0.04$; d > 0.56), with differences in favour of the girls' group, were observed. Moreover, significant differences of large magnitude are observed in the core EF ($p < 0.001$; d > 1.22) in favour of girls.

Table 10. Descriptive and contrasting statistics by sex group factors.

	Eating Scale			Personal Hygiene Scale			Dressing Scale	Daily Functioning Scale	
Sex	Oral Sensitivity	Good Manners	Manual Dexterity	Brushing	Toilet Management	General Hygiene	Dressing	Higher-Order EF Factor	Core EF Factor
Boys	5.3 ± 1.4	17.7 ± 2.1	10.6 ± 3.1	13.6 ± 2.6	24.3 ± 2.2	35.1 ± 6.0	50.9 ± 7.8	19.4 ± 2.7	12.5 ± 3.2
Girls	5.5 ± 1.3	17.9 ± 2.1	10.5 ± 3.5	13.7 ± 2.7	24.9 ± 2.5	35.7 ± 6.0	52.1 ± 6.9	19.7 ± 2.5	13.7 ± 3.0
t	−1.21	−0.48	0.30	−0.14	−2.04	−0.82	−1.51	−0.83	−3.40
p	0.22	0.62	0.76	0.88	0.04 *	0.41	0.131	0.40	0.001 **
d	0.19	0.12	0.11	0.04	0.56	0.57	1.29	0.25	1.22

t: Two-sample t-tests; p: statistical signification (* 0.05; ** 0.01); d: Cohen'd (Small = 0.2; Medium = 0.5; Large = 0.8).

Table 11 describe descriptive and contrast statistics after grouping participants according to the age of the two stages within early childhood education (3–4 and 5–6 years). Participants' scores indicate significant and high magnitude differences in almost all the dimensions, except in oral sensitivity ($p < 0.22$; $d > 0.19$) and core EF ($p < 0.001$; $d > 1.22$). These findings indicate a strong effect of age on the acquisition of BADLs (Table 11).

Table 11. Descriptive and contrasting statistics by age group factors.

	Eating Scale			Personal Hygiene Scale			Dressing Scale	Daily Functioning Scale	
Years	Oral Sensitivity	Good Manners	Manual Dexterity	Brushing	Toilet Management	General Hygiene	Dressing	Higher-OrderEF Factor	Core EF Factor
3–4	5.4 ± 1.2	17.3 ± 2.2	9.0 ± 2.9	12.6 ± 2.8	23.9 ± 3.1	32.9 ± 6.4	46.9 ± 7.3	18.7 ± 2.2	12.7 ± 2.9
5–6	5.4 ± 1.4	18.1 ± 2.0	11.6 ± 3.1	14.3 ± 2.3	25.0 ± 1.7	37.1 ± 5.1	54.5 ± 5.7	20.1 ± 2.7	13.3 ± 3.3
t	−0.01	−3.1	−7.0	−5.4	−3.8	−6.2	−10.1	−4.5	−1.5
p	0.992	0.002 **	0.000 **	0.000 **	0.000 **	0.000 **	0.000 **	0.000 **	0.111
d	0.00	0.77	2.56	1.72	1.08	4.21	7.67	1.33	0.59

t: Two-sample *t*-tests; *p*: statistical signification (* 0.05; ** 0.01); *d*: Cohen'd (Small = 0.2; Medium = 0.5; Large = 0.8).

3.6. The Basic Activities of Daily Living Assessment in Preschoolers Discrimination Ability between Typically Developing Participants and a Sample of ASD Participants

Although this manuscript presents the preschool version of our tool in typically developing children, our goal is that it can be used with children with neurodevelopmental disorders. Thus, a preliminary comparison of 11 typical children compared to 11 children with ASD (not included in our study sample) is presented to test the ability of the BADL-P to discriminate between performance on ADLs between typical development and ASD.

As illustrated in Figure 4 and Table 12, the area under the curve (AUC) shows that the tool can classify beyond chance between typically developing participants and participants with ASD ($p < 0.00$). The ability to classify between the two groups of greater magnitude is related to the personal hygiene scale and the total score of the questionnaire.

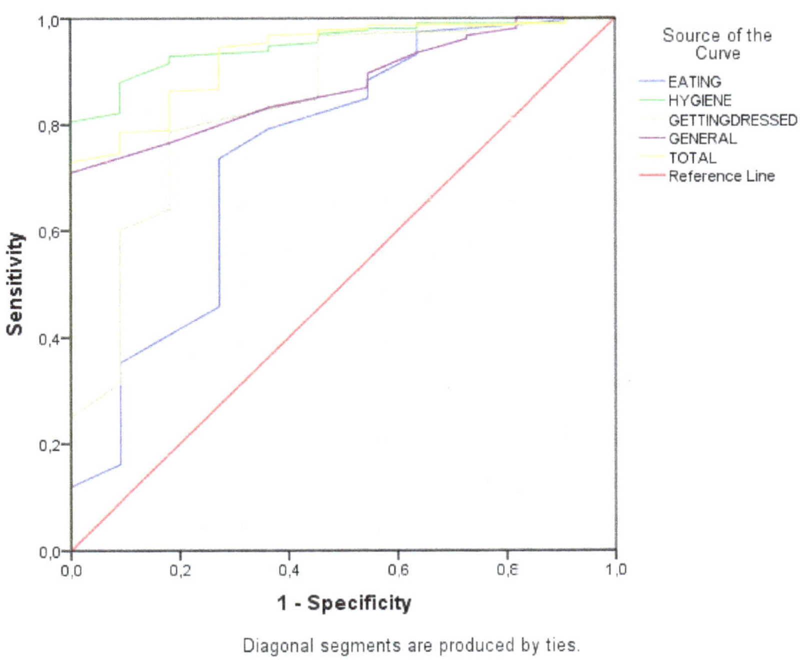

Figure 4. Graphical representation from the receiver operating characteristic (ROC curves).

Table 12. Statics from the receiver operating characteristic (ROC curves).

Scales	Typical	ASD	AUC (CI 95%)	p	d
Eating	33.9 ± 4.4	29.1 ± 5.6	0.74 (0.57–0.91)	0.005	0.936
Hygiene	73.8 ± 9.2	51.6 ± 11	0.95 (0.91–0.98)	0.000	2.327
Dressing	51.5 ± 7.4	39 ± 10.1	0.84 (0.71–0.96)	0.000	1.406
General	32.7 ± 0.4.5	25.7 ± 4.6	0.87 (0.81–0.93)	0.000	1.613
Total	192 ± 20.3	145.5 ± 25.6	0.93 (0.87–0.98)	0.000	2.088

AUC = Area under the curve; CI = Confidence interval; p = significance level; d = effect size following Cohen criteria [67].

4. Discussion

4.1. The Basic Activities of Daily Living Assessment in Preschoolers Theoretical Model

This study presents the BADL-P theoretical model, a novel tool for Spanish children between 3–6 years, with good psychometric properties according to preliminary data provided, practical and useful for both, early school educators and early care services educators and therapists. It was initially composed of 113 items, and after the study, they were reduced to 84. The model is divided into four scales: eating, personal hygiene, dressing, and daily functioning scales. The last scale offers a screening of cognitive factors which may influence during ADLs performance. In the eating scale, we got a structure with three factors and 16 items: oral sensitivity (three items), good manners (seven items) and manual dexterity (six items). In the personal hygiene scale, three factors and 30 items: brushing teeth (six items), toileting management (nine items) and hygiene and grooming (15 items). The dressing scale is composed of only one factor with 21 items. Finally, the daily functioning scale is composed of two factors and 17 items: higher-order EF (eight items) and core EF (nine items) during ADLs performance.

In our previous study [68], we presented the scholar version for children between six and 12 years (ADL-E). It was formed by a total of 84 quantitative items and six additional qualitative items only for girls about menstruation management. All items were distributed in the same four scales, but with different factors that outlined the progressive specialization in the BADLs from birth through lifetime. Thus, comparing the preschool version (BADL-P) with the school version (ADL-E), we observe how the dimensions are gradually expanded, as the skills are subdivided as the children grow up, which presents an indicator of validity [17,69].

As observed in Table 7, which shows correlations between factors, core EF, is closely related to BADLs performance. Thus, it is important to determine how problems in both of them could be affecting BADLs performance [30,70,71]. Therefore, our tool might help clinicians to determine whether a more in-depth assessment in one or another direction is needed.

4.2. The Basic Activities of Daily Living Assessment in Preschoolers and Other Tools

As exposed, ADLs performance is influenced by both internal and external factors. Occupational development is the result of the dynamic interaction of person, activity and environment [6]. In Spain, some instruments for measuring BADLs are available, but as previously exposed, they present some limitations. On the one hand, sometimes occupational assessment is inferred from instruments that assess adaptive behaviour, described as suitable behaviours for independent living. However, this concept includes some or other areas or activities depending on the classification consulted. For example, Kamphaus (1987) talks about physical/motor, self-help/independence, interpersonal/social, cognitive/communication and responsibility. Meanwhile, Widaman et al. (1993) mention cognitive competence, social competence, social maladaptation, and personal maladaptation [53]. On the other hand, ADLs conceptualization has reached a huge agreement [2,72,73]. The BADL-P structure is focused on ADLs, which is concrete and unambiguous. Some of the most widely used instruments based on adaptive behaviour concept, mix BADLs performance with other social aspects, not covering the BADLs full range of activities, or being their items divided into different sections or categories not according to their nature. For example, the Battelle Developmental Inventory [51], or the Inventory for Client and Agency Planning [49] include few items on BADLs performance. In the Adaptive Behavior Assessment System II [74], the items are divided into different sections which make them difficult to understand. It is also important to note that some tools, such as the Carolina Curriculum [75] or the Merrill–Palmer Revised Scales [52], do not cover the full preschooler stage. Moreover, many of these instruments are available in Spanish, but we have not found information about their validation; e.g., the Pediatric Evaluation of Disability Inventory [76] or the Vineland Adaptive Behavior Scales II [44], with the risk of not being culturally adapted.

4.3. The Basic Activities of Daily Living Assessment in Preschoolers Psychometric Properties

We have created our instrument after performing an exhaustive review, using an experts' group, carrying out a pilot study with families, conducting the study itself and carrying out the corresponding statistical analysis. In relation to statistics, we have carried out the factorial analysis with FACTOR software, which can perform SCFA what means that while performing an exploratory factor analysis shows goodness-of-fit indices to prove if the factorial solution offers a suitable adjustment. The SCFA has been used to validate instruments in natural [77,78], social [79–85], and health sciences [30,86,87]. Thus, it is a widely contrasted procedure.

As reflected in results section, the goodness-of-fit indices related to the construct validity of the test structure are highly adequate. The descriptive and contrast statistics indicate significant differences related to the two age groups analyzed (2–4 and 5–6 years). It demonstrates that ADLs performance is acquired throughout development and our instrument seems sensitive for analyzing this progression. Furthermore, construct validity is reinforced by additional data on the instrument's ability to classify between typical participants and a small group of ASD individuals. ROC curves show the instrument's ability to discriminate adequately on some of the dimensions (Hygiene = 0.95 and Total = 0.93). As it can be noticed, the scores that most discriminate between typical development and ASD preschoolers are the personal hygiene scale and the total score. Concerning hygiene activities, they have a greater contextual load (noises, smells, visual stimulation by mirrors and reflections) and are longer and more precise than feeding and dressing. Therefore, they have a greater demand of core EF. The reliability index provided by the ordinal alpha [88–91] shows an acceptable level of internal consistency ($\alpha > 0.70$). In summary, this preliminary study offers promising indicators of reliability and construct validity.

4.4. Limitations and Future Lines

This research has some limitations. We are aware that we need to check the concurrent validity using well-established tools and predictive validity, conducting longitudinal studies to check the capacity of the instrument to detect occupational performance issues development of the children. However, we have not found validated tools that support BADLs construct in Spanish preschoolers. Another limitation is the small sample size of ASD children. This is the reason why we are talking about preliminary results, and we are working to get a larger sample size to increase the power of results.

Several future lines will be developed. In this manuscript, we have presented the BADL-P for preschoolers. In a previous study, the scholar version was tested [68]. We are also interested in exploring the skills required to achieve BADLs during the 0–3 years stage. In this line, IADLs (caring for others, communication management, community mobility, financial and home management, spiritual activities, safety and emergency maintenance, and health management [2]), which are performed at home and in the community, gain importance during adolescence. Thus, it could be interesting to explore an instrument in this scope.

Furthermore, our final goal is testing our tools in children and adolescents with neurodevelopmental disorders diagnosis [11], which includes intellectual disability, ASD, attention deficit and hyperactivity, specific learning, motor, and communication disorders. These children usually have poorer ADLs performance compared with typical development children, and some studies draw different occupational profiles in these individuals [12,13,92,93]. At the stage studied, the development of ADLs is closely linked to maturational processes, in addition to other contextual processes, such as the patterns of parenting in each cultural setting. The translation of the scale into other languages and its adaptation to other cultural contexts will bring greater clarity to the influence of both aspects on the development of ADLs. Although this paper presents preliminary discrimination data with a small sample of ASD subjects, we intend to check the specificity–sensitivity of our tools in clinical samples of children with neurodevelopmental disorders.

Finally, we want to highlight the importance of carrying out practices and policies to support children with disabilities to participate in society, even those with "invisible disabilities" like children with neurodevelopmental disorders. Thus, this project is aligned with objectives 3 ("Good-health and well-being") and 4 ("Quality education") of the 2030 Agenda for Sustainable Development [94].

5. Conclusions

Based on our preliminary results, we conclude that BADL-P is a practical and easy to use tool with good construct validity and reliability properties for assessing BADLs occupational performance in Spanish preschoolers between three and six years.

Although this tool was developed to test BADLs occupational performance in typical development preschoolers aged from three to six years, preliminary results suggest that this tool could discriminate between typically developed children and their peers with neurodevelopmental disorders. However, future studies with larger sample sizes are needed to increase the power of results.

Supplementary Materials: The following are available online at https://www.mdpi.com/article/10.3390/children8060496/s1. Supplementary materials: The Basic Activities of Daily Living Assessment in Preschoolers (Spanish version).

Author Contributions: Conceptualization, S.B.-F., J.C.-V., M.G. and D.R.-A.; methodology, A.G.-G.; software, A.G.-G.; formal analysis, A.G.-G. and D.R.-A.; writing—original draft preparation, S.B.-F. and J.C.-V.; writing—review and editing, S.B.-F., M.G. and D.R.-A.; supervision, S.B.-F. and M.G.; funding acquisition, S.B.-F. All authors have read and agreed to the published version of the manuscript.

Funding: This research was partially funded by the Occupational Therapy Association of Extremadura (Colegio Profesional de Terapeutas Ocupacionales de Extremadura), grant number Ayudas a proyectos de investigación en Terapia Ocupacional/convocatoria 2019.

Institutional Review Board Statement: The study was conducted according to the guidelines of the Declaration of Helsinki and approved by the Committee on Biomedical Ethics of the University of Extremadura (198/2019).

Informed Consent Statement: Informed consent was obtained from all subjects involved in the study.

Data Availability Statement: The datasets used during the current study are available from the corresponding author on reasonable request.

Conflicts of Interest: The authors declare no conflict of interest.

References

1. Gronski, M.; Doherty, M. Interventions Within the Scope of Occupational Therapy Practice to Improve Activities of Daily Living, Rest, and Sleep for Children Ages 0–5 Years and Their Families: A Systematic Review. *Am. J. Occup. Ther.* **2020**, *74*, 7402180010p1–7402180010p33. [CrossRef]
2. American Occupational Therapy Association. Occupational Therapy Practice Framework: Domain and Process—Third Edtion. *Am. J. Occup. Ther.* **2017**, *68*, S1–S48. [CrossRef]

3. Romero, D.M. Actividades de la vida diaria desde una perspectiva evolutiva. In *Actividades de la Vida Diaria*; Moruno, P., Romero, D.M., Eds.; Masson: Barcelona, Spain, 2006; pp. 23–34.
4. Edemekong, P.F.; Bomgaars, D.L.; Sukumaran, S.; Levy, S.B. *Activities of Daily Living*; StatPearls Publishing: Treasure Island, FL, USA, 2020.
5. Delval, J.A. *El Desarrollo Humano*; Siglo Veintiuno Editores: Mexico DF, Mexico, 2006; ISBN 978-968-23-1990-7.
6. Duncan, E.A.S. *Foundations for Practice in Occupational Therapy*; Elsevier Health Sciences: Saint Louis, MO, USA, 2014; ISBN 978-0-7020-4661-2.
7. Moruno Miralles, P.; Romero Ayuso, D.M. *Actividades de la Vida Diaria*; Masson: Madrid, Spain, 2006; ISBN 978-84-458-1561-8.
8. Rodger, S.; Ziviani, J. (Eds.) *Occupational Therapy with Children: Understanding Children's Occupations and Enabling Participation*; Blackwell Pub: Oxford, UK; Malden, MA, USA, 2006; ISBN 978-1-4051-2456-0.
9. Rodger, S.; Ziviani, J. *Hand Function in the Child: Foundations for Remediation*, 2nd ed.; Henderson, A., Pehoski, C., Eds.; Mosby/Elsevier: Saint Louis, MO, USA, 2006; ISBN 978-0-323-03186-8.
10. Shepherd, J. Self care: A primary occupation. I can do it myself! In *Kids Can Be Kids: A Childhood Occupations Approach*; FA Davis: Baltimore, MD, USA, 2012; pp. 125–158.
11. American Psychiatric Association. *Diagnostic and Statistical Manual of Mental Disorders*, 5th ed.; American Psychiatric Association Publishing: Washington, DC, USA, 2013; ISBN 978-0-89042-555-8.
12. Gantschnig, B.E.; Page, J.; Nilsson, I.; Fisher, A.G. Detecting Differences in Activities of Daily Living Between Children With and Without Mild Disabilities. *Am. J. Occup. Ther.* **2013**, *67*, 319–327. [CrossRef] [PubMed]
13. Bal, V.H.; Kim, S.-H.; Cheong, D.; Lord, C. Daily Living Skills in Individuals with Autism Spectrum Disorder from 2 to 21 Years of Age. *Autism* **2015**, *19*, 774–784. [CrossRef]
14. Van der Linde, B.W.; van Netten, J.J.; Otten, B.; Postema, K.; Geuze, R.H.; Schoemaker, M.M. Activities of Daily Living in Children With Developmental Coordination Disorder: Performance, Learning, and Participation. *Phys. Ther.* **2015**, *95*, 1496–1506. [CrossRef]
15. Günal, A.; Bumin, G.; Huri, M. The Effects of Motor and Cognitive Impairments on Daily Living Activities and Quality of Life in Children with Autism. *J. Occup. Ther. Sch. Early Interv.* **2019**, 1–11. [CrossRef]
16. Goyal, N.; Siddiqui, S.; Chatterjee, U.; Kumar, D.; Siddiqui, A. Neuropsychology of Prefrontal Cortex. *Indian J. Psychiatry* **2008**, *50*, 202. [CrossRef]
17. Best, J.R.; Miller, P.H. A Developmental Perspective on Executive Function: Development of Executive Functions. *Child. Dev.* **2010**, *81*, 1641–1660. [CrossRef]
18. Miyake, A.; Friedman, N.P.; Emerson, M.J.; Witzki, A.H.; Howerter, A.; Wager, T.D. The Unity and Diversity of Executive Functions and Their Contributions to Complex "Frontal Lobe" Tasks: A Latent Variable Analysis. *Cogn. Psychol.* **2000**, *41*, 49–100. [CrossRef]
19. Tirapu Ustárroz, J.; Bausela Herreras, E.; Cordero Andrés, P. Modelo de funciones ejecutivas basado en análisis factoriales en población infantil y escolar: Metaanálisis. *Rev. Neurol.* **2018**, *67*, 215. [CrossRef] [PubMed]
20. Diamond, A. The early development of executive functions. In *Lifespan Cognition: Mechanisms of Change*; Oxford University Press: New York, NY, USA, 2006; pp. 466–503.
21. Martos Pérez, J.; Paula Pérez, I. Una aproximación a las funciones ejecutivas en el trastorno del espectro autista. *Rev. Neurol.* **2011**, *52*, S147. [CrossRef]
22. Diamond, A. Executive Functions. *Annu. Rev. Psychol.* **2013**, *64*, 135–168. [CrossRef]
23. Aydmune, Y.S.; Introzzi, I.M.; Zamora, E.V.; Lipina, S.J. Diseño, Implementación y Análisis de Transferencia de Una Tarea de Entrenamiento de Inhibición Cognitiva Para Niños Escolares. Un Estudio Piloto. *Psicl. Educ.* **2018**, *24*, 63–74. [CrossRef]
24. Collins, A.; Koechlin, E. Reasoning, Learning, and Creativity: Frontal Lobe Function and Human Decision-Making. *PLoS Biol.* **2012**, *10*, e1001293. [CrossRef] [PubMed]
25. García-Molina, A.; Enseñat-Cantallops, A.; Tirapu-Ustárroz, J.; Roig-Rovira, T. Maduración de La Corteza Prefrontal y Desarrollo de Las Funciones Ejecutivas Durante Los Primeros Cinco Años de Vida. *Rev. Neurol.* **2009**, *48*, 435. [CrossRef] [PubMed]
26. Papazian, O.; Alfonso, I.; Luzondo, R.J. Trastornos de Las Funciones Ejecutivas. *Rev. Neurol.* **2006**, *42*, 45–50. [CrossRef]
27. Howard, S.J.; Vasseleu, E. Self-Regulation and Executive Function Longitudinally Predict Advanced Learning in Preschool. *Front. Psychol.* **2020**, *11*, 49. [CrossRef] [PubMed]
28. Howard, S.J.; Vasseleu, E.; Batterham, M.; Neilsen-Hewett, C. Everyday Practices and Activities to Improve Pre-School Self-Regulation: Cluster RCT Evaluation of the PRSIST Program. *Front. Psychol.* **2020**, *11*, 137. [CrossRef]
29. Romero-Ayuso, D.; Toledano-González, A.; Segura-Fragoso, A.; Triviño-Juárez, J.M.; Rodríguez-Martínez, M.C. Assessment of Sensory Processing and Executive Functions at the School: Development, Reliability, and Validity of EPYFEI-Escolar. *Front. Pediatr.* **2020**, *8*, 275. [CrossRef] [PubMed]
30. Fogel, Y.; Rosenblum, S.; Josman, N. Environmental Factors and Daily Functioning Levels among Adolescents with Executive Function Deficits. *Br. J. Occup. Ther.* **2020**, *83*, 88–97. [CrossRef]
31. Kellegrew, D.H. Constructing Daily Routines: A Qualitative Examination of Mothers With Young Children With Disabilities. *Am. J. Occup. Ther.* **2000**, *54*, 252–259. [CrossRef]
32. Aguilar-Yamuza, B.; Raya-Trenas, A.F.; Pino-Osuna, M.J.; Herruzo-Cabrera, J. Relación Entre El Estilo de Crianza Parental y La Depresión y Ansiedad En Niños Entre 3 y 13 Años. *RPCNA* **2019**, *6*, 36–43. [CrossRef]

33. Ministerio de Educación y Ciencia. *Orden ECI/3960/2007, de 19 de Diciembre, por la que se Establece el Currículo y se Regula la Ordenación de la Educación Infantil*; Ministerio de Educación y Ciencia: Madrid, Spain, 2007; Volume 5, pp. 1016–1036.
34. Ministerio de Educación. *Decreto 4/2008, de 11 de enero, por el que se aprueba el Currículo de Educación Infantil para la Comunidad Autónoma de Extremadura*; Ministerio de Educación: Madrid, Spain, 2008; Volume 12, pp. 1226–1276.
35. Lipkin, P.H.; Macias, M.M. Promoting Optimal Development: Identifying Infants and Young Children With Developmental Disorders Through Developmental Surveillance and Screening. *Pediatrics* **2020**, *145*, e20193449. [CrossRef]
36. Filipek, P.A.; Accardo, P.J.; Ashwal, S.; Baranek, G.T.; Cook, E.H.; Dawson, G.; Gordon, B.; Gravel, J.S.; Johnson, C.P.; Kallen, R.J.; et al. Practice Parameter: Screening and Diagnosis of Autism: Report of the Quality Standards Subcommittee of the American Academy of Neurology and the Child Neurology Society. *Neurology* **2000**, *55*, 468–479. [CrossRef]
37. Federación Estatal de Asociaciones de Profesionales de Atención Temprana. *Libro Blanco de La Atención Temprana*; Real Patronato sobre Discapacidad: Madrid, Spain, 2005.
38. Heredia, M.C. Influencia del contexto familiar y social en el desarrollo del niño y sus alteraciones. In *Psicopatología, Riesgo y Tratamiento de los Problemas Infantiles*; Gómez-Maqueo, E.L., Heredia, M.C., Eds.; Manual Moderno: Mexico DF, Mexico, 2014; pp. 27–48.
39. Ministerio de Sanidad, Servicios Sociales e Igualdad. *Encuesta Nacional de Salud: España 2011/12. Salud Mental y Calidad de Vida En La Población Infantil. Serie Informes monográficos No. 2*; Ministerio de Sanidad, Servicios Sociales e Igualdad: Madrid, Spain, 2014.
40. Díaz Sánchez, C. *Guía Básica Sobre Atención Temprana y Transformación. Cuadernos de Buenas Prácticas*; Plena Inclusión: Madrid, Spain, 2019.
41. Mcwilliam, R. Metanoia En Atención Temprana: Transformación a Un Enfoque Centrado En La Familia. *Rev. Latinoam. Educ. Inclusiva* **2016**, *10*, 133–153. [CrossRef]
42. McWilliam, R.A. *Routines-Based Early Intervention: Supporting Young Children and Their Families*; Paul H. Brookes: Baltimore, MD, USA, 2010; ISBN 978-1-59857-062-5.
43. Hughes-Scholes, C.H.; Gavidia-Payne, S. Development of a Routines-Based Early Childhood Intervention Model. *Educ. Rev.* **2016**, 141–154. [CrossRef]
44. Sparrow, S.S.; Cichetti, D.V.; Balla, D.A. *Vineland Adaptive Behavior Scales*, 2nd ed.; American Guidance Service: Circle Pines, MN, USA, 2005.
45. Sparrow, S.S.; Cichetti, D.V.; Saulnier, C.A. *Vineland Adaptive Behavior Scales*, 3rd ed.; Pearson: San Antonio, TX, USA, 2016.
46. Harrison, P.L.; Oakland, T. *Adaptive Behavior Assessment System*, 2nd ed.; Psychological Corp.: San Antonio, TX, USA, 2003; ISBN 978-0-15-400452-9.
47. Harrosin, P.; Oakland, T. *Adaptive Behavior Assessment System*, 3rd ed.; Pearson: San Antonio, TX, USA, 2015.
48. Morreau, L.E.; Bruininks, R.H.; Montero Centeno, D. *Inventario de Destrezas Adaptativas (CALS): Manual*; Instituto de Ciencias de la Educación: Oaxaca de Juárez, Spain; Universidad de Deusto, Mensajero: Bilbao, Spain, 2006; ISBN 978-84-271-2480-6.
49. Bruininks, R.K.; Hill, B.K.; Weatherman, R.F.; Woodcock, R.W. *Inventary for Client and Agency Planning*; The Riverside Pub. Co.: Chicago, IL, USA, 1986.
50. Haley, S.M.; Coster, W.J.; Dumas, H.M.; Fragala-Pinkham, M.A.; Moed, R. *PEDI-CAT: Development, Standardization and Administration Manual*; Boston University: Boston, MA, USA, 2012.
51. de la Cruz, M.V.; González Criado, M.; Newborg, J. *Battelle, Inventario de Desarrollo: Manual de Aplicación*; TEA: Madrid, Spain, 1996; ISBN 978-84-7174-421-0.
52. Sánchez, F.; Santamaría, P.; Fernández-Pinto, I.; Arribas, D. *Escalas de Desarrollo Merrill-Palmer Revisadas*; TEA: Madrid, Spain, 2011.
53. Romero, D.M. Actividades de La Vida Diaria. *An. Psicol.* **2007**, *23*, 264–271.
54. World Medical Association. A Fifth Amendment for the Declaration of Helsinki. *Lancet* **2000**, *356*, 1123. [CrossRef]
55. Ferrando, P.J.; Lorenzo-Seva, U. Program FACTOR at 10: Origins, Development and Future Directions. *Psicothema* **2017**, 236–240. [CrossRef]
56. Watkins, M.W. Exploratory Factor Analysis: A Guide to Best Practice. *J. Black Psychol.* **2018**, *44*, 219–246. [CrossRef]
57. Lloret, S.; Ferreres, A.; Hernández, A.; Tomás, I. The Exploratory Factor Analysis of Items: Guided Analysis Based on Empirical Data and Software. *An. Psicol.* **2017**, *33*, 417–432. [CrossRef]
58. Lorenzo-Seva, U.; Ferrando, P.J. *FACTOR v. 10.10.02. Windows*; Universitat Rovira i Virgili: Tarragona, Spain, 2020.
59. Lorenzo-Seva, U.; Ferrando, P.J. FACTOR 9.2: A Comprehensive Program for Fitting Exploratory and Semiconfirmatory Factor Analysis and IRT Models. *Appl. Psychol. Meas.* **2013**, *37*, 497–498. [CrossRef]
60. Ferrando, P.J.; Lorenzo-Seva, U. El Análisis Factorial Exploratorio de Los Ítems: Algunas Consideraciones Adicionales. *An. Psicol.* **2014**, *30*, 1170–1175. [CrossRef]
61. Jöreskog, K.G.; Sörbom, D. *LISREL 8: User's Reference Guide*, 2nd ed.; Scientific Software International: Chicago, IL, USA, 1996.
62. Frías-Navarro, M.D.F.; Pascual-Soler, M.P. Prácticas del análisis factorial exploratorio (AFE) en la investigación sobre conducta del consumidor y marketing. *Suma Psicol.* **2012**, *19*, 47–58.
63. Beavers, A.S.; Lounsbury, J.W.; Richards, J.K.; Huck, S.W.; Skolits, G.J.; Esquivel, S.L. Practical Considerations for Using Exploratory Factor Analysis in Educational Research. *PARE* **2013**, *18*, 1–13.
64. Ferrando, P.J.; Anguiano-Carrasco, C. El análisis factorial como técnica de investigación en psicología. *Pap. Psicólogo* **2010**, *31*, 18–33.

65. Gadermann, A.; Guhn, M.; Zumbo, B.D. Ordinal Alpha. In *Encyclopedia of Quality of Life and Well-Being Research*; Michalos, A.C., Ed.; Springer: Dordrecht, The Netherlands, 2014; pp. 4513–4515. ISBN 978-94-007-0752-8.
66. Dominguez-Lara, S. Fiabilidad y alfa ordinal. *Actas Urológicas Españolas* **2018**, *42*, 140–141. [CrossRef]
67. Cohen, J. *Statistical Power Analysis for the Behavioral Sciences*, 2nd ed.; L. Erlbaum Associates: Hillsdale, MI, USA, 1988; ISBN 978-0-8058-0283-2.
68. Barrios-Fernández, S.; Gozalo, M.; García-Gómez, A.; Romero-Ayuso, D.; Hernández-Mocholí, M.Á. A New Assessment for Activities of Daily Living in Spanish Schoolchildren: A Preliminary Study of Its Psychometric Properties. *Int. J. Environ. Res. Public Health* **2020**, *17*, 2673. [CrossRef] [PubMed]
69. Chevalier, N.; Jackson, J.; Revueltas Roux, A.; Moriguchi, Y.; Auyeung, B. Differentiation in Prefrontal Cortex Recruitment during Childhood: Evidence from Cognitive Control Demands and Social Contexts. *Dev. Cogn. Neurosci.* **2019**, *36*, 100629. [CrossRef]
70. Jefferson, A.; Paul, R.; Czonoff, A.; Cohen, R. Evaluating Elements of Executive Functioning as Predictors of Instrumental Activities of Daily Living (IADLs). *Arch. Clin. Neuropsychol.* **2006**, *21*, 311–320. [CrossRef] [PubMed]
71. Poncet, F.; Swaine, B.; Dutil, E.; Chevignard, M.; Pradat-Diehl, P. How Do Assessments of Activities of Daily Living Address Executive Functions: A Scoping Review. *Neuropsychol. Rehabil.* **2017**, *27*, 618–666. [CrossRef]
72. American Occupational Therapy Association. Occupational Therapy Practice Framework: Domain & Process 2nd Edition. *Am. J. Occup. Ther.* **2008**, *62*, 625–683. [CrossRef]
73. American Occupational Therapy Association. Occupational Therapy Practice Framework: Domain and Process—Fourth Edition. *Am. J. Occup. Ther.* **2020**, *74*, 7412410010p1. [CrossRef]
74. Montero, D.; Fernández-Pinto, I. *ABAS® II: Sistema Para la Evaluación de la Conducta Adaptativa: Manual*; TEA: Madrid, Spain, 2013; ISBN 978-84-15262-76-3.
75. Johnson-Martín, N.M.; Jens, K.G.; Attermeier, S.M.; Hacker, B.J. *Curriculo Carolina*; TEA: Madrid, Spain, 1997.
76. Fragala-Pinkham, M.A.; Miller, P.E.; Dumas, H.M.; Shore, B.J. Development and Validation of Equations to Link Pediatric Evaluation of Disability Inventory (PEDI) Functional Skills Scores to PEDI-Computer Adaptive Test Scores for Youth with Cerebral Palsy. *Phys. Occup. Ther. Pediatr.* **2020**, *40*, 106–120. [CrossRef]
77. Dzhambov, A.M. Perceived Benefits of Nature Questionnaire: Preliminary Results. *Ecopsychology* **2014**, *6*, 109–115. [CrossRef]
78. Leveau, L.M. Bird Traits in Urban–Rural Gradients: How Many Functional Groups Are There? *J. Ornithol.* **2013**, *154*, 655–662. [CrossRef]
79. Ginns, P.; Marsh, H.W.; Behnia, M.; Cheng, J.H.S.; Scalas, L.F. Using Postgraduate Students' Evaluations of Research Experience to Benchmark Departments and Faculties: Issues and Challenges. *Br. J. Educ Psychol.* **2009**, *79*, 577–598. [CrossRef]
80. Ficapal-Cusí, P.; Boada-Grau, J.; Torrent-Sellens, J. Spanish Adaptation of the Internal Functioning of the Work Teams Scale (QFI-22). *Psicothema* **2014**, *26*, 273–278. [CrossRef] [PubMed]
81. Maki, W.S.; Buchanan, E. Latent Structure in Measures of Associative, Semantic, and Thematic Knowledge. *Psychon. Bull. Rev.* **2008**, *15*, 598–603. [CrossRef]
82. Özer, B.U.; Saçkes, M.; Tuckman, B.W. Psychometric Properties of the Tuckman Procrastination Scale in a Turkish Sample. *Psychol. Rep.* **2013**, *113*, 874–884. [CrossRef]
83. Barbu, O.C.; Marx, R.W.; Yaden, D.B.; Levine-Donnerstein, D. Measuring Approaches to Learning in Preschoolers: Validating the Structure of an Instrument for Teachers and Parents. *Education* **2016**, *44*, 698–714. [CrossRef]
84. Begega, A.; Méndez López, M.; de Iscar, M.J.; Cuesta-Izquierdo, M.; Solís, G.; Fernández-Colomer, B.; Álvarez, L.; Méndez, M.; Arias, J.L. Assessment of the Global Intelligence and Selective Cognitive Capacities in Preterm. *Psicothema* **2010**, *22*, 648–653.
85. Daset, L.R.; Fernandez-Pintos, M.E.; Costa-Ball, D.; López-Soler, C.; Vanderplasschen, W.P. Development and validation of adolescent self-report: ADA. *Ciencias Psicol.* **2015**, *9*, 85–104.
86. Ortuño-Sierra, J.; Fonseca-Pedrero, E.; Paino, M.; Sastre i Riba, S.; Muñiz, J. Screening Mental Health Problems during Adolescence: Psychometric Properties of the Spanish Version of the Strengths and Difficulties Questionnaire. *J. Adolesc.* **2015**, *38*, 49–56. [CrossRef] [PubMed]
87. Gómez-Campelo, P.; Bragado-Álvarez, C.; Hernández-Lloreda, M.J.; Sánchez-Bernardos, M.L. The Spanish Version of the Body Image Scale (S-BIS): Psychometric Properties in a Sample of Breast and Gynaecological Cancer Patients. *Support. Care Cancer* **2015**, *23*, 473–481. [CrossRef] [PubMed]
88. Hennegan, J.; Nansubuga, A.; Smith, C.; Redshaw, M.; Akullo, A.; Schwab, K.J. Measuring Menstrual Hygiene Experience: Development and Validation of the Menstrual Practice Needs Scale (MPNS-36) in Soroti, Uganda. *BMJ Open* **2020**, *10*, e034461. [CrossRef]
89. Stene, K.L.; Dow-Fleisner, S.J.; Ermacora, D.; Agathen, J.; Falconnier, L.; Stager, M.; Wells, S.J. Measuring the Quality of Care in Kinship Foster Care Placements. *Child. Youth Serv. Rev.* **2020**, *116*, 105136. [CrossRef]
90. Pucciarelli, G.; Årestedt, K.; Simeone, S.; Bolgeo, T.; Alvaro, R.; Vellone, E. Psychometric Characteristics of the WHOQOL-SRPB Scale in a Population of Stroke Survivors and Caregivers. *Qual. Life Res.* **2020**, *29*, 1973–1985. [CrossRef]
91. Rosen, C.; Chase, K.A.; Perona-Garcelán, S.; Marvin, R.W.; Sharma, R.P. The Psychometric Properties of the DAIMON Scale, a Translation from Spanish to English: An Instrument to Measure the Relationship with and between Voices. *Psychosis* **2020**, *12*, 45–56. [CrossRef] [PubMed]
92. Kottorp, A.; Bernspang, B.; Fisher, A.G. Activities of Daily Living in Persons with Intellectual Disability: Strengths and Limitations in Specific Motor and Process Skills. *Aust. Occup. Ther. J.* **2003**, *50*, 195–204. [CrossRef]

93. Rosenblum, S.; Frisch, C.; Deutsh-Castel, T.; Josman, N. Daily Functioning Profile of Children with Attention Deficit Hyperactive Disorder: A Pilot Study Using an Ecological Assessment. *Neuropsychol. Rehabil.* **2015**, *25*, 402–418. [CrossRef] [PubMed]
94. United Nations. Proceedings of the The United Nations Conference Sustainable Development (UNCSD or "Rio+20"), Rio de Janiero, Brazil, 20–22 June 2012.

children

MDPI

Article

A Complementary Sensory Tool for Children with Autism Spectrum Disorders

Sabina Barrios-Fernández [1,*], Margarita Gozalo [2], Beatriz Díaz-González [3] and Andrés García-Gómez [4]

1 Medical-Surgical Therapeutics Department, University of Extremadura, 10003 Cáceres, Spain
2 Psychology and Anthropology Department, University of Extremadura, 10003 Cáceres, Spain; mgozalo@unex.es
3 Nursing and Occupational Therapy College, University of Extremadura, 10003 Cáceres, Spain; bdiazgon@alumnos.unex.es
4 Education Sciences Department, University of Extremadura, 10003 Cáceres, Spain; agarcil9@unex.es
* Correspondence: sabinabarrios@unex.es

Received: 30 September 2020; Accepted: 18 November 2020; Published: 20 November 2020

Abstract: Background: Sensory integration (SI) issues are widely described in people with autism spectrum disorder (ASD), impacting in their daily life and occupations. To improve their quality of life and occupational performance, we need to improve clinical and educational evaluation and intervention processes. We aim to develop a tool for measuring SI issues for Spanish children and adolescents with ASD diagnosis, to be used as a complementary tool to complete the Rivière's Autism Spectrum Inventory, a widely used instrument in Spanish speaking places to describe the severity of ASD symptoms, recently updated with a new sensory scale with three dimensions. Methods: 458 Spanish participants complemented the new questionnaire, initially formed by 73 items with a 1–5 Likert scale. Results: The instrument finally was composed of 41 items grouped in three factors: modulation disorders (13 items), discrimination disorders (13 items), and sensory-based motor disorders (15 items). The goodness-of-fit indices from factor analyses, reliability, and the analysis of the questionnaire's classification capability offered good values. Conclusions: The new questionnaire shows good psychometric properties and seems to be a good complementary tool to complete new the sensory scale in the Rivière's Autism Spectrum Inventory.

Keywords: sensory processing; emotional regulation; assessment; autism spectrum disorders

1. Introduction

1.1. Sensory Integration Process

Sensory integration (SI) is "the neurological process that organizes sensations from one's own body (internal) and the environment (external) and makes it possible to use the body effectively within the environment" [1] (p. 11). An adequate organization of sensory information is necessary for producing adaptive responses in daily life, which includes different end products: motor, cognitive, behavioral, emotional, or learning outcomes [2]. SI is considered a prerequisite so that more complex functions, as perceptual-motor and cognitive ones, can be appropriately developed [3].

The SI process runs through a series of stages. Firstly, the sensory organs capture fragments of sensory information, which can have either an internal or an external origin. Later, that information is integrated in the central nervous system (CNS) to become a meaningful whole [4]. The SI process takes place in different brain structures in a coordinated way, classifying, and organizing the sensory flow through a series of stages. Firstly, in registration, the CNS detects the sensory sensations from our sensory receptors and we become aware of those sensations [5]. Next, in modulation, the CNS regulates and processes the sensory stimuli [6]. Then, during discrimination the CNS distinguishes between different sensory stimuli, perceiving their specific qualities and becoming meaningful [6–8]. Finally, we elicit a response, intended to adaptive, which can include attention, organization, self-esteem, self-confidence, movement, reasoning, and learning outcomes [1,7,9]. Within that end products, and in the group of adaptive motor-based responses, we must refer to praxis. Praxis is the ability to conceptualize, plan, and execute unusual motor actions. Thus, it allows us to organize and manage a purposeful interaction with the physical world, thus involving both motor and cognitive skills [8,10].

Although traditionally we have focused in five senses (vision, hearing, smell, taste, and touch), there are three more sensory systems essential to be successful in daily life: proprioception, vestibular system, and interoception. Proprioceptive sense reports on sensations from muscles, ligaments, and joints, providing information about the compression and stretching of muscles and joints. Proprioception and touch together form the somatosensory pathway, considered essential for praxis and movement [11,12]. The vestibular system provides information on movement, gravity and balance, so it is crucial for the building of spatial and temporal relationships [13]. It also provides information about the speed and the direction of the head movement and our position with relation to gravity [9]. Interoception sense processes sensory stimuli within the body, including body sensations (hunger, thirst, body temperature, heart, breathing rate, etc.) and emotional states (happiness, sadness, shame, anger), being intimately related to self-regulation and well-being [14,15].

1.2. Sensory Processing Disorders

When sensations flow in an organized and integrated way, our brain can use those sensations to form perceptions, behaviors, and learning; when the flow of sensations is disorganized, perception, behavior, and learning are like a traffic jam at a rush hour [16]. Therefore, when SI is not working properly, motor, cognitive, emotional, behavioral, and adaptive issues produce a decrease in daily living functioning and learning [17–20]. This dysfunction can be mild, medium, or severe [21]. Sensory processing disorder (SPD) is a neurological disorder in which the ability to process and interpret sensory stimuli results in abnormal responses, causing a decrease in the quality of life and occupational performance [22,23]. Several models have been developed to understand the SPD [1,6,24], being Miller's model one of the most accepted. According to it, SPD can be classified into three categories with their corresponding subtypes: sensory modulation disorders, sensory discrimination disorders, and sensory-based motor disorders. Sensory modulation disorders happen when the CNS has problems in regulating the sensory information (degree, nature, or intensity) resulting in the following subtypes: sensory over-responsivity (exaggerated response), sensory under-responsivity (lack or insufficient response), or sensory craving (desperate seeking for sensory information). Sensory discrimination disorders happen when there is difficulty interpreting the qualities of the sensory stimuli. As a result, the responses are often slow, and sometimes, wrong. Finally, sensory-based motor disorders cause difficulty with motor planning and movement, resulting in postural disorder or dyspraxia subtypes [6,25].

1.3. Autism Spectrum Disorders and SPD Relationships

Taking the latest version of the Diagnostic and Statistical Manual of Mental Disorders (DSM-5) as a reference [26], ASD are included in the neurodevelopmental disorders group, and they are defined by the presence of (a) persistent deficits in social communication and interaction, and (b) restricted, repetitive patterns of behavior, interests, or activities. Within the (b) criterion and, for the first time in the DSM, sensory abnormalities were included as "Hyper- or hyporeactivity to sensory input or unusual interest in sensory aspects of the environment (e.g., apparent indifference to pain/temperature, adverse response to specific sounds or textures, excessive smelling or touching of objects, visual fascination with lights or movement)" (p. 50).

With regards to etiology, and although it is widely recognized that genetic and environmental factors and their interactions contribute to the phenotypes of ASD. the precise causal mechanisms keep still unclear [27]. On a neuroanatomical basis, it is hypothesized that ASD symptoms should be a consequence of brain disconnection since hypomyelination of the brain nerves occurs simultaneously with the main behavioral symptoms [28]. Other studies complement this hypoconnectivity hypothesis by suggesting that in addition to hypoconnectivity in some regions of the cerebral cortex and at an interhemispheric level, a compensatory hyperconnectivity between the thalamus and the cerebral cortex, explaining sensory, and social symptoms [29]. Under this assumption, sensory issues in ASD have as origin atypical connectivity of neuronal structures. Nevertheless, it seems that topography of hypoconnectivity in ASD is unique and different from other conditions, such as SPD. In ASD, areas related to socio-emotional processing are highly affected; whereas, in SPD, there is lower connectivity in the brain's perception and integration pathways, which serve as connections for the auditory, visual, and somatosensory systems involved in SI [30].

SI issues are commonly reported in ASD, compared to their peers [31] Various studies have tried to explain the most frequent sensory profiles or those issues that cause the biggest issues in children with ASD, as well as the proposals of intervention to improve their occupational performance [19,31–37]. With regards to ASD specific sensory profiles, hyporeactivity/under-responsivity is one of the most consistent issues found [24], although hyperreactivity/over-responsivity and sensory seeking have been also reported [38]. Several studies have found relationships between the core symptoms of ASD and sensory impairments, such as repetitive behaviors [34,39], with social communication and interaction [31,40,41], but also, with movement issues, including coordination, planning, and timing [42,43], impacting in their daily life [44]. With regards to the interventions, some of the studies focused on Ayres's Sensory Integration Therapy [36,45], and others in using specific sensory techniques and environmental modifications, thus the promotion of ecological approaches to improve occupational performance [4,37].

1.4. Autism Spectrum Disorders and SPD Assessment

There are different tools to measure SI functioning, including questionnaires, observational tools, and comprehensive tests administered to the children or adolescents. Some reviews have been performed to resume information about SI tools, noticing that there are a large number of proposals [46,47]. Other reviews have checked for the most used SI tools in ASD, providing information about their characteristics and limitations [48–50]. Some of the most representative instruments are the Sensory Profile (SP) [51] and its second version (SP2) [52], a group of standardized questionnaires for assessing sensory processing including the infant, toddler, child, short, and school companion forms, from birth to 14.11 years. The Sensory Processing Measure (SPM), formed by a set of questionnaires to assess SI in home and the school, in children between 5–12 years. It also includes self-evaluation forms to be completed by the children and adolescents. There is a preschool version from 2–5 years [53]. The Sensory Integration and Praxis Test (SIPT) is a comprehensive test formed by 17 subtests to assess visual, tactile, kinesthetic, and motor tasks in children from 4–8.11 years [16]. There are several emerging SI assessment tools. The Sensory Processing 3-Dimensions (SP3D) is a tool composed of a series of task to elicit typical and atypical behavioral responses in children, covering sensory modulation, discrimination, and sensory-based motor disorders; and by a questionnaire with five subscales: sensory over-responsiveness, sensory under-responsiveness, sensory craving, postural disorder, dyspraxia, and sensory discrimination disorder [25,54]. The Evaluation in Ayres Sensory Integration (EASI) is a comprehensive assessment test for SI which includes measures related to sensory perception, sensory responsiveness, postural, ocular and bilateral integration, and praxis [24,55].

Tools for ASD assessment, including detection [56,57], diagnosis and measuring changes after interventions [58,59] are also available. In any case, the assessment of the severity of ASD should be complete and comprehensive and must include the measure of the SI and its impact in daily life. Within these tools, the Autism Spectrum Disorders Inventory developed by Rivière [60,61], is a widely used tool both in Spain and Latin America. It examines the severity of ASD by establishing four disease groups: relationship disorders, communication disorders, anticipation and flexibility, and symbolization, resulting in 12 dimensions, all of which can be scored from 0 to 8 points. The Rivière's Autism Spectrum Inventory was set up before the importance of the SI was spread so, recently, a new sensory scale has been incorporated [62] updating the tool to the current knowledge of ASD. Now it is formed by five disease groups and 15 dimensions (Figure 1). An advantage of the Rivière's Autism Spectrum Inventory is the fact that, as being designed by severity levels, it can help the clinicians' in their judgment to determine the levels of severity required in DSM-5 [26]. However, and although this instrument explains the four levels of affectation in each dimension, it does not define specific behaviors to observe, so using complementary tools to collect information is strongly recommended.

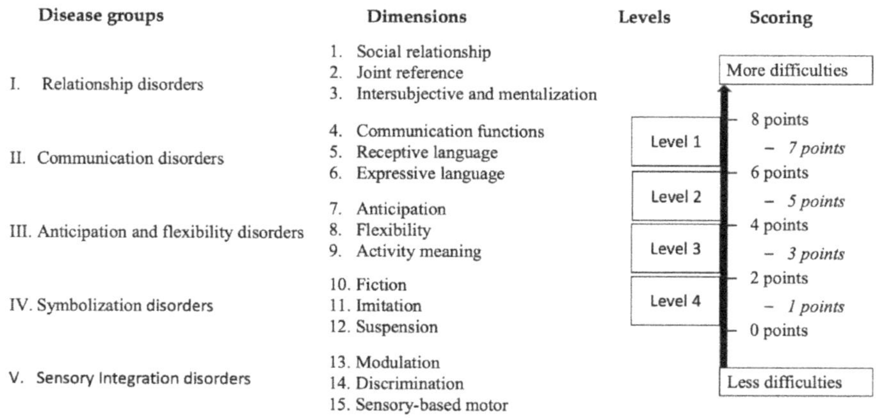

Figure 1. Summary of Rivière's Autism Spectrum Inventory [60,61]. Disease groups from I–IV with their 12 dimensions correspond to Rivière's original version. The V scale with the dimensions 13–15 was added by García-Gómez [62]. Preferred scores for rating the Inventory are the even ones, while odd scores are used to describe intermediate stages.

1.5. Aim

We aim to create a questionnaire to be used as a support for scoring the new sensory scale in the Rivière's Autism Spectrum Inventory, a widely used tool to assess ASD severity in Spanish speaking places.

2. Methods

2.1. Participants

The sample was formed by 458 children and adolescents (308 males, 68.7%, and 144 females, 31.3%) from 4 to 19 years ($x = 9.6$, $dt = 4.42$). Of these, 259 were individuals with typical development (57.2%), 145 presented ASD clinical diagnosis (32%) and 54 had other diagnoses different than ASD resulting in intellectual, sensory, and/or motor disabilities (11.95%).

2.2. Procedure

After conducting a literature review, a group of experts in the fields of Occupational Therapy and Psychology, with clinical experience, created a preliminary version of the tool composed of 73 items. Then a pilot study was carried out with 31 ASD families with diagnosed children. The 50 items with the best indicators were selected. Participants were recruited using the snowball technique in the case of typical development children, and through different associations, in the case of diagnosed children. The data collection was carried out between May and August 2020. This protocol adheres to the updates of the Declaration of Helsinki, and the study was approved by the Committee on Biomedical Ethics of the University of Extremadura (97/2020).

Our instrument, the Behavioral Observation on Sensory Stimuli Questionnaire for Parents (BOSS-P) was administered to the families. They were also asked for socio-demographic data, including age, sex, clinical diagnosis, intellectual capacity, language level, comorbidities, and the need for aids in their daily life. Once the questionnaire was administered to the sample, the items were analyzed by the group of experts, discarding those which did not fit on the theoretical model, being the final version composed of 41 items (Supplementary Table S1). The BOSS-P was administered together with the Sensory Profile 2 (SP2) Short Form [63,64] to 31 participants, to obtain validity indicators.

2.3. Instrument

The BOSS-P, a new instrument to better characterize ASD children and adolescents to fulfil the three new sensory dimensions from Rivière's Autism Spectrum Inventory based on Miller's model, must be completed interviewing with main caregivers, which may answer the 41 items through a Likert scale with five response options, from 1 to 5 (higher scores mean greater SI dysfunction). It takes about 25–30 min to complete the interview.

2.4. Statistics

To perform the validation process of the BOSS-P we have carried out: (1) an exploratory factor analysis (EFA), (2) confirmatory factor analysis (CFA), (3) reliability analysis, (4) the assessment of concurrent validity through the correlations with the SP2, and (5) provide descriptive statistics from the typical development and the ASD subsamples.

Because we are handling ordinal variables from a Likert-type scale with five response categories, the EFA was carried out with the FACTOR software [65–67] using polychoric correlations and robust methods [68]. Items with factorial weights below 0.30 were excluded. The CFA was carried out with the IBM SPSS AMOS™ 24 [69] using the Maximum Likelihood estimation procedure, suitable for Likert-type scales of five response categories. The CFA supports the factorial solution provided by the EFA and also offers the model of relations between the variables that best fits with the data [70–72].

The evaluation of the model fit was made taking into account the Chi-Square divided by degrees of freedom (CMIN/DF) and the p of Chi-square following Byrne's criteria [73]. The statistical p of Chi-square is dependent on the sample size, so it was convenient to use other goodness-of-fit indicators choosing the Tucker–Lewis index (TLI), the comparative fit index (CFI) following Hu and Bentler's criteria [74], the root-mean-square error of approximation (RMSEA), and the root-mean-square residuals (RMSR) [75,76].

Ordinal alpha coefficients were calculated [77,78] to assess reliability, considering values >0.70 acceptable and >0.90, excellent [79]. The analysis of the correlations between our tool and the SP2, the descriptive statistics of the subsamples and the relative operating characteristic (ROC) analysis were carried out to check the instrument's ability to classify between the two subsamples, using the IBM SPSS™ 24 [80] statistical package. Cohen's d statistic [81] was also calculated to check the magnitude of the effect size of the differences between the subsamples scores.

3. Results

3.1. Exploratory Factor Analysis

After administering the experimental version of the questionnaire to the sample, a solution of 41 items grouped into three correlated factors was obtained. Bartlett's (5025.4; $df = 820$; $p = 0.000$) and Kaiser–Meyer–Olkin test (0.912) statistics showed a very good sample suitability [82]. In Table 1, can be found both the rotated factorial matrix and factorial weights of each item. The three factors obtained represent (F1) modulation disorders with 13 items, (F2) discrimination disorders with 13 items, and (F3) sensory-based motor disorders with 15 items.

Table 1. Rotated factorial matrix and factorial weights of each item.

Items	F1	F2	F3
1. Shows disproportionate reactions if touched.	0.491		
2. Shows panic reactions to loud noises.	0.624		
3. Shows rejection of water when showering or washing.	0.340		
4. He is bothered by noisy and crowded places.	0.829		
5. When something goes wrong, it takes a long time to calm down.	0.566		
6. Shows discomfort with activities that involve spinning.	0.507		
7. Cannot concentrate or perform tasks when background noise.	0.627		
8. He gets agitated in the presence of very powerful light sources.	0.760		
9. Frequently touches or puts body parts or objects in his mouth.	0.394		
10. He is bothered with strong smells.	0.702		
11. Some clothes bother him; he feels itchy about some fabrics.	0.730		
12. He dislikes personal hygiene or grooming activities.	0.452		
13. Quick movements are unpleasant for him.	0.643		
14. Attends to his name or when he is called.		0.492	
15. Communicates feelings aimed at satisfying basic needs.		0.620	
16. Realizes when he is tired or exhausted.		0.639	
17. Shows comfort when hugged by parents or close relatives.		0.837	
18. Shows satisfaction when basic needs are met		0.959	
19. When he is disconsolate, he gets calmed by his parents.		0.720	
20. Expresses enjoyment or feels comfortable in certain situations.		0.897	
21. Can perceive danger in situations that could harm.		0.475	
22. Can identify basic emotions in himself and others.		0.442	
23. Can orientate himself in the environment.		0.418	
24. Notices that his heart is racing when he is tired or excited.		0.522	
25. Recognizes the elements that make him nervous.		0.578	
26. Has difficulty in recognizing people's faces.		0.374	
27. Has difficulty identifying parts of his own body.			0.655
28. Presents inability to reproduce speech movements.			0.737
29. Can ride a bicycle, rollerblades or a skateboard.			0.623
30. Can perform simple motor imitations.			0.724
31. Can fasten buttons or make loops to get dressed.			0.927
32. Can stack small blocks or string beads on a string.			0.569
33. Can use cutlery with both hands.			0.634
34. Can make copies from simple drawings.			0.930
35. Shows clumsiness in typing or using the computer keyboard.			0.814
36. Shows insecurity going downstairs/hills, holds on to railings.			0.485
37. Can adjust his strength when grasping objects.			0.452
38. Can cut with scissors properly for his age.			0.929
39. Can draw or colour within the proposed margins.			0.924
40. Can follow motor imitations containing multiple steps.			0.892
41. Can complete drawings with one half of it missing.			0.930

(F1) Modulation disorders; (F2) discrimination disorders; and (F3) sensory-based motor disorders. Items translated for readability; no cross-cultural adaptation performed.

With regards to the correlation between factors, moderate relationships were found between F1–F2 (0.38); F1–F3 (0.61), and F2–F3 (0.53) [81], which was to be expected since they are different stages within the same neurobiological process.

3.2. *Confirmatory Factor Analysis*

The CFA confirms the exploratory factorial solution revealing three latent variables which group the 41 observable variables (items). Figure 2 shows the graphical representation of the analyzed model, being (F1) modulation disorders, (F2) discrimination disorders, and (F3) sensory-based motor disorders. The factorial weights of every item and the covariation relations between the latent variables are shown.

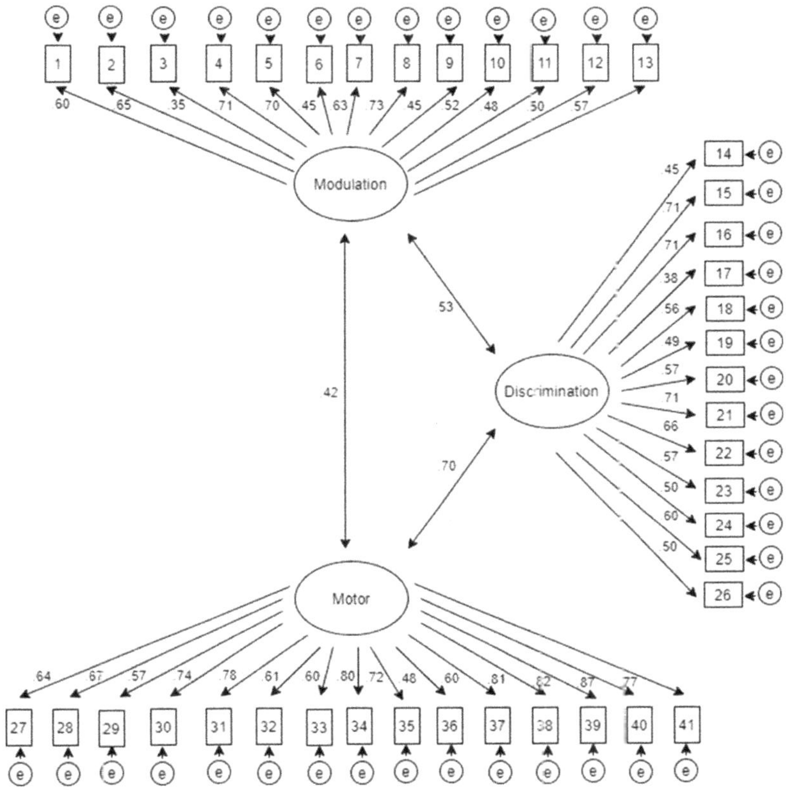

Figure 2. The Behavioral Observation on Sensory Stimuli Questionnaire for Parents' (BOSS-P) graphical representation after confirmatory factor analysis (CFA).

In Table 2, are represented the goodness-of-fit indices from the CFA, showing good values.

Table 2. BOSS-P goodness-of-fit indices from the confirmatory factor analysis (CFA).

Indices	Cut-Off	Value
CMIN/DF	<2	1.995
p (χ^2)	>0.05	0.000
TLI	>0.90	0.912
CFI	>0.90	0.925
RMSEA	<0.06	0.047 (0.043–0.051)
RMSR	<0.08	0.071

p (χ^2): chi-squared probability; CFI: comparative fit index; NNFI: non-normed fit index, RMSEA: root mean square error of approximation; RMSR: root mean square of residuals.

3.3. Reliability

To analyze the concurrent validity, we compared the BOSS-P with the SP2, a tool for SI assessment validated for Spanish children and adolescents. Both questionnaires were administered to 31 participants with ASD to study their correlations. As shown in Table 3, the modulation disorders factor (F1) from the BOSS-P was the only with significant and moderate correlations with the factors analyzed in the SP2.

Table 3. Correlation matrix between the Behavioral Observation on Sensory Stimuli Questionnaire for Parents (BOSS-P) and the Short Sensory Profile 2 (SP2).

	BOSS-P				SP2		
	F1	**F2**	**F3**	**Total**	**Sensory**	**Behavioral**	**Total**
F1	1						
F2	−0.076	1					
F3	−0.134	0.297	1				
Total	0.438 *	0.636 **	0.701 **	1			
Sensory	0.448 *	0.084	0.027	0.309	1		
Behaviour	0.600 **	0.034	0.147	0.446 *	0.613 **	1	
total	0.590 **	0.063	0.103	0.426 *	0.879 **	0.915 **	1

*. Correlation is significant at the 0.05 level (2-tailed). **. Correlation is significant at the 0.01 level (2-tailed) F1 = Modulation Disorders factor; F2 = Discrimination Disorders factor; F3 = Sensory-Based Motor Disorders factor; Sensory = Sensory Processing; Behavioral = Behavioral Responses associated with Sensory Processing.

3.4. *Questionnaire's Capability to Classify between ASD and Typical Development*

Descriptive statistics of participants with ASD (n = 145) and with typical development (n = 259) subsamples are shown in Table 4. It can be checked that both, mean and standard deviation of every subsample offer different scores.

Table 4. Descriptive statistics of ASD and typical development samples.

	Autism Spectrum Disorder				Typical Development			
	F1	**F2**	**F3**	**Total**	**F1**	**F2**	**F3**	**Total**
x	33.8	31.9	40.3	106	24.8	20.5	23.1	68.4
SD	8.9	8.0	11.9	19	7.7	5.5	7.8	16.0

x: mean; SD: standard deviation.

In Figure 3, graphical representation and statistics from ROC curves are provided. The area under the curve (AUC) shows differences with large effect magnitudes between the three factors, being the BOSS-P total score the most capable dimension to establish a correct classification of subjects according to their reference group.

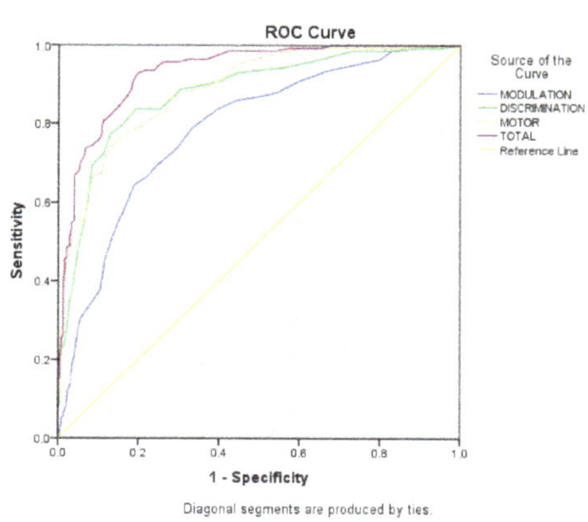

(a)

Dimensions	AUC (CI 95%)	p	d
Modulation	0.80 (0.75–0.84)	0.000	1.190
Discrimination	0.88 (0.84–0.91)	0.000	1.669
Motor	0.89 (0.85–0.92)	0.000	1.735
Total	0.93 (0.91–0.96)	0.000	2.176

AUC = Area under the curve; CI = confidence interval; p = significance level; d = size effect following Cohen criteria [81].

(b)

Figure 3. Graphical representation (**a**) and statistics (**b**) from the receiver operating characteristic (ROC) curves.

Considering the Rivière's Autism Spectrum Inventory scoring system, an approximation to the level of SI severity using the level of affectation in the Rivière's inventory and the BOSS-P interquartile scores was obtained in the ASD sample (see Table 5).

Table 5. Combination of the level of affectation in the Rivière's Inventory and the Behavioral Observation on Sensory Stimuli Questionnaire for Parents' (BOSS-P) interquartile scores.

		BOSS-P		
		F1	F2	F3
Rivière's inventory levels of severity	1 (8 points)	>40	>36	>50
	2 (6 points)	34–40	30–36	40–50
	3 (4 points)	27–34	27–30	31.5–40
	4 (2 points)	<27	<27	<31.5

F1 = modulation disorders factor; F2 = discrimination disorders factor; F3 = sensory-based motor disorders factor.

4. Discussion

4.1. About the BOSS-P Questionnaire

We aimed to create a questionnaire to support the new SI scale [62] added to the Rivière's Autism Spectrum Inventory [60,61]. The Rivière's Inventory is a widely used instrument in Spain and Latin America, which allows us to establish the level of the ASD severity, in line with the levels proposed in the DSM-5 [26]. The Rivière's Inventory is useful both during the diagnosis and intervention processes.

The BOSS-P is a screening instrument, administered through an interview with parents or carers, which is not intended to replace other comprehensive assessments, existing or emerging, with good psychometric properties on SI. However, our instrument has several advantages: (1) it is a quick test which is administered in 25–30 min; (2) that does not require specific training; (3) is open access; (4) is a complete tool, as it assesses items within the three areas described by Miller [6]: sensory modulation, sensory discrimination, and sensory-based motor disorders; (5) with good psychometric properties in terms of validity, reliability, and discrimination capacity; (6) created in Spain and therefore, adapted to the cultural characteristics of this country; (7) which fills a gap in terms of SI tools in Spanish-speaking population; and (8) which complements a psychological test widely used in the Spanish-speaking world, the Rivière's Inventory for people with ASD.

We have also provided an attempt to the combined use of the BOSS-P and the Rivière's Inventory, by linking the Rivière's level of severity and the BOSS-P quartile scores. Our instrument showed good psychometric values, offering a factorial structure formed by the three groups proposed by Miller [6]. These data are interesting because let us verify that Miller's model is consistent in different cultures and because. The BOSS-P's ability to classify between participants with ASD and typical development children seems adequate (AUC = 0.938), corresponding to a large effect size between the scores of both subsamples (d = 2.176) [83].

4.2. The BOSS-P and Other Instruments

Some reviews have found that psychometric properties of some of the SI tools are from poor to moderate, so the professionals must use the obtained data with caution [48,50], selecting appropriate SI assessments depending on the detected SI needs [47]. However, as aforementioned, there are few available instruments for Spanish children and adolescents. According to our best knowledge, neither the SIPT—considered as a Gold Standard for SI assessment [84]—nor the SPM are available for Spanish population, while the SP3D and the EASI are not yet published, being the SP2 the only tool of choice in Spain. The SP2 Spanish version covers a little shorter age range than the original, from 3 to 14.11 years. The BOSS-P covers from 4 to 19 years, a wider range including the full adolescent stage. The correlations between the BOSS-P and the SP2 only find relationships in modulation disorders, which could lead us to consider the necessity of using different tools to obtain information about SI if using the SP2.

Concerning its psychometric properties, the BOSS-P items present excellent internal consistency (alpha > 0.87), similar or superior other questionnaires used in the international context [46]. The ability of the questionnaire to discriminate between sub-samples offers a large effect size (d = 2.176), which is slightly higher than the size effect of the difference reported in other instruments [85].

4.3. Limitations and Future Lines

This research has some limitations. The information was completed through parents, and although instruments completed by families are considered to be valid [86], we must be careful because some parents should overestimate or underestimate the development of their children [87]. The sample was one of convenience. Another limitation was that we could not perform a test–retest. As future lines, we will try to improve the psychometric properties of the questionnaire, as well as to perform studies for its use in other Spanish-speaking countries different than Spain.

5. Conclusions

The preliminary study of the psychometric properties of Behavioral Observation on Sensory Stimuli Questionnaire for Parents (BOSS-P) shows good values for its use in Spanish children and adolescents diagnosed with ASD between 4 and 19 years. This tool was designed to help clinicians and educational professionals to establish the level of severity in children and adolescents with ASD diagnosis through the new SI scale in the Rivière's Autism Spectrum Inventory.

Supplementary Materials: The following are available online at http://www.mdpi.com/2227-9067/7/11/244/s1, Table S1: Behavioral Observation on Sensory Stimuli Questionnaire for Parents (BOSS-P) Versión original española: Cuestionario de Observación de la Conducta ante Estímulos Sensoriales para Padres de niños/as y adolescentes con Autismo/TEA (OCS-P).

Author Contributions: Conceptualization, S.B.-F., M.G., and B.D.-G.; Methodology, A.G.-G.; Software, A.G.-G.; Formal analysis, A.G.-G.; Writing—original draft preparation, S.B.-F., M.G.; Writing—review and editing, S.B.-F. and M.G.; Supervision, A.G.-G. All authors have read and agreed to the published version of the manuscript.

Funding: This research received no external funding.

Acknowledgments: We want to thank all the participants who kindly dedicated their time to help us in this research.

Conflicts of Interest: The authors declare no conflict of interest.

References

1. Ayres, A.J. *Sensory Integration and Learning Disorders*; Western Psychological Services: Los Angeles, CA, USA, 1972; ISBN 978-0-87424-303-1.
2. Humphries, T.; Wright, M.; McDougall, B.; Vertes, J. The Efficacy of Sensory Integration Therapy for Children with Learning Disability. *Phys. Occup. Ther. Pediatr.* **1990**, *10*, 1–17. [CrossRef]
3. Williams, M.S.; Shellenberger, S. *The Alert Program for Self-Regulation*; TherapyWorks Inc.: Albuquerque, NM, USA, 1995; ISBN 978-0-9643041-1-6.
4. Dunn, W. Supporting Children to Participate Successfully in Everyday Life by Using Sensory Processing Knowledge. *Infants Young Child.* **2007**, *20*, 84–101. [CrossRef]
5. Kilroy, E.; Aziz-Zadeh, L.; Cermak, S.A. Ayres Theories of Autism and Sensory Integration Revisited: What Contemporary Neuroscience Has to Say. *Brain Sci.* **2019**, *9*, 68. [CrossRef]
6. Miller, L.J.; Anzalone, M.E.; Lane, S.J.; Cermak, S.A.; Osten, E.T. Concept Evolution in Sensory Integration: A Proposed Nosology for Diagnosis. *Am. J. Occup. Ther.* **2007**, *61*, 135–140. [CrossRef]
7. Sher, B. *Everyday Games for Sensory Processing Disorder: 100 Playful Activities to Empower Children with Sensory Differences*; Althea Press: Berkeley, CA, USA, 2016; ISBN 978-1-62315-700-5.
8. Lane, S.J.; Bundy, A.C. *Kids Can Be Kids: A Childhood Occupations Approach*; Lane, S., Bundy, A.C., Eds.; F.A. Davis Co.: Philadelphia, PA, USA, 2012; ISBN 978-0-8036-1228-0.

9. Lane, S.J.; Mailloux, Z.; Schoen, S.; Bundy, A.; May-Benson, T.A ; Parham, L.D.; Roley, S.S.; Schaaf, R.C. Neural Foundations of Ayres Sensory Integration®. *Brain Sci.* **2019**, *9*, 153. [CrossRef]
10. Cermak, S.A. Reflections on 25 Years of Dyspraxia Research. In *Ayres Dyspraxia Monograph*; Pediatric Therapy Network: Torrance, CA, USA, 2011.
11. Ackerley, R.; Kavounoudias, A. The role of tactile afference in shaping motor behaviour and implications for prosthetic innovation. *Neuropsychologia* **2015**, *79*, 192–205. [CrossRef]
12. Beaudry Bellefeuille, I.; Sánchez Padrón, O. *Tengo Duendes en Las Piernas*. Nobel: Oviedo, Spain, 2011; ISBN 978-84-8459-654-7.
13. Pfeiffer, C.; Serino, A.; Blanke, O. The vestibular system: A spatial reference for bodily self-consciousness. *Front. Integr. Neurosci.* **2014**, *8*, 31. [CrossRef]
14. Mahler, K.J.; Craig, A.D. *Interoception: The Eighth Sensory System: Practical Solutions for Improving Self-Regulation, Self-Awareness and Social Understanding of Individuals with Autism Spectrum and Related Disorders*; AAPC Publishing: Shawnee Mission, KS, USA, 2016; ISBN 978-1-942197-14-0.
15. Farb, N.A.S.; Daubenmier, J.; Price, C.J.; Gard, T.; E Kerr, C.; Dunn, B.D.; Klein, A.C.; Paulus, M.P.; Mehling, W.E. Interoception, contemplative practice, and health. *Front. Psychol.* **2015**, *6*, 763. [CrossRef]
16. Ayres, A.J. *Sensory Integration and Praxis Tests*; Western Psychological Services: Los Angeles, CA, USA, 1989.
17. Gourley, L.; Wind, C.; Henninger, E.M.; Chinitz, S. Sensory Processing Difficulties, Behavioral Problems, and Parental Stress in a Clinical Population of Young Children. *J. Child Fam. Stud.* **2013**, *22*, 912–921. [CrossRef]
18. Miller, L.J.; Nielsen, D.M.; Schoen, S.; Brett-Green, B.A. Perspectives on sensory processing disorder: A call for translational research. *Front. Integr. Neurosci.* **2009**, *3*, 3. [CrossRef]
19. Galiana-Simal, A.; Vela-Romero, M.; Romero-Vela, V.M.; Oliver-Tercero, N.; García-Olmo, V.; Benito-Castellanos, P.J.; Muñoz-Martinez, V.; Beato-Fernandez, L. Sensory processing disorder: Key points of a frequent alteration in neurodevelopmental disorders. *Cogent Med.* **2020**, *7*. [CrossRef]
20. Butera, C.; Ring, P.; Sideris, J.; Jayashankar, A.; Kilroy, E.; Harrison, L.; Cermak, S.; Aziz-Zadeh, L. Impact of Sensory Processing on School Performance Outcomes in High Functioning Individuals with Autism Spectrum Disorder. *Mind Brain Educ.* **2020**, *14*, 243–254. [CrossRef]
21. Baranek, G.T.; David, F.J.; Poe, M.D.; Stone, W.L.; Watson, L.R. Sensory Experiences Questionnaire: Discriminating sensory features in young children with autism, developmental delays, and typical development. *J. Child Psychol. Psychiatry* **2006**, *47*, 591–601. [CrossRef] [PubMed]
22. Dunn, W. The Sensations of Everyday Life: Empirical, Theoretical, and Pragmatic Considerations. *Am. J. Occup. Ther.* **2001**, *55*, 608–620. [CrossRef] [PubMed]
23. Ismael, N.; Lawson, L.M.; Hartwell, J. Relationship Between Sensory Processing and Participation in Daily Occupations for Children with Autism Spectrum Disorder: A Systematic Review of Studies That Used Dunn's Sensory Processing Framework. *Am. J. Occup. Ther.* **2018**, *72*. [CrossRef]
24. Schaaf, R.C.; Mailloux, Z. *Clinician's Guide for Implementing Ayres Sensory Integration: Promoting Participation for Children with Autism*; AOTA Press: Bethesda, MD, USA, 2015; ISBN 978-1-56900-365-7.
25. Mulligan, S.; A Schoen, S.; Miller, L.J.; Valdez, A.; Magalhaes, D. The Sensory Processing 3-Dimensions Scale: Initial Studies of Reliability and Item Analyses. *Open J. Occup. Ther.* **2019**, *7*, 4 [CrossRef]
26. APA. *Diagnostic and Statistical Manual of Mental Disorders*, 5th ed.; American Psychiatric Association: Washington, DC, USA, 2013; p. 5.
27. Bölte, S.; Girdler, S.; Marschik, P.B. The contribution of environmental exposure to the etiology of autism spectrum disorder. *Cell. Mol. Life Sci.* **2019**, *76*, 1275–1297. [CrossRef]
28. Steinman, G.; Mankuta, D. Molecular biology of autism's etiology—An alternative mechanism. *Med. Hypotheses* **2019**, *130*, 109–272. [CrossRef]
29. Linke, A.C.; Keehn, R.J.J.; Pueschel, E.B.; Fishman, I.; Müller, R.-A. Children with ASD show links between aberrant sound processing, social symptoms, and atypical auditory interhemispheric and thalamocortical functional connectivity. *Dev. Cogn. Neurosci.* **2018**, *29*, 117–126. [CrossRef]
30. Chang, Y.-S.; Owen, J.P.; Desai, S.S.; Hill, S.S.; Arnett, A.B.; Harris, J.; Marco, E.J.; Mukherjee, P. Autism and Sensory Processing Disorders: Shared White Matter Disruption in Sensory Pathways but Divergent Connectivity in Social-Emotional Pathways. *PLoS ONE* **2014**, *9*, e103038. [CrossRef]
31. Schaaf, R.C.; Lane, A.E. Toward a Best-Practice Protocol for Assessment of Sensory Features in ASD. *J. Autism Dev. Disord.* **2015**, *45*, 1380–1395. [CrossRef] [PubMed]

32. Posar, A.; Visconti, P. Sensory abnormalities in children with autism spectrum disorder. *J. Pediatr.* **2018**, *94*, 342–350. [CrossRef]
33. Marco, E.J.; Hinkley, L.B.N.; Hill, S.S.; Nagarajan, S.S. Sensory Processing in Autism: A Review of Neurophysiologic Findings. *Pediatr. Res.* **2011**, *69*, 48R–54R. [CrossRef] [PubMed]
34. Suarez, M.A. Sensory Processing in Children with Autism Spectrum Disorders and Impact on Functioning. *Pediatr. Clin. North Am.* **2012**, *59*, 203–214. [CrossRef] [PubMed]
35. Glod, M.; Riby, D.M.; Rodgers, J. Sensory processing profiles and autistic symptoms as predictive factors in autism spectrum disorder and Williams syndrome. *J. Intellect. Disabil. Res.* **2020**, *64*, 657–665. [CrossRef] [PubMed]
36. Schoen, S.; Lane, S.J.; Mailloux, Z.; May-Benson, T.; Parham, L.D.; Roley, S.S.; Schaaf, R.C. A systematic review of ayres sensory integration intervention for children with autism. *Autism Res.* **2019**, *12*, 6–19. [CrossRef] [PubMed]
37. Bodison, S.C.; Parham, L.D. Specific Sensory Techniques and Sensory Environmental Modifications for Children and Youth with Sensory Integration Difficulties: A Systematic Review. *Am. J. Occup. Ther.* **2017**, *72*, 72011–90040. [CrossRef]
38. Ben-Sasson, A.; Hen, L.; Fluss, R.; Cermak, S.A.; Engel-Yeger, B.; Gal, E. A Meta-Analysis of Sensory Modulation Symptoms in Individuals with Autism Spectrum Disorders. *J. Autism Dev. Disord.* **2009**, *39*, 1–11. [CrossRef]
39. Di Renzo, M.; Di Castelbianco, F.B.; Vanadia, E.; Petrillo, M.; Racinaro, L.; Rea, M. Sensory Processing and Repetitive Behaviors in Clinical Assessment of Preschool Children with Autism Spectrum Disorder. *J. Child Adolesc. Behav.* **2017**, *5*, 5. [CrossRef]
40. Dakopolos, A.J.; Jahromi, L.B. Differences in sensory responses among children with autism spectrum disorder and typical development: Links to joint attention and social competence. *Infant Child Dev.* **2018**, *28*, e2117. [CrossRef]
41. Thye, M.D.; Bednarz, H.M.; Herringshaw, A.J.; Sartin, E.B.; Kana, R.K. The impact of atypical sensory processing on social impairments in autism spectrum disorder. *Dev. Cogn. Neurosci.* **2018**, *29*, 151–167. [CrossRef] [PubMed]
42. Miller, M.; Chukoskie, L.; Zinni, M.; Townsend, J.; Trauner, D. Dyspraxia, motor function and visual–motor integration in autism. *Behav. Brain Res.* **2014**, *269*, 95–102. [CrossRef] [PubMed]
43. Kaur, M.; Srinivasan, S.M.; Bhat, A.N. Comparing motor performance, praxis, coordination, and interpersonal synchrony between children with and without Autism Spectrum Disorder (ASD). *Res. Dev. Disabil.* **2018**, *72*, 79–95. [CrossRef] [PubMed]
44. Günal, A.; Bumin, G.; Huri, M. The Effects of Motor and Cognitive Impairments on Daily Living Activities and Quality of Life in Children with Autism. *J. Occup. Ther. Sch. Early Interv.* **2019**, *12*, 444–454. [CrossRef]
45. Wong, C.; Odom, S.L.; Hume, K.A.; Cox, A.W.; Fettig, A.; Kucharczyk, S.; Brock, M.E.; Plavnick, J.B.; Fleury, V.P.; Schultz, T.R. Evidence-Based Practices for Children, Youth, and Young Adults with Autism Spectrum Disorder: A Comprehensive Review. *J. Autism Dev. Disord.* **2015**, *45*, 1951–1966. [CrossRef]
46. Jorquera-Cabrera, S.; Romero-Ayuso, D.; Rodriguez-Gil, G.; Triviño-Juárez, J.-M. Assessment of Sensory Processing Characteristics in Children between 3 and 11 Years Old: A Systematic Review. *Front. Pediatr.* **2017**, *5*, 57. [CrossRef]
47. Eeles, A.L.; Spittle, A.J.; Anderson, P.J.; Brown, N.; Lee, K.J.; Boyd, R.; Doyle, L.W. Assessments of sensory processing in infants: A systematic review. *Dev. Med. Child Neurol.* **2012**, *55*, 314–326. [CrossRef]
48. Burns, C.O.; Dixon, D.R.; Novack, M.; Granpeesheh, D. A Systematic Review of Assessments for Sensory Processing Abnormalities in Autism Spectrum Disorder. *Rev. J. Autism Dev. Disord.* **2017**, *4*, 209–224. [CrossRef]
49. Dubois, D.; Lymer, E.; Gibson, B.E.; Desarkar, P.; Nalder, E.J. Assessing Sensory Processing Dysfunction in Adults and Adolescents with Autism Spectrum Disorder: A Scoping Review. *Brain Sci.* **2017**, *7*, 108. [CrossRef]
50. Yeung, L.H.J.; Thomacos, N. Assessments of sensory processing in infants and children with autism spectrum disorder between 0–12 years old: A scoping review. *Res. Autism Spectr. Disord.* **2020**, *72*, 101517. [CrossRef]
51. Dunn, W. *Sensory Profile User's Manual*; Pearson Psychcop: San Antonio, TX, USA, 1999.
52. Dunn, W. *Sensory Profile 2 Manual*; Pearson Psychcop: San Antonio, TX, USA, 2014.

53. Parham, L.D.; Ecker, C.; Miller Kuhaneck, H.; Henry, D.A.; Glennon, T.J. *Sensory Processing Measure (SPM): Manual*; Western Psychological Services: Los Angeles, CA, USA, 2007.
54. Mulligan, S.; Schoen, S.; Miller, L. Scientific Research Panel 304C Reliability and Item Analyses of the Sensory Processing 3-Dimensions Scale. *Am. J. Occup. Ther.* **2018**, *72*, 7211500055. [CrossRef]
55. Mailloux, Z.; Parham, L.D.; Roley, S.S.; Ruzzano, L.; Schaaf, R.C. Introduction to the Evaluation in Ayres Sensory Integration® (EASI). *Am. J. Occup. Ther.* **2017**, *72*, 72011–95030. [CrossRef]
56. Petrocchi, S.; Levante, A.; Lecciso, F. Systematic Review of Level 1 and Level 2 Screening Tools for Autism Spectrum Disorders in Toddlers. *Brain Sci.* **2020**, *10*, 180. [CrossRef]
57. Towle, P.O.; Patrick, P.A. Autism Spectrum Disorder Screening Instruments for Very Young Children: A Systematic Review. *Autism Res. Treat.* **2016**, *2016*, 1–29. [CrossRef]
58. Payakachat, N.; Tilford, J.M.; Kovacs, E.; Kuhlthau, K. Autism spectrum disorders: A review of measures for clinical, health services and cost–effectiveness applications. *Expert Rev. Pharm. Outcomes Res.* **2012**, *12*, 485–503. [CrossRef]
59. Randall, M.; Egberts, K.J.; Samtani, A.; Scholten, R.J.; Hooft, L.; Livingstone, N.; Sterling-Levis, K.; Woolfenden, S.; Williams, K. Diagnostic tests for autism spectrum disorder (ASD) in preschool children. *Cochrane Database Syst. Rev.* **2018**, *7*, CD009044. [CrossRef]
60. Rivière, Á. Tratamiento y Definición del Espectro Autista. In *Tratamiento del Autismo. Nuevas Perspectivas*; Instituto de Migraciones y Servicios Sociales: Madrid, Spain, 1998; ISBN 84-88986-70-X.
61. Rivière, A. *IDEA: Inventario de Espectro Autista*; Fundec: Buenos Aires, Argentina, 2002.
62. García-Gómez, A. A proposal of three additional dimensions to the Rivière's Autism Spectrum Inventory. *Psicol. Educ.* in press. [CrossRef]
63. Williams, Z.J.; Failla, M.D.; Gotham, K.O.; Woynaroski, T.G.; Cascio, C. Psychometric Evaluation of the Short Sensory Profile in Youth with Autism Spectrum Disorder. *J. Autism Dev. Disord.* **2018**, *48*, 4231–4249. [CrossRef]
64. Dunn, W. *Perfil Sensorial 2 Breve*; Adaptación Española; Pearson Psychcop: Madrid, Spain, 2016; ISBN 978-84-9035-547-3.
65. Ferrando, P.J.; Lorenzo-Seva, U. Program FACTOR at 10: Origins, development and future directions. *Psicothema* **2017**, *29*, 236–240.
66. Lorenzo-Seva, U.; Ferrando, P.J. Factor: A computer program to fit the exploratory factor analysis model. *Behav. Res. Methods* **2006**, *38*, 88–91. [CrossRef]
67. Manual of the Program. Available online: http://psico.fcep.urv.es/utilitats/factor/documentation/Manual-of-the-Factor-Program-v92.pdf (accessed on 20 August 2020).
68. Timmerman, M.E.; Lorenzo-Seva, U. Dimensionality assessment of ordered polytomous items with parallel analysis. *Psychol. Methods* **2011**, *16*, 209–220. [CrossRef] [PubMed]
69. Arbuckle, J. *Amos 24.0 User's Guide*; IBM SPSS: Chicago, IL, USA, 2015.
70. Flora, D.B.; LaBrish, C.; Chalmers, R.P. Old and New Ideas for Data Screening and Assumption Testing for Exploratory and Confirmatory Factor Analysis. *Front. Psychol.* **2012**, *3*, 3. [CrossRef]
71. Lloret-Segura, S.; Ferreres-Traver, A.; Hernández-Baeza, A.; Tomás-Marco, I. Exploratory Item Factor Analysis: A practical guide revised and updated. *An. Psicol.* **2014**, *30*, 1151–1169. [CrossRef]
72. Ferrando, P.J.; Anguiano-Carrasco, C. Factor analysis as a research technique in psychology. *Pap. Psicólogo* **2010**, *31*, 18–33.
73. Byrne, B.M. A Primer of LISREL. In *Texto original: Basic Applications and Programming for Confirmatory Factor Analytic Models*; Springer: New York, NY, USA, 1989; ISBN 978-1-4613-8887-6.
74. Hu, L.-T.; Bentler, P.M. Cutoff criteria for fit indexes in covariance structure analysis: Conventional criteria versus new alternatives. *Struct. Equ. Model. Multidiscip. J.* **1999**, *6*, 1–55.
75. Hair, J.F. *Multivariate Data Analysis: A Global Perspective*; Pearson Education: London, UK, 2010; ISBN 978-0-13-515309-3.
76. Browne, M.W.; Cudeck, R. Alternative Ways of Assessing Model Fit. *Sociol. Methods Res.* **1992**, *21*, 230–258. [CrossRef]
77. Gadermann, A.M.; Guhn, M.; Zumbo, B.D. Ordinal Alpha. *Encycl. Qual. Life Well Being Res.* **2014**, 4513–4515. [CrossRef]
78. Oliden, P.E.; Zumbo, B.D. Reliability coefficients for ordinal response scales. *Psicothema* **2008**, *20*, 896–901.

79. Pallant, J. *SPSS Survival Manual: A Step by Step Guide to Data Analysis Using IBM SPSS*, 5th ed.; McGraw Hill: Berkshire, UK, 2013; ISBN 978-0-335-26258-8.
80. IBM Corp IBM SPSS Statistics for Windows, Version 24.0. Available online: https://he02.tci-thaijo.org/index.php/ramajournal/statistical_software_references_format (accessed on 22 August 2020).
81. Cohen, J. Statistical Power Analysis for the Behavioral Sciences. Lawrence Earlbaum Associates Hillsdale, NJ, USA. Available online: http://www.utstat.toronto.edu/~{}brunner/oldclass/378f16/readings/CohenPower.pdf (accessed on 15 October 2020).
82. Jöreskog, K.G.; Sörbom, D. *LISREL 8: Structural Equation Modeling with the SIMPLIS Command Language*; Scientific Software International: Lincolnwood, IL, USA, 1993; ISBN 978-0-89498-033-6.
83. Salgado, J.F. Transforming the Area under the Normal Curve (AUC) into Cohen's d, Pearson's r pb, Odds-Ratio, and Natural Log Odds-Ratio: Two Conversion Tables. *Eur. J. Psychol. Appl. Leg. Context* **2018**, *10*, 35–47. [CrossRef]
84. Roley, S.S.; Blanche, E.I.; Schaaf, R.C. *Understanding the Nature of Sensory Integration with Diverse Populations*; PRO-ED: Indianapolis, IN, USA, 2007; ISBN 978-1-4164-0332-6.
85. Schoen, S.; Miller, L.J.; Sullivan, J.C. Measurement in Sensory Modulation: The Sensory Processing Scale Assessment. *Am. J. Occup. Ther.* **2014**, *68*, 522–530. [CrossRef]
86. Ministerio de Sanidad, Servicios Sociales e Igualdad. *Salud Mental y Calidad de Vida en la Población Infantil*; Serie Informes Monográficos no2; Ministerio de Sanidad, Servicios Sociales e Igualdad: Madrid, Spain, 2014.
87. Van Gameren-Oosterom, H.B.; Van Dommelen, P.; Schönbeck, Y.; Oudesluys-Murphy, A.M.; Van Wouwe, J.P.; Buitendijk, S.E. Prevalence of Overweight in Dutch Children with Down Syndrome. *Pediatrics* **2012**, *130*, e1520–e1526. [CrossRef] [PubMed]

children

MDPI

Article

Play in Children with Neurodevelopmental Disorders: Psychometric Properties of a Parent Report Measure 'My Child's Play'

Dulce Romero-Ayuso [1,*], María Ruiz-Salcedo [1], Sabina Barrios-Fernández [2], José Matías Triviño-Juárez [3], Donald Maciver [4], Janet Richmond [5] and Miguel A. Muñoz [6]

1 Physical Therapy Department, Occupational Therapy, Faculty of Health Sciences, University of Granada, 18016 Granada, Spain; mariamrs97@hotmail.com

2 Medical-Surgical Therapeutics Department, University of Extremadura, 10003 Cáceres, Spain; sabinabarrios@unex.es

3 Primary Care Center Zaidín Sur, Granada Metropolitan Sanitary District, 18007 Granada, Spain; jmtjuarez@hotmail.com

4 Occupational Therapy and Arts Therapies Subject Area, School of Health Sciences, Queen Margaret University, Edinburgh, Scotland EH21 6UU, UK; DMaciver@qmu.ac.uk

5 Occupational Therapy, School of Medical and Health Sciences, Edith Cowan University, 270 Joondalup Drive, Joondalup WA 6027, Australia; inscribeot@outlook.com.au

6 Personality, Assessment and Psychological Treatment Department, Faculty of Psychology, University of Granada, 18071 Granada, Spain; mamunoz@ugr.es

* Correspondence: dulceromero@ugr.es

Abstract: Play is essential in childhood, allowing for a positive trend in development and learning. Health professionals need useful tools to assess it, especially in the case of children with neurodevelopmental disorders. The aim of this study was to validate and cross-culturally adapt the My Child's Play questionnaire and to find out if this instrument allows us to differentiate the play of children with neurodevelopmental disorders from the play of children with neurotypical development. A total of 594 parents completed the questionnaire. A confirmatory factor analysis was conducted, which showed a similar structure to the English version: (1) executive functions; (2) environmental context; (3) play characteristics; and (4) play preferences and interpersonal interactions. The reliability of the analysis was high, both for the whole questionnaire and for the factors it comprises. The results provide evidence of the potential usefulness of the My Child's Play questionnaire for determining play needs and difficulties of children; moreover, this tool can also be used to plan intervention programs according to the needs of each child and family.

Keywords: play; assessment; executive functions; neurodevelopmental disorders; autism spectrum disorder; specific language disorder

Citation: Romero-Ayuso, D.; Ruiz-Salcedo, M.; Barrios-Fernández, S.; Triviño-Juárez, J.M.; Maciver, D.; Richmond, J.; Muñoz, M.A. Play in Children with Neurodevelopmental Disorders: Psychometric Properties of a Parent Report Measure 'My Child's Play'. *Children* **2021**, *8*, 25. https://doi.org/10.3390/children8010025

Received: 5 December 2020
Accepted: 2 January 2021
Published: 6 January 2021

1. Introduction

Play is considered a natural learning mechanism through which children explore and learn about themselves and the world around them [1]. Children spend considerable time playing, providing fun, learning, and activity [2]. Children's play has been studied by many disciplines because of its considerable influence on global development and well-being, being essential for achievement of motor, cognitive, emotional, and social milestones [3]. In fact, participation in play contributes to peer inclusion, improvement of self-concept and self-esteem, promotion of creativity and flexibility, emotional regulation, language development, and frustration tolerance during academic and daily life activities [1]. Play can be defined as a non-serious, spontaneous, or organized activity that provides enjoyment, entertainment, amusement, or diversion and its characteristics include intrinsic motivation, emphasis on process rather than product, pleasure, reward, and voluntary engagement [2,4].

In children with neurodevelopmental disorders (NDD), especially those with autism spectrum disorder (ASD), developmental delay (DD), and specific language disorder (SLD), differences are observed in the way they participate in play [5,6]. In ASD diagnosed children, deficits in joint attention, imagination, imitation, and communicative intention can affect their play development [7]. Usually, their play interests are oriented toward sensory and physical aspects [8], and together with their repetitive and stereotypical behaviors [9] produce issues while interacting with their peers and achieving a proper play engagement [10,11]. Children with DD spend more time in passive activities rather than playing and with adults more than with their peers [12]. Although children with ASD and SLD diagnosis face different challenges around play, there are few studies that address them, and the instruments to assess them are limited [1,13,14].

Educational and health professionals may use different tools for play assessment [6], such as the Test of Playfulness, Test of Environmental Supportiveness, Revised Know Preschool Play Scale, The McDonald Play Inventory, The Play Assessment for Group Settings, and My Children's Play. Test of Playfulness [15] is designed to measure play in children between 6 months and 18 years, observing their individual free play both indoors and outdoors and its extension. The Test of Environmental Supportiveness assesses how the environment influences play. The Revised Knox Preschool Play Scale [16] uses observation to assess participation in play, taking into consideration the use of space and materials, sensory and motor processing, social behavior, communication, and symbolic play. The McDonald Play Inventory [17] is a two-part self-report instrument that provides information about play activities and play style. For the pretend play evaluation, the Play Assessment for Group Settings [18] and the Child-Initiated Pretend Play Assessment [19,20] are available, having this second one an extension for measuring social aspects of play called the Indigenous Play Partner Scale, both using professional observation.

On the other hand, as parents are often the primary caregivers of their children, it is important to know the way in which they interact during play situations [21]. It is also important to consider parents' beliefs about their children's play, influencing how they organize their contexts, activities, and interactions [1,22,23]. Although parents are able to adapt their play to their child's play level, parents with ASD children can use fewer symbolic solicitations, not giving the opportunity to make their play more complex [24]. For all the above, parents must be considered as important agents for a proper play assessment and intervention.

The My Children's Play (MCP) questionnaire [25] is a measure that provides information about parent's perception about their child's play performance, where they indicate the response that best describes their child's play behavior on a 5-point Likert scale. This instrument has a total of 43 items divided in four factors: executive functions, interpersonal relationships, play choices, and preferences and opportunities in the environment, which makes it a tool with a broad view on a phenomenon as complex as children's play.

The availability of valid, reliable, and appropriate tools to assess play using parental perceptions and beliefs is important for a complete understanding of children's play. The first aim of this study was to conduct a cross-cultural adaptation of the My Child's Play questionnaire for the Spanish-speaking population. Secondly, we studied whether the My Child's Play questionnaire would allow us to know the characteristics of the play of children with NDD, such as ASD, DD, and SLD, and to differentiate them from children with neurotypical development.

2. Materials and Methods

2.1. Participants

The participants were recruited through different educational centers and associations of children with functional diversity: CEIP Parque de la Infantas de Granada, CEIP Maruja Mallo de Málaga, Asociación Serranía de Churriana, Federación Española de Autismo (FESPAU), Autismo España, and Asperger España. Two researchers with experience in child therapy contacted the different entities (M.R.-S. and D.R.-A.) A researcher with clinical experience in children with ASD and SLD recruited the parents of children with NDD (S.B.-F.) Authorization was requested from those responsible for each entity. Once authorization was obtained, the interested parents were contacted, and the questionnaire was provided in digital format. The participation of all parents was voluntary. Before starting to fill in the questionnaire, the objective of the study was explained to them, and their written informed consent was requested. The researchers resolved the doubts that arose to the parents while completing the questionnaire. Similar to the original questionnaire in the English version, the responses were based on parents' perceptions of their children's play. The same procedure was followed in all centers.

The inclusion criteria in the neurotypical group were to be the main caregiver of a child aged between 3 and 9 years old without any neurological or psychiatric illness, without learning disorders, Spanish nationality, and consent to participate in the study. The criteria in neurodevelopmental disorder group in addition to age were to have a clinical diagnosis of NDD (ASD, DD, or SLD).

2.2. Instruments

The My Child's Play (MCP) is the original English version of the questionnaire that has been translated and validated into Spanish in this study, and it is a tool that has strong psychometric qualities, with good validity and reliability of internal consistency (Cronbach's $\alpha = 0.86$) [26]. The original tool consisted of 50 items, the last version reduced the number of items to 43, being divided into four dimensions: interpersonal relationships and social participation, executive functions, choices and preferences in play, and opportunities in the environment. Parents should indicate in each item the response that best reflects their child's behavior during play using a 5-point Likert scale ranging from 1 = never to 5 = always. It also includes the option of not applicable to assess an item as not relevant in that specific case. The total score obtained in the questionnaire is interpreted taking into account that higher scores reflect better performance.

The participants answered a series of questions about sociodemographic aspects that included age, gender, place of residence, educational level, and general questions about their children such as premature or full-term birth Likewise, the parents were asked if the children had any type of learning difficulty and if they did other activities regularly in addition to school, such as sports, playing an instrument, or another hobby. Subsequently, all parents completed the translated version of the MCP questionnaire.

2.3. Design and Procedure

For the development of this study, the methodology of the validation of health questionnaires was followed [27]. Before conducting the study, the authors of the original questionnaire were contacted to inform them about our study and request their authorization to carry out the translation, adaptation, and validation of the questionnaire with the Spanish population. This study was approved by the Ethics and Research Committee of the University of Granada (code 1426/CEIH/2020).

The first phase included the direct and inverse translation of the Spanish version and the cultural adaptation that was generated. In the second phase, a pilot study of the Spanish version of the questionnaire was carried out with participants recruited by the research team. The selection of the sample was by non-probabilistic method, and data collection was carried out over six months. Finally, in the third phase, the analysis of the psychometric properties was carried out to check the validity and reliability of the questionnaire in its Spanish version and the confirmatory factor analysis of the structure of the original questionnaire. The original English version of the MCP questionnaire was translated into Spanish by two people independently, a bilingual translator and one of the researchers in the study who has an adequate knowledge of the original language. Both translations were compared simultaneously by the research team to identify and discuss the discrepancies between the two versions until a consensus was reached, generating a first version of the questionnaire in Spanish. The first Spanish version of the questionnaire generated in the previous step was translated back into English by a translator. An expert panel made up of members of the research team was set up to review and compare the translation of each item with the original version and the Spanish version. This allowed us to check whether the translation generated relevant conceptual differences between the version translated into Spanish and the original. A total of five items were modified to improve their understanding, corresponding to numbers 5, 14, 15, 31, and 50 and considering the rest of the questions as correct (Table 1). These changes gave rise to the second version in Spanish of the questionnaire with which the pilot study was carried out.

Table 1. Items modified by experts.

Item	First Spanish Version	Second Spanish Version
5	El niño es capaz de imitar movimientos.	El niño imita movimientos.
14	El niño se adapta fácilmente a la intervención de nuevos adultos o niños.	El niño se adapta fácilmente a nuevos adultos o niños.
15	El niño es capaz de afrontar situaciones de frustración durante el juego.	El niño afronta situaciones de frustración durante el juego.
31	El niño pierde el interés cuando juega por sí mismo.	El niño pierde el interés cuando juega solo.
50	Estoy contento con la forma en que mi hijo juega.	Estoy satisfecho con la manera con la que juega el niño.

In a second phase, a pilot test was performed. The Spanish version of MCP was used to carry out a pilot test with 30 parents of children with neurotypical development. An intentional sampling was used. None of the participants reported having problems understanding the instructions of the questionnaire or any of its items. However, one of the participants suggested a possible change toward a more inclusive terminology, modifying the terms "fathers" and "mothers" by parents to also contemplate gay or single parent families. No other changes were made to the wording of the items or instructions of the translated version of the questionnaire.

Once the final questionnaire was obtained, it was administered to parents of children with neurotypical development and NDD. A total of 591 responses were obtained for total sample, of which 17 did not meet any of the established inclusion criteria, leaving 574 valid responses from parents living in Spain. To complete the questionnaire, parents were asked to indicate the answer that best described their children's play on a 5-point Likert scale from 1 = never to 5 = always. The same instructions were followed as in the original questionnaire. Parents completed the questionnaire at home. In case any questions arose while completing the questionnaire, they were provided with the email of the main researcher and the telephone number of the contact researcher. All parents who agreed to participate in the study completed the questionnaire. Once the questionnaire was completed, it was reviewed by the group of researchers, and in case of doubts or observations made by the parents, they were contacted to resolve possible doubts or suggestions.

2.4. Statistical Analysis

Construct validity allows knowing the degree to which the items of the instrument measure the theoretical construct that they intend to measure. The construct validity of the questionnaire was determined through factor analysis, which is a statistical technique that allows structuring a dataset into factors or components. AMOS extension (version 18.0) is structural equation modeling software that was used to conduct confirmatory factor analysis (CFA). The maximum likelihood method was used for the estimation of the goodness of fit parameters. Once it was verified that the goodness of fit parameters did not allow confirming the model with Pearson's correlations and neither did they improve after eliminating with less weight in each factor, a new CFA was carried out with the FACTOR software (version 10.10.03) [28], since the answer options of the questionnaire are through a Likert scale with 5 answer options. Polychoric correlations with robust analysis and unweighted least squares (ULS) were used, and the method for factor extraction was normalized varimax [29,30]. CFA was performed to verify that the dimensions identified by the authors of the original tool were valid in the translated version of the questionnaire. For this, the measures of the quality of the fit of the model were evaluated through the absolute fit measures: the Chi-square divided by degrees of freedom (CMIN/DF), the Root Mean Square Error of Approximation (RMSEA), incremental adjustment measures such as the comparative fit index (CFI), Tucker–Lewis index (TLI), and other adjusted goodness fit statistics: goodness of fit index (GFI), adjusted goodness of fit index (AGFI).

Reliability of internal consistency of the MCP questionnaire was calculated using Cronbach's alpha. Reliability for each factor was carried out by calculating this coefficient for the items with respect to the global score and the other coefficient for the items of each domain with respect to its value. Cronbach's alpha values >0.70 were considered acceptable to guarantee the internal consistency of the questionnaire [31].

Furthermore, relative operating characteristic (ROC) analysis was performed to know the MCP's ability to classify between children with NDD and neurotypical development. The characteristics of the participants were analyzed using simple descriptive statistics. These statistical analyses were performed using IBM SPSS Statistics for Windows software (version 26.0, IBM Corp., Armonk, NY, USA), for others statistical analysis of the data. Statistical significance was set at $p < 0.05$ (bilateral).

3. Results

The sample in this study was 574 families of children (326 boys, 56.8%, and 248 girls, 43.2%) between 3 and 9 years old. Of these, 469 (81.7%) were children with neurotypical development and 105 (18.3%) were children with NDD: DD (n = 47; 8.2%), SLD (n = 23; 4%), and ASD (n = 34; 5.9%). The mean age of the children was 5.55 years (SD = 1.92), and the mean age of the parents was 39.41 (SD = 5.36) and 39.38 (5.23) respectively. Regarding the characteristics of the children, birth was premature in 59 cases (10.3%) and at term in 515 (89.7%).

3.1. Construct Validity

The construct validity was verified using a CFA with the factor model proposed by the authors of the original questionnaire conforming to the data that we have obtained in the Spanish population (Figure 1). The CFA with FACTOR Software confirmed the four-factor structure for the MCP (Table 2).

Table 2. My Children's Play goodness-of-fit index from the confirmatory factor analysis.

	Index	Cut-Off	Original Model Value	Alternative Model Value
Model Fit				
	p (χ2)	>0.05	2161.378 $p < 0.001$	817.584 $p = 0.020$
	RMSEA	<0.05	0.058	0.023 CI 95%, (0.010–0.050)
Incremental Adjusted Measures				
	CFI	>0.90–1	0.792	0.991
	NNFI	>0.90–1	0.780	0.990
	CMIN/DF	<2	2.937	1.108
	RMSR	<0.08	-	0.0479

p (χ2): Chi-squared probability; RMSEA: root mean square error of approximation; CFI: comparative fit index; NNFI: non-normed fit index, RMSR: root mean square of residuals.

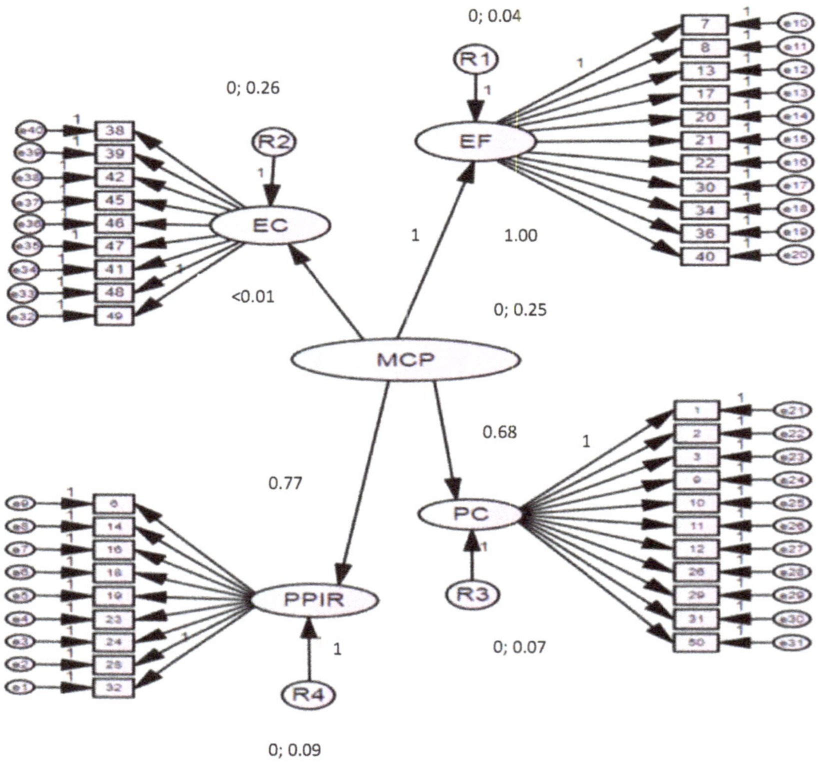

Figure 1. Model for neurotypical, specific language disorder (SLD), and autism spectrum disorder (ASD) children. $\chi2$ = 817.584, gl = 737.89 *p* = 0.020.

The composition of the four factors and their factor loading are shown in Table 3. The four MCP factors explain 42.98% of the variance. The first factor, flexibility and executive attention, explained 25.40% of the variance. The second factor, the environmental context, explained 7.11% of the variance. The third factor, play characteristics, explained 5.69%, and the last factor, play preferences and interpersonal relationships, explained 4.77%. Items 27, 15, and 35 were not included in any factor.

Table 3. Factor loading for the 40 items of the My Child's Play questionnaire.

Item No.	Item	Factor 1	Factor 2	Factor 3	Factor 4	
	Executive Functions: Flexibility and Executive Attention					
7	Child has difficulty concentrating with background noise	0.381				Eigenvalue: 10.92 Cronbach's alpha: 0.861 IC95% (0.844–0.878)
8	Child bumps into or drops things during play	0.650				
13	Child adapts easily to changes in play conditions	0.572				
17	Child plays with kids according to the rules	0.619				
20	Child is willing to share toys with others	0.420				
21	Child adapts play behavior to setting	0.503				
22	Child controls impulses during play with others	0.693				

Table 3. *Cont.*

Item No.	Item	Factor 1	Factor 2	Factor 3	Factor 4	
	Executive Functions: Flexibility and Executive Attention					
30	Child needs lots of breaks to stay attentive	0.557				
34	Child doesn't play games that have rules	0.538				
36	Child purposely bumps into objects or surfaces	0.583				
40	Child has difficulty playing with too many visual stimuli	0.476				
	Environmental Context					
38	There is accessible space outside house for play		0.347			Eigenvalue: 3.058 Cronbach's alpha: 0.639 IC95% (0.593–0.682)
39	There is accessible space inside house for play		0.446			
41	Child has enough toys for varied enjoyable play		0.468			
42	Toys at home are organized for easy access		0.364			
45	I consider my child's play preferences		0.331			
46	I offer help after my child tries playing alone		0.614			
47	I model play according to my child's abilities		0.639			
48	I define rules clearly so my child can play enjoyably		0.521			
49	Daily routine includes time for play with the child		0.568			
	Play Characteristics					
1	Child plays with toys according to intended use			0.352		Eigenvalue: 2.44 Cronbach's alpha: 0.838 IC95% (0.818–0.857)
2	Child varies play with toys			0.458		
3	Child loses interest in toy			0.574		
9	Child persists at play even when having difficulty			0.404		
10	Child tries to problem solve by him- or herself during play			0.521		
11	Child can't get organized for play without adult help			0.525		
12	Child needs adult help to stay focused on play			0.695		
26	Child finds opportunity to play everywhere			0.561		
29	Child enjoys imaginative play			0.581		
31	Child loses interest when playing by him- or herself			0.663		
50	I'm pleased with the way my child plays			0.601		
	Play Preferences and Interpersonal Relationships					
6	Child uses both hands to play				0.322	Eigenvalue: 2.05 Cronbach's alpha: 0.821 IC95% (0.798–0.842)
14	Child adapts easily to new adults or children				0.687	
16	Child relates to other children during play				0.819	
18	Child is able to initiate play				0.612	
19	Child takes on role of group leader during play				0.522	
23	Child needs adult help to join group of children playing				0.696	
24	Child prefers to play only with familiar toys				0.570	
28	Child avoids play that requires movement				0.488	
32	Child prefers to play with adults over children				0.447	

The final questionnaire in the Spanish version consisted of 40 items instead of 43 in the original version (Table 4 & Appendix A).

Table 4. Distribution of items for each factor in original and for Spanish version of My Children's Play.

Factor Original Version	Items Original Version (43 Items)	Factor Spanish Version	Items Spanish Version (40 Items)
Factor 1. Interpersonal Relationships, Social Participation	10, 14, 15, 16,17, 18, 19, 20, 21, 23, 24	Factor 4. Play Preferences and Interpersonal Relationships	6, 14, 16, 18, 19, 23, 24, 28, 32
Factor 2. Executive Functions	3, 7, 8, 11, 12, 22, 27, 30, 31, 32, 34, 36	Factor 1. Executive Functions: Flexibility and Executive attention	7, 8, 13, 17, 20, 21, 22, 30, 34, 36, 40
Factor 3. Play Characteristics and Behavior	1, 9, 13, 26, 28, 29, 35,38, 39, 40, 41	Factor 3. Play Characteristics	1, 2, 3, 9, 10, 11, 12, 26, 29, 31, 50
Factor 4. Environmental Context	2, 6, 42, 45, 46, 47, 48, 49, 50	Factor 2. Environmental Context	38, 39, 41, 42, 45, 46, 47, 48, 49

3.2. *Reliability*

The reliability analysis showed a Cronbach's alpha for total score (0.695) that is acceptable. Despite being slightly below the level of acceptability that was set, we can assume that it is practically 0.7, and therefore, it is an acceptable value, indicating that the internal consistency is adequate (Table 3).

3.3. *Interpretability*

Table 5 shows the mean scores obtained by neurotypical children and by those with NDD in MCP and in each of its four factors. There were significant differences between neurotypical children and children with NDD with lower scores in the first group (Table 5). Likewise, Figure 2 shows the ROC curve for the predictive level of MCP in the children with NDD. The area under the curve was 0.876 (CI 95%, 0.840–0.912).

Table 5. Mean scores in neurotypical and neurodevelopmental children.

	Neurotypical Group		Neurodevelopmental Group			
	Mean	**SD**	**Mean**	**SD**	**Dif Mean**	**Cohen's d**
Flexibility and executive attention	43.06	5.63	32.12	7.24	10.94	1.837
Environmental context	38.35	4.12	38.26	4.10	0.089	0.057
Play characteristics	41.21	5.50	34.55	7.56	6.66	1.123
Play preferences and interpersonal relationships	36.10	4.06	28.55	5.50	7.55	1.733
Total Score	158.75	13.50	133.49	17.31	25.25	1.770

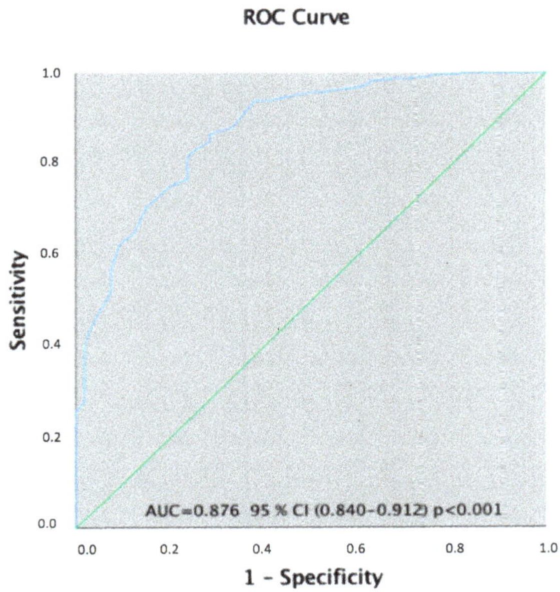

Figure 2. Relative operating characteristic (ROC) curve used to determine the predictive value of MCP in the diagnosis of children with neurodevelopmental disorder.

Accordingly, the optimal cut-off score to differentiate children from the neurotypical group versus children with NDD was 142 points. Thus, the score <142 in the MCP is indicative of NDD according to the MCP.

4. Discussion

The objective of this study was to translate and culturally adapt the MCP questionnaire to the Spanish population, in addition to studying its reliability and validity, providing a new assessment resource for pediatric health and educational professionals that allows them to learn about participation in play in children with neurotypical development and children with NDD. Play is of great importance and very significant in childhood, the assessment of which has been hampered by the complexity for defining the concept and because it is a behavior that is difficult to standardize and quantify. For professionals and those interested in assessment, the lack of time and resources and having only clinical environments where the behavior during play is different from that manifested in the family environment means that many professionals do not use the existing standardized tools [32,33]. These problems can be addressed with questionnaires such as My Child's Play. Scores on the MCP questionnaire represent the parental perceptions on daily living. Although MCP does not include observations or tests of the child's play performance, it could also be considered a strength, since it is relevant from the point of view of family-centred practice, allowing to know the functioning of the child in everyday life and showing good ecological validity. MCP has good psychometric properties [25]. The MCP allows knowing different factors underlying the play that are relevant in the assessment of children with neurodevelopmental disorders: (1) cognitive such as executive functioning; (2) socio-emotional, such as social interaction and participation; (3) the behavior during play; and (4) characteristic of play and child's play preference. Finally, the MCP is a short questionnaire, easily understandable by parents, and easy to complete.

4.1. Reliability

The questionnaire shows good reliability. Cronbach's alpha coefficient indicates that the internal consistency is acceptable ($\alpha = 0.695$ for the total score, while in the original, it is 0.86). In addition, in the four dimensions Cronbach's alpha were 0.861, 0.639, 0.838, and 0.821, respectively. These values were similar to those of the original questionnaire, which were 0.80, 0.81, 0.67, and 0.63. As with the original questionnaire, the factor referring to the environmental context was the one that presented lower reliability.

4.2. Construct Validity

Regarding the construct validity, the results obtained in the CFA of the Spanish translation of the questionnaire do not allow us to support the same original factorial solution of the English version. However, both versions have four factors, although the weight of each of them is different for the two populations. The factor analysis of the original questionnaire revealed the existence of four factors (executive functions, interpersonal relationships and social participation, preferences and choices in the game, and opportunities in the environment) that explained 30% of the total variance and supported the original concept of the authors of the elaboration of a questionnaire based on the person–occupation–environment relationship. The CFA of the version translated into Spanish determines that the construct validity is not completely adequate, as indicated by the values produced by the adjustment variables (RMSEA = 0.058, CFI = 0.792, NNFI = 0.780, and CIM/DF = 2.937); therefore, the model proposed in the original questionnaire did not fit the data obtained in the Spanish population. However, the new factorial solution obtained also supports the person–environment–participation relationship proposed by the original authors. It is important to note that both populations can identify the same factors, although in a different order, and that therefore, the overall structure of the questionnaire is similar in both versions. In the Spanish version, the first factor was executive functions, the second factor was the environmental context, the third factor referred to the characteristics of the play, and the fourth factor can be understood as referring to preferences in the play and interpersonal relationships.

The differences between the original model and the Spanish version may be due to different factors. Probably the most important is that the sample used in our study included children not only with neurotypical development but also with NDD according to the prevalence in the Spanish population [34]. This allows us to differentiate between children with neurotypical development and NDD through the MCP, as indicated by the results of the ROC curve.

This explains the fact that the first factor, referring to executive functions, refers fundamentally to cognitive flexibility and self-regulation of attention, which can be a weak point in children with ASD and SLD. In addition, these functions keep changing between 3 and 9 years [35,36], so it is relevant that it emerges as an important factor in the child's play. Executive functions develop during childhood and are complex mental activities that allow the child to plan, make decisions, show a flexible behavior, to change from one task to another, or have inhibitory control during play. In addition, the play contributes to the self-controlled development of executive functions, obtaining greater benefits when it is slightly structured [37]. Furthermore, the development of executive functions has been related to parenting patterns. In this way, it is possible that these differences are showing different customs and traditions than in the way in which parents understand the play, the type of context in which it is played, the rules, and demands of the context. These aspects are coherent if one takes into account that the play, as a human occupation, has a social and anthropological component and not merely a cognitive one [38].

Another possible explanation for the differences found is that, in the original research, only mothers were included, compared to the inclusion of both parents in our study. The relationship of mothers and fathers with their children is different, and many authors have agreed that today, there is still a greater involvement and presence of women in parenting, that leads to a greater appearance of positive interactions compared to fathers [39]. Furthermore, the sociocultural context has a fundamental role in explaining the play [40].

The Spanish version consisted of 40 items. Removed items from the updated version of the MCP were the following: 27 (My child persists at play only with toys/games that he likes and finds interesting), 15 (My child is able to cope with frustrating situations that arise during play), and 35 (My child prefers to play for long periods with toys and materials that enable him to touch different textures). The first and second items can be related to both executive functions and self-regulation of attention and can be related to items 7, 22, and even item 10. On the other hand, the elimination of item 35 may be due to this type of play in Spanish culture being considered suitable between 18 and 36 months [41,42].

4.3. Interpretability

This study provides preliminary evidence of the discriminant validity of the MCP among children with neurotypical development and NDD, as shown by the scores for factors 1, 3, and 4. In addition, the total MCP score allows for the consistent differentiation of children with disorders of NDD with neurotypical development, with the established cut-off point of 142.

4.4. Implications in the Practice

This study is especially relevant since it is the first one to provide a version in Spanish for the assessment of the play. It provides a simple and quick tool for the evaluation of the play by health professionals and educators, allowing the detection not only whether there are differences between the play of children with NDD or neurotypical development, but it also allows us to know the dimensions in which there are differences, such as executive functions, play preferences, and interpersonal interactions, environmental context, and/or play characteristics. The MCP has a series of advantages for the assessment of play in childhood, allowing guiding treatment on the underlying factors that affect successful participation in the play.

In addition, it is a short, simple, and easy questionnaire for parents to fill out that allows for relatively easy screening. This questionnaire can facilitate professionals working in the field of childhood, to establish intervention programs and treatment plans in children between 3 and 9 years, and with NDD, especially in those with ASD, SLD, and DD.

4.5. Limitations and Future Research

The present study has some limitations. First, we took a non-random sample. Therefore, the study should be replicated in a representative random sample of parents of neurotypical children. Second, it would be advisable to expand the sample size further and be able to establish levels according to different age groups. As a future line of research, it would be of interest to compare different clinical populations with other NDD, such as attention deficit hyperactivity disorders or motor coordination disorders and to establish different profiles in the play, which allow orienting the targeted intervention for these specific groups. Likewise, it would be of interest to be able to develop instruments for younger children and babies not only based on parental perceptions but also on the child's performance in the play.

5. Conclusions

The MCP provides a unique understanding of the processes underlying the play; especially, it allows knowing how some executive functions influence during it, such as cognitive flexibility and attentional control. The MCP allows us to assess the play from a broad perspective. In this sense, it helps us knowing which elements of the child's participation are appropriate to the context as well as whether the conditions of possibility allow the child to participate positively in the play. It also gives the opportunity of knowing the characteristics of the child's play, their preferences, and social interaction during it.

The results of cross-cultural validation and psychometric analysis confirm its internal consistency, as well as the construct validity and discriminant validity in the Spanish population and with children with ASD, SLD, and delayed development.

Author Contributions: Conceptualization, D.R.-A. and M.A.M.; methodology, D.R.-A., M.A.M. and M.R.-S.; validation, M.R.-S. and S.B.-F.; formal analysis, D.R.-A. investigation,; writing—original draft preparation, D.R.-A., S.B.-F., M.R.-S., D.M., J.R. and M.A.M.; writing—review and editing, D.R.-A., S.B.-F., M.R.-S., D.M., J.R., J.M.T.-J. and M.A.M. All authors have read and agreed to the published version of the manuscript.

Funding: This research received no external funding.

Institutional Review Board Statement: The study was conducted according to the guidelines of the Declaration of Helsinki, and approved by the Ethics and Research Committee of the University of Granada (code 1426/CEIH/2020; date of approval: 04/24/2020).

Informed Consent Statement: Informed consent was obtained from all subjects involved in the study.

Data Availability Statement: The data presented in this study are available on request from the corresponding author. The data are not publicly available due to privacy reasons.

Acknowledgments: The authors would like to acknowledge the support received from the original MCP authors, Eleanor Schneider and Sara Rosenblum, in developing this study.

Conflicts of Interest: The authors declare no conflict of interest.

Appendix A. Spanish Version of My Child's Play (MCP) of © Schneider & Rosenblum 2014

El niño juego con los juguetes según el uso previsto.
El niño varía el tipo de juego con los juguetes.
El niño pierde el interés por los juguetes.
El niño utiliza ambas manos para jugar.
El niño tiene dificultad para concentrarse con ruido de fondo.
El niño se choca contra los objetos o los deja caer durante el juego.
El niño persiste en el juego incluso cuando tiene dificultades.
El niño intenta resolver los problemas por sí mismo durante el juego.
El niño no puede organizarse para jugar sin la ayuda de un adulto.
El niño necesita ayuda de un adulto para concentrarse en el juego.
El niño se adapta fácilmente a los cambios en las condiciones de juego.
El niño se adapta fácilmente a la intervención en el juego de nuevos adultos o niños.
El niño se relaciona con otros niños durante el juego.
El niño juega con los demás niños de acuerdo con las normas del juego.
El niño puede iniciar el juego.
El niño asume el papel de líder del grupo durante el juego.
El niño está dispuesto a compartir juguetes con otros.
El niño adapta su comportamiento durante el juego al contexto.
El niño controla sus impulsos durante el juego con los demás.
El niño necesita ayuda de un adulto para unirse al juego de un grupo de niños.
El niño prefiere jugar solo con juguetes familiares.
El niño encuentra la oportunidad para jugar en cualquier lugar.
El niño evita el juego que requiere movimiento.
El niño disfruta del juego imaginativo.
El niño necesita muchos descansos para mantenerse atento.
El niño pierde el interés cuando juega solo.
El niño prefiere jugar con adultos en vez de niños.
El niño no juega a juegos que tienen reglas.
El niño se choca contra objetos y superficies a propósito.
Hay espacio accesible para el juego fuera de casa.

Hay espacio accesible dentro de casa para jugar.
El niño tiene dificultades cuando juega con demasiados estímulos visuales.
El niño cuenta con suficientes juguetes para disfrutar de un juego variado.
Los juguetes están organizados en casa para que sean fácilmente accesibles.
Tengo en cuenta las preferencias de juego de mi hijo
Le ofrezco ayuda después de que el niño haya intentado jugar solo.
Adapto el juego a las capacidades del niño.
Defino claramente las reglas para que el niño pueda divertirse.
Mi rutina diaria incluye tiempo para jugar con el niño.
Estoy satisfecho en la forma que mi hijo juega.

References

1. Warash, B.G.; Root, A.E.; Devito Doris, M. Parents' perceptions of play: A comparative study of spousal perspectives. *Early Child. Dev. Care* **2017**, *187*, 1–9. [CrossRef]
2. Nijhof, S.L.; Vinkers, C.H.; van Geelen, S.M.; Duijff, S.N.; Achterberg, E.J.M.; van der Net, J.; Veltkamp, R.C.; Grootenhuis, M.A.; van de Putte, E.M.; Hillegers, M.H.J.; et al. Healthy play, better coping: The importance of play for the development of children in health and disease. *Neurosci. Biobehav. Rev.* **2018**, *95*, 421–429. [CrossRef] [PubMed]
3. Yogman, M.; Garner, A.; Hutchinson, J.; Hirsh-Pasek, K.; Golinkoff, R.M.; Baum, R.; Gambon, T.; Lavin, A.; Mattson, G.; Wissow, L. The power of play: A pediatric role in enhancing development in young children. *Pediatrics* **2018**, *142*, e20182058. [CrossRef] [PubMed]
4. Nestor, O.; Moser, C.S. The importance of play. *J. Occup. Ther. Sch. Early Interv.* **2018**, *11*, 247–262. [CrossRef]
5. Wolfberg, P.; Bottema-beutel, K.; Dewitt, M. Including Children with Autism in Social and Imaginary Play with Typical Peers: Integrated Play Groups Model. *Am. J. Play* **2012**, *5*, 55–80.
6. Schaaf, R.C.; Toth-Cohen. S.; Johnson, S.L.; Outten, G.; Benevides, T.W. The everyday routines of families of children with autism: Examining the impact of sensory processing difficulties on the family. *Autism* **2011**, *15*, 373–389. [CrossRef]
7. Ten Eycke, K.D.; Müller, U. Brief Report: New Evidence for a Social-Specific Imagination Deficit in Children with Autism Spectrum Disorder. *J. Autism Dev. Disord.* **2014**, *45*, 213–220. [CrossRef]
8. Frey, J.R.; Kaiser, A.P. The Use of Play Expansions to Increase the Diversity and Complexity of Object Play in Young Children with Disabilities. *Top. Early Child. Spec. Educ.* **2011**, *31*, 99–111. [CrossRef]
9. Barton, E.E. Teaching Generalized Pretend Play and Related Behaviors to Young Children with Disabilities. *Except. Child.* **2015**, *81*, 489–506. [CrossRef]
10. Movahedazarhouligh, S. Teaching Play Skills to Children with Disabilities: Research-Based Interventions and Practices. *Early Child. Educ. J.* **2018**, *46*, 587–599. [CrossRef]
11. Kasari, C.; Chang, Y.; Patterson, S. Pretending to play or playing to pretend: The case of autism. *Am. J. Play* **2013**, *6*, 124–135. [PubMed]
12. Case-Smith, J.; Kuhaneck, H.M. Play Preferences of Typically Developing Children and Children with Developmental Delays between Ages 3 and 7 Years. *Otjr Occup. Particip. Health* **2008**, *28*, 19–29. [CrossRef]
13. Hancock, C.L. We don't play that way, we play this way: Functional Play Behaviours of Children with Autism and Severe Learning Difficulties. *Res. Dev. Disabil.* **2020**, *103*, 103688. [CrossRef]
14. Esmaili, S.K.; Mehraban, A.H.; Shafaroodi, N.; Yazdani, F.; Masoumi, T.; Zarei, M. Participation in Peer-Play Activities among Children With Specific Learning Disability: A Randomized Controlled Trial. *Am. J. Occup.* **2019**, *73*, 73022051101. [CrossRef] [PubMed]
15. Skard, G.; Bundy, A.C. Test of playfulness. In *Play in Occupational Therapy for Children*; Mosby Elsevier: Sl. Louise, MO, USA, 2008; pp. 71–93. ISBN 978-0-323-02954-4.
16. Jankovich, M.; Mullen, J.; Rinear, E.; Tanta, K.; Deitz, J. Revised knox preschool play scale: Interrater agreement and construct validity. *Am. J. Occup. Ther.* **2008**, *62*, 221–227. [CrossRef]
17. McDonald, A.E.; Vigen, C. Reliability and validity of the Mcdonald play inventory. *Am. J. Occup. Ther.* **2012**, *66*, e52–e60. [CrossRef]
18. Lautamo, T.; Laakso, M.L.; Aro, T.; Ahonen, T.; Törmäkangas, K. Validity of the Play Assessment for Group Settings: An evaluation of differential item functioning between children with specific language impairment and typically developing peers. *Aust. Occup. Ther. J.* **2011**, *58*, 222–230. [CrossRef]
19. Swindells, D.; Stagnitti, K. Pretend play and parents' view of social competence: The construct validity of the Child-Initiated Pretend Play Assessment. *Aust. Occup. Ther. J.* **2006**, *53*, 314–324. [CrossRef]
20. Stagnitti, K. *The Child-Initiated Pretend Play Assessment 2 (ChIPPA 2): Manual*; Learn to Play: Melbourne, Australia, 2019; ISBN 978-0-9944647-8-1.
21. Menashe-Grinberg, A.; Atzaba-Poria, N. Mother-child and father-child play interaction: The importance of parental playfulness as a moderator of the links between parental behavior and child negativity: Parental playfulness and child negativity. *Infant Ment. Health J.* **2017**, *38*, 772–784. [CrossRef]

22. Fisher, K.R.; Hirsh-Pasek, K.; Golinkoff, R.M.; Gryfe, S.G. Conceptual split? Parents' and experts' perceptions of play in the 21st century. *J. Appl. Dev. Psychol.* **2008**, *29*, 305–316. [CrossRef]
23. Veitch, J.; Bagley, S.; Ball, K.; Salmon, J. Where do children usually play? A qualitative study of parents' perceptions of influences on children's active free-play. *Health Place* **2006**, *12*, 383–393. [CrossRef] [PubMed]
24. Bentenuto, A.; De Falco, S.; Venuti, P. Mother-Child Play: A Comparison of Autism Spectrum Disorder, Down Syndrome, and Typical Development. *Front. Psychol.* **2016**, *7*, 7. [CrossRef] [PubMed]
25. Schneider, E.; Rosenblum, S. Development, reliability, and validity of the my child's play (MCP) questionnaire. *Am. J. Occup. Ther.* **2014**, *68*, 277–285. [CrossRef] [PubMed]
26. Argimon, J.; Jiménez, J. *Métodos de Investigación Clínica y Epidemiológica*; Elsevier: Amsterdam, The Netherlands, 2013; ISBN 9788480869416.
27. Lorenzo-Seva, U.; Ferrando, P.J. FACTOR: A computer program to fit the exploratory factor analysis model. *Behav. Res. Methods* **2006**, *38*, 88–91. [CrossRef] [PubMed]
28. Muthén, B.; Kaplan, D. A comparison of some methodologies for the factor analysis of non-normal Likert variables. *Br. J. Math. Stat. Psychol.* **1985**, *38*, 171–189. [CrossRef]
29. Muthen, B.; Kaplan, D. A comparison of some methodologies for the factor analysis of non-normal Likert variables: A note on the size of the model. *Br. J. Math. Stat. Psychol.* **1992**, *45*, 19–30. [CrossRef]
30. Tavakol, M.; Dennick, R. Making sense of Cronbach's alpha. *Int. J. Med. Educ.* **2011**, *2*, 53–55. [CrossRef]
31. Stagnitti, K.; Unsworth, C. The importance of pretend play in child development: An occupational therapy perspective. *Br. J. Occup. Ther.* **2000**, *63*, 121–127. [CrossRef]
32. Miller, E.; Kuhaneck, H. Children's perceptions of play experiences and play preferences: A qualitative study. *Am. J. Occup. Ther.* **2008**, *62*, 407–415. [CrossRef]
33. Romli, M.H.; Wan Yunus, F. A Systematic Review on Clinimetric Properties of Play Instruments for Occupational Therapy Practice. *Occup. Ther. Int.* **2020**, *2020*. [CrossRef]
34. Carballal Mariño, M.; Gago Ageitos, A.; Ares Alvarez, J.; del Rio Garma, M.; García Cendón, C.; Goicoechea Castaño, A.; Pena Nieto, J. Prevalence of neurodevelopmental, behavioural and learning disorders in Pediatric Primary Care. *An. Pediatr.* **2018**, *89*, 153–161. [CrossRef] [PubMed]
35. Diamond, A. The Early Development of Executive Functions. In *Lifespan Cognition: Mechanisms of Change*; Oxford University Press: Oxford, UK, 2012; ISBN 9780199847204.
36. Diamond, A. Executive functions. In *Handbook of Clinical Neurology*; Elsevier: Amsterdam, The Netherlands, 2020.
37. Van Den Bergh, S.F.W.M.; Scheeren, A.M.; Begeer, S.; Koot, H.M.; Geurts, H.M. Age related differences of executive functioning problems in everyday life of children and adolescents in the autism spectrum. *J. Autism Dev. Disord.* **2014**, *44*, 1959–1971. [CrossRef] [PubMed]
38. Taylor, R.R.; Kielhofner, G. *Kielhofner's Model of Human Occupation: Theory and Application*; Wolters Kluwer: Alphen Aan Den Rijn, The Netherlands, 2017; ISBN 9781496385925.
39. Attili, G.; Vermigli, P.; Roazzi, A. Children's social competence, peer status, and the quality of mother-child and father-child relationships: A multidimensional scaling approach. *Eur. Psychol.* **2010**, *15*, 23–33. [CrossRef]
40. Pierce, D. Untangling occupation and activity. *Am. J. Occup. Ther.* **2001**, *55*, 138–146. [CrossRef]
41. Linaza, J.L.; Bruner, J. La importancia del contexto cultural en el desarrollo del juego infantil. In *Construyendo Mentes. Ensayos en Homenaje a Juan Delval. Constructing Minds. Essays in Honor of Juan Delval*; UNED: Madrid, Spain, 2012; ISBN 8436263553.
42. Delval, J. *El Desarrollo Humano*; Siglo XXI de España Editores: Madrid, Spain, 2004.

children

MDPI

Article

A New Instrument to Assess Children's Understanding of Death: Psychometrical Properties of the EsCoMu Scale in a Sample of Spanish Children

Manuel Fernández-Alcántara [1], Macarena de los Santos-Roig [2], María Nieves Pérez-Marfil [2,*], Francisco Cruz-Quintana [2], Juan Manuel Vázquez-Sánchez [3] and Rafael Montoya-Juárez [2,4]

1 Department of Health Psychology, University of Alicante, 03690 Alicante, Spain; mfernandeza@ua.es
2 Mind, Brain and Behavior Research Center (CIMCYC), University of Granada, 18071 Granada, Spain; dlsantos@ugr.es (M.d.l.S.-R.); fcruz@ugr.es (F.C.-Q.); rmontoya@ugr.es (R.M.-J.)
3 Niño Jesús Hospital, 28009 Madrid, Spain; juanmvazquezsanchez@gmail.com
4 Faculty of Health Sciences, University of Granada, 18016 Granada, Spain
* Correspondence: nperez@ugr.es

Citation: Fernández-Alcántara, M.; de los Santos-Roig, M.; Pérez-Marfil, M.N.; Cruz-Quintana, F.; Vázquez-Sánchez, J.M.; Montoya-Juárez, R. A New Instrument to Assess Children's Understanding of Death: Psychometrical Properties of the EsCoMu Scale in a Sample of Spanish Children. *Children* **2021**, *8*, 125. https://doi.org/10.3390/children8020125

Academic Editor: Douglas L. Hill
Received: 15 December 2020
Accepted: 6 February 2021
Published: 9 February 2021

Publisher's Note: MDPI stays neutral with regard to jurisdictional claims in published maps and institutional affiliations.

Abstract: The acquisition of the death concept in children may influence how these children cope with the losses that they will confront throughout their lives. At the present time, there is a lack of psychometric instruments in Spanish-speaking countries in order to evaluate the components of the death concept in children. The aim of this study was to create and validate a scale (EsCoMu-Escala sobre el Concepto de Muerte) in order to provide insight about the concept of death in children. The sample was formed by 358 children from ages 6 to 13 years. The final EsCoMu version has 27 items which serve to evaluate universality, irreversibility, non-functionality and causality. The results of the confirmatory factor analysis show an adequate fit index for the four dimensions model, reliability (α = 83) and validity evidence, specifically based on the children's age. In conclusion, EsCoMu is an instrument that shows adequate reliability and validity indices in order to assess the concept of death and its four components among children. Due to its simplicity, this instrument can be very useful if applied to the field of neurodevelopmental disorders.

Keywords: death concept; school; causality; irreversibility; universality; non-functionality; children; scale development; neurodevelopment; grief

1. Introduction

In Western societies, death is often considered a taboo subject. In the case of children, in addition to the social reticence to talk about death, the way that the concepts of death and dying are learned is extremely important [1] and may influence how they cope with grief and loss. Previous research seems to indicate that children grief manifestations are directly associated to the knowledge they have about death [2]. Also, the possibility to talk about death and understand its meaning may help children to overcome the mistaken ideas or the appearance of unnecessary fears that can have an impact on children's emotional life even in adulthood, interfering in the normal elaboration of bereavement processes that they will have to deal with in the future [3]. Recent reviews also consider the concept of death as a core aspect when communicating bad news to children and adolescents [4]. The concept of death is very complex, as it is influenced by variables such as social beliefs, cultural norms, emotions, biological development, cognitions or previous experiences with death [5,6].

Several studies highlight four core components related to the concept of death: universality, irreversibility, non-functionality and causality [7]. Universality implies that death is conceptualized as a natural phenomenon that applies to all living beings. Irreversibility is linked to the understanding that the dead cannot come back to life. Non-functionality includes the acknowledgement that, once a person has died, their bodily functions cease, as well as their internal and external actions. Lastly, causality implies the understanding of the possible internal or external factors which can cause the end of life. Other authors have proposed other dimensions, such as inevitability, personal mortality or unpredictability [8], but most of them agree on the model proposed by Speece and Brent [7].

There are multiple factors that can influence the understanding of the death concept, even if the scientific evidence of previous investigations is contradictory. Age is one of the most consistent variables, as the death concept is more defined the older the child is. However, each component (universality, irreversibility, non-functionality and causality) seems to follow different patterns [9–12]. The child's previous experience with death or illness has also been positively linked to the understanding of the components of the death concept [9]. However, other studies did not find any differences [3,10,13]. The cognitive ability of the children has also been considered an important aspect, especially in the background of the cognitive development model by Jean Piaget. During the preoperational stage, there is a predominance of magical thinking and egocentricity, so it is harder for the child to understand the different aspects of the concept of death. However, De la Herrán et al. [14,15] noted that, as early as 3 years old, children are able to distinguish between life and absence of it. Moreover, between 3 and 5 years old, children start to be curious about the signs of devitalization and the causes of death [16,17]. In subsequent stages, such as in the concrete-operational (7–11 years), the child begin to understand the logical operations and reversibility of thought [18], so they can develop a more mature understanding of death by including components such as irreversibility, non-functionality and causality [19]. Different studies have also indicated the existence of two complementary approaches to death in children that include the biological aspect and the meta-psychological, afterlife or religious conception of death [20]. Both conceptions of death seem to be influenced by culture [21,22].

Keeping in mind the construct complexity, it is necessary to have valid and reliable assessment instruments in order to evaluate the concept of death in children. Previous investigations have used open qualitative interviews, as well as other art-related approaches, such as drawings, storytelling or play in order to investigate the understanding of the death concept [3,9,23]. However, there is a lack of quantitative instruments showing adequate reliability and validity indices in order to assess the concept of death, as, to our knowledge, a Spanish adapted quantitative scale that meets such conditions has yet to be created.

One of the classic resources is the Death Concept Questionnaire [24], which is formed by two groups of 13 questions about death in people and animals. The factor analysis displayed four main factors: irreversibility, non-functionality, causality and inevitability of death and old age [9]. The rating of each item depends on the correctness of the reply (ranging from 0 to 3) and the sophistication of the child's explanation, finding an overall Cronbach's alpha of 0.77 [24]. The main limitations of the Death Concept Questionnaire are that each factor is composed of a small number of items and that the responses of the child need to be categorized.

In Spanish, we can find two qualitative instruments. First, we can find the interview developed by Viñas et al. [25,26], named "Entrevista Estructurada del Concepto de Muerte—ECM" ("Structured Interview on Death Concept"), which evaluates the universality, irreversibility and non-functionality through 11 closed questions with dichotomous answers. Another series of 17 questions are included in order to assess beliefs related to afterlife and the child's personal experience with death, as well as three open questions where the child is asked to specify three causes of death (animal, person and own) and a final question about the definition of suicide [26]. In Mexico, Gutiérrez et al. [27] have recently developed a qualitative interview in Spanish, where 14 items assessing universality, finality, non-functionality and causality where used. The main limitation of both instruments is that they don't report evidence involving instrument validity, reliability or factorial structure.

In accordance with the above, it is essential to develop a new instrument in the Spanish language which allows us to assess the components of the death concept in children while having proper psychometric features. The main benefit of having an instrument of this kind is that it can be easily completed and quickly distributed among a large number of participants, without having to invest too much time codifying or correcting the results (as in interviews or other qualitative approaches). Also, the scores from the scale can be easily compared between studies and populations. Finally, we need to establish a reliable measure of the death concept among primary school children which will serve as a starting point to assess other populations of children, such as those with intellectual disabilities or other neurodevelopmental disorders.

Due to this, the main aim of this study is to develop and present the psychometric properties (factorial structure, reliability and validity) of a scale which is able to assess the acquisition of the components of the concept of death in primary school children (6–13 years). The factorial structure of the scale will be tested through confirmatory factor analysis, and reliability will be calculated through internal consistency analysis. The main validity evidence was assessed through the comparison of the scale between different age groups. We hypothesized that younger children will have lower scores in the four dimension of the death concept, in comparison with older children. In addition, we wanted to explore the differences in the following variables: sex, existence of a previous loss and school setting.

2. Materials and Methods

The study was formed by 358 primary school students (6–13 years) coming from five schools of the Spanish provinces of Granada, Jaén and Cádiz (see Table 1).

Table 1. Schools in which the sample is taken.

Town	Province	Setting	Management	Religious	Participants
La Zubia	Granada	Semi-urban	Public	No	105
Granada	Granada	Urban	Semi-private	Yes	83
Arjonilla	Jaén	Rural	Public	No	81
Chiclana	Cádiz	Urban	Public	No	44
Chiclana	Cádiz	Urban	Public	No	45

The mean age of children was 9.92 years (SD = 1.57). Different schools of the provinces mentioned before were contacted to select the participant sample. The inclusion criteria were: school's willingness to participate, informed consent signed by children's parents or legal guardians, and children who were between 6 and 13 years old. Data were collected about each student's sex, age and their school setting. Given the foreseeable differences between children of different ages, they were grouped into four levels (see Table 2).

Table 2. Sociodemographic data sample divided by age group.

		Groups			
		6–7 Years	**8–9 Years**	**10–11 Years**	**12–13 Years**
	n (%)	**34 (9.5%)**	**96 (26.9%)**	**189 (52.9%)**	**38 (10.6%)**
Sex	Female	17 (50%)	56 (58.3%)	95 (50.5%)	16 (43.2%)
	Male	17 (50%)	40 (41.7%)	93 (49.5%)	21 (56.8%)
School Setting	Rural	18 (52.9%)	19 (33.9%)	24 (12.8%)	11 (29.7%)
	Semi-urban	0	22 (26.8%)	74 (39.4%)	0
	Urban	16 (47.1%)	15 (40.5%)	90 (47.9%)	26 (70.3%)
Recent Loss	Yes	21 (61.8%)	63 (65.6%)	118 (62.45%)	22 (57.9%)
	No	13 (38.2%)	33 (34.4%)	71 (37.6%)	16 (42.18%)

2.1. Instruments

Ad-hoc demographic data questionnaire:

Age, sex and school setting (rural/urban/semi-urban) were considered. When the school setting was not fully rural or urban (e.g., towns located in a range of less than 10 km from the province capital), it was coded as semi-urban. A question asking whether they have suffered a recent loss (yes/no) was also added.

Scale to assess the concept of death—EsCoMu (Escala sobre el Concepto de Muerte):

This dichotomous scale was developed by four of the authors of this study who are professionals and researchers specialized on the field of bereavement and end of life processes. The dichotomous rating (yes/no) was based on previous instruments and interviews used in the field [25,28]. The items were evaluated by a panel of experts, who established items relevancy, adequacy and belonging to each of the four dimensions or theoretical components: irreversibility, universality, non-functionality and causality [29]. Each item was rated on a likert scale ranging from 0 to 100 assessing its relevancy (if the item was significantly relevant for the dimension assessed) and adequacy (if the item was appropriate for the proposed dimension of the concept of death). Experts could also include qualitative commentaries about the items. The initial version of the scale consisted on 38 items, of which 10 were eliminated as they showed mean values less of than 70 in any of the dimensions assessed (relevancy and/or adequacy), as well as those that experts identified as difficult to understand for children (in the qualitative part of the survey). An additional item was removed because of their lower factor loadings in the exploratory analysis.

The definitive EsCoMu version is formed by a group of 27 dichotomous items (yes/no answer), grouped into four dimensions: 6 for universality, 7 for irreversibility, 7 for non-functionality and 7 for causality (see Supplementary Material for the Spanish version of the scale). Each item has a score of 1 (if the answer is correct) or 0 (if the answer is incorrect), with some items being reversed. The total score is calculated by adding all items from each component. The scale global Cronbach's alpha of this investigation was $\alpha = 0.83$.

2.2. Procedure

Two informative meetings were held in order to inform the management of each school participating in the study. After obtaining the school's permission, with the help of Parent Associations (AMPA—Asociación de Madres y Padres de Alumnos), an informative meeting with parents was held in order to explain the aim of the study. Secondly, each student was given an informative sheet and an informed consent in order to be signed by their parents. Subsequently, this consent was returned to the school teacher along with each parent's or legal guardian's signature. The students whose parents did not fill in the informed consent performed a different activity unrelated to the study.

The assessment was performed in groups, in the students' regular classroom. In one session, they filled in all the sociodemographic data as well as the scale EsCoMu. The evaluation lasted around 20 min, and all students received similar guidelines. The evaluation was performed by a team of experts experienced in end-of-life processes.

At the beginning of the evaluation, all students were given the option of not participating in the activity if they did not want to, regardless of the parent's consent. Each participant's emotional state was evaluated during and after the assessment in order to provide them with emotional support if needed, but none of the participants had reported issues in this regard.

2.3. Ethical Considerations

Prior to the data collection and the inclusion of participants in the study, both school management and parents were informed about the aim, purpose and confidentiality of the study. In every case, the evaluation was performed after obtaining both the school authorization and after collecting parent-signed informed consent for their children's participation. The present study was approved by the University of Granada's Ethics Committee on Human Research (Ref. 1056/CEIH/2020).

2.4. Data Analysis

To perform the descriptive analysis, the frequency of each answer was calculated for every item. To verify the factor structure, a confirmatory factor analysis (CFA) was performed. Given the dichotomous condition of data, the WLSMV (Variance-Adjusted Weighted Least Squares) estimation method was used. The following indices were used in order to calculate items' fit with the proposed model: RMSEA (Root Mean Square Error of Approximation), TLI (Tucker–Lewis Index), CFI (Comparative Fit Index) and WRMR (Weighted Root Mean Square Residual).

To gather validity evidence about possible relations between EsCoMu's ratings and other external variables, multivariate analysis of variance (MANOVA) was applied, with variables including age, sex, having suffered a loss (yes/no) and school setting (urban, semi-urban and rural) for each subcomponent of the scale. For post-hoc contrasts, Bonferroni correction and partial eta-squared effect size were used. Statistical software SPSS 22 (IBM, 2013) was used. For gathering structural validity evidence, MPLUS 6.11 [30] was used.

3. Results

3.1. Descriptive Analysis of EsCoMu's Response

In Table 3, the percentage of correct answers for each age group is shown in each EsCoMu scale item, based on their dimension.

Table 3. Descriptive analysis of the EsCoMu scale items for each age group.

		Correct Answer (%)			
Item	**Content**	**6–7 Years (n = 34)**	**8–9 Years (n = 96)**	**10–11 Years (n = 198)**	**12–13 Years (n = 38)**
U1	Do you think that your grandparents will die someday?	85.3	92.7	96.8	81.6
U2 *	Can a mum live forever?	88.2	93.7	98.4	81.0
U3	Can you die?	81.3	93.7	94.7	86.8
U4 *	Are there living beings that do not die?	69.7	88.5	90.4	84.2
U5	Do all people die?	79.4	89.6	98.4	92.1
U6	Do you think that a very good person can die?	64.7	86.2	95.8	86.5
IR1 *	If we die, can someone wake us up?	76.5	84.2	96.8	86.8
IR2 *	Can a dead animal come back to life?	72.7	94.6	96.3	86.8
IR3 *	If someone close to you died, could they come back to life?	78.8	88.4	93.0	83.8
IR4 *	If a child died, could they live again?	73.5	91.5	92.6	78.9
IR5 *	Can a dead person come back to life if you really want it?	85.3	90.4	96.3	91.9
IR6 *	Can a dead person come back to life?	82.4	96.2	87.7	92.1
IR7 *	After dying, do you think that it is possible to come back to life?	85.3	87.1	86.1	78.9
NF1 *	When someone dies, can they feel cold?	81.8	74.0	72.6	65.8
NF2 *	Do animals feel hunger or thirst when they are dead?	82.4	90.5	96.3	92.1
NF3 *	Can a dead person move?	70.6	89.6	93.1	97.4
NF4 *	Does a dead person keep breathing?	87.9	93.7	98.4	94.7
NF5	When someone dies, does their body stop working?	70.6	89.2	91.0	92.1
NF6 *	When an animal dies, do they still want to play?	75.8	91.6	96.8	81.6
NF7 *	Can a dead person hear or feel?	76.5	81.9	87.2	91.9
C1	Can a person kill themselves?	79.4	93.6	98.9	86.8
C2	Can people die of hunger or thirst?	67.6	85.1	87.8	86.5

Table 3. *Cont.*

Item	Content	Correct Answer (%)			
		6–7 Years (n = 34)	8–9 Years (n = 96)	10–11 Years (n = 198)	12–13 Years (n = 38)
C3	Can a person die from falling off a high place?	91.2	94.8	97.4	97.2
C4 *	Can someone be killed by the force of imagination?	68.8	86.3	84.5	83.8
C5	Can a person die from being very old?	81.8	86.5	97.3	91.9
C6	Can people die after suffering an illness for a long time?	93.9	98.9	98.9	97.3
C7	Can a person die if they have a serious accident?	97.1	97.9	96.8	94.7

* Reverse items, U = Universality, IR = Irreversibility, NF = Non-Functionality, C = Causality.

3.2. EsCoMu Factor Structure

Two one-order models (One-Factor and Four-Factor) were tested. However, fit indices for the one-factor model (see Table 4) were not adequate. As correlation values were not appropriate for causality-universality dimensions on the Four-Factor model (with a coefficient bigger than 1), a second-order model was tested (Second order with Four Factor model). CFA results showed adequate fit indices in this model (see Table 4 and Figure 1). The dimensions showed medium-high values of intercorrelation (see Table 5).

Table 4. Fit indices for EsCoMu factor models.

Model	X^2	*df*	CFI/TLI	RMSEA	WRMR
One factor	449.86 **	324	0.885/0.876	0.033 [C.I. $_{95\%}$ = 0.025–0.040]	1.071
Four factors	398.08 **	318	0.927/0.919	0.027 [C.I. $_{95\%}$ = 0.017–0.035]	0.951
Second-order four factors	406.37 **	320	0.921/.914	0.028 [C.I. $_{95\%}$ = 0.018–0.035]	0.971

Note. ** = $p < 0.001$, X^2 = Chi Square goodness of fit statistic, *df* = degrees of freedom, CFI = Comparative Fit Index, TLI = Tucker–Lewis Index, RMSEA = Root Mean Square Error of Approximation, WRMR = Weighted Root Mean Square.

3.3. Evidence of Validity

As observed in Table 6, the MANOVA results indicate a significative medium-low effect size with age in all EsCoMu dimensions as well as in the total score. Post-hoc analysis (Bonferroni) indicate lower scores in Universality, Irreversibility, and Non-functionality in the 6–7 years age group if compared with the 8–9 years age group ($p < 0.01$) and with the 10–11 years age group ($p < 0.01$). There were no statistically significant differences among the youngest and oldest age groups. However, both in the Causality dimension and in the total score, the youngest children showed statistically significant differences (both $p < 0.01$) if compared with other groups, where such differences do not occur.

As observed in Tables 7 and 8, there were no differences between any of the instrument dimensions involving sex, nor between the participants who have suffered a recent loss and those who did not.

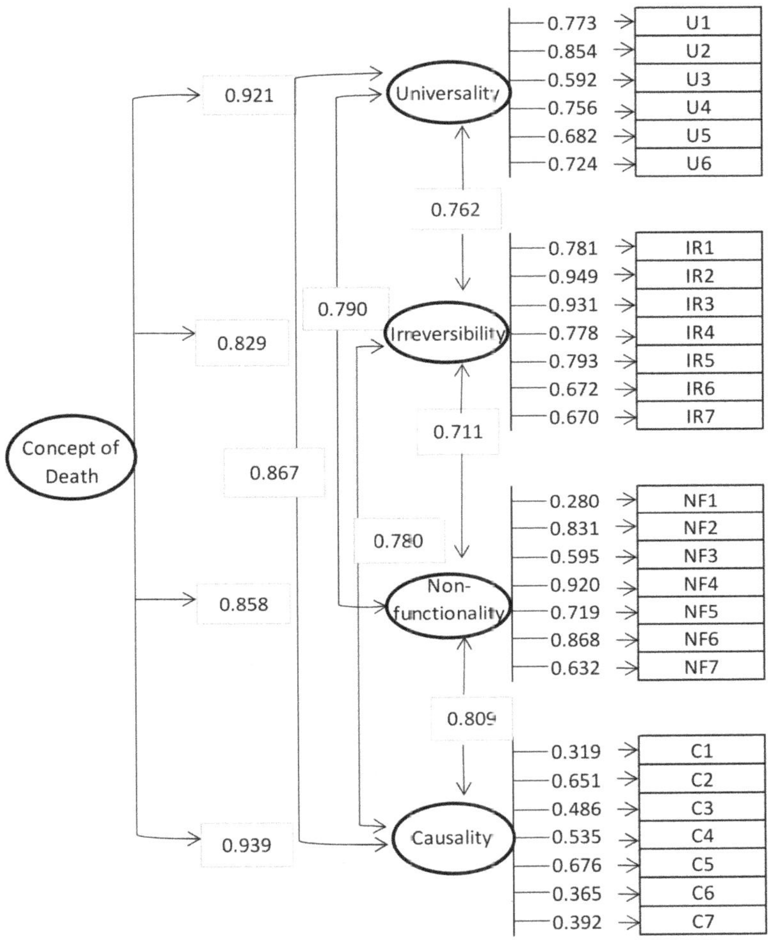

Figure 1. Second-order four factors EsCoMu model. Latent variables are represented by ellipses and measured variables are represented by rectangles. Values are standardized estimated correlations between factors.

Table 5. Intercorrelations between EsCoMu dimensions.

	Irreversibility	Non-Functionality	Causality
1. Universality	0.431 **	0.363 **	0.552 **
2. Irreversibility		0.424 **	0.376 **
3. Non-functionality			0.312 **

Note. ** = $p < 0.01$.

Table 6. MANOVA results for school setting with EsCoMu dimensions and total scores.

EsCoMu Dimension	Age (n)	Mean (SD)	F (df)	Power	η^2
1	6–7 (24) 8–9 (75) 10–11 (177) 12–13 (31)	4.79 (1.35) 5.65 (0.84) 5.74 (0.63) 5.35 (1.35)	$F_{(3,303)} = 9.65$ **	0.99	0.08
2	6–7 (24) 8–9 (75) 10–11 (177) 12–13 (31)	5.37 (2.22) 6.44 (0.87) 6.45 (1.20) 6.12 (1.70)	$F_{(3,303)} = 5.29$ **	0.92	0.05
3	6–7 (24) 8–9 (75) 10–11 (177) 12–13 (31)	6.20 (2.08) 7.14 (1.15) 7.22 (1.24) 7.00 (1.57)	$F_{(3,303)} = 4.14$ **	0.84	0.04
4	6–7 (24) 8–9 (75) 10–11 (177) 12–13 (31)	5.62 (1.05) 6.53 (0.74) 6.61 (0.64) 6.38 (1.35)	$F_{(3,303)} = 10.82$ **	0.99	0.09
Total Score	6–7 (24) 8–9 (75) 10–11 (177) 12–13 (31)	21.25 (5.30) 24.90(2.24) 25.14 (2.40) 24.09 (5.00)	$F_{(3,303)} = 12.11$ **	1.00	0.10

Note. 1. = Universality, 2. = Irreversibility, 3. = Non-functionality, 4. = Causality, SD = Standard Deviation, df = degree of freedom, η^2 = partial eta-squared effect size, ** = $p < 0.01$.

Table 7. MANOVA results for gender with EsCoMu dimensions and total scores.

EsCoMu Dimension	Sex (n)	Mean (SD)	F (df)	Power	η^2
1	Male (150) Female (156)	5.58 (0.80) 5.63 (0.97)	$F_{(1,304)} = 0.28$	—	—
2	Male (150) Female (156)	6.35 (1.36) 6.31 (1.30)	$F_{(1,304)} = 0.06$	—	—
3	Male (150) Female (156)	7.18 (1.25) 7.03 (1.45)	$F_{(1,304)} = 0.90$	—	—
4	Male (150) Female (156)	6.54 (0.69) 6.44 (0.96)	$F_{(1,304)} = 1.02$	—	—
Total Score	Male (150) Female (156)	24.76 (2.92) 24.58 (3.44)	$F_{(1,304)} = 0.23$	—	—

Note. 1. = Universality, 2. = Irreversibility, 3. = Non-functionality, 4. = Causality, SD = Standard Deviation, df = degree of freedom, η^2 = partial eta-squared effect size

Finally, when analyzing the children's school setting, MANOVA showed lower results in rural areas (Table 9). The effects appear in the four dimensions as well as in the instrument's total score, with medium-to-low effect sizes. The post-hoc analysis results (Bonferroni) indicate differences only between rural and semi-urban settings ($p < 0.01$) in terms of Universality, Irreversibility and Non-functionality. Again, in this case, Causality and the EsCoMu total score are the dimensions with more differences between rural settings and the other two groups ($p < 0.05$).

Table 8. MANOVA results for recent loss with EsCoMu dimensions and total scores.

EsCoMu Dimension	Loss (*n*)	Mean (SD)	F (df)	Power	η^2
1	Yes (198) No (110)	5.60 (0.90) 5.61 (0.86)	$F_{(1,306)} = 0.001$	–	–
2	Yes (198) No (110)	6.33 (1.31) 6.30 (1.36)	$F_{(1,306)} = 0.034$	–	–
3	Yes (198) No (110)	7.05 (1.42) 7.15 (1.30)	$F_{(1,306)} = 0.363$	–	–
4	Yes (198) No (110)	6.548 (0.86) 6.49 (0.79)	$F_{(1,306)} = 0.001$	–	–
Total Score	Yes (198) No (110)	24.61 (3.20) 24.71 (3.23)	$F_{(1,305)} = 0.07$	–	–

Note. 1. = Universality, 2. = Irreversibility, 3. = Non-functionality, 4. = Causality, SD = Standard Deviation, df = degree of freedom, η^2 = partial eta-squared effect size

Table 9. MANOVA results for school setting with EsCoMu dimensions scores.

EsCoMu Dimension	School Setting (*n*)	Mean (SD)	F (df)	Power	η^2
1	Urban (135) Rural (77) Semi-urban (96)	5.57 (0.95) 5.38 (1.10) 5.83 (.45)	$F_{(2,305)} = 5.67$ *	0.86	0.03
2	Urban (135) Rural (77) Semi-urban (96)	6.32 (1.37) 5.89 (1.63) 6.67 (.81)	$F_{(2,305)} = 7.64$ **	0.94	0.05
3	Urban (135) Rural (77) Semi-urban (96)	7.70 (1.41) 6.75 (1.58) 7.38 (1.07)	$F_{(2,305)} = 4.60$ *	0.77	0.03
4	Urban (135) Rural (77) Semi-urban (96)	6.57 (.85) 6.16 (.95) 6.63 (.63)	$F_{(2,305)} = 8.02$ **	0.95	0.05
Total Score	Urban (135) Rural (77) Semi-urban (96)	24.70 (3.46) 23.41 (3.82) 25.57 (1.59)	$F_{(2,305)} = 10.24$ **	0.98	0.06

Note. 1. = Universality, 2. = Irreversibility, 3. = Non-functionality, 4. = Causality, SD = Standard Deviation, df = degree of freedom, η^2 = partial eta-squared effect size, * = $p < 0.05$, ** = $p < 0.01$.

4. Discussion

The aim of this study was to develop and present the psychometric properties (factor structure, reliability and validity) of a scale which was able to assess the acquisition of the components of the concept of death in primary school children (6–13 years). Results prove that the scale has an adequate reliability and factor structure, showing promising validity evidences.

The scale global alpha shows acceptable values, in the same direction as the value reported to this date by the Death Concept Questionnaire ($\alpha = 0.77$ in the original study and $\alpha = 0.81$ in the study by Bonoti et al. [9]). Test–retest measures could not be included, so future research should investigate whether the EsCoMu scale maintains its reliability over time, as well as whether it is sensitive to death education-based interventions [2,14].

The four scale factors showed positive and moderate correlations between each other. Furthermore, the CFA model showed that the four components of the concept are closely related to each other, suggesting that they are part of an underlying construct, in this case the concept of death. This is supported by the results of the second-order CFA, where the concept of death is explained by the four factors, which are also explained by their respective items. Following this rationale, previous research has highlighted the relevance of these four components to explain the concept of death [6,10].

Age is one of the factors that seems to systematically influence the acquisition of the concept of death. In the present study, age-dependent differences were found in the four evaluated dimensions, in line with previous investigations [10,31]. In the dimensions of universality, irreversibility and non-functionality, differences were identified between younger and older children, whereas, in causality, statistically significant differences were found between 6–7-year-old children and the rest of the age groups. This seems to indicate that not all dimensions are acquired by following the same pattern. However, we do observe that, from the age of 8–9 years, all four subcomponents are well acquired in children [7,9]. In their sample, Gutiérrez et al. [27] found that not all the components of the death concept differed according to age, finding no significant differences in universality and causality based of this variable, but rather between finality and non-functionality. However, results for these variables were very close to significance ($p < 0.08$ in both cases).

Regarding the school setting, lower scores have been found in rural schools as compared to these semi-urban and urban schools. Previous studies have shown different results, pointing to greater acquisition in children living in rural environments. Panagiotaki et al. [31] found significant differences in the irreversibility component when comparing three children groups (British living in London, British Muslims living in London, and Muslims living in rural areas of Pakistan), being higher in the latter group. However, in this study, since the groups were not equivalent due to a series of key cultural variables, no conclusive evidence can be drawn regarding the area of origin. Lastly, other studies did not find significative differences regarding the death concept in urban and rural settings [32].

In the present study, we also did not find significant differences in any of the components of the death concept based on the child's sex or in the event of having a recent loss. These findings are consistent with one prior study [3], but differ from another study that found differences on this variable [9]. Future studies must investigate the influence of the loss type and the appearance of specific symptoms in terms of bereavement, which sheds light on to what extent it is the experience of loss itself, or the intensity of the child's experience that will affect the acquisition of the concept of death [33].

The development of a scale that serves to evaluate the concept of death has important clinical implications. On one hand, death is not a common topic in school subjects or academic curricula. On the other hand, adults and families are often hesitant about how to respond to the questions that children raise about the concept of death and the dying process. Moreover, in spite of children's curiosity, some adults are unsure about the appropriateness of discussing death with their children [34]. Therefore, it is a common situation that children are not able to find the adequate space to clarify their doubts regarding what death means. This may prevent them from developing more adaptive coping responses, which can lead to emotional issues. Therefore, it is essential to have valid and reliable instruments which allow us to evaluate the conceptualization of death in different ages and contexts, as well as to work in education, as many teachers are currently demanding [35,36].

The EsCoMu scale, due to its fast and easy application, can be widely used in populations with neurodevelopmental disorders or problems. Previous qualitative studies have shown that, in cases involving diagnosed intellectual disabilities or neurodevelopmental conditions, the acquisition of the death concept seems to follow a different pattern. Markell and Hoover [37] highlight how even learning problems or physical and emotional issues in children can affect the bereavement process and understanding of death. Children diagnosed with intellectual disability (ID) have shown confusion and difficulty understanding the concepts of non-functionality, irreversibility (associating death with the illness) and universality [37]. Finally, recent studies in adults diagnosed with ID show that they do acquire the components of the death concept, but in a different and, in many cases, partial way [38,39], showing greater difficulty understanding concepts such as causality and universality [40]. Future studies that use the EsCoMu scale may explore the concept of death in these populations, as well as the effectiveness of interventions related to death education and supporting methods for bereavement and end-of-life processes in this population [41].

However, this research has a series of limitations: Firstly, the child age groups were not equivalent, the 10–11-year-old group being the biggest one. Moreover, it is necessary for future research to examine the usefulness of EsCoMu among populations under 6 years of age as well as to include test–retest measures to evaluate the temporal reliability of the scale. We did not perform a pilot study or cognitive interviews prior to the initial assessment, so it may be useful to perform pilot testing when applying this scale to children less than 6 years old. However, the assessed population did not have any problem understanding any of the items. No measures of anxiety or depression were taken in the children who completed the scale, so it would be necessary in the future to control such variables and check their effect and connection to the EsCoMu score. Future studies should verify if the acquisition of the components of the death concept correlates with the most common themes regarding death, such as biological, psychological or metaphysical death [3,9]. In the present study, age was considered as the main evidence of validity, but there are other variables associated with the concept of death, such as religious, cognitive or socioeconomic aspects, that should be included in future studies to have measures of convergent validity of the EsCoMu scale. Finally, the use of mixed methods design to explore the relationship between the acquisition of the components of the concept of death and the subjective experience of the child [27] will give additional information about the validity of the EsCoMu scale.

5. Conclusions

In conclusion, the EsCoMu scale is an instrument with adequate factor structure that shows adequate reliability and validity indices in order to assess the concept of death and its four components (universality, irreversibility, non-functionality and causality) among children.

Supplementary Materials: The following are available online at https://www.mdpi.com/2227-9067/8/2/125/s1, Table S1: Escala sobre el Concepto de Muerte (EsCoMu).

Author Contributions: Conceptualization, M.F.-A., M.N.P.-M., F.C.-Q. and R.M.-J.; Data curation, M.d.l.S.-R., F.C.-Q., J.M.V.-S. and R.M.-J.; Formal analysis, M.F.-A., M.d.l.S.-R. and J.M.V.-S.; Investigation, M.N.P.-M. and R.M.-J.; Methodology, M.F.-A., M.d.l.S.-R., M.N.P.-M. and R.M.-J.; Software, M.d.l.S.-R.; Supervision, M.N.P.-M. and F.C.-Q.; Writing—original draft, M.F.-A.; Writing—review and editing, M.d.l.S.-R., M.N.P.-M., F.C.-Q., J.M.V.-S. and R.M.-J. All authors have read and agreed to the published version of the manuscript.

Funding: This research received no external funding.

Institutional Review Board Statement: The study was conducted according to the guidelines of the Declaration of Helsinki, and approved by the University of Granada's Ethics Committee on Human Research (Ref. 1056/CEIH/2020).

Informed Consent Statement: Informed consent was obtained from all subjects involved in the study.

Data Availability Statement: Data will be available upon request to the corresponding author.

Acknowledgments: We thank the Alma y Vida Association in Chiclana (Spain) for their help in the data collection.

Conflicts of Interest: The authors declare no conflict of interest.

References

1. Pla, A.R.; Guàrdia, R.C. Fundamentos para una pedagogía preventiva sobre la muerte en la escuela. *Rev. Complut. Educ.* **2018**, *29*, 527–538. [CrossRef]
2. Serrano-Pastor, F.J.; Martínez-Segura, M.J. *Las Cosas Que No Me Cuentas. Propuesta de Innovación Educativa para la Pérdida y el Duelo*; Editorial Octaedro: Madrid, Spain, 2019.

3. Vázquez-Sánchez, J.M.; Fernández-Alcántara, M.; García-Caro, M.P.; Cabañero-Martínez, M.J.; Martí-García, C.; Montoya-Juárez, R. The concept of death in children aged from 9 to 11 years: Evidence through inductive and deductive analysis of drawings. *Death Stud.* **2019**, *43*, 467–477. [CrossRef] [PubMed]
4. Stein, A.; Dalton, L.; Rapa, E.; Bluebond-Langner, M.; Hanington, L.; Fredman-Stein, K.; Ziebland, S.; Rochat, T.; Harrop, E.; Kelly, B.; et al. Communication with children and adolescents about the diagnosis of their own life-threatening condition. *Lancet* **2019**, *393*, 1150–1163. [CrossRef]
5. Krepia, M.; Krepia, V.; Tsilingiri, M. School children's perception of the concept of death. *Int. J. Caring Sci.* **2017**, *10*, 1717–1722.
6. Kronaizl, S.G. Discussing death with children: A developmental approach. *Pediatr. Nurs.* **2019**, *45*, 47–50.
7. Speece, M.W.; Brent, S.B. Children's understanding of death: A review of three components of a death concept. *Child Dev.* **1984**, 1671–1686. [CrossRef]
8. Slaughter, V. Young children's understanding of death. *Aust. Psychol.* **2005**, *40*, 179–186. [CrossRef]
9. Bonoti, F.; Leondari, A.; Mastora, A. Exploring children's understanding of death: Through drawings and the death concept questionnaire. *Death Stud.* **2013**, *37*, 47–60. [CrossRef]
10. Panagiotaki, G.; Hopkins, M.; Nobes, G.; Ward, E.; Griffiths, D. Children's and adults' understanding of death: Cognitive, parental, and experiential influences. *J. Exp. Child Psychol.* **2018**, *166*, 96–115. [CrossRef] [PubMed]
11. Longbottom, S.; Slaughter, V. Sources of children's knowledge about death and dying. *Philos. Trans. R. Soc. B Biol. Sci.* **2018**, *373*, 20170267. [CrossRef]
12. Norero, V. La maduración cerebral en el niño. El caso de la adquisición del concepto de muerte y su evolución. *Rev. Chil. Pediatr.* **2018**, *89*, 137–142. [CrossRef]
13. Miller, P.J.; Rosengren, K.S.; Gutiérrez, I.T. Children's understanding of death: Toward a contextualized and integrated account: I. Introduction. *Monogr. Soc. Res. Child Dev.* **2014**, *79*, 1–18. [CrossRef] [PubMed]
14. De la Herrán, A.; Cortina, M. La muerte y su enseñanza. *Diálogo Filosófico* **2009**, *75*, 499–516.
15. De la Herrán, A.; Herrero, P.R.; de Miguel Yubero, V. Is death in the Spanish curriculum? *Rev. Educ.* **2019**, *385*, 201–226.
16. Tau, R.; Lenzi, A. Acerca del desarrollo de la noción de muerte en niños. *Anu. Investig. Fac. Psicol.* **2012**, *1*, 1–6.
17. Mahmood Ashiri, R.; Khodabakhshi-Koolaee, A. Explaining the concept of death from the perspective of children aged 4 to 8: A descriptive phenomenological study. *J. Qual. Res. Health Sci.* **2020**, *9*, 10–17.
18. Piaget, J. *The Origins of Intelligence in Children*; Intl Universities: New York, NY, USA, 1963.
19. Paul, S. Is Death Taboo for Children? Developing Death Ambivalence as a Theoretical Framework to Understand Children's Relationship with Death, Dying and Bereavement. *Child. Soc.* **2019**, *33*, 556–571. [CrossRef]
20. Harris, P.L. Children's understanding of death: From biology to religion. *Philos. Trans. R. Soc. B Biol. Sci.* **2018**, *373*, 20170266. [CrossRef]
21. Giménez, M.; Harris, P. Children's acceptance of conflicting testimony: The case of death. *J. Cogn. Cult.* **2005**, *5*, 143–164. [CrossRef]
22. Astuti, R.; Harris, P.L. Understanding mortality and the life of the ancestors in rural Madagascar. *Cogn. Sci.* **2008**, *32*, 713–740. [CrossRef]
23. Yang, S.; Park, S. A sociocultural approach to children's perceptions of death and loss. *Omega J. Death Dying* **2017**, *76*, 53–77. [CrossRef] [PubMed]
24. Smilansky, S. *On Death: Helping Children Understand and Cope*; Peter Lang Editorial: New York, NY, USA, 1987.
25. Viñas i Poch, F.; Jané i Ballabriga, M.; Domènech, E. Assessment of self-report suicidal ideation severity in 8 to 12 years old school children. *Psicothema* **2000**, *12*, 549–598.
26. Viñas i Poch, F.; Domènech, E. El concepto de muerte en un grupo de escolares con ideación suicida. *Rev. Psicol. Gen. Appl.* **1999**, *52*, 89–104.
27. Gutiérrez, I.T.; Menendez, D.; Jiang, M.J.; Hernandez, I.G.; Miller, P.; Rosengren, K.S. Embracing death: Mexican parent and child perspectives on death. *Child Dev.* **2020**, *91*, e491–e511. [CrossRef] [PubMed]
28. Speece, M.W.; Brent, S.B. The acquisition of a mature understanding of three components of the concept of death. *Death Stud.* **1992**, *16*, 211–229. [CrossRef]
29. Fernández-Alcántara, M.; Cruz-Quintana, F.; Pérez-Marfil, M.N. Mecanismos emocionales y neuropsicológicos en procesos de duelo complicado. In *Neurociencias Aplicadas. Medioambiente, Desarrollo Humano y Bienestar Comunitario*; Saforcada, E., Fariña, O., Eds.; Nuevos Tiempos: Avellaneda, Argentina, 2017; pp. 227–252.
30. Muthén, L.K.; Muthén, B.O. *Mplus User's Guide*, 6th ed.; Muthén & Muthén: Los Angeles, CA, USA, 2007.
31. Panagiotaki, G.; Nobes, G.; Ashraf, A.; Aubby, H. British and Pakistani children's understanding of death: Cultural and developmental influences. *Br. J. Dev. Psychol.* **2015**, *33*, 31–44. [CrossRef]
32. Hopkins, M. The Development of Children's Understanding of Death. Ph.D. Thesis, University of East Anglia, Norwich, UK, 2014.
33. Speece, M.W. Children's concepts of death. *Mich. Fam. Rev.* **1995**, *134*, 141–153. [CrossRef]
34. Flahault, C.; Dolbeault, S.; Sankey, C.; Fasse, L. Understanding grief in children who have lost a parent with cancer: How do they give meaning to this experience? Results of an interpretative phenomenological analysis. *Death Stud.* **2018**, *42*, 483–490. [CrossRef]

35. Siracusa, F.; Cruz-Quintana, F.; Perez-Marfil, M.N.; Garcia-Caro, M.P.; Schmidt-Riovalle, J.; Vera-Martinez, M. Actitudes y afrontamiento ante la muerte en padres de niños de primaria. *Psicol. Conduct.* **2011**, *19*, 627–642.
36. Morell-Velasco, C.; Fernández-Alcántara, M.; Hueso-Montoro, C.; Montoya-Juárez, R. Teachers' Perception of Grief in Primary and Secondary School Students in Spain: Children's Responses and Elements Which Facilitate or Hinder the Grieving Process. *J. Pediatr. Nurs.* **2020**, *51*, e100–e107. [CrossRef]
37. Markell, M.A.; Hoover, J.H. Children with developmental disabilities, death, and grief. In *Children's Encounters with Death, Bereavement, and Coping*; Corr, C.A., Balk, D.E., Eds.; Springer Pusblishing Company: New York, NY, USA, 2010; pp. 395–412.
38. McEvoy, J.; MacHale, R.; Tierney, E. Concept of death and perceptions of bereavement in adults with intellectual disabilities. *J. Intellect. Disabil. Res.* **2012**, *56*, 191–203. [CrossRef] [PubMed]
39. McEvoy, J.; Treacy, B.; Quigley, J. A matter of life and death: Knowledge about the body and concept of death in adults with intellectual disabilities. *J. Intellect. Disabil. Res.* **2017**, *61*, 89–98. [CrossRef] [PubMed]
40. Chow, A.Y.M.; McEvoy, J.; Chan, I.K.N.; Borschel, M.; Yuen, J.H.L.; Lo, J.Y.M. Do men and women with intellectual disabilities understand death? *J. Intellect. Disabil. Res.* **2017**, *61*, 1130–1139. [CrossRef] [PubMed]
41. Fernández-Ávalos, M.I.; Pérez-Marfil, M.N.; Ferrer-Cascales, R.; Cruz-Quintana, F.; Fernández-Alcántara, M. Feeling of grief and loss in parental caregivers of adults diagnosed with intellectual disability. *J. Appl. Res. Intellect. Disabil.* **2020**, 1–12. [CrossRef]

children

MDPI

Article

An Autoencoder-Based Deep Learning Classifier for Efficient Diagnosis of Autism

Harshini Sewani and Rasha Kashef *

Department of Electrical, Computer, and Biomedical Engineering, Ryerson University, Toronto, ON M5B 2K3, Canada; harshini.sewani@ryerson.ca
* Correspondence: rkashef@ryerson.ca

Received: 25 September 2020; Accepted: 8 October 2020; Published: 14 October 2020

Abstract: Autism spectrum disorder (ASD) is a neurodevelopmental disorder characterized by a lack of social communication and social interaction. Autism is a mental disorder investigated by social and computational intelligence scientists utilizing advanced technologies such as machine learning models to enhance clinicians' ability to provide robust diagnosis and prognosis of autism. However, with dynamic changes in autism behaviour patterns, these models' quality and accuracy have become a great challenge for clinical practitioners. We applied a deep neural network learning on a large brain image dataset obtained from ABIDE (autism brain imaging data exchange) to provide an efficient diagnosis of ASD, especially for children. Our deep learning model combines unsupervised neural network learning, an autoencoder, and supervised deep learning using convolutional neural networks. Our proposed algorithm outperforms individual-based classifiers measured by various validations and assessment measures. Experimental results indicate that the autoencoder combined with the convolution neural networks provides the best performance by achieving 84.05% accuracy and Area under the Curve (AUC) value of 0.78.

Keywords: autism; diagnosis; autoencoder; convolution neural network; machine learning

1. Introduction

Autism spectrum disorder (ASD) is one of the brain development disorders. According to the World Health Organization (WHO), 1 in 60 children has an autism spectrum disorder [1]. Difficulties in social communication and interaction characterize this disorder; individuals on the spectrum also tend to have restricted interest and repetitive behaviour. ASD is an intellectual disability; many of those on the autism spectrum have extraordinary abilities and skills Roughly 40% are intellectually above average and have a unique ability to see the world with pride from a different perspective. According to the National Autism Spectrum Disorder Surveillance System (NASS), the most up-to-date Canadian prevalence rate is: 1 in 66 Canadian children and youth (ages 5–17) were diagnosed with autism spectrum disorder [2]. According to the National Institute of Mental Health (NIHM) [3], scientists do not know how and what causes autism, but some research suggests that genes and environmental factors cause autism. Some of the potential risk factors associated with ASD include having a sibling with ASD, older parents, pre-existing genetic conditions like Down syndrome, fragile X syndrome, and Rett syndrome, and finally, a low birth weight. Additionally, it is worth mentioning that researchers found differences in the brains of babies born before 27 weeks [4], i.e., babies born very prematurely are at higher risk for developing ASD. Early diagnosis in the first few years of life significantly improves results for people on the autism spectrum, but there are often delays in recognizing and diagnosing ASD. If health systems were better capable of identifying children at high risk for ASD and bringing them in earlier for a comprehensive evaluation, more children could benefit from early intervention. Many machine learning and neural network methods have recently shown an improvement in autism diagnosis [4–7]. The classification accuracy and the required computational time for building an automatic diagnosis system are significant challenges for many classifiers. In the paper, we focus on classifying individuals who have ASD from typically developing controls subjects using functional magnetic resonance imaging (fMRI) images provided by the autism brain imaging data exchange (ABIDE) [8] to study brain activities. There are 17 different brain imaging centers from where these images are collected. The dataset contains 539 individuals who have ASD and 573 typical controls (TC). ABIDE is preprocessed by four different pipelines like the connectome computation system (CCS), the configurable pipeline for the analysis of connectomes (CPAC), the data processing assistant for resting-state fMRI (DPARSF), and the neuroimaging analysis kit. We used the CPAC pipeline with preprocessing steps, including slice time correction, motion correction, nuisance signal remover, low-frequency drift, and voxel intensity normalization. We propose a hybrid classifier that combines an autoencoder with some well-known supervised machine learning algorithms and deep learning methods. For the deep learning methods, we focused on the convolution neural network (CNN). The autoencoder, combined with CNN, has shown a maximum accuracy of 83.39%. This paper is structured as follows: In Section 2, a literature survey is provided. Section 3 discusses the algorithms used from the machine learning and the neural network literature and essential parameters in each algorithm. In Section 4, we introduced the autoencoder-based hybrid diagnosis model. Section 5 provides details on the performance of the individual and hybrid algorithms using rs-fMRI experimental datasets. In Section 6, we concluded the paper along with some future directions.

2. Literature Review

Various machine learning and deep neural network methods distinguish between ASD and non-ASD. These methods are categorized into three main categories as image-based, questionnaire-based, or behavioural-based.

2.1. Image-Based Classification

Several studies have employed deep neural network learning on large brain image datasets obtained from the autism brain imaging data exchange [8] to identify ASD individuals from the typical control (TC). In [4], the authors used the deep learning model to perform binary classification of ASD and the typical control based on their neural patterns using rs-fMRI data. There were 505 ASD participants and 530 typically developing controls from 17 different imaging sites. They opted for using two stacked autoencoders to extracted lower-dimensional features. The model achieved 70% accuracy, a sensitivity of 74%, and a specificity of 63%, which is better than support vector machines (SVMs) and random forest (RF) models used in a previous study; these models used 10-fold cross-validation. Due to the high probability of noise in the image dataset obtained from several sites, the model does not achieve promising results despite using a dedicated Graphical Processing Unit (GPU) to speed up the training time. The entire model took about 33 h for training. Another model that diagnosed ADHD and autism from 3-D structural MRI and 4-D (fMRI) is presented in [9]. There are three learners in their work, including texture-based filters obtained using the sparse encoders that extracts features from MRI datasets. The fMRI scans are used to compute spatial non-stationary independent components, which decompose the subject's scans into the sequence order in time from the obtained component. The multimodal features obtained from the learner serves as input to the SVM model. The accuracy of the ADHD-200 dataset is 67.3%, and the accuracy of the ABIDE dataset is 64.3%. These learning models have found a "Signal" in the data to identify differences between case and control. The current results are not yet clinically applicable. In [10], authors have used 6 personal characteristic data (PCD) of 851 subjects (421 ASD and 430 non-ASD) from the ABIDE database to predict autism. The authors have evaluated the performance of nine machine learning models. Comparing to the other eight models, the neural network-based stacked sparse encoder performance is better with an area under the curve of 0.646. The advantage of their work includes understanding the predictive power of PCD for ASD classifications. The limitation of their work was that the dataset is from 17 different clinical and research sites; this fact leads to heterogeneity in the data and might underfit the models' accuracy; the database's size is another issue. In [5], a hybrid approach is introduced to detect autism using fMRI data [5]. In their work, they have proposed the ASD-DiagNet framework. Their experimental dataset is preprocessed using the C-PAC pipeline and parcellated into 200 functionally regions. They have used data augmentation techniques using the synthetic minority over-sampling technique (SMOTE). SMOTE uses the nearest neighbour method to generate augmented data. The process is performed using two phases; the first phase evaluates the model's performance on the whole dataset to find functional connectivity between regions, which is acquired using Pearson's correlation. The results achieved an accuracy of 69.4% on the original dataset, whereas data generated using augmentation shows some improvement, i.e., 70.3% accuracy. The second phase of their work includes 5-fold cross-validation on every 17 sites separately. The average result of all sites with the ASD-DiagNet model without augmented data is 60.7% accuracy, and 63.8% with augmented data. Another experiment was performed on automated anatomical labelling (AAL) and Talairach and Tournoux (TT). For AAL, 67.5% is the highest accuracy obtained (using augmented data), whereas TT achieved an accuracy of 65.3% (using augmented data). The convolutional neural network has been applied to detect the autism spectrum disorder using the ABIDE dataset [11] and has achieved 70.22% accuracy using fewer parameters. The authors pointed out four essential regions for ASD classification: C115, C188, C247, and C326 for the CC400 functional parcellation. The performance of SVM, K-nearest neighbour (KNN), and the random forest was evaluated, and achieved accuracy 69%, 62%, and 60%, respectively, after hyperparameter tuning. Their work has used fewer parameters, which helped in the reduction of computational cost.

2.2. Questionnaire-Based Classification Methods

In [12], a research study had attempted to detect ASD and ADHD using a crowdsource recruitment procedure. The survey database contains 248 (ASD) and ADHD (174) subjects, aged 2–17. The second dataset collected from the previous study is called archival, including 2775 ASD and 150 ADHD. Five machine learning models, ENet, Lasso, SVM [13], linear discriminant analysis (LDA) [14], and Ridge, were used. These models are applied to three independent datasets and combinations of the archival and survey datasets. All five models achieved Area under the Curve (AUC) that exceeds 0.90 when the archival dataset was used as training. When considering the survey sample as training, the ENet and LDA models work well. By using the mixture of two datasets, they have achieved an AUC equal to 0.89. The disadvantages are that the data obtained in archival ADHD is composed of siblings of children with autism. This data is biased, and therefore, results are compromised. In [15], authors have used two algorithms to train a structure parent-reported questionnaires and significant behaviours from short videos of children [15]. The dataset is obtained from multiple repositories of Autism Diagnostic Observation Schedule (ADOS) and Autism Diagnostic Interview Revised (ADI-R) score-sheets of children between 18 and 84 months. The random forest (RF) is trained over the ADI-R instrument data on a parent questionnaire (2299 with ASD, 585 with TC, and 364 with other conditions). The video of the subject (i.e., a 1-min home video taken by parents) was required to evaluate the target label's presence. The responses of all the questionnaires and short clips collaborated using L2-regularized logistic regression. The Receiver Operating Characteristics (ROC) of the combined data shows a boost in the performance of the clinical study samples. The advantage is that the ROC curve outperforms when compared with tools like Modified Checklist for Autism in Toddlers (M-CHAT) and Child Behaviour Checklist (CBCL). Additionally, allowing some subjects with lower certainty output from the algorithms to be classified as inconclusive. Their work utilizes experts who have used ADI-R and ADOS tools. These tools consumed hours to evaluate the results since parents were conducting it without experts and not more than a minute to complete the test, which caused significant data degradation and adding bias with an expected loss of screening accuracy. The authors have utilized machine learning algorithms for detecting autism in the below-explained study [16]. They have used three ASD datasets available from the University of California Irvine (UCI) repository (https://archive.ics.uci.edu). The dataset has 20 attributes, of which 1–10 are screening questions, and the remaining 10 attributes are personal information. The dataset has missing values, which were handled during the preprocessing steps before applying machine learning models. They have evaluated SVM, random forest, and KNN by splitting the dataset into five different sets. The results show that the random forest has performed very well for the classification compared to SVM and KNN. The authors recommend in their study to use a large data set and fewer missing values. Authors have worked on the UCI dataset [17] to predict autism using machine learning and neural network models [18]. The accuracy of the CNN and SVM models on the adult dataset exceeds 98%, while CNN's accuracy on the youth data set exceeds 96%. The CNN, Artificial Neural Networks (ANN), logistic regression, and SVM achieve accuracy above 98% on the children dataset.

2.3. *Behavioural-Based Classification Methods*

In [19], the authors identified a few behavioural measures that were enough to differentiate ASD from ADHD. The data set is from the Boston Autism Association and Autism Genetic Resources Exchange of 2775 autistic individuals and 150 ADHD subjects. Using Social Responsiveness Scale (SRS) items containing responses of a child's behaviour, six machine learning models like SVM, LDA, categorical Lasso, and logistic regression, random forest, and decision tree was trained and tested. Minimal redundancy, maximal relevance, undersampling, forward feature selection, and 10-fold cross-validation applied to the dataset before training. The results show out of six algorithms, four algorithms, including SVM, LDA, categorical Lasso, and logistic regression, achieved an accuracy ranging from 96.2% to 96.5%. Each model used only 5 of the 65 behaviour indicators. The models mentioned were able to do classification tasks optimally, not only due to less error but probabilistic qualities. The disadvantages of their work include the massive imbalance between subjects of ASD and ADHD. This subject imbalance was overcome with undersampling but prevented authors from devoting a part of data exclusively for validation because of the constrained sample data. In [20], authors have designed a normalization layer and activation layer into a single tensor to tensor computation graph, which forms high sparse and large search space. The normalization layer and activation function are essential components of deep learning that stabilize optimization and improved generalization. The authors have shown an experiment of Evo Norms (normalization-activation layer) on image classification models such as Res Nets, Mobile Nets, and Efficient Nets. Evo Norms consist of two series: (1) the B-series, which is batch dependent, and (2) the S-series, which works on independent samples introduced by rejecting any batch dependent operation. Their method discovered novel layers with structures that achieved strong generalization across many architectures and tasks.

3. Machine Learning and Deep Learning Classifiers

In our proposed hybrid model, we combined an autoencoder for dimensionality reduction with one of the well-known classifiers, including support vector machines (SVMs), random forest (RF), K-nearest neighbours (KNNs), and convolutional neural network (CNN). This section introduces each of the adopted methods in our hybrid model.

3.1. *Autoencoder*

The autoencoder is a type of neural network that does not require the labeling of data, and therefore it is an unsupervised learning algorithm. The aim is to learn an input function to reconstruct the input to an output of fewer dimensions. It approximates the identity function to get the outcome of a neural network similar to the input. In order words, it tries to copy the input to its output. Mathematically, if x is the input (also called an encoder), x' is the network (also called a decoder). The architecture of autoencoders reduces dimensionality using non-linear optimization. In Equation (1), h is the hidden layer, which can be calculated by multiplying the vector x with weights and adding the bias and passing it to the activation function. The decoder x' is calculated in Equation (2).

$$h = \sigma(W \times x + b) \tag{1}$$

$$x' = (W \times h + b) \tag{2}$$

There are many autoencoder variants, such as the undercomplete autoencoder, denoising autoencoder, sparse autoencoder, and adversarial autoencoder. A research study in [21] has demonstrated that when the input has a relation or a basic structure, the input reconstruction will be painless. They have described several applications that involve the use of the autoencoder algorithm, one of which is brain disorders. Whenever clinical neuroimaging studies are considered, they always opt for an autoencoder before feeding data to any other classification model because of the high dimensionality of genetic and neuroimaging data. The difficulty lies in constructing and learning output from a high dimensional input. In [22], the authors have evaluated the performance by comparing an autoencoder with other models that can do a similar task of reduction, for example, models like principal component analysis, linear discriminant analysis (linear models), locally linear embedding, and Isomap (non-linear models). They have applied their model on various datasets and concluded that the number of hidden layer nodes affects the autoencoder's performance. When the hidden nodes adjusted around the dataset's inherent dimensionality, the Modified National Institute of Standards and Technology (MNIST) data set performs well. Other experiments in their paper involved a synthetic dataset and Olivetti dataset. Experimental analysis on the synthetic dataset showed stable performance by principal component analysis (PCA), linear discriminant analysis (LDA), and Isomap. However, an autoencoder and locally linear embedding (LLE) were not stable. The unstable models retain the original data's geometric characteristics, so the result is still acceptable. Experiments on the MNIST dataset showed that the autoencoder performed better than PCA. The autoencoder projected points to represent the digit "1". An autoencoder tends to project images of the same class to edges and corners. The results showed that the autoencoder not only helps in dimensionality reduction but also in detecting the recurrent structures. The lower-dimensional data generated during the encoding process contains useful patterns from the original input, is provided to a convolutional neural network or a machine learning algorithm [23–25].

3.2. Support Vector Machines (SVMs)

Support vector machines (SVMs) are a supervised machine learning model applied in regression and classification tasks. The SVM aims to find a hyperplane in an N-dimensional space that classifies the data points. Let us consider an example of two classes. Figure 1 shows multiple hyperplanes (Y1, Y2, and Y3) that divide these data points into their respective classes. We had to choose a hyperplane that assures data points are on the right side of the graph. From Figure 1, we could conclude that Y2 segregated data points more efficiently. Two points were closest to the two lines (Y1 and Y3) and had less margin. These points (pink filled shapes) were a little further from hyper-plane Y2. Hence, we set Y2 as the right hyperplane with a high margin.

In this paper, we perform binary classification such that the SVM predicts the binary outcome on brain image data. The knowledge of the SVM is incomplete without understanding kernels. Kernel functions play a vital role in SVM. They transform inputs space into feature space in any required form. Kernels provide shortcuts to avoid heavy calculations. The significant fact about the kernel is that we can go to higher dimensions and perform effortless calculations. With the kernels, we can go up to an infinite number of dimensions using kernels. There are various types of kernels; some of these kernels are discussed as follows: [26–29].

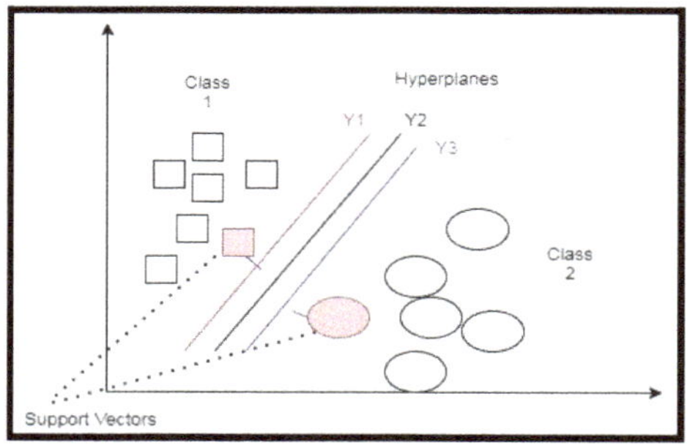

Figure 1. Hyperplane of the support vector machine (SVM).

- Linear: This form of kernel function is very simple, straightforward. It is given by the inner product of (*x*,*y*) plus an optional constant bias, as shown in Equation (3):

$$k(x, y) = x^T y + bias \quad (3)$$

- Sigmoid: The sigmoid kernel is also called hyperbolic tangent kernel and as a multilayer perceptron kernel. The sigmoid kernel is obtained from the neural network field, where the bipolar sigmoid function is used as an activation function for the neurons.

$$k(x, y) = \propto \times \tanh\left(x^T y + bias\right) \quad (4)$$

- Radial basis function (RBF): is used when we have no prior knowledge of data.

$$k(x, y) = \exp\left(\frac{\|x - y\|^2}{2\sigma^2}\right) \quad (5)$$

The SVM is an effective classifier when the number of dimensions is greater than the number of data samples. SVM has high-efficiency memory functions and has various forms of kernels [13].

3.3. Random Forest

An ensemble of decision trees forms the random forest (RF). The disadvantage of using decision trees is that they are not flexible enough to classify new sets of data points. Random forest combines the simplicity of a decision tree with flexible results and improves performance metrics. The following steps are required to build a random forest tree, as in Figure 2.

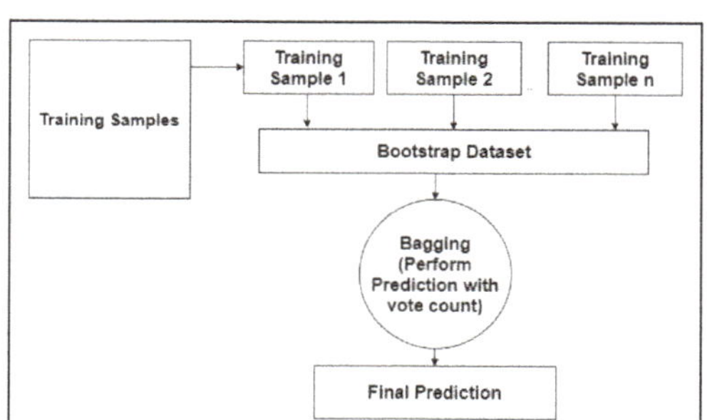

Figure 2. The random forest algorithm.

- Step 1: Building decision trees using a bootstrap dataset.
- Step 2: Consider a random subset of variables at each step.
- Step 3: Perform a vote for a new dataset by sending it to all the trees.
- Step 4: Select the prediction result with the highest votes as the final prediction.

The bootstrap dataset does not select all columns to determine the root of the tree. Step 1 mentioned above is performed again until varieties of trees are built. The idea of creating multiple trees leads to an efficient performance of the random forest. Assume a new input dataset (also called the out of bag dataset) is added to all the bootstrap datasets, the decision from each bootstrap is recorded. The aggregated decision is the decision for the new input. This type of decision-making using a bootstrap dataset is called bagging [28,29].

The algorithm is used for binary classification and regression problems. RF is considered an accurate and robust method because of the number of decision trees constructed to provide a prediction for the new dataset. RF does not suffer from the overfitting problem. The random forest is a time-consuming algorithm because decisions are made from many trees [30–32].

3.4. K-Nearest Neighbours

The K-nearest neighbours (KNN) is a simple supervised, non-parametric algorithm used for classification and regression problems. For a data point x to be classified, its K-nearest neighbours are retrieved, as a neighbourhood of x. Voting among the neighbourhood data is usually used to decide the classification for the point x. The critical point is to select the value for the k. If the value of k is not appropriate, there is a low chance of obtaining promising results for any dataset. The algorithm becomes slow when we increase the number of k values [30,31].

3.5. Convolutional Neural Network (CNN)

CNN is a deep learning algorithm that is very helpful for image classification. The CNN model on image datasets generally takes an image as the input, and the output is the likelihood of the class to which it belongs. The critical layers in the CNN are the convolution layer and the max pooling layers. The input image is given to the convolution layer, and it applies different kernels/filters that extract the low-level features. The following are the fundamental building blocks on CNN [33].

3.5.1. Stride

It is the number of picture elements the kernel/filter shifts over the input at a time. Figure 3 shows an example of how the stride process works. In the example, the filter convolved around the input by shifting two units at a time. To calculate the first block of the resulting image after a stride operation with stride = 2 was performed. We applied a cross product between the image pixel and the filter pixel as $(0 \times 0) + (1 \times 2) + (2 \times 1) + (3 \times 2) = 10$; such that the first number (in orange color) was the image pixel and second number (in blue color) was the filter pixel.

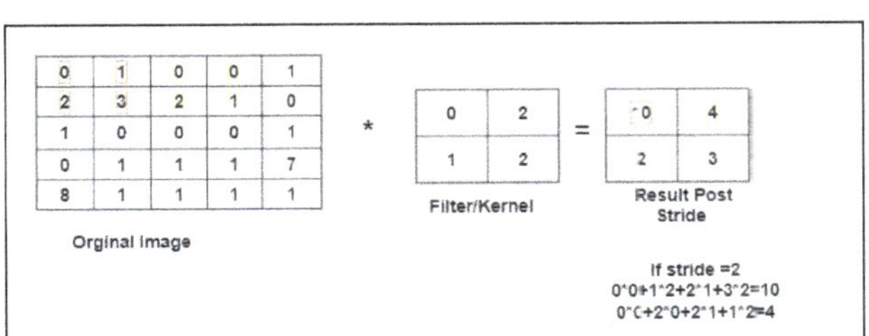

Figure 3. A Stride Example.

The image was of size 5 × 5 with a filter of size 2 × 2, and a stride value equal to 2. The size of the reduced image was calculated using Equation (6): where n_{in} (in our case, 5) is the number of input features, n_{out} is the number of output features, k is kernel size (in our case, 2), p is the convolution padding size (in our case, 0), and s is convolution stride size (in our case, 2). The resulting image was of size 2 × 2.

$$n_{out} = \left| \frac{n_{in} + 2p - k}{s} \right| + 1 \tag{6}$$

3.5.2. Padding

The convolution layer without padding does not preserve the spatial size of the input image. When the input is given to the convolution layer with padding, we add zeros to the border of input, which helps in extracting the features from the corner of the image. The input image dimensions in Figure 4 are 6 × 6 × 1, where 6 × 6 is the image size, and the number of channels is 1, which means the image has only one channel. If we set the padding size = 2, we get the image size of image 8 × 8 × 1. Figure 4 shows the original image and the matrix after applying the padding process.

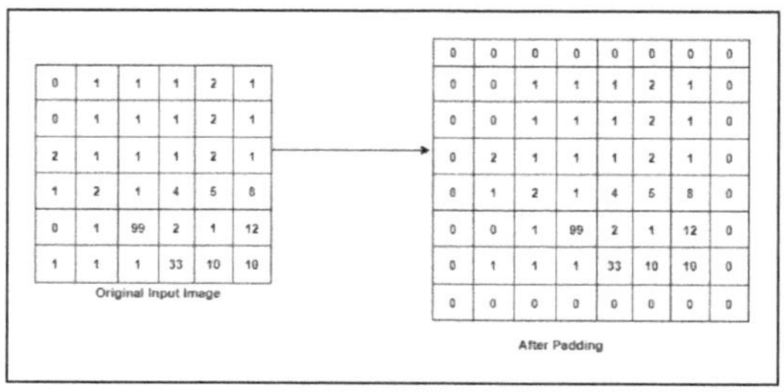

Figure 4. The Padding Example.

3.5.3. Max Pooling

The max pooling reduces the size of the feature maps. The advantage of using this layer is to reduce the computational power. Although the size of the image is reduced, the vital information is still maintained. There are different types of pooling, which are as follows max pooling and average pooling. Max pooling chooses the highest/topmost value from the image covered by the kernel. In contrast, average pooling calculates the midpoint/mean value from the portion of an image covered by the filter. An example is shown in Figure 5, where the input image is 4 × 4; if we apply stride = 2 and perform max pooling, the results are obtained in each block as the max value out of the selected block.

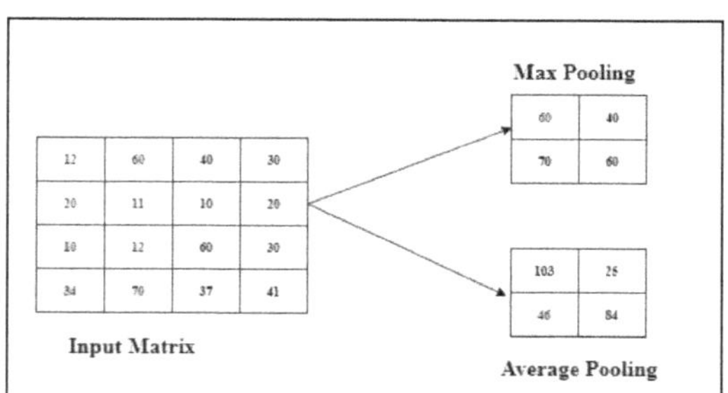

Figure 5. Max pooling.

3.5.4. Activation Function

The activation function is also called a transfer function, computes a weighted sum of the input and biases. The activation function decides if the weights and bias' values will activate/fire the neuron. The activation function aims to convert a linear input signal of the model into non-linear output signals. The simple CNN model consists of an input layer hidden layer (having a convolution layer, activation, and max pooling layer) and the output layer. The activation function choice will help us perform classification or regression tasks when throwing the model's output. After the hidden layer, the activation function is invoked to learn a non-linear form of linear mapping before making any predictions. Some activation functions are Rectilinear, sigmoid, SoftMax, and tanh [28].

- Sigmoid function: The sigmoid function exists between 0 and 1, and its shape looks like an S shape. Sigmoid is the correct choice when we have to predict the likelihood of a model. Equation (7) illustrates the sigmoid function. Since the sigmoid function is differentiable, the sigmoid function's derivative is shown in Equation (8) to calculate the slope of the sigmoid curve.

$$\sigma(x) = \frac{1}{1 + e^{-z}} \tag{7}$$

$$\sigma' = \sigma(x)(1 - \sigma(x)) \tag{8}$$

- Rectilinear function: The Rectilinear function, also called ReLU. It has values between 0 and infinity, and it provides better performance than the sigmoid function. Equation (9) shows the derivative of the ReLU function.

$$R(z) = \left\{ \begin{array}{ll} 1 & if\, z > 0 \\ 0 & if\, z < 0 \end{array} \right\} \tag{9}$$

In one of the proposed models, we used the sigmoid activation function since our problem evolved to predict whether the candidate has autism or not, making it a binary classification.

4. The Proposed Hybrid Autoencoder-Based Classifier

Autoencoders play a vital role in extracting low dimensional features, and these features can be given to machine learning models or deep learning models to perform classification tasks. The architecture of autoencoders reduces dimensionality using non-linear optimization. Our proposed method focused on using the undercomplete autoencoder to extract useful information from the input layer by having fewer neurons in the hidden layer than the input. The architecture of an undercomplete autoencoder is shown in Figure 6. It is the simplest form of constructing an autoencoder by limiting the amount of information that can flow through the network. This can be achieved by reducing the number of neurons in the hidden layer. This helps to obtain essential features from the data. By penalizing the structure according to the reconstruction error, our architecture learns the most important input data attributes and show how to reconstruct the original input from an "encoded" state.

The input fMRI was fed to the Pearson's correlation function to compute the pairwise correlation. This data was provided as input to an autoencoder, which will help extract lower-dimensional features (in our case, 4975 features from 9950) to send it to the classification models. In the paper, we focused on using four main classifiers, including KNN, SVM, RF, and CNN. Figure 7 shows the flowchart of combing the autoencoder and the adopted machine learning classifiers. In the autoencoder–KNN model, for calculating the distance between k points, the value of p was set to 2, which was for the Euclidean distance and 100 neighbours. For the autoencoder–SVM model, in the parameter list, we chose C = 2.0, which is a regularization parameter. For the autoencoder–RF model, we assigned the estimators value to 1050 and the depth value to 90.

In the proposed autoencoder–CNN, the CNN consisted of two 1D convolution layer followed by batch normalization, an activation function, and a max pooling layer. After flattening the CNN layer, it worked as a fully connected neural network, and we had two linear layers with an activation function. Since the output predicts whether an individual is diagnosed with autism or not, we applied the sigmoid activation function. Figure 8 shows the workflow of combining an autoencoder with CNN.

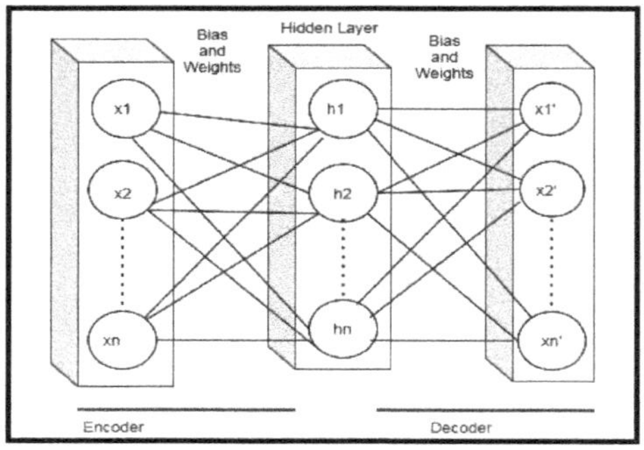

Figure 6. The autoencoder architecture.

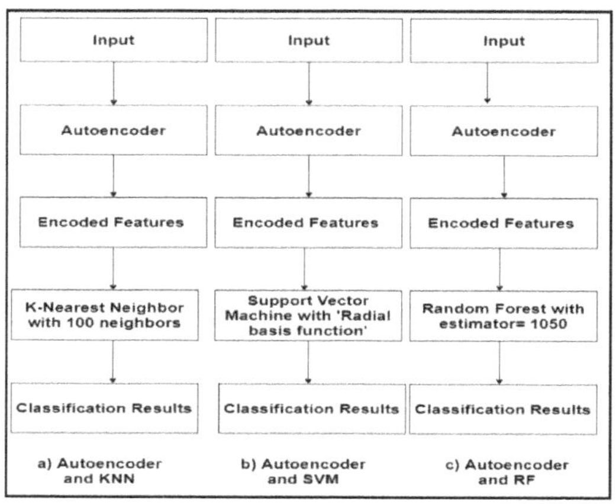

Figure 7. The hybrid autoencoder-based machine learning classifier. KNN: K-nearest neighbour; RF: random forest.

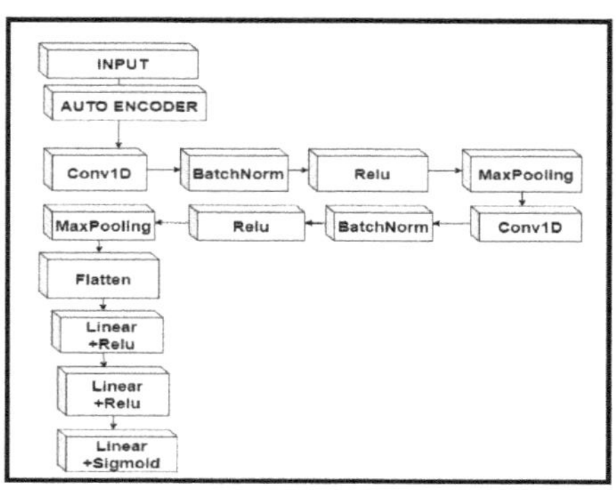

Figure 8. The hybrid model of an autoencoder and convolutional neural network (CNN).

5. Experiment Results

The Google Colaboratory (Colab) was used to perform experiments, a free online cloud-based Jupyter notebook that allowed us to train our machine learning and deep learning models on CPUs, GPUs, and TPUs. The ABIDE-I dataset has rs-fMRI data for 1112 candidates, along with phenotypic information. This data is slice time corrected, motion-corrected, and normalized. In our study, all rs-fMRI data were from the CPAC preprocessing pipeline and band-pass filtered (0.01–0.1 Hz). From these 1112 subjects, 1035 subjects were considered for our study since only these subjects had completed phenotypic information. To limit the variance between outputs to just preprocessing, statistical derivatives for each pipeline and strategy were calculated using the CPAC software [8]. The rs-fMRI (shown in Figure 9) stands for resting-state fMRI, a type of functional magnetic resonance imaging (fMRI) used in brain mapping to evaluate regional interactions in a resting or task-negative state when an explicit task is not performed. The resting-state process helps explore the brain's functional organization and examine if altered in neurological or mental disorders. Figure 9 shows the brain structure of a child having ASD [34].

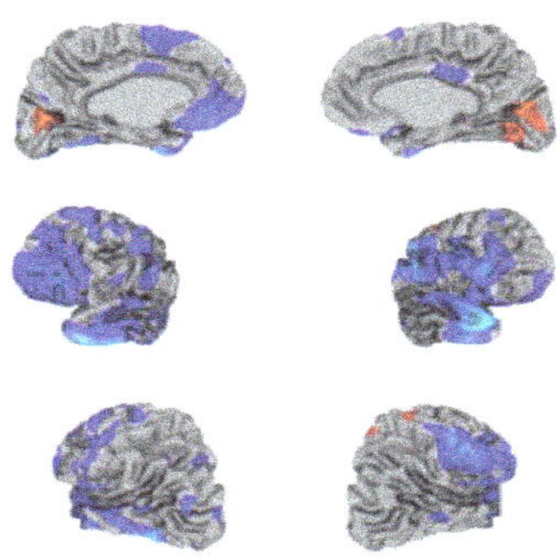

Figure 9. The brain structure variations in an autistic child.

Experimental Analysis

To evaluate the performance, we used k-fold cross-validation. We used three machine learning algorithms and two forms of neural networks to detect ASD. Table 1 compares the accuracy, sensitivity, and specificity of the four proposed models with individual-based classifiers. The accuracy refers to the number of correct predictions made by the predictive model over the rest of the predictions. Sensitivity refers to how sensitive the classifier is in detecting positive instances, and specificity is the proportion of the true negatives correctly identified by a diagnostic test. The results show that an autoencoder, combined with CNN, had achieved 84.05% accuracy, which outperformed other methods. The percentage of improvement in each measure is illustrated in Table 2

Figures 10–13 compare the performance of the proposed hybrid models against individual classifiers. We could observe that the hybrid autoencoder-based models outperformed the individual methods measured by the increased value of the accuracy, sensitivity, and the low values of the specificity measures. The Receiver Operating Characteristic (ROC) curve for each hybrid model, compared to the individual classifier, is shown in Figures 14–17. We could observe that the ROC curve for autoencoder–CNN was better than any other model. ROC is a probability curve, and AUC represents the degree or measure of separability. The higher the AUC, the better the model was at the prediction.

Table 1. Sensitivity and specificity.

Model	Accuracy %	Sensitivity %	Specificity %
Autoencoder–CNN	84.05	80	75.3
Evo Norm CNN	74	71.33	65.2
SVM	60.2	35.1	84.1
Autoencoder–SVM	69.1	66.5	71.69
Random Forest (RF)	61.5	53.8	68.8
Autoencoder–RF	65.3	58.3	72.1
KNN	58.1	68.2	55.5
Autoencoder–KNN	60.1	35	84

CNN: convolution neural network; SVM: support vector machine; KNN: K-nearest neighbour.

Table 2. Percentage of improvement in accuracy, sensitivity, and specificity.

Model	Accuracy %	Sensitivity %	Specificity %
Autoencoder–CNN	10.05%	8.67%	10.1%
Autoencoder–SVM	8.9%	31.4%	−12.41%
Autoencoder–RF	3.8%	−0.5%	3.3%
Autoencoder–KNN	2%	−33.2%	28.5%

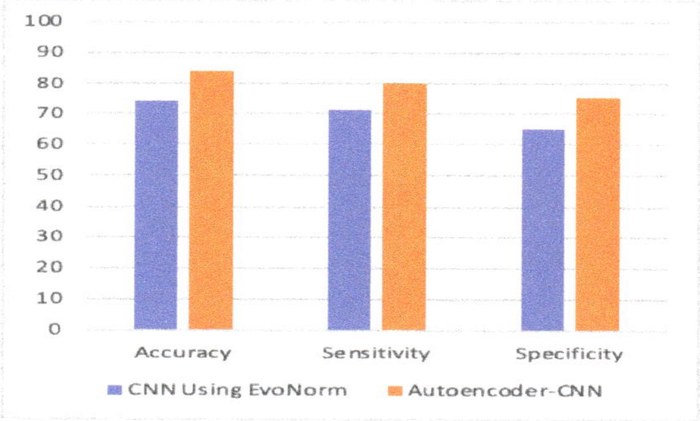

Figure 10. Autoencoder-CNN vs. CNN. CNN: convolution neural network.

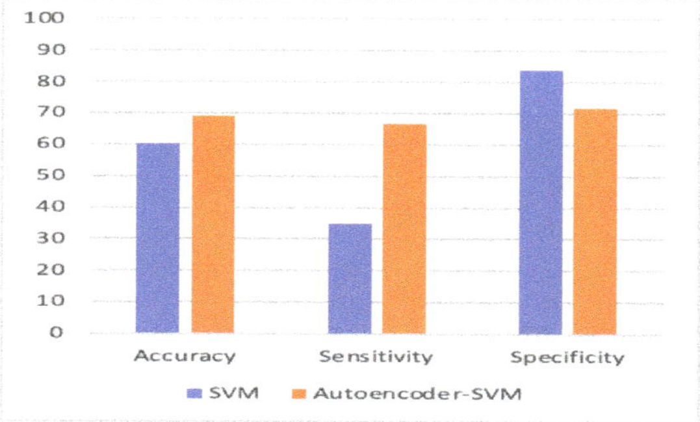

Figure 11. Autoencoder-SVM vs. SVM.

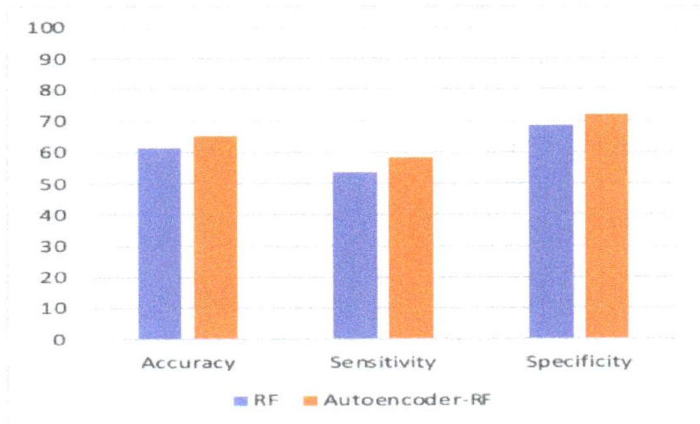

Figure 12. Autoencoder-RF vs. RF.

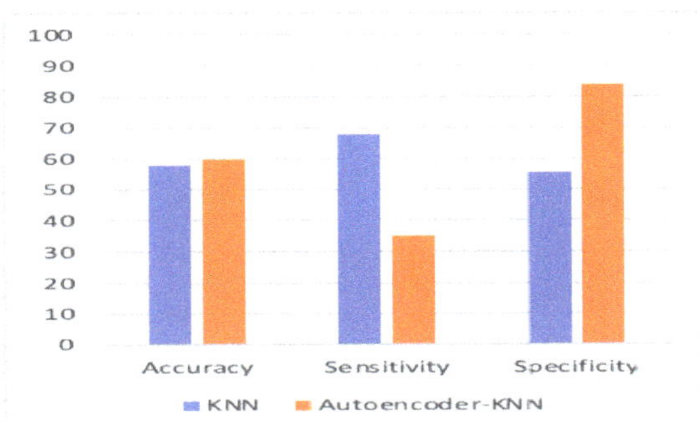

Figure 13. Autoencoder-KNN vs. KNN.

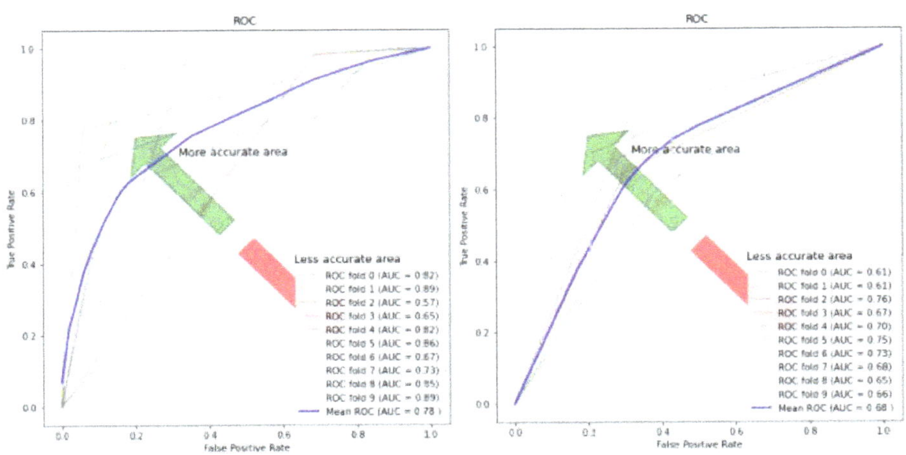

Figure 14. ROC curve and AUC values for autoencoder–CNN (**Left**) and CNN (**Right**). ROC: Receiver Operating Characteristics; AUC: Area under the Curve.

Table 3 shows the values of accuracy, sensitivity, specificity, and AUC [35]. The first value indicates the average of all the 10 k-folds, and the second value is the standard deviation. The standard deviation helps to calculate the amount of variation in a set of values [36]. A low standard deviation indicates that the values tend to be close to the mean, while a high standard deviation indicates that the values are dispersed over a broader range [37,38].

The F1 score was also calculated for all the proposed models, as shown in Figure 18. CNN achieved better results compared to other models. The F1 score can be interpreted as a weighted average of precision and recall. The relative contribution of precision and recall to the F1 score are equal. The F1 score [39,40] is calculated as:

$$\mathrm{F1} = 2 \times (precision \times recall) / (precision + recall) \tag{10}$$

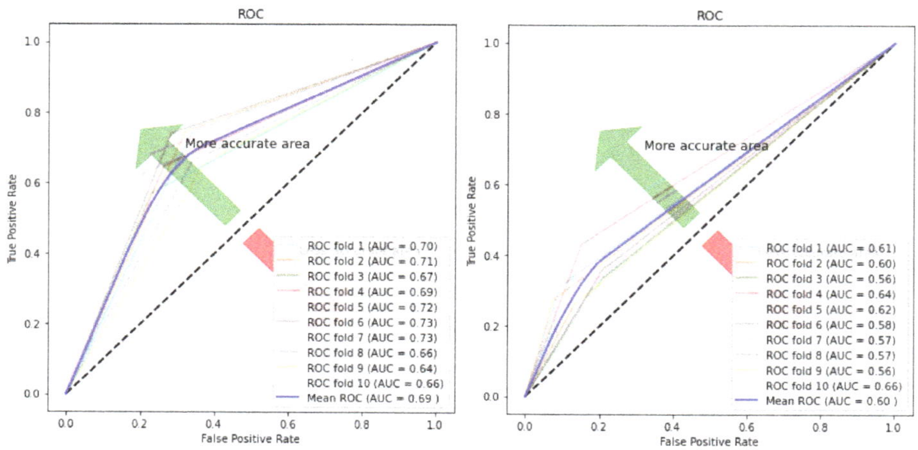

Figure 15. ROC curve and AUC values for autoencoder–SVM (**Left**) and SVM (**Right**).

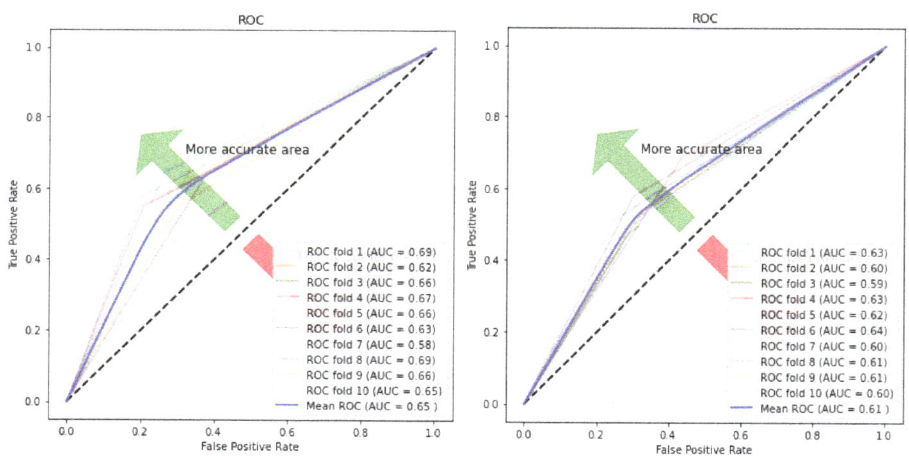

Figure 16. ROC curve and AUC values for autoencoder–RF (**Left**) and RF (**Right**).

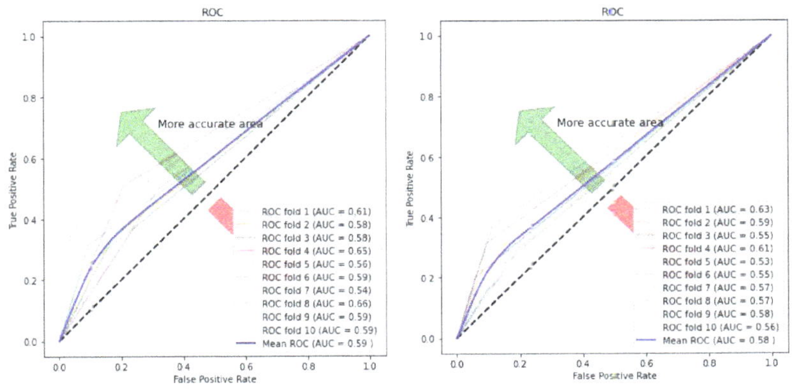

Figure 17. ROC curve and AUC values for autoencoder–KNN (**Left**) and KNN (**Right**).

Table 3. Average and standard deviation in accuracy, sensitivity, specificity, and AUC.

Model	Accuracy %	Sensitivity %	Specificity %	AUC
KNN	0.582 (+/−) 0.02	0.682 (+/−) 0.07	0.555 (+/−) 0.02	0.58 (+/−) 0.02
Autoencoder–KNN	0.601 (+/−) 0.035	0.35 (+/−) 0.09	0.84 (+/−) 0.08	0.595 (+/−) 0.03
Evo Norm CNN	0.743 (+/−) 0.05	0.713 (+/−) 0.07	0.652 (+/−) 0.09	0.68 (+/−) 0.05
Autoencoder–CNN	0.84 (+/−) 0.07	0.8 (+/−) 0.19	0.753 (+/−) 0.22	0.78 (+/−) 0.11
RF	0.615 (+/−) 0.01	0.583 (+/−) 0.06	0.688 (+/−) 0.04	0.612 (+/−) 0.01
Autoencoder–RF	0.653 (+/−) 0.02	0.583 (+/−) 0.06	0.721 (+/−) 0.05	0.651 (+/−) 0.03
SVM	0.603 (+/−) 0.03	0.351 (+/−) 0.07	0.841 (+/−) 0.04	0.6 (+/−) 0.03
Autoencoder–SVM	0.691 (+/−) 0.03	0.665 (+/−) 0.06	0.716 (+/−) 0.06	0.69 (+/−) 0.03

AUC: Area under the Curve.

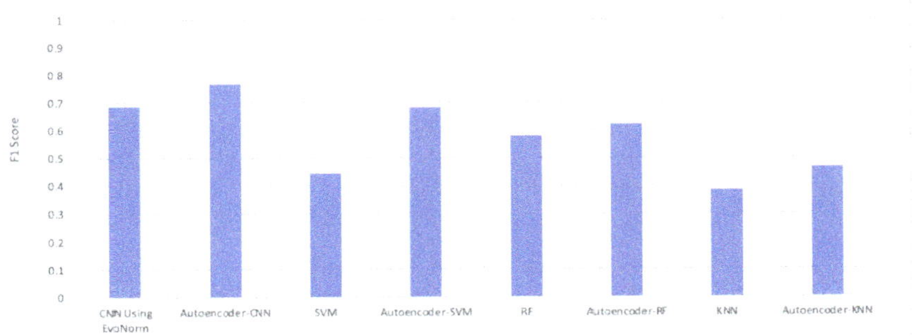

Figure 18. The F1 score.

The experimental results in Figure 18 show that the autoencoder with CNN was the best performing hybrid model for our problem. The computational time taken by each model is illustrated in Figure 19. The autoencoder combined with CNN has the highest computational time for training, while the autoencoder–KNN had the lowest computational time.

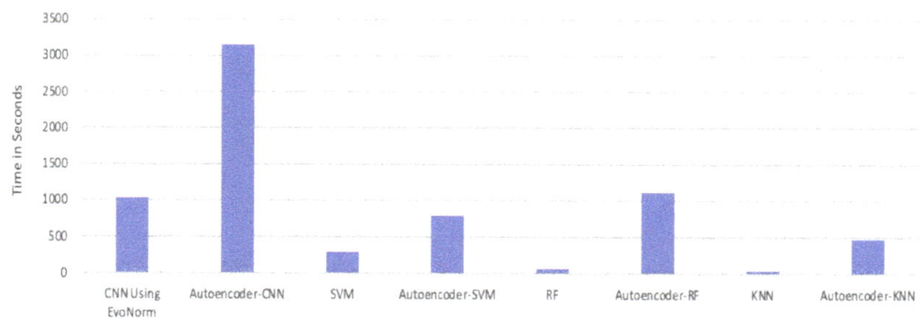

Figure 19. Computational time (s).

6. Conclusions and Future Direction

The purpose of this paper was to provide an automatic diagnosis algorithm that classifies individuals with ASD and non-ASD. Experimental results show that the hybrid autoencoder with convolution networks gave a better performance by achieving 84.05% accuracy and an AUC value of 0.78. An autoencoder with CNN consumed approximately 55 min to train the model. The autoencoder performed feature selection, and those features can be given as input to any classification model. The AUC score for an autoencoder combined with SVM, random forest, and KNN was 0.69, 0.65, and 0.59, respectively. The main drawback of our experiment was the size of the dataset. We had a small dataset with 1112 rs-fMRI images. In the future, personal characteristics data like birth weight, mother's age, and family history could give us more promising results. Survey data related to the child's daily behaviour or a short clip of the participant could help detect autism, which can add more weightage to the number of features. Complex models like ResNet-50 can be applied to the data of fMRI through the approach of transfer learning. Future directions also include a combative analysis to compare the performance of other dimensionality reduction methods such as the principal component analysis, linear discriminant analysis (linear models), locally linear embedding, and Isomap (non-linear models) when combined with machine learning or deep learning classifiers. The results of KNN can be improved by using the Grid Search CV method, and it helps to loop through predefined hyperparameters and fit your estimator (model) on your training set. So, in the end, we could select the best parameters from the listed hyperparameters. In summary, we developed and compared an autoencoder's performance combined with other models to the performance of the individual models to understand how much the emphasis of encoded features helps classify ASD candidates from fMRI images.

Author Contributions: Software, H.S.; Supervision, R.K.; Visualization, H.S.; Writing—original draft, H.S. and R.K.; Writing—review & editing, H.S. and R.K.; Validation, R.K.; Source, H.S. and R.K. All authors have read and agreed to the published version of the manuscript.

Funding: This research received no external funding.

Conflicts of Interest: The authors declare no conflict of interest.

References

1. World Health Organization (WHO). Autism Spectrum Disorders. Available online: https://www.who.int/news-room/fact-sheets/detail/autism-spectrum-disorders (accessed on 3 June 2020).
2. Autism Spectrum Disorder among Children and Youth in Canada 2018. Available online: https://www.canada.ca/en/public-health/services/publications/diseases-conditions/autism-spectrum-disorder-children-youth-canada-2018.html(accessedon22May2020).
3. Autism Spectrum Disorder. Available online: https://www.nimh.nih.gov/health/topics/autism-spectrum-disorders-asd/index.shtml (accessed on 22 May 2020).

4. Heinsfeld, A.S.; Franco, A.R.; Craddock, R.C.; Buchweitz, A.; Meneguzzi, F. Identification of autism spectrum disorder using deep learning and the ABIDE dataset. *NeuroImage: Clin.* **2018** *17*, 16–23. [CrossRef] [PubMed]
5. Eslami, T.; Mirjalili, V.; Fong, A.; Laird, A.R.; Saeed, F. ASD-DiagNet: A Hybrid Learning Approach for Detection of Autism Spectrum Disorder Using fMRI Data. *Front. Aging Neurosci.* **2019**, *13*, 70. [CrossRef] [PubMed]
6. Iidaka, T. Resting state functional magnetic resonance imaging and neural network classified autism and control. *Cortex* **2015**, *63*, 55–67. [CrossRef] [PubMed]
7. Khosla, M.; Jamison, K.; Kuceyeski, A.; Sabuncu, M.R. 3D Convolutional Neural Networks for Classification of Functional Connectomes. In *Deep Learning in Medical Image Analysis and Multimodal Learning for Clinical Decision Support*; Springer: Quebec City, QC, Canada, 2018; pp. 137–145.
8. Craddock, R.C.; Yassine, B.; Carlton, C.; Francois, C.; Alan, E.; András, J.; Budhachandra, K.; John, L.; Qingyang, L.; Michael, M.; et al. The Neuro Bureau Preprocessing Initiative: Open sharing of preprocessed neuroimaging data and derivatives. *Front. Aging Neurosci.* **2013**, *7*. [CrossRef]
9. Sen, B.; Borle, N.C.; Greiner, R.; Brown, M.R.G. A general prediction model for the detection of ADHD and Autism using structural and functional MRI. *PLoS ONE* **2018**, *13*, e0194856. [CrossRef] [PubMed]
10. Parikh, M.N.; Li, H.; He, L. Enhancing Diagnosis of Autism with Optimized Machine Learning Models and Personal Characteristic Data. *Front. Comput. Neurosci.* **2019**, *13*. [CrossRef] [PubMed]
11. Sherkatghanad, Z.; Akhondzadeh, M.; Salari, S.; Zomorodi-Moghadam, M.; Abdar, M.; Acharya, U.R.; Khosrowabadi, R.; Salari, V. Automated Detection of Autism Spectrum Disorder Using a Convolutional Neural Network. *Front. Neurosci.* **2020**, *13*, 1325. [CrossRef] [PubMed]
12. Duda, M.; Haber, N.; Daniels, J.; Wall, D.P. Crowdsourced validation of a machine-learning classification system for autism and ADHD. *Transl. Psychiatry* **2017**, *7*, e1133. [CrossRef] [PubMed]
13. Support Vector Machines. Available online: https://scikit-learn.org/stable/modules/svm.html# (accessed on 17 May 2020).
14. Linear Discriminant Analysis in Python. Available online: https://towardsdatascience.com/linear-discriminant-analysis-in-python-76b8b17817c2 (accessed on 3 June 2020).
15. Abbas, H.; Garberson, F.; Glover, E.; Wall, D.P. Machine learning approach for early detection of autism by combining questionnaire and home video screening. *J. Am. Med. Inform. Assoc.* **2018**, *25*, 1000–1007. [CrossRef] [PubMed]
16. Erkan, U.; Thanh, D.N.H. Autism Spectrum Disorder Detection with Machine Learning Methods. *Curr. Psychiatry Res. Rev.* **2020**, *15*, 297–308. [CrossRef]
17. Raj, S.; Masood, S. Analysis and Detection of Autism Spectrum Disorder Using Machine Learning Techniques. *Procedia Comput. Sci.* **2020**, *167*, 994–1004. [CrossRef]
18. University of California Irvine (UCI). Available online: http://archive.ics.uci.edu/ml/index.php (accessed on 11 May 2020).
19. Duda, M.; Ma, R.; Haber, N.; Wall, D.P. Use of machine learning for behavioral distinction of autism and ADHD. *Transl. Psychiatry* **2016**, *6*, e732. [CrossRef] [PubMed]
20. Liu, H.; Brock, A.; Simonyan, K.; Le, Q.V. Evolving Normalization-Activation Layers. *arXiv* **2020**, arXiv:2004.02967v5.
21. Pinaya, W.H.L.; Vieira, S.; Garcia-Dias, R.; Mechelli, A. Autoencoders. In *Machine Learning*; Academic Press: Cambridge, MA, USA, 2020; pp. 193–208. [CrossRef]
22. Wang, Y.; Yao, H.; Zhao, S. Auto-encoder based dimensionality reduction. *Neurocomputing* **2016**, *184*, 232–242. [CrossRef]
23. Karen, S.; Andrew, Z. Very Deep Convolutional Networks for Large-Scale Image Recognition. *arXiv* **2014**, arXiv:1409.1556.
24. Traore, B.B.; Kamsu-Foguem, B.; Tangara, F. Deep convolution neural network for image recognition. *Ecol. Inform.* **2018**, *48*, 257–268. [CrossRef]
25. Activation Functions Neural Networks. Available online: https://towardsdatascience.com/activation-functions-neural-networks-1cbd9f8d91d6 (accessed on 22 May 2020).
26. Kernel Functions for Machine Learning Applications. Available online: http://crsouza.com/2010/03/17/kernel-functions-for-machine-learning-applications/ (accessed on 22 May 2020).
27. Ridge Regression and Classification. Available online: https://scikit-learn.org/stable/modules/linear_model.html#ridge-regression-and-classification (accessed on 22 May 2020).

28. Random Forests Classifier Python. Available online: https://www.datacamp.com/community/tutorials/random-forests-classifier-python (accessed on 17 May 2020).
29. Random Forest Classifier. Available online: https://scikit-learn.org/stable/modules/generated/sklearn.ensemble.RandomForestClassifier.html (accessed on 3 June 2020).
30. KNeighbors Classifier. Available online: https://scikit-learn.org/stable/modules/generated/sklearn.neighbors.KNeighborsClassifier.html (accessed on 22 May 2020).
31. Mitchell, T. *Machine Learning*; MIT Press: Cambridge, MA, USA; McGraw-Hill: New York, NY, USA, 1997.
32. Nwankpa, C.; Ijomah, W.; Gachagan, A.; Marshall, S. Activation Functions: Comparison of trends in Practice and Research for Deep Learning. *arXiv* **2018**, arXiv:1811.
33. Large set Brain Scans. Available online: https://www.spectrumnews.org/news/large-set-brain-scans-reveals-no-telltale-signs-autism/ (accessed on 13 May 2020).
34. Deep Learning. Available online: https://www.deeplearningbook.org/ (accessed on 3 June 2020).
35. Model Evaluation. Available online: https://scikit-learn.org/stable/modules/model_evaluation.html (accessed on 11 July 2020).
36. Kashef, R.; Kamel, M. Distributed cooperative hard-fuzzy document clustering. In Proceedings of the Annual Scientific Conference of the LORNET Research Network, Montreal, QC, Canada, November 2006; Available online: http://citeseerx.ist.psu.edu/viewdoc/download?doi=10.1.1.612.3974&rep=rep1&type=pdf (accessed on 11 July 2020).
37. Ibrahim, A.; Rayside, D.; Kashef, R. Cooperative based software clustering on dependency graphs. In Proceedings of the 2014 IEEE 27th Canadian Conference on Electrical and Computer Engineering (CCECE), Toronto, ON, Canada, 4–7 May 2014.
38. Abu-Zeid, N.; Kashif, R.; Badawy, O.M. Immune based clustering for medical diagnostic systems. In Proceedings of the 2012 International Conference on Advanced Computer Science Applications and Technologies (ACSAT), Kuala Lumpur, Malaysia, 26–28 November 2012.
39. F1-Score. Available online: https://scikit-learn.org/stable/modules/generated/sklearn.metrics.f1_score.html (accessed on 11 July 2020).
40. Kashef, R.; Kamel, M.S. Towards better outliers detection for gene expression datasets. In Proceedings of the 2008 International Conference on Biocomputation, Bioinformatics, and Biomedical Technologies, Bucharest, Romania, 29 June–5 July 2008.

Publisher's Note: MDPI stays neutral with regard to jurisdictional claims in published maps and institutional affiliations.

children

MDPI

Article

Using Stakeholder Involvement, Expert Knowledge and Naturalistic Implementation to Co-Design a Complex Intervention to Support Children's Inclusion and Participation in Schools: The CIRCLE Framework

Donald Maciver [1,*], Cathleen Hunter [1], Lorna Johnston [1,2] and Kirsty Forsyth [1]

[1] School of Health Sciences, Queen Margaret University, Edinburgh EH21 6UU, UK; chunter@qmu.ac.uk (C.H.); LJohnston2@qmu.ac.uk (L.J.); kforsyth@qmu.ac.uk (K.F.)

[2] Additional Support for Learning Service, Communities and Families, City of Edinburgh Council, Edinburgh EH8 8BG, UK

* Correspondence: dmaciver@qmu.ac.uk

Abstract: Whist inclusion is recommended for most children most of the time it remains difficult to implement. In this paper, we present the process undertaken to review and redesign a pre-existing complex intervention (The CIRCLE Framework) which was designed to enhance teachers confidence and competence in provision of universal first level supports for 5–12 year old children with additional support needs. The approach presented draws on the Medical Research Council guidance for the development of complex interventions. A series of ten co-design workshops with 70 stakeholders was completed, applying interactive and participatory methods. Analysing outputs of each workshop revealed recurring design ideas that became the main aspects of the new framework and associated manuals. Intervention content, theoretical frameworks, manuals to support use in practice and implementation strategies were developed. On completion, the updated intervention was extended up to 18 years of age and redistributed to all teachers in the participating local authority. We present the main conclusions and interpretations around the design and naturalistic implementation of the framework, and reflections on use in practice, including a detailed list of recommendations for implementation across schools and staff.

Keywords: inclusive education; complex interventions development; teachers; health professionals; qualitative; co-production; co-design

Citation: Maciver, D.; Hunter, C.; Johnston, L.; Forsyth, K. Using Stakeholder Involvement, Expert Knowledge and Naturalistic Implementation to Co-Design a Complex Intervention to Support Children's Inclusion and Participation in Schools: The CIRCLE Framework. *Children* **2021**, *8*, 217. https://doi.org/10.3390/children8030217

Academic Editor: Sari A. Acra

Received: 10 December 2020
Accepted: 9 March 2021
Published: 11 March 2021

1. Introduction

Increasingly, children with additional support needs are educated alongside peers in inclusive schools [1–5]. There are numerous studies and theoretical perspectives associated with what makes an effective inclusive school [6] Core principles that should underpin comprehensive school reform to facilitate inclusion are widely accessible. However, teachers still have difficulty operationalising these concepts, and including learners with additional needs. There are issues with attitudes to inclusion and disability [7], understanding of specific needs, for example autism and other neurodevelopmental disorders [8], and level of knowledge of staff [9], leading to ongoing calls for more training, support, and resources [10]. Attempting to reduce unequal outcomes for all children is the primary goal [11]. Within this context, we developed a novel intervention to improve the confidence and competence of teachers around inclusion and participation in the school setting [12]. This paper presents an analysis of the steps taken to improve and extend this intervention.

Modern methods of intervention development, for example the Medical Research Council complex interventions development framework [13], are systematic and theory-driven approaches to developing novel interventions. Developing the evidence base for new interventions may include a range of methods. Taking an approach based on quantitative statistical techniques, such as meta-analysis or controlled trial, whilst desirable, is not possible when robust quantitative data does not exist for the intervention or population [14]. Qualitative research is a useful alternative [15,16]. Qualitative methodologies can be used to develop new understanding about how to deliver interventions, mechanisms and outcomes of interventions, and key features of interventions believed to be important [17]. Extensive stakeholder involvement is of fundamental importance, helping to identify priorities, understand problems and find solutions that will work in the real world, ensuring that interventions are realistic and effective for their context [18].

This paper presents an intervention development process, drawing on techniques of qualitative research and stakeholder involvement. The process covers the review and redevelopment of the CIRCLE Framework, an intervention that was designed to support teachers to be inclusive practitioners and to work effectively with children with additional support needs in schools.

1.1. Background and Context

In Scotland, where this research was carried out, "additional support needs" is the term used to describe children who require support over and above that which is typically required. Direct comparison across countries are complicated by differing systems and definitions, however, analogous terms internationally are Special Educational Needs (SEN) and/or Special Educational Needs and Disabilities (SEND). In line with international trends, numbers of children with additional support needs in the school system have been rising significantly in Scotland. In 2012, 16.9% of 5–12 year old children (62,572 children) were recorded as having one or more additional support need, rising to 27% in 2019 (107,635 children) [19]. For secondary schools (12–18 year old learners), 16.5% of learners were recorded as having one or more additional support need in 2012 (48,486 learners) compared to 35% in 2019 (101,130 learners) [19]. Additional support needs are commonly identified for autistic children, children with social and emotional needs, children with learning difficulties and children with speech or language disorders [19] [for more information, including a breakdown of neurodevelopmental disorders, see Supplemental Materials A1–A4]. Segregated specialist schools are available, but this is for a very small minority. In 2019 there were 7132 children registered for special education in Scotland (across primary and secondary education) [19]. Therefore, it is clear that the focus on inclusion has led to the majority of children being educated in general education, leading to a subsequent interest in tools and methods to improve inclusion for this group [20].

Placement is no longer the key determinant, i.e., special vs. other schools [21]. From a rights-based perspective, inclusion is an ethical priority [22]. Contemporary practice focusses on ensuring children's participation and inclusion through changes to the school, with particular emphasis on staff behaviours, environments, routines and structures. Most commentators broadly support the case for inclusion, indicating that there is a strong argument, and some empirical evidence, that inclusive educational settings confer benefits [23,24]. However, the strength of the evidence is variable [25] and hampered by lack of clear definitions and theoretical frameworks [26]. A recent review has identified that the field has a large preponderance of theory and policy; however, research that actually develops, applies, and adds evidence on how support should be provided is less common [27]. A key issue is an overt focus on individual conditions leading to a "program for every problem" [28]. An overabundance of programs makes getting it right for children with additional needs difficult. There are also rights-based issues around making sure children are not reduced to their limitations [21]. Research indicates that teachers often require new skills and knowledge to work with diverse learners, leading to recommendations that additional training around inclusive education is necessary within initial teacher training and continuing professional development [29].

Considering the above, a cross-discipline partnership was developed between education staff, health professionals and academics to address these issues. The title of the partnership was the Child Inclusion: Research into the Curriculum, Learning and Education (CIRCLE) Collaboration. This group undertook the development of the CIRCLE framework [12]. This framework was in response to a requirement for a classroom teacher focussed intervention for use in mainstream schools to improve teachers' practices.

1.2. Initial CIRCLE Development and Evaluation

The first version of the CIRCLE framework was developed using a literature review and a 2-year period of qualitative research [12]. The qualitative studies involved in-depth interviews and observation of professionals from education (working in mainstream and specialist settings), health staff and parents/carers of children aged 5–12 years [12]. The CIRCLE development team included Head (Principle) Teachers, Educational Psychologists, a range of specialists in inclusive practice and additional support for learning, and senior paediatric specialists from occupational therapy, speech and language therapy, and physiotherapy, in addition to academics and clinical researchers. The development team helped to synthesise key practices identified from analysis of the preceding research. Through a cyclical process of review and refinement, this led to the development of the CIRCLE framework and a manual that was considered reflective of best practice.

The CIRCLE framework and associated manual were designed to provide a universal first level framework for teachers and other related staff. Reflecting the social model of disability, the CIRCLE framework emphasises embracing difference and the importance of considering and adapting environmental factors. As such, the framework and manual include strategies based on this set of ideas to support adaptations to structures and routines, modifications to the physical environment and teacher approaches for individual children. A key underpinning concept is the premise that supporting children of all abilities is not the remit of specialists, but the duty of everybody; and that all teachers within the school can and should provide support for all children.

Initial research found that the CIRCLE framework was received well [12]. Teachers and other school staff reported it was a useful resource [12]. Teachers reported that the framework and associated manual were feasible and acceptable, and supported them to be systematic in their approach to meeting the needs of children with additional needs [12]. Users reported that the framework and manual were useful in supporting joint working by providing a common language for collaboration [12]. Following the initial research, CIRCLE was disseminated across the local education authority, which was an urbanised area encompassing c85 primary schools, c1400 teachers, c30,000 primary aged children.

In view of its perceived utility, the local authority commissioned further development of the CIRCLE framework and expanded the remit to include support for older children (12–18 years). This process is covered in this paper.

2. Materials and Methods

2.1. Ethical Approval

Ethical approval was provided by University Research Ethics committee (Queen Margaret University "CIRCLE Project" 01052013) and permission to work with teachers and schools was granted by the Local Authority Research Access Service. Written informed consent was obtained from workshop participants and anyone who provided qualitative data. All participants were volunteers and given the opportunity to withdraw at any time without giving a reason.

2.2. Process in Development of the Updated CIRCLE Framework

Following the Medical Research Council complex interventions development framework [13] several steps were completed, encompassing co-design workshops, stakeholder involvement, theory development, and naturalistic implementation. See Figure 1. This paper presents each of these stages in turn, covering methods and outputs sequentially.

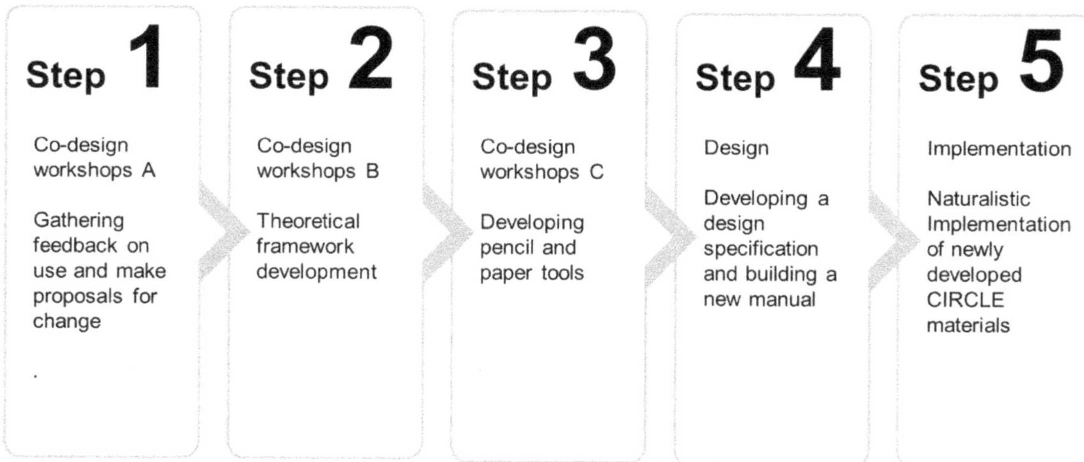

Figure 1. Process for development of CIRCLE framework.

3. Results

3.1. Co-Design Workshops A: Initial Review and Feedback

3.1.1. Procedure and Analysis

The next iteration of the CIRCLE framework was targeted at 5–12 and 12–18 year age ranges. A qualitative study including 125 teachers and other staff, focussing on best practices for use with older children with additional needs, was completed. Details of which are published elsewhere [30]. This study provided the detail for interventions, supports and strategies that would underpin development for older learners' content.

Next, a series of ten co-design workshops applying interactive and participatory methods [31,32] were completed over a 2-year period. Seventy stakeholders participated. Participants in the workshops included the research team, specialist additional support for learning teachers, classroom teachers, specialist therapists, managers of education and health services, psychologists, medical doctors, and parents/carers. The research team included combined expertise in complex intervention development, education, rehabilitation, autism, occupational therapy, physiotherapy, and speech and language therapy.

A core group of stakeholders attended most of the workshops and acted as an Advisory Group with additional responsibilities for consultation, review and leadership. This core group comprised a senior local authority education manager, a senior additional support for learning manager, a senior educational psychologist, senior members of the additional support for learning service, a head teacher, class teachers and senior therapists from speech and language therapy and occupational therapy.

In the workshops, which included open discussion, small group work and brainstorming, participants were presented with updates and ideas for development of the CIRCLE resources. Facilitators led the workshops, and recorded notes. The aim of the workshops was to review the existing CIRCLE manual, gather feedback on current use, determine the validity of development ideas and develop new ideas. Detailed notes capturing each group's discussion, how the participants tackled each activity, and feedback on the intervention ideas were produced and analysed. The analytic procedure drew on qualitative approaches of thematic and framework analysis involving familiarisation, identification of a thematic framework, coding of the data according to the framework, charting the themes, and mapping and interpreting the data [33–36]. To safeguard trustworthiness and transparency, peer checking was undertaken with colleagues about emergent ideas. The facilitators prepared detailed presentations to reflect group discussions. These presentations were given to the next workshop in the sequence. In this way, the analysis and outputs from each workshop were verified and built upon at the next workshop in sequence, leading to the design ideas (i.e., broad goals for the CIRCLE update) which became the new aspects of the framework and associated materials.

3.1.2. Outputs

Overall utility of CIRCLE. Feedback from participants in the early workshops emphasised that the utility of CIRCLE was perceived to be high, indicating that the existing materials had a positive impact on staff and children in terms of improving the practices of teachers. Use of the resources were perceived to increase understanding of children's needs and related supports. As a reference point for busy teachers, the current manuals were perceived as easy to use, clearly laid out, comprehensive and comprehensible. School leaders and experienced teachers reported that CIRCLE was a useful part of the strategy to increase the amount of support provided directly by teachers in schools, and to effectively deal with issues in schools via school pathways (prior to requiring external support). It was reported that using the resource had helped staff to shift towards meeting the needs of all children along the lines of a more inclusive classroom, rather than a "pull out" or "expert" model. CIRCLE resources were perceived to raise awareness of the inclusion "agenda."

Uses in practice. As well as use by classroom teachers, specialist staff had been using the resource to share information between colleagues (e.g., at times of transition), or between the teacher and the additional support for learning services, or for meetings. The CIRCLE manual had been used as a resource by teachers to photocopy and tick strategies to try with individual pupils. The resources were also perceived to give teachers ideas as to what to do next, help to guide staff through the referral process for extra support, and in some cases prevent unnecessary referrals. It was also reported that there was a function for clear and transparent documentation about which strategies had been used in school.

Requirement for pencil and paper tools and other issues. Participants reported that they were frustrated that there was no formal method presented in the manuals to record information on children's progress, and no formal way to communicate information using the existing CIRCLE framework. How to use the manuals to facilitate recording of information, and the associated tools required for this, was a key area of discussion. Participants reported that it would be helpful if the manual contained specific checklists and other pages, which could be photocopied and shared between teachers and related services personnel. Concerns around duplication of content across the resource were also reported. Descriptions and acronyms used in the resource were felt to be confusing, and some of the sections (particularly the inclusive classroom section) was perceived to be too short and lacking in content. Additionally navigation of the main document was described as problematic, and there were reported difficulties in finding the relevant sections to support a specific child.

Theoretical aspects. Presentation of a more coherent theoretical framework was requested. It was considered necessary to move the focus away from the child's perceived deficits towards wider aspects of inclusion. It was felt that there should be more content related to inclusive environments. The overall presentation of strategies was to be reviewed, particularly to highlight the importance of environmental adaptations. The participants in the early workshops unanimously agreed the documents should be carefully written to reduce emphasis on child deficits. Throughout, it was felt terms should be replaced by positive headings wherever possible. Although the resources were largely felt to be clear, it was requested that a systematic process should be developed to facilitate use of the materials.

3.2. Co-Design Workshops B: Theoretical Framework

3.2.1. Procedure and Analysis

The Medical Research Council guidance on development of complex interventions includes conceptual framework development as a necessary step [13]. The main ideas considered in the development of the CIRCLE framework focussed on person-environment interactions [37] and models of participation [38]. The primary theoretical framework used was the Model of Human Occupation (MOHO) [39]. The MOHO is a rehabilitation model that aims to enhance people's participation, and includes concepts related to how people engage in everyday life focusing on values, attitudes, habits, routines, skills and the environment [39]. The relevance of the MOHO to understanding psychosocial and environmental factors in community, home and school situations for children is well-established [40–44]. The MOHO uses a holistic understanding of people, their daily life activities, interests and needs, and relationship with their environment to develop interventions [39]. People are conceptualised as being participation driven, with satisfactory engagement in personally and socially valued activities and roles seen as the fundamental outcome of interventions [39]. MOHO theory encourages interventions at multiple levels, and provides a structure for assessment and application of supports and strategies. It was agreed, due to its known utility for understanding the needs of children, and person-environment approach, to use the MOHO to guide the development of the CIRCLE framework. Using this model as the broad basis for CIRCLE meant several aspects had to be considered in tandem. The MOHO examines personal (i.e., motivation, habits and skills) and environmental (e.g., physical and social environment) influences [39]. This means understanding that "impairment" and "disability" are not person focussed, but linked to, and oftentimes driven by the environment. Adopting such a model is in response to critique around the labelling issues, stigma and disadvantage associated with a deficit or "medical" model approach [45]. A model that focuses on participation provides a beneficial alternative structure, meeting calls for a "social" or "biopsychosocial" approach [38,39].

Using MOHO theory as a guiding structure, common themes and features that related to the core intervention concepts were developed, discussed, modified, debated and eventually ratified in the co-design workshops. Across workshops, the focus was towards developing a framework that could be used to organise and present important ideas to the users, and how to "translate" MOHO concepts, some of which were unfamiliar to teachers, into a useable format and language. To our knowledge, this was the first application of these ideas for teachers. Using the above review, discussion and analysis led to the development of a new CIRCLE theoretical framework.

3.2.2. Outputs

The updated CIRCLE Framework, which encompasses a streamlined and education focussed application of MOHO concepts, presents children's inclusion and participation in terms of four main areas (see Figure 2 and Table 1):

1. The environment (physical and social),
2. Structures and routines
3. Motivation
4. Skills

We presented the framework as a jigsaw puzzle to highlight the interconnectedness of the component parts. Workshop participants had perceived that there was a tendency by some teachers and others to focus on a child's physical, sensory or behavioural deficits. They agreed that it was important to shift focus towards different areas (including environment and attitudes) rather than on deficits. Within this framework, it was important to stress some key ideas. Firstly, that participation and inclusion are a function of the child and environment together [38,39] with particular reference to the social model of disability [22]. We also took from MOHO the idea that people and environments are a complex dynamic system, and that children's needs are best understood within a framework that considers motivation, structures and routines, and skills together. A key aspect identified was that the support for children should continue to take place in typical classrooms—and that this was the main and best place for most children. A key focus was therefore the environment. The idea of "environment first" was consistently highlighted as important by the workshop participants. Therefore, environmental adaptation and review of the environment should be the first step. Rather than thinking about what a learner can and cannot do, or only thinking about their underlying ability, the framework encourages teachers to think more widely, particularly paying attention to the disabling aspects of the environment. Using MOHO theory, the environment is understood to contain physical and social components, each of which requires attention [39].

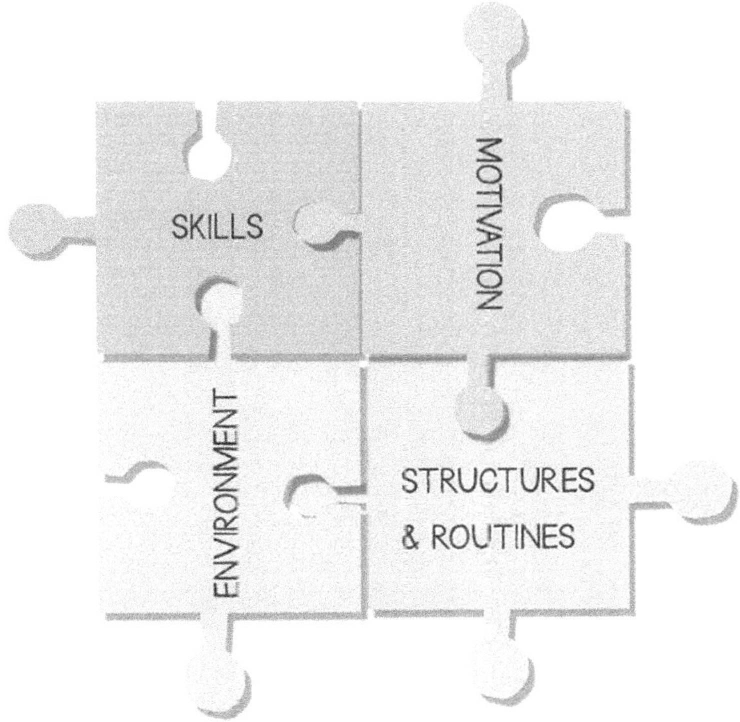

Figure 2. Updated CIRCLE framework. Reproduced from CIRCLE manuals [46,47].

Structures and routines were also included as an explicit aspect of the model [39]. Routines (i.e., daily structures of the school) support children to be able to anticipate transitions and required actions. Order and consistency are clearly helpful for children, and for some, school is the place where this is most apparent and helpful. For example, children may benefit from strategies including explicit structuring of the day/week or provision of visual supports (i.e., visual timetables) to help them follow routines or understand what comes next.

Motivation was included as an explicit aspect of the model, again drawing on MOHO theory. This focused across three overarching themes: "interests," "values," and "abilities." Children's "interests" is related to motivation and activities that are engrossing, enjoyable or satisfying to them. Supportive practices include utilising learners' own specific ideas, hobbies, or cultural background, and ensuring individualisation and options. "Values" refers to what children find important and meaningful to them. Supportive practices include listening to and valuing children's views, jointly setting goals, and self-assessment. Lastly, "abilities" refers to how children perceive themselves in terms of their ability and capacity. Supportive practices associated with this idea include differentiating work, setting achievable goals whilst ensuring challenge, giving positive feedback, and affirming interests, languages and cultures.

Table 1. Overview of CIRCLE framework components *.

Framework Component	Description
Physical environment	The physical environment refers to the physical layout of the classroom and the resources used within it.
Social environment	The social environment is concerned with the attitudes, expectations and actions of those within the class and how these can affect children either positively or negatively.
Structures and routines	Structures and routines are events that happen in the same way with regularity. The start, middle and end of the routine becomes predictable through repetition.
Motivation	Motivation gives children incentive, enthusiasm and interest when engaging with activities and the people around them. Children are motivated by their own feelings, desires, self-esteem and confidence.
Skills	Skills refer to a learner's skills in the key areas: attention and concentration; organisation and planning; posture and mobility; dexterity and manipulation; socialising, emotions and relationships; verbal and non-verbal communication.

* reproduced from CIRCLE manuals [46,47].

The presentation of supports and strategies was split into areas that were felt to be "neutral" labels (rather than condition specific or deficit focused). For younger learners these were: Attention and Concentration Skills; Organisational and Planning Skills; Posture and Mobility (Gross Motor) Skills; Dexterity and Manipulation (Fine Motor) Skills; Social, Emotional and Relationship Skills; and Verbal and Non-verbal Communication Skills. For older learners these were Attention and Concentration Skills; Organisation and Planning Skills; Motor Skills; Social, Emotional and Relationship Skills; Verbal and Non-Verbal Communication Skills. These categories and labels were agreed by the co-design workshop participants, who identified them as the main underlying areas of challenge experienced by children in schools. Each area was described and suggestions of strategies were developed using positive language, with culturally diverse examples. In line with the theoretical framework, throughout the manuals the strategies were split into "modifications to the learning environment" first, followed by "establishing structures and routines" second and "approaches to enhance motivation" third [for examples, see Supplementary Materials A5 and A6].

3.3. *Co-Design Workshops C: Developing Pencil and Paper Tools*

3.3.1. Procedure and Analysis

To reflect the conceptual framework, and at the request of the stakeholders in the co-design workshops, pencil and paper tools to support information gathering and information sharing were developed. Two tools were developed: the CIRCLE Participation Scale (CPS) and the CIRCLE Inclusive Classroom Scale (CICS). These tools were designed to form the assessment portion of the CIRCLE intervention, to facilitate teachers' engagement with the manual, and as a method for identifying where to target supports and strategies for children.

Workshop participants had indicated that teachers valued and tended to engage with tools that were quick and easy to use. They also reported that teachers were looking for tools that could be used to record input/change in order to support communication with colleagues, partner services and agencies, parents, and with the children themselves. Furthermore, a key output of the co-design workshops was to have tools that would shift teacher focus from children's impairments towards one where they considered environmental factors first. It was also important to develop easy to use tools that would support teachers to consider their role in the inclusion of children, rather than considering this a role devolved to specialists.

The CPS and CICS were developed as first level tools to be used sequentially (environment tool first, followed by the participation tool). They were designed to be concise and easy to use by all education and related services personnel irrespective of training or level. To develop these tools, factors considered to have a potential influence on children's participation were identified drawing on our previous research [12,30] and using the Model of Human Occupation (MOHO) [39] as a theoretical guide. To ensure content validity, face validity and utility, over the course of three meetings the co-design workshop Advisory Group reviewed and provided commentary. Items were identified for inclusion and exclusion at this point. In the next phase, a longstanding independent group (N = 9) of senior professionals was asked for further comment. This group included managers, educational psychologists and researchers. This group met four times. Based on these activities, pilot versions were designed. A pilot version of the CPS was field tested in three schools by teachers, who provided detailed feedback. Classroom teachers, head teachers and representatives from a parent organisation also provided feedback and commentary on the CICS. Comments helped the research team to clarify and revise the tools, including wording of items and instructions for use, before finalisation.

3.3.2. Outputs

Circle Inclusive Classroom Scale (CICS): The CICS is a pencil and paper rating tool which identifies environmental barriers/supports to inclusion and participation. The tool comprises 3 domains developed using MOHO theory: the physical environment, the social environment, and structures and routines within the environment. Sub-domains for consideration include children's participation in decision making, routines, appeal of activities, expectations, activity demands, empowerment, provision of information, relationships, support and facilitation, attitudes, availability of objects, visual supports, sensory space, and accessibility/adequacy of physical spaces. The CICS utilises a 4-point rating scale for all the items within each sub-domain. Using this scale, based on the judgement of the teacher completing the assessment, a "4" rating indicates a domain that strongly supports participation of learners, whereas a "1" rating indicates aspects that strongly interfere with participation of learners where improvement is required. As well as a rating sheet and recording format, the CICS also includes a set of reflective questions that help users when considering the quality of the classroom environment. Scoring is based on observation and a "walk through" of the classroom. The CICS can be completed by one individual, or by colleagues working together [see Supplementary Materials A7–A9 for examples of content].

CIRCLE Participation Scale (CPS): The aim of the CPS is to facilitate identification and measurement of factors impacting on children's participation in school. The CPS was designed for use in general classrooms by teachers and other related staff for children aged 5–18 years with additional support needs, including physical, developmental or learning needs. The CPS consists of 10 short sections that cover the environment, structures and routines, motivation, and skills. The item pool contains items assessing the potential determinants of school participation across these areas. Each section of the CPS contains five items, which are positively framed statements with a 4 point Likert scale in which teachers rate the frequency with which, in their opinion, each item is observed for a given child. A lower score on the CPS indicates presence of barriers or needs for the child in that area, and potential requirement for additional support from staff. Once the CPS is completed, it directs users to relevant sections of the CIRCLE resources containing supports and strategies for teachers to try with children [see Supplementary Materials A7–A9 for examples of content].

Feedback: Feedback received on the tools indicated they were functional and straightforward to use. Teachers highlighted the benefit of tools that could be used for a broad range of children that directed them towards appropriate supports and strategies within the CIRCLE manuals. Feedback indicated they were a useful way to consider provision of supports for children and a useful way to share information between colleagues, e.g., between teachers at times of transition, or between the teacher and the specialist team, or at meetings. Specialist staff reported that the tools could be useful in supporting communication between classroom teachers and specialist teachers. It was felt that the CPS and CICS encouraged teachers to look at areas of the child (e.g., motivation) or the environment (e.g., peer support) that they might not have initially considered and encouraged teachers to complete assessment of the child and the environment. Although feedback was mainly positive, a few teachers expressed concerns. These included anxieties around the time that it might take to complete the tools and anxieties around the replacement of more comprehensive or specialised (e.g., dyslexia) assessments. Others were concerned that some of the items related to the environment were outside their control. Several suggestions were made on how the tools could be used to support collaborative working.

3.4. Design Specification and Building a New Manual

3.4.1. Procedure and Analysis

This stage of the research developed the ideas and outputs from the previous manual and new research into new materials, principally new intervention manuals. Workshop participants were supportive of developing the manuals, as they stressed the usefulness of having useable, physical copies of the CIRCLE Framework (including the tools and supports/strategies) easily available in the classroom setting. To develop the new manuals a tendering process to identify a graphics design company was undertaken. The design brief and specification were included in the tender. Low-fidelity prototype documents were created in Microsoft publisher and sent to the contracted company. The research team worked with the contracted company using the following specification:

- Creative design of document elements (cover, tables, diagrams, lists, text styles, section navigation, glossary)
- To create a resource that is functional and easy to use
- To reduce reliance on text (e.g., design of diagrams) and improve use of colour
- To create a professional finish
- Improve readability

Following development of high-fidelity prototypes, a final co-design workshop took place in a university space, including several members of the target audience, i.e., teachers. Copies of the manuals were also sent to the Advisory Group and representatives from paediatric therapy services, head teachers, senior managers within the local authority, parents and experts in inclusive education, with feedback requested. Participants were provided with a draft copy of the manual and asked to "use" the manual with a child in mind with the aim of testing its usability and validity. Feedback, was recorded and transcribed. A list of required revisions was approved.

3.4.2. Outputs

A list of revisions was developed. Issues were identified including document structure and signposting to relevant initiatives nationally and locally. Issues were attended to, and comments were fed back to the design company and a final version of the younger (5–12 years) [46] and older children's (12–18 years) manual was published [47].

3.5. Naturalistic Implementation

3.5.1. Procedure and Analysis

The newly developed manuals were distributed within the local authority who commissioned the work from 2016/2017 onwards. Across primary (elementary) and secondary (senior) provision this included c85 primary schools (5–12 years), c20 secondary schools (12–18 years), and c3000 teachers.

The roll out of the resources was managed by a senior member of the Additional Support for Learning Service. To facilitate training, a senior educational psychologist also worked with colleagues to develop a training structure for teaching staff, focused on self-evaluation and using the various tools in the resources effectively. The training and implementation was fully led by the local authority. Designing the implementation in this way ensured that it was absorbed into naturally occurring practices. This aspect was designed to foster informal networks, to leverage existing organisational structures, to ensure that knowledge of the framework and ability to train and educate using the framework was distributed, and to have the change be led by insiders rather than external "experts." This ensured that the implementation was resilient and robust, and met the needs of the target community.

Once the manuals had been made available to schools, and training completed, we collected feedback from individuals representing a convenience sample of 10 schools (staff from 8 primary schools and 2 secondary schools), as well as from a group of 20 senior professionals including senior managers, head teachers, and senior additional support for learning teachers.

3.5.2. Outputs

Evaluation of implementation reach across the authority. After approximately 18 months, all schools had been trained and were in possession of CIRCLE manuals. Specialist additional support for learning staff had also received training and were given resources with agreement that they would train additional staff as required. One copy each of the relevant resource had been printed for all teachers in the local authority (primary, secondary and special). Additional arrangements for further training were that leadership and support for learning teachers could attended specialist training, and cascade this training as appropriate. All teaching staff were expected to have an awareness of the resource and use it in their practice. Use in formal local authority processes was instigated, including requests from schools for extra support for children, school self-evaluation and school policies for inclusion. CIRCLE implementation was therefore supported by senior management within the authority and through strategic planning, making CIRCLE a core tool for the authority that teachers were expected to engage with. Several schools reported using CIRCLE as part of formal processes, including writing individual education plans, referrals to specialist providers, and communication with parents. Some schools reported making the use of the CICS a feature of their school calendar, where teachers carried the assessment out at the start of a new school year, ensuring that all started the year engaged with the CIRCLE framework. However, implementation between schools was varied. Schools reported that implementation was more robust where training had been completed as a 'whole school' strategy, rather than led by individuals. Some schools reported that implementation was still in the early stages.

Feedback from users. The CIRCLE resources have been well received in terms of usefulness, structure and ease of use. CIRCLE was reported to be an effective first level universal intervention for new staff, as well as a guide for more experienced staff. Teachers reported that use of the manuals supported them to clearly articulate strategies that they may include as part of their routine practice. This encouraged teachers to focus on their own individual responsibility for pupils within their class and provided a framework for discussions with other teachers and colleagues. The resources were felt to support teachers and related services personnel to look at areas of the child and environment that they might not have initially considered—and encourage teachers to do "detective work" around the child and what could help that child. The parts of the resource most commonly used were the CIRCLE Inclusive Classroom Scale, the CIRCLE Participation Scale and the various Supports and Strategies pages. Most feedback about these sections was positive, but some teachers reported that the resource, whilst helpful, was long, and required time to read and understand.

A few teachers also reported that they found it challenging to complete the tools without discussion with others. Some secondary school teachers highlighted that they did not have their own specific teaching space, so that they perceived that they had little control over many aspects of the environment. Concern was also expressed that some teachers were reluctant to change some aspects of the environment to suit one or a small group of children if they thought that there was no benefit for the larger group. Additionally it was noted that the process, as recommended in the manual, would be difficult to complete at the start of a new session/school year, as the class would be new at that point, so that the teacher would not know the children. Not unexpectedly, a few teachers reported concerns around the time taken to complete the tools possibly in addition to other assessments; however, others thought they could be completed in a timely manner.

4. Discussion

The development process described in this paper included qualitative research, stakeholder involvement and naturalistic implementation, to develop, refine and implement a complex intervention.

Principles underlying the CIRCLE intervention are that activities and interventions should be collaborative, preventative, high frequency, and based in the classroom. The thinking on this approach is that interventions should be embedded in daily lessons and routines, provided by classroom teachers as part of routine practice, rather than creating an isolated strategy or event, provided by "experts." High frequency refers to use in the daily routines of the class. Given the opportunity to provide this first level support in the natural environment of the classroom, this might reduce the need for specialist services (i.e., the CIRCLE intervention might be preventative). The CIRCLE intervention supports collaborative working with others as required, by providing a common framework and language to support communication and discussion with a range of education and health staff, parents and the child.

Within CIRCLE, the child's difficulties are not the primary concern and a combination of strategies, in particular those focusing on the environment, are required. Rather than thinking about what a learner can and cannot do, the CIRCLE Framework encourages teachers to consider what affects learner's inclusion and participation within the context of the environment, and to take responsibility for "delivering" inclusion within their classroom. Such approaches support professionals to embrace the complexity of the child's needs, create a "working hypothesis" about a child's situation and provide transparency of reasoning. They also support a consistency of service provision and provide a common language for communication and research.

It is likely that a key mechanism underpinning CIRCLE is focused discussions on inclusion. It is possible that other frameworks with similar aims, but developed with different content in different ways, might also achieve similar outcomes. Although this may be the case, it remains true that there is considerable debate in the field on the best methods of achieving inclusion-focused change [23–27]. A framework underpinning inclusion must be clear and unambiguous in order to support understanding, improve practices and influence policies. Within the CIRCLE framework, a key strength is the clarity and combination of components across child and environment.

With reference to other approaches, there are several other inclusion-focused frameworks [48–51]. However, these have tended to focus on measurement of whole school inclusive practice [49], theoretical principles [50], or require a whole system approach [51]. It is arguably the case that previous efforts to develop inclusion-focused frameworks have sometimes involved "ivory-tower" efforts failing to take account of stakeholder perspectives and real-world problems faced by schools. Our research suggests that what teachers require is a practical framework that is easy to understand, with supports and strategies for use in the classroom, which are applicable to the range of needs and abilities that are increasingly common in schools. Reflection on practice, a common language and a structure for communication and information sharing are also important. As noted, there is a very significant literature on ideas around inclusion. Along with the extensive range of different specialised interventions, this makes application for teachers, who have a general responsibility for an age-based cohort with varying support needs, difficult. The

CIRCLE framework is an intervention that any teacher can use. The framework has been designed with significant collaboration from stakeholders, including teachers and school leadership, with excellent ecological and face validity, and proven feasibility for use in the school context. This meets the need for a universal inclusion focused framework that can be applied in schools as a first level support.

Within the CIRCLE framework, the CICS and CPS pencil and paper measurement tools were developed to provide individual teachers, departments or schools a means of assessing the environment and children's participation, and of documenting and sharing this. The CICS was intended to allow the user to formally rate the classroom. Together with strategies oriented for developing an inclusive classroom, this was designed to encourage focus on the environmental aspects of inclusion. The CPS was considered the next step and intended to enable identification of a learner's strengths and also areas requiring development. It was designed to help identify which groups of supports and strategies to try by directing the user to further specific sections within the CIRCLE manual. It is a truism noted within any system, including education, that what is measured will become what is done. Therefore, the CPS and CICS provide an avenue for encouraging a beneficial focus on inclusion across child and environment.

A final issue of interest concerns the role of external specialists, who may be part of the multidisciplinary team involved with schoolchildren. Many countries have multidisciplinary and multiagency teams involved with diagnosis, assessment and intervention. A key challenge is engagement of these teams across services; particularly as inclusion and participation in school is increasingly accepted as an important component of a holistic health intervention [52]. Recent priority setting exercises for children with learning difficulties [53] and neurodisability [54] have emphasised the importance of schools and teachers in terms of training, identifying optimal learning environments and facilitating interagency collaboration. There is therefore inherent value in working with and considering the views of multiple professional groups. External professionals collaborating with teachers can support ecological assessment and intervention, as well as facilitating a focus on school participation within their own practice. CIRCLE could provide a framework and language to support discussions between external staff and education staff around implementation of first level supports for children.

4.1. Recommendations

Since the initial evaluation, the CIRCLE manuals continue to be used within schools in the local authority where the research was originally carried out. The CIRCLE manuals have also been adopted in other areas across Scotland. Feedback indicates positive influence in terms of practice, through improved teacher confidence and competence in delivering early interventions and first level supports. To support dissemination, all CIRCLE manuals are freely available online [55]. To accompany the materials, a detailed list of recommendations for implementation across different school levels and individual roles was developed (Table 2). A key emphasis of CIRCLE is that teachers take responsibility for inclusion, without overt focus on specific diagnoses or needs. However, it is known that children with a range of needs for example autistic children, have particular needs which require greater understanding and more focused interventions. Use of CIRCLE represents the first universal level of intervention that should be in place. This will support all children, as well as providing a basis for support of children with more specific needs. Such first level support comprises core information and key messages required by all staff. With this foundation in place, training in more specific evidence based approaches or ways of working is still recommended. Using CIRCLE will provide staff with a foundation on which to build their knowledge and skills around supporting children with additional needs in schools.

Table 2. Recommendations for implementation of CIRCLE across various levels of practice.

Group	Recommendations for Implementation
Classroom Teachers	1. Download the CIRCLE manual 2. Complete CIRCLE Inclusive Classroom Scale each term 3. Use CIRCLE assessment processes and CIRCLE supports and strategies with specific children 4. Use CIRCLE paperwork for communication and collaboration with colleagues in school 5. Know how and when to ask for support 6. Use photocopied CIRCLE pages ticked around what supports and strategies have already put in place at point of referral/request for support 7. Use CIRCLE assessments in collaborative working with parents and other partners
Specialist teachers, senior teachers, psychologists, health and therapy staff	1. Download the CIRCLE manual 2. Encourage teachers to download CIRCLE manual 3. Regularly encourage teachers to complete CIRCLE processes before seeking out support 4. Routinely ask for CIRCLE paperwork (e.g., printed sheet with ticked off supports, classroom assessment or child assessment) when working with teachers 5. Promote the 'Inclusive Classroom' as a core strategy in school 6. Regularly encourage teachers to take increased responsibility for inclusive practice and anticipatory supports 7. Use CIRCLE resources in communication and collaborative working with parents and partner services 8. Use CIRCLE in providing training to teachers on universal supports
School Leadership	1. Understand and promote CIRCLE across the school 2. Use CIRCLE as part of student teacher and new teacher induction 3. Encourage staff to download the CIRCLE manual 4. Provide funding to print manuals and materials for ease of use 5. Reference CIRCLE in school policy and school web-site 6. Use CIRCLE to provide professional learning for staff on universal supports 7. Promote CIRCLE as first step pf professional learning pathway for developing knowledge and skills 8. Use CIRCLE paperwork in school processes 9. Promote the 'Inclusive Classroom' as a core strategy in school 10. Use the CIRCLE Inclusive Classroom Scale in quality assurance and/or audit processes 11. Use CIRCLE paperwork to support referrals to partner services and other agencies 12. Use CIRCLE resources to support communication and collaborative working between school staff, parents and partner services
Area or local government	1. Published Policies and plans reference CIRCLE and encourage the use of CIRCLE materials 2. CIRCLE paperwork is used in relevant official processes (e.g., referrals for extra support) 3. Government or "official" web-site references CIRCLE 4. All relevant staff are aware of CIRCLE resources 5. Recommend CIRCLE as the first step of professional learning pathway for developing knowledge and skills 6. Ensure that professional learning refers to CIRCLE

4.2. Limitations

This paper focusses on the processes used to develop a complex intervention. The preliminary findings are positive as outlined, providing good data on adequacy of theoretical underpinnings and feasibility and acceptability of CIRCLE in a variety of real-world conditions. However, although there has been extensive stakeholder involvement, feedback represents a convenience sample, which may not have been representative of the views of all teachers in the authority. Additionally, it is beyond the scope of this paper to discuss investigation into the efficacy of the CIRCLE intervention in terms of outcomes for children and young people. Future study will be required to ascertain these wider outcomes.

5. Conclusions

Building application of inclusion-fostering theory and interventions into practice is fundamentally important. In this research, the Medical Research Council guidance on the development of complex interventions has been used to improve and implement a new intervention. The methods and processes undertaken mean that professionals, academics and experts with a wide range of backgrounds and expertise have been involved, including teachers, educational psychologists, a range of specialist teachers, and senior representatives from children's therapy services. The research provides a useful and novel example of developing a complex intervention in schools including co-design and stakeholder involvement.

Supplementary Materials: The following are available online at https://www.mdpi.com/2227-9067/8/3/217/s1, Supplementary Material A1 Pupils in primary mainstream schools, 2007–2019 Scotland. Supplementary Material A2 Pupils in secondary mainstream schools, 2007–2019, Scotland. Supplementary Material A3 Pupils in primary mainstream schools, 2012, 2017, 2019, Local Authority where CIRCLE was implemented. Supplementary Material A4 Pupils in secondary mainstream schools, 2012, 2017, 2019, Local Authority where CIRCLE was implemented. Supplementary Material A5 CIRCLE manual examples ages 12–18 year (4x pages). Supplementary Material A6 CIRCLE manual examples ages 5–12 years (4x pages). Supplementary Material A7 Domains, sub-domains and examples of from CIRCLE Inclusive Classroom Scale (CICS). Supplementary Material A8 Circle Inclusive Classroom Scale (CICS) reflective question examples. Supplementary Material A9 Overview of the CIRCLE Participation Scale (CPS).

Author Contributions: Conceptualization, D.M., C.H., L.J., and K.F.; methodology, D.M., C.H., L.J., and K.F.; software, D.M., C.H., L.J., and K.F.; validation, D.M., C.H., L.J., and K.F.; formal analysis, D.M., C.H., L.J., and K.F.; investigation, D.M., C.H., L.J., and K.F.; resources, D.M., C.H., L.J., and K.F.; data curation, D.M., C.H., L.J., and K.F.; writing—original draft preparation, D.M.; writing—review and editing, D.M., C.H., L.J., and K.F.; visualization, D.M., C.H., L.J., and K.F.; supervision, D.M., C.H., L.J., and K.F.; project administration, D.M., C.H., L.J., and K.F.; funding acquisition, K.F. and D.M. All authors have read and agreed to the published version of the manuscript.

Funding: This work was supported by the City of Edinburgh Council.

Institutional Review Board Statement: The study was conducted according to the guidelines of the Declaration of Helsinki, and approved by Institutional Review Board (Queen Margaret University "CIRCLE Project" 01062013).

Informed Consent Statement: Written informed consent was obtained from workshop participants and anyone who provided qualitative data. All participants were volunteers and given the opportunity to withdraw at any time without giving a reason.

Data Availability Statement: Please contact the corresponding author for study data. Data are not publically available due to confidentiality and ethical requirements. The Scottish Government Pupil Census Supplementary Statistics data are available online: https://www.gov.scot/publications/pupil-census-supplementary-statistics.

Acknowledgments: Thanks are due to the Head Teachers and staff from the participating schools. Thanks to the Additional Support for Learning Service, City of Edinburgh Council. Thanks to the parents and children who have supported the research. We are grateful for a final implementation support, which has been development of an online module based on CIRCLE that has been developed by a Scottish Government agency with responsibility for professional development in education (Education Scotland) [56].

Conflicts of Interest: The authors declare no conflict of interest. The funders had no role in the design of the study; in the collection, analyses, or interpretation of data; in the writing of the manuscript, or in the decision to publish the results.

References

1. Bitta, M.; Kariuki, S.M.; Abubakar, A.; Newton, C.R. Burden of neurodevelopmental disorders in low and middle-income countries: A systematic review and meta-analysis. *Wellcome Open Res.* **2017**, *2*, 121. [CrossRef]
2. Beckman, L.; Janson, S.; von Kobyletzki, L. Associations between neurodevelopmental disorders and factors related to school, health, and social interaction in schoolchildren: Results from a Swedish population-based survey. *Disabil Health* **2016**, *9*, 663–672. [CrossRef]
3. Bonati, M.; Cartabia, M.; Zanetti, M.; Reale, L.; Didoni, A.; Costantino, M.A.; Lombardy ADHD Group. Age level vs. grade level for the diagnosis of ADHD and neurodevelopmental disorders. *Eur. Child. Adolesc. Psychiatry* **2018**, *27*, 1171–1180. [CrossRef] [PubMed]
4. Zablotsky, B.; Black, L.I.; Maenner, M.J.; Schieve, L.A.; Danielson, M.L.; Bitsko, R.H.; Blumberg, S.J.; Kogan, M.D.; Boyle, C.A. Prevalence and trends of developmental disabilities among children in the United States: 2009–2017. *Pediatrics* **2019**, *144*, e20190811. [CrossRef] [PubMed]
5. Sokal, L.; Katz, J. Inclusive and Special Education in Canada and the United States. In *Oxford Research Encyclopedia of Education*; Oxford University Press: New York, NY, USA, 2020.
6. De Bruin, K. The impact of inclusive education reforms on students with disability: An international comparison. *Int. J. Incl. Educ.* **2019**, *23*, 811–826. [CrossRef]
7. Krischler, M.; Pit-ten Cate, I.M. Pre-and in-service teachers' attitudes toward students with learning difficulties and challenging behavior. *Front. Psychol.* **2019**, *25*, 327. [CrossRef] [PubMed]
8. Vincent, J.; Ralston, K. Trainee teachers' knowledge of autism: Implications for understanding and inclusive practice. *Oxf. Rev. Educ.* **2020**, *46*, 202–221. [CrossRef]
9. Attwood, S.; MacArthur, J.; Kearney, A. Beginner secondary teacher preparedness for inclusion. *Int. J. Incl. Educ.* **2019**, *23*, 1032–1048. [CrossRef]
10. Lewis, I.; Corcoran, S.L.; Juma, S.; Kaplan, I.; Little, D.; Pinnock, H. Time to stop polishing the brass on the Titanic: Moving beyond 'quick-and-dirty' teacher education for inclusion, towards sustainable theories of change. *Int. J. Incl. Educ.* **2019**, *23*, 722–739. [CrossRef]
11. Woodcock, S.; Moore, B. Inclusion and students with specific learning difficulties: The double-edged sword of stigma and teacher attributions. *Educ. Psychol.* **2018**, *15*, 1–20. [CrossRef]
12. Maciver, D.; Hunter, C.; Adamson, A.; Grayson, Z.; Forsyth, K.; McLeod, I. Development and Implementation of the CIRCLE Framework. *Intl. J. Disabil. Dev. Educ.* **2020**, *67*, 608–629. [CrossRef]
13. Craig, P.; Dieppe, P.; Macintyre, S.; Michie, S.; Nazareth, I.; Petticrew, M. Developing and evaluating complex interventions an introduction to the new Medical Research Council guidance. *Evid. Based Public Health Eff. Effic.* **2009**, *2010*, 185–202. [CrossRef]
14. Mays, N.; Pope, C.; Popay, J. Systematically reviewing qualitative and quantitative evidence to inform management and policy-making in the health field. *J. Health Serv. Res. Policy* **2005**, *10* (Suppl. 1), 6–20. [CrossRef] [PubMed]
15. Mannell, J.; Davis, K. Evaluating complex health interventions with randomized controlled trials: How do we improve the use of qualitative methods? *Qual. Health Res.* **2019**, *29*, 623–631. [CrossRef]
16. Wigginton, B.; Thomson, Z.O.; Sandler, C.X.; Reeves, M.M. Reflexive intervention development: Using qualitative research to inform the development of an intervention for women with metastatic breast cancer. *Qual. Health Res.* **2020**, *30*, 666–678. [CrossRef]
17. Lewin, S.; Glenton, C.; Oxman, A.D. Use of qualitative methods alongside randomised controlled trials of complex healthcare interventions: Methodological study. *BMJ* **2009**, *10*, b3496. [CrossRef]
18. O'Cathain, A.; Croot, L.; Duncan, E.; Rousseau, N.; Sworn, K.; Turner, K.M.; Yardley, L.; Hoddinott, P. Guidance on how to develop complex interventions to improve health and healthcare. *BMJ Open* **2019**, *9*, e029954. [CrossRef] [PubMed]
19. Scottish Government Pupil Census Supplementary Statistics 2007–2019. Available online: https://www.gov.scot/publications/pupil-census-supplementary-statistics/ (accessed on 15 October 2020).
20. Children and Families Directorate. Legal Act. Edinburgh. Available online: https://www.gov.scot/children-and-families/ (accessed on 25 November 2020).
21. Browne, M.; Millar, M. A rights-based conceptual framework for the social inclusion of children and young persons with an intellectual disability. *Disabil. Soc.* **2016**, *31*, 1064–1080. [CrossRef]
22. Oliver, M. The social model of disability: Thirty years on. *D isabil. Soc.* **2013**, *28*, 1024–1026. [CrossRef]
23. Hehir, T.; Grindal, T.; Freeman, B.; Lamoreau, R.; Borquaye, Y.; Burke, S. *A Summary of the Evidence on Inclusive Education*; Abt Associates: Boston, MA, USA, 2016.

24. Szumski, G.; Smogorzewska, J.; Karwowski, M. Academic achievement of students without special educational needs in inclusive classrooms: A meta-analysis. *Educ. Res. Rev.* **2017**, *1*, 33–54. [CrossRef]
25. Ruijs, N.M.; Peetsma, T.T. Effects of inclusion on students with and without special educational needs reviewed. *Educ. Res. Rev.* **2009**, *4*, 67–79. [CrossRef]
26. Florian, L. What counts as evidence of inclusive education? *Eur. J. Spec. Needs Educ.* **2014**, *29*, 286–294. [CrossRef]
27. Amor, A.M.; Hagiwara, M.; Shogren, K.A.; Thompson, J.R.; Verdugo, M.Á.; Burke, K.M.; Aguayo, V. International perspectives and trends in research on inclusive education: A systematic review. *Int. J. Incl. Educ.* **2019**, *23*, 1277–1295. [CrossRef]
28. Domitrovich, C.E.; Bradshaw, C.P.; Greenberg, M.T.; Embry, D.; Poduska, J.M.; Ialongo, N.S. Integrated models of school-based prevention: Logic and theory. *Psychol. Sch.* **2010**, *47*, 71–88. [CrossRef] [PubMed]
29. Crispel, O.; Kasperski, R. The impact of teacher training in special education on the implementation of inclusion in mainstream classrooms. *Int. J. Incl. Educ.* **2019**, *4*, 1–2. [CrossRef]
30. Maciver, D.; Hunter, C.; Adamson, A.; Grayson, Z.; Forsyth, K.; McLeod, I. Supporting successful inclusive practices for learners with disabilities in high schools: A multisite, mixed method collective case study. *Disabil. Rehabil.* **2018**, *40*, 1708–1717. [CrossRef]
31. Langley, J.; Wolstenholme, D.; Cooke, J. 'Collective making' as knowledge mobilisation: The contribution of participatory design in the co-creation of knowledge in healthcare. *BMC Health Serv. Res.* **2018**, *18*, 585. [CrossRef]
32. Gibson, A.; Welsman, J.; Britten, N. Evaluating patient and public involvement in health research: From theoretical model to practical workshop. *Health Expect.* **2017**, *20*, 826–835. [CrossRef]
33. Ritchie, J.; Spencer, L. Qualitative data analysis for applied policy research. In *The Qualitative Researcher's Companion*; Huberman, A.M., Miles, M.B., Eds.; Sage: Thousand Oaks, CA, USA, 2002; pp. 305–331.
34. Seale, C. *The Quality of Qualitative Research*; SAGE Publications: London, UK, 1999.
35. McGhee, G.; Marland, G.R.; Atkinson, J. Grounded theory research: Literature reviewing and reflexivity. *J. Adv. Nurs.* **2007**, *60*, 334–342. [CrossRef]
36. Stringer, E. *Action Research*, 3rd ed.; Sage: Los Angeles, CA, USA, 2007.
37. Bronfenbrenner, U. *The Ecology of Human Development*; Harvard University Press: Cambridge, MA, USA, 1979.
38. World Health Organization. *International Classification of Functioning, Disability, and Health: Children & Youth Version: ICF-CY*; World Health Organization: Geneva, Switzerland, 2007.
39. Kielhofner, G. *Model of Human Occupation: Theory and Application*, 4th ed.; Lippincott Williams & Wilkins: Philadelphia, PA, USA, 2008.
40. Crowe, M.; Maciver, D.; Rush, R.; Forsyth, K. Psychometric evaluation of the ACHIEVE assessment. *Front. Pediatr.* **2020**, *29*, 245. [CrossRef]
41. OBrien, J.; Hoffman, J.; Moreau, E. Measuring OT Intervention Outcomes Using the Short Child Occupational Profile (SCOPE). *Am. J. Occup. Ther.* **2019**, *73* (Suppl. 1). [CrossRef]
42. Bowyer, P.L.; Kramer, J.; Kielhofner, G.; Maziero-Barbosa, V.; Girolami, G. Measurement properties of the Short Child Occupational Profile (SCOPE). *Phys. Occup. Ther. Pediatr.* **2007**, *27*, 67–85. [CrossRef] [PubMed]
43. Yokoi, K.; Kurasawa, S.; Utsumi, M.; Miyai, N. Relationship between Child Occupational Self-Assessment and Quality of Life in Elementary School Children. *J. Occup. Ther. Sch. Early Interv.* **2020**, *13*, 7–18. [CrossRef]
44. Esmaili, S.K.; Mehraban, A.H.; Shafaroodi, N.; Yazdani, F.; Masoumi, T.; Zarei, M. Participation in Peer-Play Activities among Children with Specific Learning Disability: A Randomized Controlled Trial. *Am. J. Occup. Ther.* **2019**, *73*. [CrossRef]
45. Norwich, B. Conceptualizing special educational needs using a biopsychosocial model in England: The prospects and challenges of using the international classification of functioning framework. *Front. Educ.* **2016** *1*, 5. [CrossRef]
46. CIRCLE Collaboration. Inclusive Learning and Collaborative working—Primary School Resource (Ages 5–12) International Version. Available online: https://www.thirdspace.scot/circle/education-resources/ (accessed on 13 October 2020).
47. CIRCLE Collaboration. Inclusive Learning and Collaborative working—Secondary School Resource (Ages 12–18) International Version. Available online: https://www.thirdspace.scot/circle/education-resources (accessed on 13 October 2020).
48. Barrett, L.; Beaton, M.; Head, G.; McAuliffe, L.; Moscardini, L.; Spratt, J.; Sutherland, M. Developing inclusive practice in Scotland: The National Framework for Inclusion. *Pastor. Care Educ.* **2015**, *33*, 180–187. [CrossRef]
49. Booth, T.; Ainscow, M. *Index for Inclusion: Developing Learning and Participation in Schools*; Centre for Studies on Inclusive Education (CSIE): Bristol, UK, 2002.
50. EADSNE [European Agency for Development in Special Needs Education). *Profile of Inclusive Teachers*; EADSNE: Odense, Denmark, 2012.
51. Shogren, K.A.; McCart, A.B.; Lyon, K.J.; Sailor, W.S. All means all: Building knowledge for inclusive schoolwide transformation. *Res. Pract. Pers. Sev. Disabl.* **2015**, *40*, 173–191. [CrossRef]
52. Anaby, D.R.; Campbell, W.N.; Missiuna, C.; Shaw, S.R.; Bennett, S.; Khan, S.; Tremblay, S.; Kalubi-Lukusa, J.; Camden, C.; GOLDs (Group for Optimizing Leadership and Delivering Services). Recommended practices to organize and deliver school-based services for children with disabilities: A scoping review. *Child. Care Health Dev.* **2019**, *45*, 15–27. [CrossRef] [PubMed]
53. James Lind Alliance. Learning Difficulties (Scotland) Top 10. 2016. Available online: http://www.jla.nihr.ac.uk/top-10-priorities (accessed on 18 February 2021).

54. Morris, C.; Simkiss, D.; Busk, M.; Morris, M.; Allard, A.; Denness, J.; Janssens, A.; Stimson, A.; Coghill, J.; Robinson, K.; et al. Setting research priorities to improve the health of children and young people with neurodisability: A British Academy of Childhood Disability-James Lind Alliance Research Priority Setting Partnership. *BMJ Open* **2015**, *5*, e006233. [CrossRef]
55. CIRCLE Collaboration Website. Available online: https://www.thirdspace.scot/circle/ (accessed on 13 October 2020).
56. Education Scotland Online Learning Resources. Available online: https://education.gov.scot/improvement/learning-resources/inclusion-in-practice (accessed on 13 October 2020).

children

MDPI

Article

Application of Low-Intensity Modified Constraint-Induced Movement Therapy to Improve the Affected Upper Limb Functionality in Infantile Hemiplegia with Moderate Manual Ability: Case Series

Rocío Palomo-Carrión [1], Rita-Pilar Romero-Galisteo [2,*], Elena Pinero-Pinto [3,*], Purificación López-Muñoz [1], Helena Romay-Barrero [1] and Francisco García-Muro San José [4]

1 Department of Nursery, Physiotherapy and Occupational Therapy, Faculty of Physiotherapy, University of Castilla-La Mancha, 13001 Ciudad Real, Spain; rocio.palomo@uclm.es (R.P.-C.); purificacion.lopez@uclm.es (P.L.-M.); helena.romay@uclm.es (H.R.-B.)

2 Department of Physiotherapy, Faculty of Science Health, University of Málaga, 29016 Málaga, Spain

3 Department of Physical Therapy, Faculty of Nursery, Physiotherapy and Podiatry, University of Seville, 41004 Sevilla, Spain

4 Department of Physiotherapy, Faculty of Medicine, University San Pablo-CEU, 28003 Madrid, Spain; fgarciamuro@ceu.es

* Correspondence: rpromero@uma.es (R.-P.R.-G.); epinero@us.es (E.P.-P.); Tel.: +34-95-1952862 (R.-P.R.-G.)

Received: 15 July 2020; Accepted: 2 September 2020; Published: 4 September 2020

Abstract: Objective: To assess the functionality of the affected upper limb in children diagnosed with hemiplegia aged between 4 and 8 years after applying low-intensity modified Constraint-Induced Movement Therapy (mCIMT). Methods: Prospective case series study. A mCIMT protocol was applied for five weeks, with two hours of containment per day. The study variables were quality of movement of the upper limb, spontaneous use, participation of the affected upper limb in activities of daily living, dynamic joint position, grasp–release action, grasp strength, supination and extension elbow movements. Four measurements were performed, using the quality of upper extremity test (QUEST) scale, the Shriners Hospital for Children Upper Extremity Evaluation (SHUEE) Evaluation, a hand dynamometer and a goniometer. Results: The sample was composed of eight children with moderate manual ability. Statistically significant differences were detected in all the studied variables ($p < 0.05$) between the pre-treatment and post–treatment results (Week 0–Week 5), except for upper limb dressing, putting on splints and buttoning up. In the first week, the changes were statistically significant, except for protective extension, grasp strength, grasp–release and all functional variables (level of functionality and participation of the patient's upper limbs) in the SHUEE Evaluation ($p > 0.05$). The greatest increase occurred in spontaneous use from Assessment 1 to Assessment 4 ($p = 0.01$), reaching 88.87% active participation in bimanual tasks. The quality of movement of the upper limb exhibited a significant value due to the increase in dissociated movements and grasp ($p = 0.01$). Conclusion: A low dose (50 h) of mCIMT increased the functionality of children diagnosed with congenital hemiplegia between 4 and 8 years of age with moderate manual ability.

Keywords: family; infantile hemiplegia; modified Constraint-Induced Movement Therapy; physical therapy modalities; upper extremity

1. Introduction

Infantile hemiplegia is a subtype of infantile cerebral palsy, characterized by the affectation of one of the hemibodies as a consequence of brain injury. Its prevalence is 1 case per 1300 live births [1].

There is more affectation of the upper limb than the lower limb due to the alteration of the corticospinal tract. The affected hand has a deficit in proprioception and tactile perception, which hinders fine motor skills, generally those of the fingers and the strength exerted by them [2]. Sensory abnormalities, weak grasp and loss of manual ability (fine movements) may appear, specifically in the fingers, with slower movements, poorer coordination and longer phases associated with mirror movements. This leads to a decrease in the use of the affected hand and often interferes with the manual ability of the healthy upper limb [3].

From early childhood, children with hemiplegia, even the least affected, use their healthy hand as the dominant hand in all tasks. Therefore, they learn "not to use" their affected upper limb, which is known as developmental disregard [4]. This "non-use" of the affected upper limb produces an increase in muscle tone in the affected segment, poor motor control, decreased active and passive range of motion, generalized weakness and delayed musculoskeletal maturation. The non-use affectation is caused by neural dysfunction as a result of brain injury. This neuronal alteration [5] can be improved through the activation of certain brain areas that remained inactive after the brain lesion and also through experience and learning (trial–error).

Thus, in order to improve the affected upper limb "non-use", Constraint-Induced Movement Therapy (CIMT) is used [6,7], which consists of constraining the healthy upper limb with a whole or partial containment (glove), thus promoting the use of the affected upper limb in activities of daily living. The programmed tasks integrate the repetition of the motor action with a variety of exercises. The use of CIMT has spread in recent years among physiotherapists and occupational therapists, due to the large number of studies that support the effectiveness of this intervention compared to traditional interventions that do not restrict the use of the healthy side [8]. However, in its original conception, two premises had to be met: the restriction of the less-affected upper limb and the application of an intensive treatment applied in a structured way to the upper limbs [9]. Different variants of CIMT have emerged over the years, under the term "modified Constraint-Induced Movement Therapy" (mCIMT). Likewise, there are a variety of protocols used for CIMT, in which different containment systems are proposed [10–15] in which it is the dose that varies [6,12,14,16–27]. In this line, one of the modifications widely used in pediatrics is the one based on mCIMT, which constrains the healthy upper limb for less than 3 h [23,28–30]. McConnell et al. [31] found that a less intensive treatment (63 h of treatment over 21 days) produced similar benefits compared to a more intensive approach (126 h of treatment over 21 days). Functional gains may be feasible for some children with a less intense program adjusted to 20 h of therapy in more than two consecutive weeks [31]. According to Schweighofer et al. [32], the existence of a "functional threshold" would be necessary for the maintenance of functionality after therapy, below which the use of the upper limb decreases while the benefits to the individual remain above such threshold. It would be useful to determine the specific doses of therapy in each patient.

McConnell et al. [31] applied mCIMT for 2 weeks with two hours of dose per day in a clinical setting, designed for children aged 8–15 years, and the therapist increased the dose to continue with the use of the affected upper limb for 30 min at home. The children executed 20 h of total dose with functional changes. We proposed to apply 50 h of total dose, with the same distribution per day according to this study, although increasing the dose by 30 h, since the participants in our study were younger than those in McConnell et al. [31] and the therapy was performed at home, thus the children and their families needed more time to obtain significant results. Thus, we decided to assess the children at Week 2 of treatment (20 h) in order to verify whether the changes would be the same at Week 5 (after treatment with a total dose of 50 h). The systematic review [33] included 31 papers, each of which applied different doses per day, total doses, measurement tools, etc. All 31 studies were compared, with the main difficulty being that the children had different manual ability levels, and it would be ideal to know the correct dose for each level. In this systematic review, the manual ability levels were assessed with the Manual Classification System, MACS; some studies show Levels I–III, I–IV or I–V [34]. We could consider a moderate hand ability level for children classified as Level I–II in MACS. These levels reflect that the children are independent in the execution of activities using one or two hands or including compensation strategies (neck, trunk, mouth, etc.) to complete the bimanual task; they also show that the movement restrictions do not impede the complete use of the affected upper limb.

However, most of the published studies include functional activities in their treatment proposals. To our knowledge, a few of them contemplate an ecological vision of human development as initially proposed by Bronfenbrenner [35]. According to this perspective, it is crucial to incorporate the principles of therapy to the environment in which the child develops, which is essential to ensure the long-term persistence of the achieved results [36]. From the ecological point of view, the evolution of the child is understood as a process of progressive differentiation of the activities that he/she carries out, his/her role and his/her interactions with the environment. The interactions and transactions established between the child and the elements of his/her environment are very important, especially with his/her parents.

One of the latest reviews on the use of CIMT [8] showed that the risk of bias of the analyzed clinical trials was between moderate and high; therefore, a new randomized controlled trial is proposed in this work, whose main objective was to analyze the effectiveness of the use of CIMT by modifying the applied dose. Moreover, the ecological perspective of development was considered, introducing functional tasks that children usually carry out in their usual environment. To our knowledge, no study has been published in Spain that combines a low dose of treatment with the performance of functional activities at home with the parents. For this reason, we consider assessing the functionality of the affected upper limb in children diagnosed with congenital hemiplegia with moderate manual ability between 4 and 8 years of age after applying low-intensity modified constraint-induced movement therapy (50 h) at home

2. Materials and Methods

This is a case series, prospective and longitudinal study with non-probability sampling (clinical.gov NCT02178371). The study was approved (060-13) by the ethics committee of the CEU-San Pablo University of Madrid in accordance with the Declaration of Helsinki of the World Medical Association. Before initiating the study, an informed consent form was given to the children's families to participate, which guaranteed the right to withdraw from the study at any time, if required by the participants.

The inclusion criteria were a medical diagnosis of left/right congenital infantile hemiplegia, age between 4 and 8 years, lack of activity of the affected upper limb, ability to exceed 10° extension in the metacarpophalangeal and interphalangeal joint, ability to complete a 20° extension of the wrist of the affected upper limb, adequate cognitive development to understand the verbal orders given for the execution of tasks and cooperation in their execution. In the same way, the exclusion criteria were visual problems that prevented the individual from carrying out the intervention, suffering from significant balance disturbances that put the child at risk of falling as a consequence of having the healthy upper limb contained, presenting uncontrolled epilepsy and having received botulinum toxin within 6 months prior to the intervention.

All the children were selected according to the inclusion criteria by their rehabilitation doctor of the "Virgen de la Salud" Hospital in Toledo for the execution of the therapy.

2.1. Intervention Method

The study was carried out over a period of 5 weeks of treatment, containing the healthy upper limb for 2 h per day [11,13] (not continuously) from Monday to Friday. McConnell et al. [31] and Al-Oraibi 2011 [21] used mCIMT for 2 h per day, obtaining positive results, and the children wore the hand containment for 96% of the total dose [13]. Thus, in our study, the children were requested to perform the structured activities for two non-consecutive hours, with the aim of increasing the adherence and avoiding great physical effort. The tasks were separated by at least 30 min of rest to allow the children to concentrate on the next activities, perform properly and stay motivated. The families were advised to set aside one hour in the early afternoon and another hour in the late afternoon to ensure that the child was attentive, frustration-free and effort-tolerant. The families were also instructed to run a full hour, repeating the activity and designing a story, in which the child was the protagonist and the activity was an enjoyable game to complete. Each of the proposed hours could be divided into periods of 30 min to improve the child's attention and motivation in case the child was tired during the treatment. We chose this minimum period of time, since it is the smallest dose of mCIMT used to treat babies aged 3 to 8 months with babyCIMT, in order to ensure sustained attention to activity [37]. This minimum dose of 30 min was used also in a systematic review [11]. When dealing with children from 4 to 8 years old, attention is greater and maintained for a longer time, which allows establishing a continuity of 1 h of intervention. The intervention was carried out by the family at home. Previously, an informative meeting was held with the parents, in which all the details of the study were explained to them and a program of unimanual activities was given to them to be executed with the affected upper limb every treatment week (Table 1). The activities were programmed to work different movements that were limited in the affected upper limb: shoulder flexion, elbow extension, forearm supination, wrist extension and grasp. Each activity was repeated for around 15 min to obtain a lesson about a functional strategy to use in their usual activities. Each intervention hour was completed with four activities (Table 1), which were repeated in the second hour to increase the movement learning and the possibility to modify and obtain new functional strategies to perform the activity. The same activities were performed every week (first and second hours from Monday to Friday) to improve the movement (shoulder flexion, forearm supination, elbow extension, wrist extension and grasp–release).

Table 1. Example of "modified Constraint-Induced Movement Therapy" (mCIMT) designed tasks.

Movements to Work in the Affected Upper Limb	Examples of mCIMT Designed Tasks
Shoulder flexion and elbow extension	• Put stickers at different heights on the wall and try to cover them with the affected hand. • Take a small and light ball and try to throw it higher towards a target. • The parents will put a cardboard or continuous paper stuck on the wall; using finger paint, the child will try to draw a picture or put his/her hand with paint on the paper. • The parents will throw balloons or bubbles, which the child will try to hit with his/her hand. • The parents will give the child a small and light ball, which he/she will try to throw higher and higher or towards a target.
Forearm supination	• Put stickers on the palm of the affected hand or forearm. • Fishing game. • The parents will place a light object on the palm of the affected hand (for example, a colored pompom) and the child will keep it for a while. • The child will use the affected hand to remove objects stuck on his/her t-shirt (at the level of the abdomen). • Playing the trumpet or other instruments ...
Wrist extension	• The parents will push cardboard boxes or other elements and the child will try to throw them off the table. • The child will smash packing paper, balls and/or soft objects with the palm of his/her hand. • The child must roll a ball, bottle. • The child must hit a piano or a drum placed vertically. • The child will remove pieces fallen from the wall.

Table 1. *Cont.*

Movements to Work in the Affected Upper Limb	Examples of mCIMT Designed Tasks
Grasp–release	• Grasp, hold and transfer light and long objects. • Grasp, hold and transfer heavy, long and rough objects. • Grasp, hold and transfer rough, light and spherical objects. • Grasp, hold and transfer rough, heavy and spherical objects. • Grasp, hold and transfer different objects with a variety of the previous characteristics.

The parents were instructed to correctly carry out the intervention avoiding possible errors during the treatment protocol. The weekly exercises, the containment technique and its correct use were also taught to them. The treatment was only initiated when the families and children were confident about it. The family and therapist met every week to assess the activities and make adjustments if necessary.

The containment applied was partial, such as a glove or a bandage [21]. In this way, manipulation with the healthy hand was prevented and the wrist and elbow joints were also free to allow the child to react effectively to an external disturbance (Figure 1).

Figure 1. Child with left hemiplegia wearing a bandage as a partial containment in the right hand (dominant hand). In this task, the child is working the grasp–release action.

Each week, the therapist and the parents of the participants had a meeting to follow-up the tasks and solve problems. The follow-up with the families was conducted online, reviewing all the activities and modifying those that were too difficult for the child, maintaining great therapist–family–child feedback. The activities were designed according to the limitations of the children and with simplicity in order for the latter to be able to perform them. In the follow-up, the activities that were not adequate were valued and changed for others considering the interest of the child.

The parents were asked to fill out a table with the performed tasks, completing these with photographs and videos of the tasks carried out daily and the execution time to complete 96% of total dose [13], in this case, 48 h (total dose: 50 h) (Figure 2).

WEEKLY FOLLOW-UP

mCIMT
Child number:
Weeks: 1-2-3-4-5

MONDAY	TUESDAY	WEDNESDAY	THURSDAY	FRIDAY
First hour (Activities)	First hour (Activities)	First hour (Activities)	First hour (Activities)	First hour (Activities)
Second hour (Activities)	Second hour (Activities)	Second hour (Activities)	Second hour (Activities)	Second hour (Activities)

Comments:

Figure 2. Weekly follow-up for the families.

2.2. Data Collection

Four assessments (Basal (T0, before therapy), T1 (Assessment 2, after Week 1 of therapy), T2 (Assessment 3, after Week 2 of therapy) and T3 (Assessment 4, after Week 5 of therapy)) were performed to measure the study variables and to compare the results before, during and after the intervention (Figure 3).

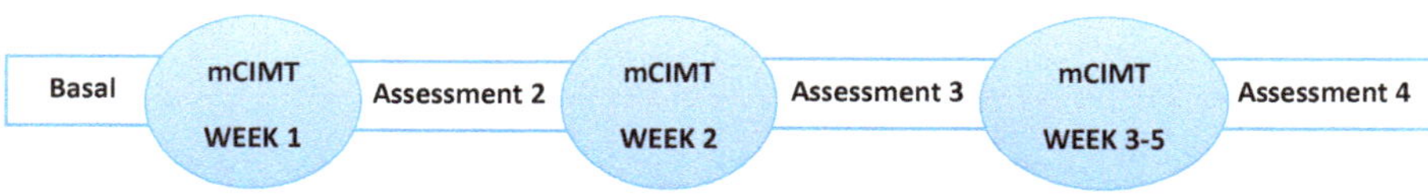

Figure 3. Representation of the assessment number in the 5 weeks of treatment (mCIMT).

2.2.1. Studied Variables and Measuring Instruments

Quality of Movement and Bimanual Dexterity of Both Upper Extremities

The quality of upper extremity test (QUEST) [38–40] was used, validated for children with neuromotor dysfunction with spasticity from 18 months to 8 years of age. It provides a numerical value that is obtained from the mean of the percentages in 36 items distributed in four categories: dissociated movements, grasp, weight bearing and protective extension of both extremities. It takes a value from 0 to 100 and can be expressed in percentages (%).

Active Extension of the Wrist and Active Supination of the Forearm in the Affected Upper Limb

Both variables were measured with an arm goniometer [41], making three measurements for each variable and selecting the best result. The measurements were made with the child sitting. Wrist extension was measured with elbow flexion, with the child leaning on a table to decrease muscle tension and associated reactions. Supination was measured with the forearm close to the body, avoiding trunk compensations to gain greater joint width.

Grasp Strength in the Affected Hand

This was measured using a hand dynamometer [18] with a scale between 0 and 150 that expressed grasp strength in PSI (pound per square inch, 1 psi = 0.0703 kg/cm^2). The test was performed with the child sitting on a chair in front of a table with the healthy hand under the table and the affected forearm resting on the table to give stability to the upper limb (Figure 4). The child was asked to press the dynamometer with the affected hand (global grasp) as hard as possible to obtain the best measurement.

Figure 4. Grasp strength measurement with a hand dynamometer.

Spontaneous Use, Dynamic Positioning of the Affected Upper Limb, Grasping and Releasing Action (Wrist Position in Neutral Flexion–Extension), and Level of Functionality and Integration of the Affected Upper Limb in Various Activities of Daily Living

The Shriners Hospital for Children Upper Extremity Evaluation (SHUEE) [40,42] was used to obtain the values in the four measurements. This evaluation consists of videotaping the children while they execute a series of tasks to observe the functionality and the joint alignment of the affected upper limb, and it has been validated for use in children with hemiplegia aged between 3 and 18 years. The results are expressed in percentages, with 100% being the best result.

The level of functionality and participation of the patient's upper limbs was determined through the SHUEE assessment as dependent, assisted or independent. Activities of daily living, such as dressing upper limbs, dressing lower limbs, buttoning, putting on socks, putting on shoes, putting on splints and personal hygiene were assessed.

2.3. Statistical Analysis

Statistical analyses were performed using [43]. Given the small sample size, we used non-parametric tests. First, a Friedman's test was used to evaluate the existence of statistical significance for the assessments performed at different times in each variable. Subsequently, a Wilcoxon test (paired samples) was performed on those variables that presented statistical significance, in order to observe statistically significant differences between paired assessments. Significance was set at a p-value of 0.05. The results are shown as medians and interquartile ranges (IQRs) with 95% confidence intervals. Those with a p-value < 0.05 were considered as significant values. The qualitative variable of "functionality" was turned into a quantitative variable, graduating it in 5 levels, from 0 = worst functionality to 4 = maximum functionality (Table 2).

Table 2. Description of the functionality levels.

Dependent	Value 0. Needs help from an adult (does not perform the action).
Assisted	Value 1. Needs help from an adult (partially performs the action).
Independent	Value 2. Uses the healthy upper limb exclusively. Value 3. Uses the upper limb to provide stability. Value 4. Uses both upper limbs to execute the action.

3. Results

Twenty-four children were recruited; 14 of them did not meet the inclusion criteria and two of them declined to participate. The final sample consisted of eight children (Figure 5), with 50% males and 50% females, diagnosed with congenital hemiplegia.

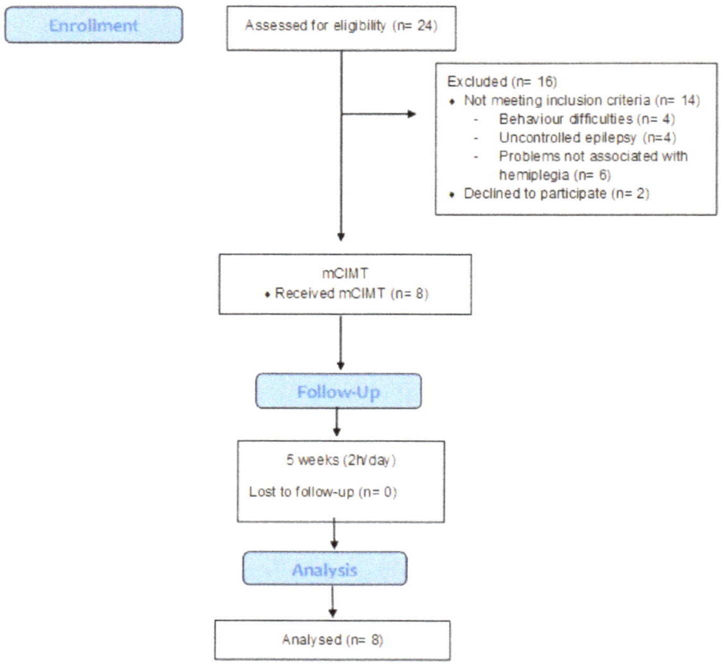

Figure 5. Flowchart of the sample selection.

Of the entire sample, 62.5% had affectation of the left upper limb. The average age was 6 years, with a standard deviation of 1.77 years. After assessing the motor ability of the children, they were classified as Level I in the Gross Motor Function Classification System (GMFCS) [44] and Level II in the manual ability classification system (MACS) [34]. (Table 3)

Table 3. Baseline characteristics of the participants.

Sample	Age	Sex	Gest. Week	Lesion	MACS Level	GMFCS Level	Hemiplegia Side	Add. Impair
Child 1	4	F	Term	Perinatal stroke	II	I	Left	No
Child 2	5	M	Term	Perinatal stroke	II	I	Right	No
Child 3	5	M	Preterm	Perinatal stroke	II	I	Left	No
Child 4	5	M	Preterm	Perinatal stroke	II	I	Left	No
Child 5	7	F	Term	Perinatal stroke	II	I	Right	Speech
Child 6	6	F	Term	Perinatal stroke	II	I	Right	Speech
Child 7	8	F	Preterm	Perinatal stroke	II	I	Left	Speech
Child 8	8	M	Term	Perinatal stroke	II	I	Left	No

Sex: F: Female; M: Male. Gest. Week: Gestational Week: preterm (>32 weeks and <36 weeks); term: >36 weeks; MACS: Manual Ability Classification System; GMFCS: Gross Motor Function Classification System. Add. Impair: Added impairment.

3.1. Quality of Movement of the Upper Limb

The total score for the quality of movement in the upper limbs exhibited an increase of 94.07%. All the variables that compose it, i.e., dissociated movements, grasp, weight bearing and protective extension, showed statistical significance ($p \leq 0.001$) in the Friedman test. When the Wilcoxon test was applied, dissociated movements and grasp obtained significant changes for all pairwise comparisons with a p-value < 0.03. However, no statistically significant differences were found for weight bearing between the second and third assessments ($p = 0.14$), second and fourth assessments ($p = 0.10$) or third and fourth assessments ($p = 0.11$), nor for protective extension between the baseline and second assessments ($p = 0.07$) or second and third assessments ($p = 0.07$). The results are shown in Table 4.

Table 4. Results and pairwise comparisons for the quality of movement in the upper limbs.

Variables	Results	Friedman's Test		Wilcoxon's Test		
	Median (IQR)	Statistical Significance	p Value	Pairwise Comparisons	Statistical Significance	p Value
Quality of Movement in the Upper Limbs (Total Score)						
Baseline	74.16 (63.55, 83.00)	24.000	0.000 *	Baseline–2nd assessment	−2.521	0.012 *
2nd assessment	83.32 (77.18, 88.49)			Baseline–3rd assessment	−2.521	0.012 *
3rd assessment	88.70 (84.42, 91.42)			Baseline–4th assessment	−2.521	0.012 *
4th assessment	94.07 (90.32, 94.92)			2nd assessment–3rd assessment	−2.521	0.012 *
				2nd assessment–4th assessment	−2.521	0.012 *
				3rd assessment–4th assessment	−2.521	0.012 *
Dissociated Movements						
Baseline	59.38 (53.90, 80.48)	23.538	0.000 *	Baseline–2nd assessment	−2.524	0.012 *
2nd assessment	75.00 (73.83, 82.82)			Baseline–3rd assessment	−2.521	0.012 *
3rd assessment	83.60 (81.24, 87.11)			Baseline–4th assessment	−2.521	0.012 *
4th assessment	89.84 (84.77, 91.79)			2nd assessment–3rd assessment	−2.201	0.028 *
				2nd assessment–4th assessment	−2.524	0.012 *
				3rd assessment–4th assessment	−2.527	0.012 *
Grasp						
Baseline	62.97 (46.30, 76.86)	21.808	0.000 *	Baseline–2nd assessment	−2.533	0.011 *
2nd assessment	79.60 (59.26, 87.96)			Baseline–3rd assessment	−2.527	0.012 *
3rd assessment	87.03 (63.89, 91.67)			Baseline–4th assessment	−2.527	0.012 *
4th assessment	96.30 (75.00, 96.30)			2nd assessment–3rd assessment	−2.200	0.028 *
				2nd assessment–4th assessment	−2.384	0.017 *
				3rd assessment–4th assessment	−2.384	0.017 *

Table 4. *Cont.*

Variables	Results	Friedman's Test		Wilcoxon's Test		
	Median (IQR)	Statistical Significance	*p* Value	Pairwise Comparisons	Statistical Significance	*p* Value
Weight Bearing						
Baseline	87.00 (76.50, 93.50)	19.154	0.000 *	Baseline–2nd assessment	−2.536	0.011 *
2nd assessment	98.00 (85.50, 99.50)			Baseline–3rd assessment	−2.524	0.012 *
3rd assessment	97.00 (93.00, 99.50)			Baseline–4th assessment	−2.521	0.012 *
4th assessment	99.00 (96.00, 100.00)			2nd assessment–3rd assessment	−1.461	0.144
				2nd assessment–4th assessment	−1.461	0.102
				3rd assessment–4th assessment	−1.604	0.109
Protective Extension						
Baseline	80.56 (75.00, 90.27)	17.431	0.001 *	Baseline–2nd assessment	−1.841	0.066
2nd assessment	83.34 (79.17, 96.53)			Baseline–3rd assessment	−2.207	0.027 *
3rd assessment	90.27 (84.73, 97.92)			Baseline–4th assessment	−2.379	0.017 *
4th assessment	94.44 (92.36, 99.31)			2nd assessment–3rd assessment	−1.826	0.068
				2nd assessment–4th assessment	−2.207	0.027 *
				3rd assessment–4th assessment	−2.023	0.043 *

* Statistically significant when the *p*-value < 0.05; quality of movement measured with quality of upper extremity test (QUEST) scale. Results expressed in percentages (%) as median (IQR).

3.2. Grasp Strength

The Friedman test showed significance in all assessments ($p < 0.001$). All pairwise comparisons between assessments were statistically significant ($p < 0.05$), except between the baseline and second assessments ($p = 1$) (Table 5). The largest increase observed occurred from the third to the fourth measurement, with 1 PSI.

Table 5. Results and pairwise comparisons of grasp strength.

Variable: Grasp Strength	Results	Friedman Test		Wilcoxon Test		
	Median (IQR)	Statistical Significance	*p* Value	Pairwise Comparisons	Statistical Significance	*p* Value
Baseline	2.00 (1.00, 2.75)	20.069	0.000 *	Baseline–2nd assessment	0.000	1.000
2nd assessment	2.00 (1.00, 2.75)			Baseline–3rd assessment	−2.000	0.046 *
3rd assessment	2.00 (1.25, 3.75)			Baseline–4th assessment	−2.640	0.008 *
4th assessment	3.00 (2.25, 4.50)			2nd assessment–3rd assessment	−2.000	0.046 *
				2nd assessment–4th assessment	−2.640	0.008 *
				3rd assessment–4th assessment	−2.449	0.014 *

* Statistically significant when *p* value < 0.05. Results expressed in median (IQR) measured in PSI units.

3.3. Active Elbow Extension and Forearm Supination

The Friedman test showed significance in all assessments ($p < 0.001$). Both variables increased their value in each of the assessments carried out, exhibiting an increase of 21° for elbow extension between the baseline and fourth measurements ($p = 0.011$), and an increase of 11.50° for the supination of the forearm ($p = 0.011$) between the baseline and fourth measurements (Table 6).

Table 6. Results and pairwise comparisons of elbow extension and forearm supination.

Variables: Active Elbow Extension	Results	Friedman Test		Wilcoxon Test		
	Median (IQR)	Statistical Significance	p Value	Pairwise Comparisons	Statistical	p Value
Baseline	12.50 (10.00, 43.75)	23.423	0.000 *	Baseline–2nd assessment	−2.565	0.010 *
2nd assessment	22.50 (20.00, 50.00)			Baseline–3rd assessment	−2.533	0.011 *
3rd assessment	27.50 (22.75, 54.50)			Baseline–4th assessment	−2.536	0.011 *
4th assessment	33.50 (25.75, 64.25)			2nd Assessment–3rd assessment	−2.456	0.014 *
				2nd assessment–4th assessment	−2.536	0.011 *
				3rd assessment–4th assessment	−2.375	0.018 *
Active Forearm Supination						
Baseline	70.00 (35.50, 75.00)	23.416	0.000 *	Baseline–2nd assessment	−2.588	0.010 *
2nd assessment	75.00 (45.00, 80.00)			Baseline–3rd assessment	−2.536	0.011 *
3rd assessment	76.50 (53.50, 82.25)			Baseline–4th assessment	−2.524	0.012 *
4th assessment	81.50 (58.75, 87.75)			2nd Assessment–3rd assessment	−2.032	0.042 *
				2nd assessment–4th assessment	−2.536	0.011 *
				3rd assessment–4th assessment	−2.527	0.012 *

* Statistically significant when $p < 0.05$. Results expressed in median (IQR), measured in degrees of movement.

3.4. Spontaneous Use, Dynamic Joint Position of the Affected Upper Limb, Grasp and Release Action (Wrist Position in Neutral Flexion–Extension), and Level of Functionality and Integration of the Affected Upper Limb in Different Activities of Daily Living

Spontaneous use increased in all evaluations, reaching 83.87% in the fourth assessment, as did dynamic joint position and grasp–release action with different wrist positions, with 88.20% and 91.67%, respectively. These three variables showed statistical significance in the Friedman test with a p-value < 0.001. The pairwise comparison showed that, in spontaneous use, the values of the second and third assessments were not significant ($p > 0.05$) when compared with the values of the fourth measurement. In dynamic joint positioning, there were no significant differences between the second and third assessments ($p = 0.237$). Grasp–release action was only significant between the baseline and fourth assessments ($p = 0.03$) and between the second and fourth assessments ($p = 0.04$). (Table 7).

An increase was observed in all the variables of functionality and integration of the affected upper limb in various activities of daily living (proposed in SHUEE). All the increases were statistically significant ($p < 0.05$) in the Friedman test, except for "buttoning buttons", where $p = 0.163$. In the pairwise comparison of the assessments for the action of dressing the upper limbs, putting on the splints and buttoning buttons, no statistical significance was detected ($p > 0.05$). In the action of dressing the lower limbs, statistically significant differences were obtained for all assessments, except between the baseline and second assessments and between the second and third assessments ($p \geq 0.05$). In the action of putting on shoes, significant differences were not found between the baseline and second assessments ($p = 0.32$), between the baseline and fourth assessments ($p = 0.06$) or between the third and fourth assessments ($p = 0.10$). In the action of putting on socks, there were no differences between the baseline and second assessments ($p = 1.00$) or between the third and fourth assessments ($p = 0.08$). Regarding personal hygiene, only the changes between the baseline and fourth assessments and between the second and fourth assessments were significant ($p = 0.02$) (Table 8).

Table 7. Results and pairwise comparisons of spontaneous use, dynamic joint position and grasp–release action.

Variable	Results	Friedman's Test		Wilcoxon's Test		
Spontaneous Use in the Affected Upper Limb	**Median (IQR)**	**Statistical Significance**	***p* Value**	**Pairwise Comparisons**	**Statistical Significance**	***p* Value**
Baseline	70.00 (49.45, 87.78)	18.932	0.000 *	Baseline–2nd assessment	−2.371	0.018 *
2nd assessment	85.56 (58.34, 95.00)			Baseline–3rd assessment	−2.366	0.018 *
3rd assessment	87.78 (72.78, 95.55)			Baseline–4th assessment	−2.521	0.012 *
4th assessment	88.87 (87.11, 97.22)			2nd assessment–3rd assessment	−2.201	0.028 *
				2nd assessment–4th assessment	−1.963	0.050
				3rd assessment–4th assessment	−1.690	0.091
Dynamic Joint Position						
Baseline	77.78 (48.24, 86.81)	23.416	0.000 *	Baseline–2nd assessment	−2.366	0.018 *
2nd assessment	80.56 (75.35, 89.93)			Baseline–3rd assessment	−2.521	0.012 *
3rd assessment	85.44 (71.87, 9132)			Baseline–4th assessment	−2.521	0.012 *
4th assessment	88.20 (84.03, 92.71)			2nd assessment–3rd assessment	−1.183	0.237
				2nd assessment–4th assessment	−2.366	0.018 *
				3rd assessment–4th assessment	−2.023	0.043 *
Grasp–Release action						
Baseline	58.34 (50.00, 91.67)	13.568	0.004 *	Baseline–2nd assessment	−1.414	0.157
2nd assessment	75.00 (54.17, 95.83)			Baseline–3rd assessment	−1.890	0.059
3rd assessment	83.33 (66.67, 100.00)			Baseline–4th assessment	−2.226	0.026 *
4th assessment	91.67 (83.33, 100.00)			2nd assessment–3rd assessment	−1.342	0.180
				2nd assessment–4th assessment	−2.041	0.041 *
				3rd assessment–4th assessment	−1.857	0.063

* Statistically significant when $p < 0.05$. Results expressed in percentages % as median (IQR) measured with SHUEE.

Table 8. Results and pairwise comparisons of upper limb participation in activities of daily living (SHUEE).

Variable	Results	Friedman's Test		Wilcoxon's Test		
Upper Limb Dressing	**Median (IQR)**	**Statistical Significance**	***p* Value**	**Pairwise Comparisons**	**Statistical Significance**	***p* Value**
Baseline	3.50 (2.25, 4.00)	10.355	0.016 *	Baseline–2nd assessment	0.000	1.000
2nd assessment	3.50 (2.25, 4.00)			Baseline–3rd assessment	−1.633	0.102
3rd assessment	4.00 (3.25, 4.00)			Baseline–4th assessment	−1.857	0.063
4th assessment	4.00 (4.00, 4.00)			2nd assessment–3rd assessment	−1.633	0.102
				2nd assessment–4th assessment	−1.857	0.063
				3rd assessment–4th assessment	−1.414	0.157

Table 8. *Cont.*

Variable	Results	Friedman's Test		Wilcoxon's Test		
Upper Limb Dressing	Median (IQR)	Statistical Significance	p Value	Pairwise Comparisons	Statistical Significance	p Value
Lower Limb Dressing						
Baseline	3.00 (2.25, 3.00)	15.245	0.002 *	Baseline–2nd assessment	−1.414	0.157
2nd assessment	3.00 (3.00, 3.75)			Baseline–3rd assessment	−2.000	0.046 *
3rd assessment	3.00 (3.00, 4.00)			Baseline–4th assessment	−2.530	0.011 *
4th assessment	4.00 (4.00, 4.00)			2nd assessment–3rd assessment	−1.414	0.157
				2nd assessment–4th assessment	−2.449	0.014 *
				3rd assessment–4th assessment	−2.000	0.046 *
Putting on Splints						
Baseline	3.00 (1.00, 3.75)	9.923	0.019 *	Baseline–2nd assessment	0.000	1.000
2nd assessment	3.00 (1.00, 3.75)			Baseline–3rd assessment	−1.633	0.102
3rd assessment	3.00 (1.00, 4.00)			Baseline–4th assessment	−1.857	0.063
4th assessment	4.00 (1.50, 4.00)			2nd assessment–3rd assessment	−1.633	0.102
				2nd assessment–4th assessment	−1.857	0.063
				3rd assessment–4th assessment	−1.414	0.157
Putting on Shoes						
Baseline	2.00 (2.00, 3.50)	15.188	0.002 *	Baseline–2nd assessment	−1.000	0.317
2nd assessment	2.00 (2.00, 3.75)			Baseline–3rd assessment	−2.121	0.034 *
3rd assessment	3.00 (3.00, 4.00)			Baseline–4th assessment	−2.271	0.023 *
4th assessment	4.00 (3.25, 4.00)			2nd assessment–3rd assessment	−1.890	0.059
				2nd assessment–4th assessment	−2.251	0.024 *
				3rd assessment–4th assessment	−1.633	0.102
Putting on Socks						
Baseline	3.00 (3.00, 3.75)	15.000	0.002 *	Baseline–2nd assessment	0.000	1.000
2nd assessment	3.00 (3.00, 3.75)			Baseline–3rd assessment	−2.000	0.046 *
3rd assessment	3.00 (3.00, 4.00)			Baseline–4th assessment	−2.333	0.020 *
4th assessment	4.00 (4.00, 4.00)			2nd assessment–3rd assessment	−2.000	0.046 *
				2nd assessment–4th assessment	−2.333	0.020 *
				3rd assessment–4th assessment	−1.732	0.083
Buttoning Up						
Baseline	1.00 (0.00, 3.00)	5.118	0.163	Baseline–2nd assessment	−1.000	0.317
2nd assessment	1.50 (0.00, 3.00)			Baseline–3rd assessment	−1.414	0.157
3rd assessment	1.50 (0.00, 3.75)			Baseline–4th assessment	−1.342	0.180
4th assessment	1.50 (0.00, 4.00)			2nd assessment–3rd assessment	−1.000	0.317
				2nd assessment–4th assessment	−1.414	0.157
				3rd assessment–4th assessment	−1.000	0.317

Table 8. *Cont.*

Variable	Results	Friedman's Test		Wilcoxon's Test		
Upper Limb Dressing	Median (IQR)	Statistical Significance	p Value	Pairwise Comparisons	Statistical Significance	p Value
Personal Hygiene						
Baseline	2.00 (2.00, 2.00)	15.000	0.002 *	Baseline–2nd assessment	0.000	1.000
2nd assessment	2.00 (2.00, 2.00)			Baseline–3rd assessment	−1.890	0.059
3rd assessment	2.50 (2.00, 4.00)			Baseline–4th assessment	−2.333	0.020 *
4th assessment	4.00 (2.25, 4.00)			2nd assessment–3rd assessment	−1.890	0.059
				2nd assessment–4th assessment	−2.333	0.020 *
				3rd assessment–4th assessment	−1.633	0.102

* Statistically significant when $p < 0.05$. Results expressed in median (IQR), measured with SHUEE on a scale of 1 to 5.

After analyzing the follow-up tables of the activities completed by each family, it was observed that five children performed the total dose (50 h), two children performed 48 h, and one of them performed 49 h. All of them completed the expected dose (48–50 h of mCIMT).

4. Discussion

The deterioration of hand functionality causes a weakness present in the execution of activities of daily living in children with hemiplegia. There is an alteration compared to the healthy upper limb that manifests in the general slowness of movement, discontinuous movements, variability in the trajectory of the hand with compensations of the trunk and the presence of inadequate coordination in the grasp strength of the affected hand [45]. The improvement in grasp strength and stability occurs from the third to the fourth measurement due to an increase in hand strength. The increase was observed only in the last measurement, which could be due to the need for a longer treatment time (5 weeks of intervention). These children with impaired fine motor adjustment, a lack of finger dissociation and deficient proprioception in their affected hand had greater experience (trial–error) to adapt the grasp to the shape, texture and weight of the object, allowing the execution of a previous thinking strategy (anticipatory control) to achieve precision in the grasp and adjustment of the strength to grasp the object adequately. The improvement of grasp stability and strength allows a functional grasp when picking up objects of different characteristics and holding them while performing selective and precision activities, such as throwing a small ball at a target, keeping a fork steady with the affected hand and bringing food to the mouth during the feeding phase. Most children with unilateral brain injury do not develop adequate grip strength in the affected upper limb to coordinate one-handed activities. There is a pathological pattern or an immature state of grasp for their age, leading to an inadequate synergy of the coordination strength that is related to the deterioration of the manual ability of the affected hand depending on the level of injury [46].

Children obtained significant changes in the functional activities of daily life assessed, except in dressing the upper limbs, putting on splints and buttoning buttons. This could suggest the need for improvements in visuomotor coordination and bimanual coordination, and greater strength and precision in the affected grasp to support objects and to perform the activities, which require great ability in the affected upper limb.

There are few studies that propose a home-based therapy intervention [12,13,17,19,25]. Among such studies, only three of them combine this proposal with a modification based on the application of low doses of treatment [12,19,25]. None of them were developed in Spain; thus, our preliminary results provide interesting and unpublished data of the application of mCIMT.

The advantage of combining a low dose of treatment with the application of therapy in the child's own home is that this modification is better accepted by both parents and the child, as reported by authors such as Eliasson et al. [12], who showed better rates of parental competence among those who had applied low doses of treatment. Likewise, some children showed higher levels of frustration or low tolerance was shown by both the child and the family with higher doses of treatment. To minimize such feelings, some authors have proposed adapting the original protocol, suggesting the use of the containment only during the intervention period, reducing the dose and using a protocol that is "child friendly" and enhances children's engagement [22,40,47]. Thus, our proposal could positively affect these aspects.

Although the objective of this study was not to analyze the cost–benefit of mCIMT, the positive results obtained in it demonstrate that this type of intervention is also a low-cost treatment compared to the application of botulinum toxin [11,14,48–50].

On the other hand, the age of the participants is also an important aspect to take into account when applying this treatment modality. The results of our study coincide with those of Chen et al. (2016), since the younger children with cerebral palsy responded better to home-based CIMT on some areas of upper limb functions than older children. When the child does not receive treatment, the choice of using the upper limbs to carry out a unimanual action will depend on the characteristics of the injury, levels of disability, experience and level of frustration and motivation in carrying out activities, among other factors. Learning "not to use" the unaffected upper limb by means of mCIMT intervention can provide an increased spontaneous participation of the affected upper limb in unimanual and bimanual tasks [32], observed in all measurements performed by SHUEE evaluation. The greatest increase was observed from the first to the second measurement, reaching 15.56% of the total value obtained in the last measurement, 18.87% being the median. This suggests that, when children do not depend on their dominant hand, they learn to use their affected upper limb early and acquire a greater representation within their body schema, developing functional strategies for the execution of daily tasks that allow them to overcome the "disuse" of the affected upper limb due to a lack of integration. Spontaneous use continued to evolve throughout the intervention as the children overcame the lack of experience of use. The improvement in functional performance was reflected in activities of daily living, where a degree of independence and greater participation of the affected limb was reached in the last measurement for the execution of the tasks of dressing upper limbs and lower limbs; putting on socks, shoes and splints; and personal hygiene. The activity carried out with the greatest ability and participation of both upper limbs was putting on pants, for which the most significant statistical results were obtained in the pairwise comparison of measurements. The increase in participation of the affected limb observed from the first measurement to the last, and in some activities accentuated in the fourth measurement, was due to an increase in the quality of bimanual coordination, as a result of the greater integration of the affected upper limb. The parents of the participants provided information about the use of the affected limb in their usual environment, such as during meals to actively support the healthy limb, without the need for the parents to give a verbal order to the child to use it; execution of school activities; playing (symbolic play with dolls); and in extracurricular activities such as dancing, where greater integration and earlier activation of the affected segment was observed, among others, which allowed reducing frustration and abandoning the disuse of the affected upper limb. The families showed great satisfaction with this protocol, which was reflected in the adherence to the therapy, since the children completed 96% of the total dose, thus suggesting the importance of the family and the setting. The natural environment (home) offered less distress during constraint-induced movement therapy practice for both children with cerebral palsy and their parents. Furthermore, the training schedule can be tailored to fit the family's daily routine. A home-based intervention can also save the family time and money in terms of commuting, and parents can be more involved throughout the process, increasing opportunities for parent–child interaction [51]. There could be a continuity in the maintenance of the gains obtained in the functionality of the affected upper limb after executing the intervention, since the daily treatment session was carried out at home, simulating the situation of normal life for the child, in addition to the design of the treatment protocol to simulate activities of daily living. The improvement in the quality of movement was shown by the greater progress in the results obtained between the baseline and fourth measurements of the variables of dissociated movements and grasp. Appreciable benefits were obtained in each measurement produced by the acquisition of a more corrected posture of the trunk, head and shoulders in the execution of the grasp activities, present from the second measurement (after a week of treatment with mCIMT). A dynamic joint position occurred in wrist and elbow extension, increasing the median value for wrist extension by 21° from the baseline to the fourth measurement. In addition, the value reached in the fourth measurement for the median was 81.50° in the active supination of the forearm, allowing for greater control and support of the body structures for the execution of dissociated movements, grasp, weight bearing and protective extension due to the improvement of both active movements. There was a favorable evolution in the dynamic joint position of the affected upper limb due to the gain of active degrees for movement restriction in extension and supination, with an increase in this variable of 10.42% at the end of the treatment. In this way, the activities proposed during the evaluation were performed with greater ease of movement, such as eating a cookie, touching the opposite ear, picking up coins, opening a bottle or throwing a large ball, which require the selective motor control of certain muscles. In comparison with the results obtained for the quality of movement of the affected upper limb in the present study, we highlight an investigation [52] on mCIMT, which showed positive results for the assessment of the quality of movement of motor skills (measured through the QUEST scale) using an intervention protocol of 3 weeks of treatment with an intensity of 6 h per day of restriction and repetitive work. This study demonstrated the effectiveness of the intervention, as it had a larger sample and a control group (18 children with hemiplegia, nine children in the experimental group and nine children in the control group). In 2011, a different study [53], conducted exclusively with a girl with hemiplegia, used mCIMT for one hour per day for two weeks. No significant results were obtained at the end of the treatment, which was thereby prolonged for one more week of intervention. This last assessment showed an increase in the overall percentage of total quality of movement (also measured by the QUEST scale), appreciable in activities that involve the affected upper limb. Thus, the protocol chosen for the intervention and the initial functionality of the patient are two important factors to take into account in increasing the results obtained in the measurements. When comparing the results obtained in the second assessment after 20 h of treatment with those obtained after the treatment (50 h), improvements were detected in the former (20 h), although the greatest improvements and relevant changes were identified in the latter (50 h). At the end of the treatment, the families observed these functional changes (daily activities assessed) at different natural moments. Thus, it would be necessary to apply 50 h of dose instead of 20 h in children aged 4–8 years to increase the affected upper limb functionality, since the manual ability and age would be factors to consider in the dose to apply.

Limitations and Future Lines of Research

As this is an uncontrolled trial [54] due to the absence of a control group, it cannot be guaranteed that the observed response (changes produced throughout the intervention with respect to the baseline situation) is exclusively due to the mCIMT protocol used, since other uncontrolled factors may also have had an influence on it. Therefore, the effectiveness of the mCIMT in increasing the functionality of the affected upper limb seen in the present study cannot be generalized to the population of children with hemiplegia, and thus, the fundamental utility of this study is descriptive. It is important to highlight the statistically significant results obtained in the different studied variables throughout the 5 weeks of the intervention (It can be seen at Figures S1–S11. Progression of different variables in the four assessments over 5 weeks of mCIMT). This suggests that, although there was no control group, it could be inferred that the changes obtained in the improvement of the functionality were due to the efficacy of the treatment, since it was a short period of time, where important differences were observed in the affected upper limb, which is unlikely to occur due to the maturation effect (learning and natural development of the child over time).

In Spain, this is the first study to provide preliminary data on the use of mCIMT. Although the results should be interpreted with caution due to the small sample size, the development of this pilot scheme is the first step for this type of therapy, which has already demonstrated its effectiveness in other contexts; therefore, it should be taken into account by therapist and researchers who develop their work with this type of children in Spain.

This study leads us to open different lines of research, such as including a control group to assess the effectiveness of the treatment in the functionality of the affected upper limb, to verify whether the gains obtained after the intervention are maintained over time (6 months or one year after therapy), and to study the influence of age on the obtained results due to neuronal plasticity and active participation of the subject. Likewise, it paves the road for clinicians and researchers to develop new treatment proposals in Spain.

5. Conclusions

A low dose (50 h) of modified Constraint-Induced Movement Therapy can increase the functionality of children diagnosed with congenital hemiplegia between 4 and 8 years of age with moderate manual ability.

Supplementary Materials: The following are available online at http://www.mdpi.com/2227-9067/7/9/127/s1. Supplementary figures: Figures S1–S11. Progression of different variables in the four assessments over 5 weeks of mCIMT.

Author Contributions: Conceptualization, R.P.-C. and R.-P.R.-G.; methodology, E.P.-P.; software, F.G.-M.S.J.; validation, R.P.-C., P.L.-M. and H.R.-B.; formal analysis, E.P.-P.; investigation, R.P.-C.; data curation, P.L.-M.; writing—original draft preparation, R.-P.R.-G. and R.P.-C.; writing—review and editing, R.-P.R.-G.; visualization, F.G.-M.S.J.; supervision, F.-G.-M.S.J. All authors have read and agreed to the published version of the manuscript.

Funding: This research received no external funding.

Acknowledgments: The authors thank the collaboration of Carmen López Zarzuela, a rehabilitation doctor of the "Virgen de la Salud" Hospital in Toledo, the parents who agreed to participate and allow the intervention to be carried out successfully due to their great dedication, and especially the children who participated in this study for their continuity and daily improvement.

Conflicts of Interest: The authors declare no conflict of interest.

References

1. Monge Pereira, E.; Molina Rueda, F.; Alguacil Diego, I.M.; Cano de la Cuerda, R.; de Mauro, A.; Miangolarra Page, J.C. Empleo de sistemas de realidad virtual como método de propiocepción en parálisis cerebral: Guía de práctica clínica. *Neurologia* **2014**, *29*, 550–559. [CrossRef]
2. Sgandurra, G.; Ferrari, A.; Cossu, G.; Guzzetta, A.; Biagi, L.; Tosetti, M.; Fogassi, L.; Cioni, G. Upper limb children action-observation training (UP-CAT): A randomised controlled trial in Hemiplegic Cerebral Palsy. *BMC Neurol.* **2011**, *11*, 80. [CrossRef]
3. Eliasson, A.C.; Forssberg, H.; Hung, Y.C.; Gordon, A.M. Development of hand function and precision grip control in individuals with cerebral palsy: A 13-year follow-up study. *Pediatrics* **2006**, *118*. [CrossRef]
4. Huang, W.C.; Chen, Y.J.; Chien, C.L.; Kashima, H.; Lin, K. Constraint-induced movement therapy as a paradigm of translational research in neurorehabilitation: Reviews and prospects. *Am. J. Transl. Res.* **2011**, *3*, 48–60.
5. Wittenberg, G. Experience, cortical remapping and recovery in brain disease. *Neurobiol. Dis.* **2010**, *37*, 252–258. [CrossRef] [PubMed]
6. Liepert, J.; Bauder, H.; Miltner, W.H.R.; Taub, E.; Weiller, C. Treatment-induced cortical reorganization after stroke in humans. *Stroke* **2000**, *31*, 1210–1216. [CrossRef] [PubMed]
7. Charles, J.; Gordon, A.M. A critical review of constraint-induced movement therapy and forced use in children with hemiplegia. *Neural Plast.* **2005**, *12*, 245–261. [CrossRef]
8. Hoare, B.J.; Wallen, M.A.; Thorley, M.N.; Jackman, M.L.; LM, C.; Imms, C. Constraint-induced movement therapy in children with unilateral cerebral palsy. *Cochrane Database Syst. Rev.* **2019**, 1–274. [CrossRef]
9. Eliasson, A.C.; Krumlinde-Sundholm, L.; Gordon, A.M.; Feys, H.; Klingels, K.; Aarts, P.B.M.; Rameckers, E.; Autti-Rämö, I.; Hoare, B. Guidelines for future research in constraint-induced movement therapy for children with unilateral cerebral palsy: An expert consensus. *Dev. Med. Child Neurol.* **2014**, *56*, 125–137. [CrossRef]

10. Deppe, W.; Thuemmler, K.; Fleischer, J.; Berger, C.; Meyer, S.; Wiedemann, B. Modified constraint-induced movement therapy versus intensive bimanual training for children with hemiplegia-a randomized controlled trial. *Clin. Rehabil.* **2013**, *27*, 909–920. [CrossRef]
11. Chen, Y.P.; Pope, S.; Tyler, D.; Warren, G.L. Effectiveness of constraint-induced movement therapy on upper-extremity function in children with cerebral palsy: A systematic review and meta-analysis of randomized controlled trials. *Clin. Rehabil.* **2014**, *28*, 939–953. [CrossRef] [PubMed]
12. Eliasson, A.C.; Nordstrand, L.; Ek, L.; Lennartsson, F.; Sjöstrand, L.; Tedroff, K.; Krumlinde-Sundholm, L. The effectiveness of Baby-CIMT in infants younger than 12 months with clinical signs of unilateral-cerebral palsy; an explorative study with randomized design. *Res. Dev. Disabil.* **2018**, *72*, 191–201. [CrossRef] [PubMed]
13. Zafer, H.; Amjad, I.; Malik, A.N.; Shaukat, E. Effectiveness of constraint induced movement therapy as compared to bimanual therapy in upper motor function outcome in child with hemiplegic cerebral palsy. *Pakistan J. Med. Sci.* **2016**, *32*, 181–184. [CrossRef]
14. Dong, V.A.; Fong, K.N.K.; Chen, Y.-F.; Tseng, S.S.W.; Wong, L.M.S. 'Remind-to-move' treatment versus constraint-induced movement therapy for children with hemiplegic cerebral palsy: A randomized controlled trial. *Dev. Med. Child Neurol.* **2017**, *59*, 160–167. [CrossRef] [PubMed]
15. Christmas, P.M.; Sackley, C.; Feltham, M.G.; Cummins, C. A randomized controlled trial to compare two methods of constraint-induced movement therapy to improve functional ability in the affected upper limb in pre-school children with hemiplegic cerebral palsy: CATCH TRIAL. *Clin. Rehabil.* **2018**, *32*, 909–918. [CrossRef] [PubMed]
16. Hosseini, S.M.S.; Sourtiji, H.; Taghizadeh, A. Effect of child friendly constraint induced movement therapy on unimanual and bimanual function in hemiplegia. *Iran. Rehabil. J.* **2010**, *8*, 50–54.
17. Rostami, H.R.; Arastoo, A.A.; Nejad, S.J.; Mahany, M.K.; Malamiri, R.A.; Goharpey, S. Effects of modified constraint-induced movement therapy in virtual environment on upper-limb function in children with spastic hemiparetic cerebral palsy: A randomised controlled trial. *NeuroRehabilitation* **2012**, *31*, 357–365. [CrossRef]
18. MostafaKhan, H.S.E.; Rassafiani, M.; Hosseini, S.A.; Akbarfahimi, N.; Hosseini, S.S.; Sortiji, H.; Nobakht, Z. Comparison of combination of CIMT and BIM training with CIMT alone on fine motor skills of children with Hemiplegic cerebral palsy. *Iran. Rehabil. J.* **2013**, *11*, 46–51.
19. Taub, E.; Ramey, S.L.; DeLuca, S.; Echols, K. Efficacy of Constraint-Induced Movement Therapy for Children with Cerebral Palsy with Asymmetric Motor Impairment. *Pediatrics* **2004**, *113*, 305–312. [CrossRef]
20. Taub, E.; Griffin, A.; Uswatte, G.; Gammons, K.; Nick, J.; Law, C. Treatment of congenital hemiparesis with pediatric constraint-induced movement therapy. *J. Child Neurol.* **2011**, *26*, 1163–1173. [CrossRef]
21. Al-Oraibi, S.; Eliasson, A.C. Implementation of constraint-induced movement therapy for youngchildren with unilateral cerebral palsy in Jordan: A home-based model. *Disabil. Rehabil.* **2011**, *33*, 2006–2012. [CrossRef] [PubMed]
22. Charles, J.R.; Wolf, S.L.; Schneider, J.A.; Gordon, A.M. Efficacy of a child-friendly form of constraint-induced movement therapy in hemiplegic cerebral palsy: A randomized control trial. *Dev. Med. Child Neurol.* **2006**, *48*, 635–642. [CrossRef] [PubMed]
23. Choudhary, A.; Gulati, S.; Kabra, M.; Singh, U.P.; Sankhyan, N.; Pandey, R.M.; Kalra, V. Efficacy of modified constraint induced movement therapy in improving upper limb function in children with hemiplegic cerebral palsy: A randomized controlled trial. *Brain Dev.* **2013**, *35*, 870–876. [CrossRef] [PubMed]
24. De Brito Brandão, M.; Mancini, M.C.; Vaz, D.V.; Pereira De Melo, A.P.; Fonseca, S.T. Adapted version of constraint-induced movement therapy promotes functioning in children with cerebral palsy: A randomized controlled trial. *Clin. Rehabil.* **2010**, *24*, 639–647. [CrossRef]
25. Eugster-Buesch, F.; De Bruin, E.D.; Boltshauser, E.; Steinlin, M.; Küenzle, C.; Müller, E.; Capone, A.; Pfann, R.; Meyer-Heim, A. Forced-use therapy for children with cerebral palsy in the community setting: A single-blinded randomized controlled pilot trial. *J. Pediatr. Rehabil. Med.* **2012**, *5*, 65–74. [CrossRef] [PubMed]
26. Facchin, P.; Rosa-Rizzotto, M.; Dalla Pozza, L.V.; Turconi, A.C.; Pagliano, E.; Signorini, S.; Tornetta, L.; Trabacca, A.; Fedrizzi, E.; Valentina, A.T.; et al. Multisite trial comparing the efficacy of constraint-induced movement therapy with that of bimanual intensive training in children with hemiplegic cerebral palsy: Postintervention results. *Am. J. Phys. Med. Rehabil.* **2011**, *90*, 539–553. [CrossRef]

27. Gharib, M.; Hosseyni, A.; Fahimmi, N.; Saleh, M. Effect of modified constraint induced movement therapy on quality of upper extremity skills in children with hemiplegic cerebral palsy. *Iran. J. Pediatr.* **2010**, *12*, 29–36.
28. Eliasson, A.C.; Krumlinde-Sundholm, L.; Shaw, K.; Wang, C. Effects of oncstraint-induced movement therapy in young children with hemiplegic cerebral palsy: An adapted model. *Dev. Med. Child Neurol.* **2005**, *47*, 266–275. [CrossRef]
29. Page, S.J.; Sisto, S.; Johnston, M.V.; Levine, P. Modified Constraint-Induced Therapy after Subacute Stroke: A Preliminary Study. *Neurorehabil. Neural Repair* **2002**, *16*, 290–295. [CrossRef]
30. Peurala, S.H.; Kantanen, M.P.; Sjögren, T.; Paltamaa, J.; Karhula, M.; Heinonen, A. Effectiveness of constraint-induced movement therapy on activity and participation after stroke: A systematic review and meta-analysis of randomized controlled trials. *Clin. Rehabil.* **2012**, *26*, 209–223. [CrossRef]
31. McConnell, K.; Johnston, L.; Kerr, C. Efficacy and acceptability of reduced intensity constraint-induced movement therapy for children aged 9-11 years with hemiplegic cerebral palsy: A pilot study. *Phys. Occup. Ther. Pediatr.* **2014**, *34*, 245–259. [CrossRef] [PubMed]
32. Schweighofer, N.; Han, C.E.; Wolf, S.L.; Arbib, M.A.; Winstein, C.J. A Functional Threshold for Long-Term Use of Hand and Arm Function Can Be Determined: Predictions From a Computational Model and Supporting Data From the Extremity Constraint-Induced Therapy Evaluation (EXCITE) Trial. *Phys. Ther.* **2009**, *89*, 1327–1336. [CrossRef] [PubMed]
33. Chiu, H.C.; Ada, L. Constraint-induced movement therapy improves upper limb activity and participation in hemiplegic cerebral palsy: A systematic review. *J. Physiother.* **2016**, *62*, 130–137. [CrossRef] [PubMed]
34. Eliasson, A.C.; Krumlinde-Sundholm, L.; Rösblad, B.; Beckung, E.; Arner, M.; Öhrvall, A.M.; Rosenbaum, P. The Manual Ability Classification System (MACS) for children with cerebral palsy: Scale development and evidence of validity and reliability. *Dev. Med. Child Neurol.* **2006**. *48*, 549–554. [CrossRef]
35. Bronfenbrenner, U. *The Ecology of Human Develpment. Experiments by Nature and Design*; Harvard University Press: Cambrigdge, UK, 1979; ISBN 0674224566.
36. Brown, W.H.; Odom, S.L.; Li, S.; Zercher, C. Ecobehavioral assessment in early childhood programs: A portrait of preschool inclusion. *J. Spec. Educ.* **1999**, *33*, 138–153. [CrossRef]
37. Eliasson, A.; Sjöstrand, L.; Ek, L.; Krumlinde-Sundholm, L.; Tedroff, K. Efficacy of baby-CIMT:study protocol for a randomised controlled trial on infants below age 12 months, with clinical signs of unilateral CP. *BMC Pediatr* **2014**, *14*, 141. [CrossRef]
38. De Matteo, C.; Law, M.; Russell, D.; Pollock, N.; Rosenbaum, P.; Walter, S. The reliability and validity of the Quality of Upper Extremity Skills Test. *Phys. Occup. Ther. Pediatr.* **1993**, *13*, 1–18. [CrossRef]
39. Thorley, M.; Lannin, N.; Cusick, A.; Novak, I.; Boyd, R. Reliability of the quality of upper extremity skills test for children with cerebral palsy aged 2 to 12 years. *Phys. Occup. Ther. Pediatr.* **2012**, *32*, 4–21. [CrossRef]
40. Gilmore, R.; Sakzewski, L.; Boyd, R. Upper limb activity measures for 5- to 16-year-old children with congenital hemiplegia: A systematic review. *Dev. Med. Child Neurol.* **2010**, *52*, 14–21. [CrossRef]
41. de Carvalho, R.M.F.; Mazzer, N.; Barbieri, C.H. Analysis of the reliability and reproducibility of goniometry compared to hand photogrammetry. *Acta Ortop. Bras.* **2012**, *20*, 139–149. [CrossRef]
42. Davids, J.R.; Peace, L.C.; Wagner, L.V.; Gidewall, M.A.; Blackhurst, D.W.; Roberson, W.M. Validation of the Shriners Hospital for Children Upper Extremity Evaluation (SHUEE) for children with hemiplegic cerebral palsy. *J. Bone Jt. Surg. Ser. A* **2006**, *88*, 326–333. [CrossRef]
43. IBM. *SPSS Statistics for Windows, Version 20.0*; IBM Corp.: Armonk, NY, USA, 2011.
44. Gray, L.; Ng, H.; Bartlett, D. The gross motor function classification system: An update on impact and clinical utility. *Pediatr. Phys. Ther.* **2010**, *22*, 315–320. [CrossRef]
45. Steenbergen, B.; Charles, J.; Gordon, A.M. Fingertip force control during bimanual object lifting in hemiplegic cerebral palsy. *Exp. Brain Res.* **2008**, *186*, 191–201. [CrossRef]
46. Forssberg, H.; Eliasson, A.C.; Redon-Zouitenn, C.; Mercuri, E.; Dubowitz, L. Impaired grip-lift synergy in children with unilateral brain lesions. *Brain* **1999**, *122*, 1157–1168. [CrossRef]
47. Charles, J.R.; Msw, P.T.; Physical, D. Movement Therapy Results in Further Improvement. *Dev. Med. Child Neurol.* **2007**, *8*, 770–773. [CrossRef]
48. Abd El-Kafy, E.M.; Elshemy, S.A.; Alghamdi, M.S. Effect of constraint-induced therapy on upper limb functions: A randomized control trial. *Scand. J. Occup. Ther.* **2014**, *21*, 11–23. [CrossRef]

49. Gordon, A.M.; Hung, Y.C.; Brandao, M.; Ferre, C.L.; Kuo, H.C.; Friel, K.; Petra, E.; Chinnan, A.; Charles, J.R. Bimanual training and constraint-induced movement therapy in children with hemiplegic cerebral palsy: A randomized trial. *Neurorehabil. Neural Repair* **2011**, *25*, 692–702. [CrossRef]
50. Boyd, R.N.; Baque, E.; Piovesana, A.; Ross, S.; Ziviani, J.; Sakzewski, L.; Barber, L.; Lloyd, O.; McKinlay, L.; Whittingham, K.; et al. Mitii™ ABI: Study protocol of a randomised controlled trial of a web-based multi-modal training program for children and adolescents with an Acquired Brain Injury (ABI). *BMC Neurol.* **2015**, *15*. [CrossRef]
51. Brusco, N.K.; Taylor, N.F.; Watts, J.J.; Shields, N. Economic evaluation of adult rehabilitation: A systematic review and meta-analysis of randomized controlled trials in a variety of settings. *Arch. Phys. Med. Rehabil.* **2014**, *95*. [CrossRef]
52. Pidcock, F.; Garcia, T.; Trovato, M.; Schultz, S.; Brady, K. Pediatric constraint-induced movement therapy: A promising intervention for childhood hemiparesis. *Top. Stroke Rehabil.* **2009**, *16*, 339–345. [CrossRef]
53. Ramachandran, S.; Thakur, P. Upper extremity constraint-induced movement therapy in infantile hemiplegia. *J. Pediatr. Neurosci.* **2011**, *6*, 29–31. [CrossRef]
54. Argimon-Pallás, J.; Jiménez-Villa, J. *Métodos de Investigación Clínica y Epidemiológica*, 5th ed.; Elsevier: Barcelona, Spain, 2019; ISBN 978-84-9113-007-9.

children

MDPI

Article

Participation in Everyday Activities of Children with and without Neurodevelopmental Disorders: A Cross-Sectional Study in Spain

Nerea Blanco-Martínez [1,2,†], Laura Delgado-Lobete [1,*,†], Rebeca Montes-Montes [3], Nuria Ruiz-Pérez [4,5], Marcos Ruiz-Pérez [6] and Sergio Santos-del-Riego [1]

1 Faculty of Health Sciences, Health Integration and Promotion Research Unit (INTEGRA SAÚDE), University of A Coruña, 15011 A Coruña, Spain; nerea.blanco1@udc.es (N.B.-M.); sergio.santos.delriego@udc.es (S.S.-d.-R.)
2 Faculty of Educational Sciences & Sports, University of Vigo, 36005 Pontevedra, Spain
3 TALIONIS Research Group, Centre for Information and Communications Technology Research (CITIC), University of A Coruña, 15008 A Coruña, Spain; rebeca.montes@udc.es
4 Faculty of Pharmacy, University of Santiago de Compostela, 15782 Santiago de Compostela, Spain; nuriamaria.ruiz@rai.usc.es
5 Faculty of Health Sciences, Catholic University of Ávila, 05005 Ávila, Spain
6 University College of Teacher Training, University of Vigo, 36214 Vigo, Spain; marcos91rp@gmail.com
* Correspondence: l.delgado@udc.es; Tel.: +34-881-014-339
† These authors contributed equally to this work.

Received: 5 August 2020; Accepted: 27 September 2020; Published: 1 October 2020

Abstract: Children with neurodevelopmental disorders (NDDs) often report significant difficulties performing activities of daily living (ADLs), which may restrict their daily participation. The aim of this study was to investigate the differences in ADLs participation between children with NDDs and typically developing (TD) children, and to explore the associations between different daily participation contexts. A cross-sectional study was conducted that included twenty children with a medical diagnosis of an NDD and 26 sex- and age-matched TD controls. The daily participation across home, community, school, and instrumental living activities was measured using the Child and Adolescent Scale of Participation (CASP). The results show that children with NDDs engaged in lower participation in all CASP contexts ($\Delta = 1.7$–5.5, $p < 0.001$) and had a significantly higher prevalence of moderate or severe restricted participation than their TD peers (OR = 23.4, 95% CI = 3.6–154.2, $p < 0.001$). Additionally, a strong association was found between the different contexts of participation ($r = 0.642$–0.856). Overall, the children with NDDs experienced significant participation restrictions on their daily activities. This study adds to the growing evidence showing that intervention strategies in this population should adopt a participation-oriented approach.

Keywords: neurodevelopmental disorders; autism spectrum disorders; attention deficit and hyperactivity disorder; motor coordination disorder; activities of daily living; participation; occupational therapy

1. Introduction

Neurodevelopmental disorders (NDDs) are a group of conditions with onset in the early developmental period and comprise a broad group of developmental deficits in the brain function that affect physical, social, academic, and occupational functioning [1,2]. These disorders constitute the most frequent conditions for disability and participation restriction during childhood and are more frequent in males than females [3]. The estimated prevalence of NDDs in school-aged children worldwide ranges from 4 to 13%, but these data vary across countries and estimation methods [3–6]. In most of the cases, the NDDs persist into late adolescence and adulthood, with persistent consequences for daily living functioning [6]. The most prevalent and usually reported NDDs in childhood are attention deficit and hyperactivity disorder (ADHD), developmental coordination disorder (DCD), and autism spectrum disorders (ASDs). In a comprehensive review on ADHD prevalence conducted by Polanczyk et al., it was reported that 9.5% of children had a lifetime diagnosis of ADHD worldwide during the past three decades [7], while this prevalence ranges between 4.1% and 8.8% among Spanish children and adolescents [8–10]. Reported estimates of the prevalence of DCD in schoolchildren usually range between 5 and 6% [11–13] but recent studies have found that up to 12.0% of Spanish children are at risk of DCD [14,15]. While the prevalence estimates of ASDs are significantly lower, with approximately 1–2% of children presenting with an ASD, the consequences of these disorders in everyday living are much more severe and restrictive, thus making ASDs some of the most studied neurodevelopmental conditions [9,16–19]. Overall, approximately 9.4% of Spanish children have a neurodevelopmental condition that interferes with their functional development [9].

Children with NDDs face significant difficulties in activity performance from early childhood onward, particularly in self-care activities, play and mobility, social cognition, and instrumental activities [20–24]. However, not only activity performance is restricted in these children but daily participation is compromised as well. Participation in meaningful activities of daily living (ADLs) is defined as involvement in life contexts or situations, where the International Classification of Functioning, Disability and Health (ICF) of the World Health Organization consider this aspect to be a crucial part of children's healthy psychological, emotional, and functional development [25].

Additionally, satisfactory participation in a particular daily context is hypothesized to be intimately related to participation in other daily contexts, and thus, restrictions or difficulties in one occupational area are expected to lead to restrictions in other activities of daily living as well [26–28]. This hypothesis is supported by research that shows an interrelation in participation between different daily contexts in typically developing (TD) children [29–31]. Moreover, performance difficulties or participation restrictions are rarely present in only one particular area but are reported in most daily contexts and activities [32].

Several studies have reported that motor, social, behavioral, and processing impairments of children with NDD lead to participation restrictions, and that this population is more likely to show lower and less meaningful participation in daily contexts than typically developing children [32–36]. Three literature reviews using the ICF have concluded that more studies should be conducted to explore the consequences of ADHD, DCD, and ASDs in the context of participation restrictions [35–37]. Investigating potential limitations in daily, naturalistic contexts is relevant for intervention strategies as well, as scientific research shows that activity- and participation-oriented approaches should be used to promote daily performance and family participation in children with neurodevelopmental conditions [11,38–42]. However, very few studies have focused on daily participation differences in Spanish children with and without NDDs. To the best of our knowledge, only two studies have explored social participation among children with ADHD, ASDs, or co-occurring disorders in Spain [43,44], but participation in self-care, instrumental, or community contexts was not assessed. Thus, little is known about daily participation restrictions in Spanish children with neurodevelopmental conditions. Additionally, exploring how children with and without typical development perform and participate during their daily activities is crucial for designing meaningful interventions [45].

Daily participation is influenced by cultural and country constraints, where this effect may differ between participation contexts, even between similar European countries. For instance, a recent study found significant differences in daily participation in self-care activities between typically developing Spanish and Dutch children [12]. Another study found that Spanish boys participated less than German boys in self- and house-care activities [46]. While this research focused on typically developing children, it was expected that differences in daily participation patterns would be found in children with neurodevelopmental conditions as well. As there is no information regarding differences in daily participation in Spanish children with and without NDDs, a study that evaluated participation restrictions between both groups in Spain was needed. Therefore, the aims of this study were (a) to explore differences in participation between Spanish children with and without NDDs and (b) to explore the association between participation in different daily contexts.

2. Materials and Methods

2.1. Research Ethics, Procedure, and Participants

A multicenter, comparative cross-sectional study was carried out. This study was approved by the Autonomic Research Ethics Committee of Galicia, Spain (code 2018-544). All participants consented to take part in the study anonymously and confidentially.

The total sample comprised forty children aged 5 to 12 years. This sample size was estimated in order to measure the differences in ADLs participation between children with and without developmental disorders with a minimal bias ($\alpha < 0.01$, power $(1 - \beta) > 0.99$) [31]. Children with NDDs ($n = 20$) were recruited from two private rehabilitation centers in Vigo and A Guarda (Spain). Children in this group had a medical diagnosis of a neurodevelopmental condition (girls = 35.0%; mean age = 7.8 years, standard deviation (SD) = 1.7 years; ASDs = 50.0%, motor coordination/psychomotor disorders = 25.0%, ADHD = 15.0%, pervasive developmental disorder/not otherwise specified = 10.0%). A second sample of children without developmental or learning disorders (TD group; $n = 20$) with a similar sex and age distribution was recruited to serve as a sex- and age-matched control group (girls = 35.0%; mean age = 8.7 years, SD = 1.9 years). Children in this group attended three different mainstream schools in Vigo (Spain) and were excluded beforehand if their parents reported a medically diagnosed neurodevelopmental condition. Table 1 shows the sociodemographic characteristics of both groups. Children of both groups were similar in age, sex distribution, education track, and type of school.

Table 1. Sociodemographic characteristics of the sample ($n = 40$).

Sociodemographic Variables	TD Group ($n = 20$)	NDDs Group ($n = 20$)	p-Value
Age (mean (SD))	8.7 (1.9)	7.8 (1.7)	0.107
Sex (n (%))			1.000
Boys	13 (65.0)	13 (65.0)	
Girls	7 (35.0)	7 (35.0)	
Type of education track (n (%))			0.311
Ordinary	20 (100.0)	19 (95.0)	
Ordinary–special combined	0 (0.0)	1 (5.0)	
Type of school (n (%))			0.197
Public	10 (50.0)	14 (70.0)	
Semiprivate	10 (50.0)	6 (30.0)	
Age at diagnosis (in months, mean (SD))	NA	37.7 (17.1)	NA
Professional that conducted the NDD diagnosis (n (%))	NA		NA
Neurologist		13 (32.5)	
Psychiatrist or clinical psychologist		5 (12.5)	
Pediatrist		2 (5.0)	

TD—typically developing, NDDs—neurodevelopmental disorders, SD—standard deviation, NA—not applicable.

Parents of the participants received the Child and Adolescent Scale of Participation (CASP) questionnaire as well as an informative letter about the study between December 2018 and June 2019 via school or rehabilitation center intermediation. The letter included the e-mail address and telephone number of the first author such that parents could reach the research team for clarification of the study or the questionnaire. Only parents who consented to anonymously participate completed and returned the CASP to the schools or rehabilitation centers from where they were retrieved by the first author.

2.2. The Child and Adolescent Scale of Participation

The Spanish parent-reported version of the CASP was used to measure daily participation and participation restrictions [31,47]. This scale is part of the Child and Family Follow-up Survey, which is a parent-reported measure informed by the ICF that was originally developed by the occupational therapist Gary Bedell to monitor the needs and outcomes of children and adolescents with an acquired brain injury and their families. The CASP has been validated in multiple settings across different countries and contexts with children and adolescents with other conditions, including NDDs [31]. The CASP has reported an excellent internal consistency and temporal stability (Cronbach's alpha = 0.96; intraclass correlation (ICC) = 0.94) and a good convergent validity with the Pediatric Evaluation of Disability Index (r = 0.51–0.75) and the Child and Adolescent Scale of Environment (r = 0.43–0.57) [31].

The CASP consists of 20 items and it is available in both parent-reported and self-administered versions. The purpose of this scale is to measure the extent of participation and participation limitations of children and adolescents in comparison to an age-expected performance in four different contexts (home = six items, community = four items, school = five items, and home and community living activities = five items) [31,47].

While "home" and "community" scales cover social-oriented or self-maintenance activities within the home and community, respectively, the "home and community living activities" scale refers to those activities that support daily life within the home and community, which often require more complex tasks and interactions (i.e., instrumental activities) [26,31]. In the present study, we did not include item 20—work activities and responsibilities (e.g., completion of work tasks, punctuality, attendance, and getting along with supervisors and co-workers)—as the Spanish legal working age is 18 years, and therefore none of the children enrolled in the study were expected to participate in that activity. This decision was made based on the recommendation of two Spanish occupational therapists who independently revised the items.

Each item describes a daily activity and it is rated on a four-point Likert scale (age expected = 4, somewhat limited = 3, very limited = 2, unable to participate = 1). An additional response of "not applicable" is available if the item is not appropriate for the child's age, and items rated as "not applicable" do not receive a score. The item scores are summed and divided by the maximum possible score based on the number of items scored. This score is then multiplied by 100 such that total scores for the subscales and total scale range from 0 to 100, where higher scores indicate a greater level of participation [48].

In addition to the standard analysis of the CASP, two different item-level score analyses of the scale were conducted in the present study to analyze the severity of participation restrictions in each context and for global ADLs [48]. First, item scores of 1, 2, or 3 were considered to explore mild or moderate participation limitations between groups. For instance, if a child was rated as "participation somewhat limited" or lower in at least one activity, they would be defined as presenting with at least mild participation restrictions. Second, we explored moderate or severe participation limitations by considering item scores of 1 or 2. In these cases, if a child was rated as "participation very limited" or "unable to participate," they would be defined as presenting with moderate or severe participation restrictions. Therefore, using the standard analysis of the CASP we could compare the level of daily participation between children with and without NDDs, while using the categorized item-level scores, we could explore how many children showed mild-to-severe participation restrictions in each context.

2.3. Data Analysis

The sample size estimation was performed using G*Power version 3.1.9.4. (Heinrich-Heine-Universität Düsseldorf, Düsseldorf, Germany) [49]. The statistical analyses were conducted using SPSS version 25 (SPSS Inc., Chicago, IL, USA). Prior to conducting the analysis of the data, the internal consistency of the CASP in the sample was tested using Cronbach's alpha to ensure that the removal of item 20 did not alter the reliability of the questionnaire. Values of 0.7 or higher were considered indicators of good internal consistency. The data were examined to determine whether it had a normal distribution using visual inspection, skewness, and kurtosis [50].

Student t-tests for independent samples were used to analyze the differences in participation scores in the CASP total and subscale scores between children with and without NDDs. The effect size of these differences was estimated with Glass's delta (Δ) using the standard deviation of the typically developing group [51]. Differences in the prevalence of participation restrictions in the different contexts and global participation between both groups were analyzed using chi-squared tests. Additionally, the odds ratios (ORs) and OR 95% confidence of intervals (95% CIs) were calculated to estimate the risk for participation restrictions between children with and without NDDs [51]. Finally, the association between the different contexts of participation was examined in both the total sample and within groups using Spearman correlation coefficients.

3. Results

The internal consistency values of the CASP were adequate for both the overall sample (Cronbach's alpha = 0.9) and for the two groups of participants (TD = 0.7, NDDs = 0.9). Most of the items were scored, indicating that the activities were relevant for the child, and only item 9, item 14, and item 19 received no applicable scores (n = 1, n = 1, and n = 14, respectively). There were no significant differences in the no applicable scores in those items between both groups (p = 0.311–0.320).

As shown in Table 2, significant and strong differences were found in all contexts of participation between children with and without NDDs. Community participation, home participation, and general participation were the contexts that revealed stronger differences between groups (Δ = 4.0–5.5, $p < 0.001$).

Table 2. Participation in activities of daily living in children with and without NDDs (n = 40).

Contexts of Participation	TD Group	NDDs Group	Δ	p-Value
	Mean (SD)	Mean (SD)		
Home participation	97.7 (5.3)	76.7 (12.5)	4.0	<0.001
Community participation	96.3 (5.1)	68.1 (20.7)	5.5	<0.001
School participation	97.8 (5.3)	77.5 (12.4)	3.8	<0.001
Home and community instrumental living activities	88.8 (17.4)	59.2 (22.7)	1.7	<0.001
CASP total score	95.6 (5.6)	71.9 (13.4)	4.2	<0.001

TD—typically developing, NDDs—neurodevelopmental disorders, SD—standard deviation, Δ—effect size, CASP—Child and Adolescent Scale of Participation.

Children with NDDs showed a higher prevalence of participation restrictions or limitations in all contexts ($p < 0.01$). While up to 35.0–60.0% of children with typical development reported a mild or moderate participation limitation in at least one ADL (see Table 3), all the children in the NDDs group reported moderate-to-severe limitations or were unable to participate in at least one instrumental ADL, and most of them faced participation restrictions in home, community, and school settings as well (Table 3). Overall, children with NDDs were 23.4 times more likely to suffer significant participation limitations during their daily living.

Finally, the Spearman correlations exposed significant and moderate-to-strong associations between the different contexts of participation in the total sample and within the NDDs group (Table 4). The TD group showed significant correlations between community and school participation, and between community and home and community instrumental living activities participation (r = 0.484–0.604), although the correlation between home and community participation was close to significance (p = 0.068). The strongest correlations were found between school and home participation, and between school and community participation in both the total sample and the NDDs group (r = 0.641–0.855).

Table 3. Participation limitations in daily living in children with and without NDDs (n = 40).

Mild Participation Limitations in at Least One ADL	TD Group N (%)	NDDs Group N (%)	p-Value	OR (95% CI)
Home participation	4 (20.0)	18 (90.0)	<0.001	36.0 (5.8–223.5)
Community participation	8 (40.0)	17 (85.0)	0.003	8.5 (1.9–38.8)
School participation	4 (20.0)	19 (95.0)	<0.001	76.0 (7.7–750.5)
Home and community instrumental living activities	10 (50.0)	20 (100.0)	<0.001	41.0 (2.2–770.1)
Overall (in at least one ADL)	12 (60.0)	20 (100.0)	0.008	27.9 (1.5–526.1)
Moderate or Severe Participation Limitations in at Least One ADL	**TD Group** N (%)	**NDDs Group** N (%)	**p-Value**	**OR (95% CI)**
Home participation	1 (5.0)	13 (65.0)	<0.001	24.4 (3.6–154.2)
Community participation	1 (5.0)	13 (65.0)	<0.001	24.4 (3.6–154.2)
School participation	4 (20.0)	19 (95.0)	<0.001	47.7 (6.7–338.7)
Home and community instrumental living activities	4 (20.0)	12 (60.0)	0.010	5.4 (1.4–21.0)
Overall (in at least one ADL)	7 (35.0)	19 (95.0)	<0.001	23.4 (3.6–154.2)

ADL—activity of daily living, TD—typically developing, NDDs—neurodevelopmental disorders, OR—odds ratio, CI—confidence interval.

Table 4. Associations between the different contexts of participation (n = 40).

Total Sample (n = 40)			
Contexts of Participation	**Home Participation**	**Community Participation**	**School Participation**
Community participation	0.818 ***	-	-
School participation	0.856 ***	0.849 ***	-
Home and community instrumental living activities	0.731 ***	0.715 ***	0.642 ***
TD Group (n = 20)			
Contexts of Participation	**Home Participation**	**Community Participation**	**School Participation**
Community participation	0.416 †	-	-
School participation	0.261	0.604 **	-
Home and community instrumental living activities	0.225	0.484 *	0.021
NDDs Group (n = 20)			
Contexts of Participation	**Home Participation**	**Community Participation**	**School Participation**
Community participation	0.542 *	-	-
School participation	0.807 ***	0.641 **	-
Home and community instrumental living activities	0.469 *	0.441 ‡	0.488 *

† $p = 0.068$, ‡ $p = 0.052$, * $p < 0.05$, ** $p < 0.01$, *** $p < 0.001$.

4. Discussion

Neurodevelopmental conditions that affect a child's typical development are present in approximately 9% of school-aged children in Spain [9]. These children usually face more performance difficulties and participation restrictions than their TD peers, which might have further consequences on their emotional and psychological wellbeing [20–24,32–38]. To the best of our knowledge, no studies on NDDs have so far compared participation restrictions in the different daily contexts in Spanish children with and without NDDs.

4.1. Differences in Daily Participation between Children with and without NDDs

Significant differences in daily participation between children with and without neurodevelopmental conditions were found in the present sample. As expected, children with ASDs, motor coordination disorders, or ADHD participated significantly less and faced more participation restrictions in all daily contexts than TD children. Such a pattern is consistent with previous research [32–38]. Our results regarding the level of participation in daily contexts between children with and without developmental disorders are highly similar to the findings of Bedell in the validation study for the CASP [31], who found significant differences between both groups with an analogous outcome in children from North America, Australia, and Israel. Additionally, children with ADHD, DCD, or ASDs usually have co-occurring sensory processing issues [44,52,53], which may further restrict their daily participation [12,44,53–56]. However, it is worth noting that children with neurodevelopmental conditions who are not currently referred to rehabilitation intervention may have different participation patterns. Although most of the NDD children in this study were enrolled in ordinary education, other children with NDDs who are not in inpatient treatment could also show potential differences in their participation and performance [52].

In the present study, participation restrictions in self-care and instrumental ADLs in home and community contexts were significantly higher in children with NDDs These activities are oriented toward taking care of one's own body and supporting daily life within the home and community [26]. Our findings in these contexts are in line with previous studies that explored children from Europe, America, and Asia, which is of particular interest given that self-care and home maintenance activities may be different between cultures. Self-care and instrumental activities are one of the most problematic contexts for children with ASDs, ADHD, and DCD [21,24,33,35]. In addition, van der Linde et al. found that children with DCD both participated significantly less and performed significantly worse than TD children in self-care activities, while daily performance and participation were interrelated as performance predicted participation [23].

In our sample, children in the NDDs group showed lower levels of participation in the school context. Previous studies have highlighted the specific school-related issues that children with developmental disabilities encounter during their daily performance. Difficulties in numerical and mathematical comprehension, reading, academic fine motor activities, and peer socialization have been reported in children with motor coordination problems [33,57,58]. Children with ASDs face significant issues with learning processing and social participation, which negatively affect their academic performance and participation [44,59]. In addition, children with ADHD are more likely to face academic difficulties and to not pursue high school or university studies due to behavioral and attention deficits [44,60].

Social participation in children with neurodevelopmental disabilities is one of the most restricted contexts and one major concern for the families of these children. While the CASP does not consider a specific context of social participation, this aspect is thoroughly evaluated in all subscales, especially in the home and community participation contexts [31,47], which were significantly restricted in the NDDs group. This outcome is consistent with previous research. While exploring the level of participation in several leisure and social activities, Kaljača et al. found that children with neurodevelopmental disabilities not only participated significantly less than TD children, but also that their activities were mainly stereotypical and highly structured, and were mostly supervised by parents [61]. Social cognition has been reported to be limited in these children as well, and it is associated with motor parameters, which further restricts daily participation [20,24,62]. Similarly, in the study conducted by Kreider et al., the social networks and participation with others of children with ASDs, ADHD, and learning disorders were explored [63]. The study concluded that children with neurodevelopmental conditions show specific limitations in physical, recreational, social, and informal activities with family and/or friends.

Children's participation in family activities in home and community contexts was significantly more restricted in children with NDDs. This finding adds to the evidence that family involvement and functioning is affected in families with children with NDDs, which was previously reported [56,64–66]. Family engagement in the child's activities is important for their overall development, quality of life, and participation involvement [67,68]. Overall, family support is essential for promoting ADLs performance and participation, as parental self-efficacy and satisfaction predict children's participation involvement and enjoyment [67,69].

An interesting finding of the present study was that 35% of the overall parents (TD = 25%, NDDs = 45%, $p = 0.320$) considered the last item of this context (item 19—using transportation to get around in the community, e.g., to and from school, work, social, or leisure activities) as not applicable, meaning that their child was not expected to participate in that particular activity regardless of the presence of a neurodevelopmental condition. While this could be related to the young age of the participants (<12 years), it would be interesting to examine the subjective relevance perceived by the children about engaging in different daily contexts.

4.2. Associations between the Daily Contexts of Participation

Finally, all daily contexts were strongly associated with each other in our sample. This finding suggests that daily participation is a complex and multifaceted construct comprised of several subareas of different but interrelated occupations, as it has been proposed by previous research [26,30]. Interestingly, school participation showed the strongest correlations with both home and community participation in the total sample and the NDDs group while being the context where children with NDDs faced greater participation restrictions. Additionally, correlations between contexts were different between children with and without NDDs, with them being significantly higher in the latter group. This particular result may suggest that participation restrictions in one daily context may have a greater influence on participation restrictions in other contexts in children with neurodevelopmental conditions in comparison with their typically developing peers, and therefore it may be necessary to pay particular attention when these children first show participation restrictions in their daily activities. Overall, these findings add to the existing literature recommending the use of family-centered and occupation- and participation-based interventions, such as occupational therapy in schools [70–73]. This is of particular relevance given than most children with DCD or ADHD are enrolled in ordinary schools, which do not usually provide this kind of intervention in Spain [52].

Overall, the findings from this study support that children with NDDs present with lower levels of daily participation and greater and more severe participation restrictions in their daily activities than typically developing children. This outcome is consistent with previous research from different countries and cultures, and altogether may point toward a cross-cultural model of participation restrictions in children with NDDs. Additionally, our results suggest that participation difficulties in one particular context may lead to participation difficulties in other contexts, especially in children with neurodevelopmental conditions. Therefore, these findings have implications for research on neurodevelopmental disabilities, both in Spain and in international populations, and they could be used on clinical intervention to assess for difficulties in overall daily participation as soon as a child shows participation restrictions in one particular area, such as school or self-care contexts.

4.3. Limitations and Future Research Directions

This study has several limitations that need to be disclosed. First, a limited sample size was used; although this sample size was calculated to examine differences in daily participation between children with and without NDDs with minimal bias [31], the study findings should be interpreted cautiously and should be supported by larger studies. Nevertheless, this. Second, it is important to note that most of the children in the NDDs group had ASDs, which is usually associated with greater daily challenges than other conditions like ADHD or DCD. This could partially explain the greater variance of the participation abilities observed in this group. Additionally, this imbalance in diagnosis distribution within the NDDs group does not allow for a more in-depth analysis of potential differences between the different diagnostic groups. Third, the participants had a large age range (5 to 12 years). Even though both groups had a similar age distribution, differences in daily participation according to age could not be explored due to the limited sample size; therefore, this may pose a further limitation that should be explored in future studies. Additionally, there are other factors that could further restrict daily participation, such as psychosocial and behavioral issues, which are present in a large percentage of children with NDDs [34–37,74,75]. Finally, we used a parent-reported questionnaire to assess daily participation, which could be subject to subjectivity. However, parental questionnaires can provide valuable information that would not have been recorded otherwise in a clinical setting [76,77], and therefore parent-based measures, such as the CASP, are useful for reporting information about children's participation in the daily, naturalistic contexts. Future studies should assess differences in participation between larger samples of children with different neurodevelopmental diagnoses that involve considering other environmental, psychosocial, and child-related factors that may be influencing daily participation.

5. Conclusions

Findings from this study support the belief that participation difficulties and restrictions are present in Spanish children with NDDs in comparison with their TD peers. Home, community, and school contexts seem to be particularly affected, which may further restrict the quality of life and future development of children with neurodevelopmental issues. These consequences for daily functioning highlight the need for tailored, participation-oriented intervention strategies.

Author Contributions: Conceptualization, N.B.-M., L.D.-L., and S.S.-d.-R.; methodology, N.B.-M. and L.D.-L.; formal analysis, N.B.-M., L.D.-L., and R.M.-M.; investigation, N.B.-M., L.D.-L., R.M.-M., N.R.-P., M.R.-P., and S.S.-d.-R.; resources, N.B.-M. and L.D.-L.; data curation, N.B.-M. and L.D.-L.; writing—original draft preparation, N.B.-M., L.D.-L., and R.M.-M.; writing—review and editing, N.B.-M., L.D.-L., R.M.-M., N.R.-P., M.R.-P., and S.S.-d.-R.; supervision, L.D.-L. and S.S.-d.-R.; funding acquisition, S.S.-d.-R. All authors have read and agreed to the published version of the manuscript.

Funding: This research received no external funding.

Acknowledgments: The authors would like to thank the participants of the study for their cooperation. The authors would like to extend their gratitude and acknowledgments to the rehabilitation centers and schools that helped with data gathering.

Conflicts of Interest: The authors declare no conflict of interest.

References

1. American Psychiatry Association. *Diagnostic and Statistical Manual of Mental Disorders*, 5th ed.; American Psychiatry Association: Washington, DC, USA, 2013.
2. Nowell, K.P.; Bodner, K.E.; Mohrland, M.D.; Kanne, S.M. Neurodevelopmental disorders. In *Handbook of Rehabilitation Psychology*; Brenner, L.A., Reid-Arndt, S.A., Elliott, T.R., Frank, R.G., Caplan, B., Eds.; American Psychological Association: Washington, DC, USA, 2019; pp. 357–370.
3. Blackburn, C.; Read, J.; Spencer, N. Children with neurodevelopmental disabilities. In *Annual Report of the Chief Medical Officer 2012. Our Children Deserve Better: Prevention Pays*; Lemer, C., Todd, K., Cheung, R., Murphy, O., Eds.; Department of Health and Social Care: London, UK, 2013.
4. Arora, N.K.; Nair, M.K.C.; Gulati, S.; Deshmukh, V.; Mohapatra, A.; Mishra, D.; Patel, V.; Pandey, R.M.; Das, B.C.; Divan, G.; et al. Neurodevelopmental disorders in children aged 2–9 years: Population-based burden estimates across five regions in India. *PLoS Med.* **2018**, *15*, e1002615. [CrossRef]
5. Dietrich, K.N.; Eskenazi, B.; Schantz, S.; Yolton, K.; Rauh, V.A.; Johnson, C.B.; Alkon, A.; Canfield, R.L.; Pessah, I.N.; Berman, R.F. Principles and practices of neurodevelopmental assessment in children: Lessons learned from the Centers for Children's Environmental Health and Disease Prevention Research. *Environ. Health Perspect.* **2005**, *113*, 1437–1446. [CrossRef]
6. Cleaton, M.A.M.; Kirby, A. Why Do We Find it so Hard to Calculate the Burden of Neurodevelopmental Disorders? *J. Child. Dev. Disord.* **2018**, *4*, 10. [CrossRef]
7. Polanczyk, G.V.; Willcutt, E.G.; Salum, G.A.; Kieling, C.; Rohde, L.A. ADHD prevalence estimates across three decades: An updated systematic review and meta-regression analysis. *Int. J. Epidemiol.* **2014**, *43*, 434–442. [CrossRef]

8. Catala-Lopez, F.; Peiro, S.; Ridao, M.; Sanfelix-Gimeno, G.; Genova-Maleras, R.; Catala, M.A. Prevalence of attention deficit hyperactivity disorder among children and adolescents in Spain: A systematic review and meta-analysis of epidemiological studies. *BMC Psychiatry* **2012**, *12*, 168. [CrossRef]
9. Mariño, M.C.; Ageitos, A.G.; Álvarez, J.A.; Del Río Garma, M.; Cendón, C.G.; Castaño, A.G.; Nieto, J.P. Prevalencia de trastornos del neurodesarrollo, comportamiento y aprendizaje en Atención Primaria. *An. Pediatría* **2018**, *89*, 153–161. [CrossRef]
10. Pérez-Crespo, L.; Canals-Sans, J.; Suades-González, E.; Guxens, M. Temporal trends and geographical variability of the prevalence and incidence of attention deficit/hyperactivity disorder diagnoses among children in Catalonia, Spain. *Sci. Rep.* **2020**, *10*, 6397. [CrossRef]
11. Blank, R.; Barnett, A.L.; Cairney, J.; Green, D.; Kirby, A.; Polatajko, H.; Rosenblum, S.; Smits-Engelsman, B.; Sugden, D.; Wilson, P.; et al. International clinical practice recommendations on the definition, diagnosis, assessment, intervention, and psychosocial aspects of developmental coordination disorder. *Dev. Med. Child. Neurol.* **2019**, *61*, 242–285. [CrossRef]
12. Delgado-Lobete, L.; Montes-Montes, R.; Pértega-Díaz, S.; Santos-del-Riego, S.; Cruz-Valiño, J.M.; Schoemaker, M.M. Interrelation of Individual, Country and Activity Constraints in Motor Activities of Daily Living among Typically Developing Children: A Cross-sectional Comparison of Spanish and Dutch Populations. *Int. J. Environ. Res. Public Health* **2020**, *17*, 1705. [CrossRef]
13. Montes-Montes, R.; Delgado-Lobete, L.; Pereira, J.; Santos-del-Riego, S.; Pousada, T. Psychometric Validation and Reference Norms for the European Spanish Developmental Coordination Disorder Questionnaire: DCDQ-ES. *Int. J. Environ. Res. Public Health* **2020**, *17*, 2425. [CrossRef]
14. Amador-Ruiz, S.; Gutierrez, D.; Martínez-Vizcaíno, V.; Gulías-González, R.; Pardo-Guijarro, M.J.; Sánchez-López, M. Motor Competence Levels and Prevalence of Developmental Coordination Disorder in Spanish Children: The MOVI-KIDS Study. *J. Sch. Health* **2018**, *88*, 538–546. [CrossRef] [PubMed]
15. Delgado-Lobete, L.; Santos-del-Riego, S.; Pértega-Díaz, S.; Montes-Montes, R. Prevalence of suspected developmental coordination disorder and associated factors in Spanish classrooms. *Res. Dev. Disabil.* **2019**, *86*, 31–40. [CrossRef]
16. Morales-Hidalgo, P.; Roigé-Castellví, J.; Hernández-Martínez, C.; Voltas, N.; Canals, J. Prevalence and Characteristics of Autism Spectrum Disorder Among Spanish School-Age Children. *J. Autism Dev. Disord.* **2018**, *48*, 3176–3190. [CrossRef]
17. Williams, J.G.; Higgins, J.P.; Brayne, C.E. Systematic review of prevalence studies of autism spectrum disorders. *Arch. Dis. Child.* **2006**, *91*, 8–15. [CrossRef] [PubMed]
18. Baxter, A.J.; Brugha, T.S.; Erskine, H.E.; Scheurer, R.W.; Vos, T.; Scott, J.G. The epidemiology and global burden of autism spectrum disorders. *Psychol. Med.* **2015**, *45*, 601–613. [CrossRef]
19. Kim, Y.S.; Leventhal, B.L.; Koh, Y.J.; Fombonne, E.; Laska, E.; Lim, E.C.; Cheon, K.-A.; Kim, S.-J.; Lee, H.; Song, D.H.; et al. Prevalence of autism spectrum disorders in a total population sample. *Am. J. Psychiatry* **2011**, *168*, 904–912. [CrossRef]
20. Bumin, G.; Günal, A. The effects of motor and cognitive impairments on daily living activities and quality of life in autistic children. *Eur. J. Paediatr. Neurol.* **2008**, *12*, S70. [CrossRef]
21. Jasmin, E.; Couture, M.; McKinley, P.; Reid, G.; Fombonne, E.; Gisel, E. Sensori-motor and daily living skills of preschool children with autism spectrum disorders. *J. Autism Dev. Disord.* **2009**, *39*, 231–241. [CrossRef] [PubMed]
22. Elbasan, B.; Kayihan, H.; Duzgun, I. Sensory integration and activities of daily living in children with developmental coordination disorder. *Ital. J. Pediatr.* **2012**, *38*, 14. [CrossRef]
23. Van der Linde, B.W.; van Netten, J.J.; Otten, E.; Postema, K.; Geuze, R.H.; Schoemaker, M.M. Activities of Daily Living in Children with Developmental Coordination Disorder: Performance, Learning, and Participation. *Phys. Ther.* **2015**, *95*, 1496–1506. [CrossRef]
24. Volkan-Yazici, M.; Elbasan, B.; Yazici, G. Motor Performance and Activities of Daily Living in Children with neurodevelopmental Disorders. *Iran. J. Pediatr.* **2018**, *28*, e65396. [CrossRef]
25. World Health Organization. *International Classification of Functioning, Disability and Health: ICF.*; World Health Organization: Geneva, Switzerland, 2001.
26. American Occupational Therapy Association. Occupational therapy practice framework: Domain and process 3a ed. *Am. J. Occup. Ther.* **2014**, *68*, S1–S48. [CrossRef]
27. Law, M. Participation in the Occupations of Everyday Life. *Am. J. Occup. Ther.* **2002**, *56*, 640–649. [CrossRef]

28. Renée, T. *Kielhofner's Model of Human Occupation: Theory and Application*, 5th ed.; Lippincott Williams & Wilkins: Philadelphia, PA, USA, 2017.
29. Van der Linde, B.W.; van Netten, J.J.; Otten, B.E.; Postema, K.; Geuze, R.H.; Schoemaker, M.M. Psychometric properties of the DCDDaily-Q: A new parental questionnaire on children's performance in activities of daily living. *Res. Dev. Disabil.* **2014**, *35*, 1711–1719. [CrossRef] [PubMed]
30. Delgado-Lobete, L.; Montes-Montes, R.; van der Linde, B.W.; Schoemaker, M.M. Assessment of Motor Activities of Daily Living: Spanish Cross-Cultural Adaptation, Reliability and Construct Validity of the DCDDaily-Q. *Int. J. Environ. Res. Public Health* **2020**, *17*, 4802. [CrossRef] [PubMed]
31. Bedell, G. Further validation of the Child and Adolescent Scale of Participation (CASP). *Dev. Neurorehabil.* **2009**, *12*, 342–351. [CrossRef]
32. Rosenberg, L.; Bart, O.; Ratzon, N.Z.; Jarus, T. Personal and Environmental Factors Predict Participation of Children With and Without Mild Developmental Disabilities. *J. Child Fam. Stud.* **2013**, *22*, 658–671. [CrossRef]
33. Magalhães, L.C.; Cardoso, A.A.; Missiuna, C. Activities and participation in children with developmental coordination disorder: A systematic review. *Res. Dev. Disabil.* **2011**, *32*, 1309–1316. [CrossRef]
34. Liberman, L.; Ratzon, N.; Bart, O. The profile of performance skills and emotional factors in the context of participation among young children with Developmental Coordination Disorder. *Res. Dev. Disabil.* **2013**, *34*, 87–94. [CrossRef]
35. De Schipper, E.; Lundequist, A.; Wilteus, A.L.; Coghill, D.; de Vries, P.J.; Granlund, M.; Holtmann, M.; Jonsson, U.; Karande, S.; Levy, F.; et al. A comprehensive scoping review of ability and disability in ADHD using the International Classification of Functioning, Disability and Health-Children and Youth Version (ICF-CY). *Eur. Child Adolesc. Psychiatry* **2015**, *24*, 859–872. [CrossRef]
36. De Schipper, E.; Lundequist, A.; Coghill, D.; de Vries, P.J.; Granlund, M.; Holtmann, M.; Jonsson, U.; Karande, S.; Levy, F.; Robison, J.E.; et al. Ability and Disability in Autism Spectrum Disorder: A Systematic Literature Review Employing the International Classification of Functioning, Disability and Health-Children and Youth Version. *Autism Res.* **2015**, *8*, 782–794. [CrossRef] [PubMed]
37. Ferguson, G.D.; Jelsma, J.; Versfeld, P.; Smits-Engelsman, B.C.M. Using the ICF Framework to Explore the Multiple Interacting Factors Associated with Developmental Coordination Disorder. *Curr. Dev. Disord. Rep.* **2014**, *1*, 86–101. [CrossRef]
38. Ibañez, L.V.; Kobak, K.; Swanson, A.; Wallace, L.; Warren, Z.; Stone, W.L. Enhancing Interactions during Daily Routines: A Randomized Controlled Trial of a Web-Based Tutorial for Parents of Young Children with ASD. *Autism Res.* **2018**, *11*, 667–678. [CrossRef] [PubMed]
39. Schreibman, L.; Dawson, G.; Stahmer, A.C.; Landa, R.; Rogers, S.J.; McGee, G.G.; Halladay, A. Naturalistic developmental behavioral interventions: Empirically validated treatments for autism spectrum disorder. *J. Autism Dev. Disord.* **2015**, *45*, 2411–2428. [CrossRef] [PubMed]
40. Smits-Engelsman, B.C.; Blank, R.; van der Kaay, A.C.; Mosterd-van der Meijs, R.; Vlugt-van den Brand, E.; Polatajko, H.; Wilson, P.H. Efficacy of interventions to improve motor performance in children with developmental coordination disorder: A combined systematic review and meta-analysis. *Dev. Med. Child Neurol* **2013**, *55*, 229–237. [CrossRef] [PubMed]
41. Offor, N.; Williamson, P.O.; Cacola, P. Effectiveness of interventions for children with developmental coordination disorder in physical therapy contexts: A systematic literature review and meta-analysis. *J. Mot. Learn. Dev.* **2016**, *4*, 169–196. [CrossRef]
42. Preston, N.; Magallon, S.; Hill, L.J.; Andrews, E.; Ahern, S.M.; Mon-Williams, M. A systematic review of high quality randomized controlled trials investigating motor skill programmes for children with developmental coordination disorder. *Clin. Rehabil.* **2016**, *31*, 857–870. [CrossRef]
43. Fernández-Andrés, M.A.; Pastor-Cerezuela, G.; Sanz-Cervera, P.; Tárraga-Mínguez, R. A comparative study of sensory processing in children with and without Autism Spectrum Disorder in the home and classroom environments. *Res. Dev. Disabil.* **2015**, *38*, 202–212. [CrossRef]
44. Sanz-Cervera, P.; Pastor-Cerezuela, G.; González-Sala, F.; Tárraga-Mínguez, R.; Fernández-Andrés, M.I. Sensory Processing in Children with Autism Spectrum Disorder and/or Attention Deficit Hyperactivity Disorder in the Home and Classroom Contexts. *Front. Psychol.* **2017**, *8*, 1772. [CrossRef]
45. Barrios-Fernández, S.; Gozalo, M.; García-Gómez, A.; Romero-Ayuso, D.; Hernández-Mocholí, M.Á. A New Assessment for Activities of Daily Living in Spanish Schoolchildren: A Preliminary Study of its Psychometric Properties. *Int. J. Environ. Res. Public Health* **2020**, *17*, 2673. [CrossRef]

46. Giménez-Nadal, J.I.; Molina, J.A.; Ortega, R. Like my parents at home? Gender differences in children's housework in Germany and Spain. *Empir. Econ.* **2017**, *52*, 1143–1179. [CrossRef]
47. Bedell, G.; Khetani, M.; Coster, J.; Law, M.; Cousins, M. Measures of participation in community, social and civic life for children with disabilities. In *Measures of Outcomes and Their Determinants for Children and Youth with Developmental Disabilities*; Majnemer, A., Ed.; Mac Keith Press: London, UK, 2012.
48. Bedell, G. The Child and Adolescent Scale of Participation (CASP)©. Administration and Scoring Guidelines. Available online: http://sites.tufts.edu/garybedell/files/2012/07/CASP-Administration-Scoring-Guidelines-8-19-11.pdf (accessed on 31 May 2020).
49. Faul, F.; Erdfelder, E.; Lang, A.-G.; Buchner, A. G*Power 3: A flexible statistical power analysis program for the social, behavioral, and biomedical sciences. *Behav. Res. Methods* **2007**, *39*, 175–191. [CrossRef] [PubMed]
50. Gravetter, F.; Wallnau, L. *Essentials of Statistics for the Behavioral Sciences*, 8th ed.; Wadsworth: Belmont, TN, USA, 2014.
51. Ferguson, C.J. An effect size primmer: A guide for clinicians and researchers. *Prof. Psychol. Res. Pract.* **2009**, *40*, 532–538. [CrossRef]
52. Delgado-Lobete, L.; Pértega-Díaz, S.; Santos-del-Riego, S.; Montes-Montes, R. Sensory Processing Patterns in Developmental Coordination Disorder, Attention Deficit Hyperactivity Disorder and Typical Development. *Res. Dev. Disabil.* **2020**, *100*, 103608. [CrossRef] [PubMed]
53. Mazurek, M.O.; Petroski, G.F. Sleep problems in children with autism spectrum disorder: Examining the contributions of sensory over-responsivity and anxiety. *Sleep Med.* **2015**, *16*, 270–279. [CrossRef] [PubMed]
54. Kuhaneck, H.M.; Britner, P.A. A preliminary investigation of the relationship between sensory processing and social play in autism spectrum disorder. *OTJR (Thorofare N. J.)* **2013**, *33*, 159–167. [CrossRef]
55. Chien, C.-W.; Rodger, S.; Copley, J.; Branjerdporn, G.; Taggart, C. Sensory Processing and Its Relationship with Children's Daily Life Participation. *Phys. Occup. Ther. Pediatr.* **2016**, *36*, 73–87. [CrossRef]
56. Kirby, A.V.; Williams, K.L.; Watson, L.R.; Sideris, J.; Bulluck, J.; Baranek, G.T. Sensory Features and Family Functioning in Families of Children With Autism and Developmental Disabilities: Longitudinal Associations. *Am. J. Occup. Ther.* **2019**, *73*. [CrossRef]
57. Izadi-Najafabadi, S.; Ryan, N.; Ghafooripoor, G.; Gill, K.; Zwicker, J.G. Participation of children with developmental coordination disorder. *Res. Dev. Disabil.* **2019**, *84*, 75–84. [CrossRef]
58. Harrowell, I.; Holien, L.; Lingam, R.; Emond, A. The impact of developmental coordination disorder on educational achievement in secondary school. *Res. Dev. Disabil.* **2018**, *72*, 13–22. [CrossRef]
59. Poon, K.K. The activities and participation of adolescents with autism spectrum disorders in Singapore: Findings from an ICF-based instrument. *J. Intellect. Disabil. Res.* **2011**, *55*, 790–800. [CrossRef] [PubMed]
60. Zendarski, N.; Mensah, F.; Hiscock, H.; Sciberras, E. Trajectories of emotional and conduct problems and their association with early high school achievement and engagement for adolescents with ADHD. *J. Atten. Disord.* **2019**. [CrossRef] [PubMed]
61. Kaljača, S.; Dučić, B.; Cvijetić, M. Participation of children and youth with neurodevelopmental disorders in after-school activities. *Disabil. Rehabil.* **2019**, *41*, 2036–2048. [CrossRef] [PubMed]
62. Günal, A.; Bumin, G.; Huri, M. The Effects of Motor and Cognitive Impairments on Daily Living Activities and Quality of Life in Children with Autism. *J. Occup. Ther. Sch. Early Interv.* **2019**, *12*, 444–454. [CrossRef]
63. Kreider, C.M.; Bendixen, R.M.; Young, M.E.; Prudencio, S.M.; McCarty, C.; Mann, W.C. Social networks and participation with others for youth with learning, attention, and autism spectrum disorders. *Can. J. Occup. Ther.* **2016**, *83*, 14–26. [CrossRef]
64. Walton, K.M. Leisure time and family functioning in families living with autism spectrum disorder. *Autism* **2019**, *23*, 1384–1397. [CrossRef]
65. Şipoş, R.; Predescu, E.; Mureşan, G.; Iftene, F. The Evaluation of Family Quality of Life of Children with Autism Spectrum Disorder and Attention Deficit Hyperactive Disorder. *Appl. Med. Inform.* **2012**, *30*, 1–8.
66. Jellet, R.; Wood, C.E.; Giallo, R.; Seymour, M. Family functioning and behaviour problems in children with Autism Spectrum Disorders: The mediating role of parent mental health. *Clin. Psychol.* **2015**, *19*, 39–48. [CrossRef]
67. Chien, C.-W.; Rodger, S.; Copley, J. Parent-reported Participation in Children with Moderate-to-severe Developmental Disabilities: Preliminary Analysis of Associated Factors using the ICF Framework. *Int. J. Disabil. Dev. Educ.* **2017**, *64*, 483–496. [CrossRef]

68. Sikora, D.; Moran, E.; Orlinch, F.; Hall, T.A.; Kovacs, E.A.; Delahaye, J.; Clemons, T.E.; Kuhlthau, K. The relationship between family functioning and behavior problems in children with autism spectrum disorders. *Res. Autism Spectr. Disord.* **2013**, *7*, 307–315. [CrossRef]
69. Soref, B.; Ratzon, N.Z.; Rosenberg, L.; Leitner, Y.; Jarus, T.; Bart, O. Personal and environmental pathways to participation in young children with and without mild motor disabilities. *Child Care Health Dev.* **2012**, *38*, 561–571. [CrossRef] [PubMed]
70. Grajo, L.C.; Candler, C.; Sarafian, A. Interventions within the Scope of Occupational Therapy to Improve Children's Academic Participation: A Systematic Review. *Am. J. Occup. Ther.* **2020**, *74*, 7402180030p1–7402180030p32. [CrossRef] [PubMed]
71. Fox, A.; Dishman, S.; Valicek, M.; Ratcliff, K.; Hilton, C. Effectiveness of Social Skills Interventions Incorporating Peer Interactions for Children with Attention Deficit Hyperactivity Disorder: A Systematic Review. *Am J. Occup. Ther.* **2020**, *74*, 7402180070. [CrossRef] [PubMed]
72. Cahill, S.M.; Egan, B.E.; Seber, J. Activity- and Occupation-Based Interventions to Support Mental Health, Positive Behavior, and Social Participation for Children and Youth: A Systematic Review. *Am. J. Occup. Ther.* **2020**, *74*. [CrossRef] [PubMed]
73. Cahill, S.M.; Beisbier, S. Occupational Therapy Practice Guidelines for Children and Youth Ages 5-21 Years. *Am. J. Occup. Ther.* **2020**, *74*. [CrossRef]
74. Crane, L.; Sumner, E.M.; Hill, E.I. Emotional and behavioural prolems in children with Developmental Coordination Disorder: Exploring parent and teacher reports. *Res. Dev. Disabil.* **2017**, *70*, 67–74. [CrossRef]
75. Lingam, R.; Jongmans, M.J.; Ellis, M.; Hunt, L.P.; Golding, J.; Emond, A. Mental Health Difficulties in Children with Developmental Coordination Disorder. *Pediatrics* **2012**, *129*, 882–891. [CrossRef]
76. Glascoe, F. Evidence-based approach to developmental and behavioural surveillance using parents' concerns. *Child Care Health Dev.* **2000**, *26*, 137–149. [CrossRef]
77. Van der Linde, B.W.; Van Netten, J.J.; Otten, E.; Postema, K.; Geuze, R.H.; Schoemaker, M.M. A systematic review of instruments for assessment of capacity in activities of daily living in children with developmental co-ordiantion disorder. *Child Care Health Dev.* **2015**, *41*, 23–34. [CrossRef]

children

MDPI

Review

Effectiveness of Virtual Reality-Based Interventions for Children and Adolescents with ADHD: A Systematic Review and Meta-Analysis

Dulce Romero-Ayuso [1,*], Abel Toledano-González [2], María del Carmen Rodríguez-Martínez [3], Palma Arroyo-Castillo [1], José Matías Triviño-Juárez [4], Pascual González [5], Patrocinio Ariza-Vega [1], Antonio Del Pino González [6] and Antonio Segura-Fragoso [2]

1 Department of Physical Therapy, Occupational Therapy Division, Faculty of Health Sciences, University of Granada, 18016 Granada, Spain; palmarroyo@correo.ugr.es (P.A.-C.); pariza@ugr.es (P.A.-V.)
2 Faculty of Health Sciences, University of Castilla-La Mancha, Talavera la de Reina, 45600 Toledo, Spain; Abel.Toledano@uclm.es (A.T.-G.); Antonio.Segura@uclm.es (A.S.-F.)
3 Faculty of Health Sciences, Universidad de Málaga, 29016 Málaga, Spain; marrodmar@uma.es
4 Primary Care Center Zaidín Sur, Granada Metropolitan Sanitary District, 18007 Granada, Spain; jmtjuarez@hotmail.com
5 LoUISE Research Group, Computing Systems Department, University of Castilla-La Mancha, 02071 Albacete, Spain; Pascual.Gonzalez@uclm.es
6 Department of Educational Orientation, IES Máximo Laguna, Consejería de Educación, Junta de Castilla-La Mancha, Santa Cruz de Mudela, 13730 Ciudad Real, Spain; antoniodelpino@hotmail.es
* Correspondence: dulceromero@ugr.es

Abstract: This review aims to evaluate the effectiveness of virtual reality-based interventions (VR-based interventions) on cognitive deficits in children with attention deficit hyperactivity disorder (ADHD). A systematic review and meta-analysis were performed according to the PRISMA statement and the Cochrane Handbook guidelines for conducting meta-analyses. The Grading of Recommendations, Assessment, Development and Evaluation (GRADE) was used to assess the quality of the evidence. Clinical trials published up to 29 October 2020 were included. The meta-analysis included four studies, with a population of 125 participants with ADHD. The magnitude of the effect was large for omissions (SMD = −1.38; p = 0.009), correct hits (SMD = −1.50; p = 0.004), and perceptual sensitivity (SMD = −1.07; p = 0.01); and moderate for commissions (SMD = −0.62; p = 0.002) and reaction time (SMD = −0.67; p = 0.03). The use of VR-based interventions for cognitive rehabilitation in children with ADHD is limited. The results showed that VR-based interventions are more effective in improving sustained attention. Improvements were observed in attentional vigilance measures, increasing the number of correct responses and decreasing the number of errors of omission. No improvements were observed in impulsivity responses.

Keywords: virtual reality; ADHD; rehabilitation; cognition; attention; impulsivity

Citation: Romero-Ayuso, D.; Toledano-González, A.; Rodríguez-Martínez, M.d.C.; Arroyo-Castillo, P.; Triviño-Juárez, J.M.; González, P.; Ariza-Vega, P.; Del Pino González, A.; Segura-Fragoso, A. Effectiveness of Virtual Reality-Based Interventions for Children and Adolescents with ADHD: A Systematic Review and Meta-Analysis. *Children* **2021**, *8*, 70 https://doi.org/10.3390/children8020070

Received: 20 December 2020
Accepted: 18 January 2021
Published: 21 January 2021

1. Introduction

Among neurodevelopmental disorders, one of the most common is attention deficit hyperactivity disorder (ADHD) [1]. It is characterized by the presence of a persistent pattern of inattention and/or hyperactivity and impulsivity that interferes with cognitive functioning and participation in different activities, at least during the last six months. The diagnosis occurs after seven years of age and lasts throughout life [2]. Attention deficits are observed, for example, because the child frequently changes the focus of attention, particularly in monotonous and repetitive activities.

Occasionally, they do not pay attention to details, causing them to make mistakes or omit relevant information in the performance of tasks. It may also appear that they are not listening, even when people speak to them directly. They are easily distracted and forget details of activities of daily living (ADL) or lose objects. In addition, when impulsivity and hyperactivity appear, they can make decisions without reasoning, or not respect their turn in a conversation or play, generate difficulties in delaying gratification and inhibiting emotional reactions. This is mainly explained as a neurodevelopmental disorder of the prefrontal lobe, which concerns the development of executive functions in childhood. It includes inhibitory control, working memory, cognitive flexibility, planning, execution of goal-oriented behaviors, as well as self-behavior monitoring [3].

Some authors indicate that there is a long delay between the onset of symptoms and diagnosis and treatment, which affects the children's functional performance, acquisition of skills, and development in a broad sense [4]. There are several systematic reviews of the use of technologies, both for assessment and intervention (serious games (SG), robots, virtual reality (VR), etc.) in children with neurodevelopmental disorders [1,4–7]. However, there are no reviews or meta-analyses on the effectiveness of virtual-reality interventions in children with ADHD. Previous studies suggest that it is necessary to perform specific research with a higher level of evidence of technological interventions [4,8]. Among the different technological systems, the potential of VR is highlighted. It began to be applied in the health field in the 1990s [9]. The differences between the applications of SG and VR systems is difficult, especially in the field of childhood, where the tasks usually consist of playing a game. Regardless of the game itself, there are aspects that clearly define VR: (1) the use of external tools that provide sensory information (mainly visual, auditory, and haptic) to interact with the virtual environment; (2) internal tools, which allow the collection of information on the user's movement and position regarding their interaction with the system (for example, through gloves, trackers, exoskeletons, or a mouse); (3) systems for reproducing graphic images created by the virtual environment; and (4) software and databases that shape objects in the virtual world, using their shape, texture, or movement [8]. Furthermore, VR shares with the brain the mechanism of generating "embodied simulations" [8]. In fact, VR could be considered as an "embodied technology" [8] that provides the sensation of presence and immersion [10], allowing interaction, enhanced by the incorporation of virtual agents [11]. According to the hypothesis of predictive coding, it is understood that VR generates simulations of one's own body in the world, through the developed scenario. It allows exploring and manipulating that environment, improving self-regulation and learning through the representation from the prediction of the internal (of the body itself) and external (environmental) sensory stimuli. These contribute to improving the movements, actions, and emotions adapted to the context [8,12]. Recent developments in augmented reality (AR), which allows the adding of information and the superimposing of information on the real world, facilitate the transfer of learning to everyday life, and achieve a high level of relevance and motivation [1]. In the case of children, both VR and AR have been considered positive technologies, since they improve the quality of experience, motivation, and learning [10]. They have the potential to allow the design of rehabilitation tasks focused on the child and according to the child's interests, increasing their motivation in a safe environment and monitoring the their performance. These make VR a relevant tool in the field of rehabilitation.

In light of the above, the aim of this study was to evaluate the effectiveness of the use of VR-based interventions in children with ADHD, which is the most frequent neurodevelopmental disorder [4].

2. Materials and Methods

The systematic review was conducted according to the Cochrane Handbook for Systematic Reviews [8] (https://handbook-5-1.cochrane.org), and it was informed by the PRISMA Declaration guidelines [10]. The Grading of Recommendations, Assessment, Development and Evaluation (GRADE) system was used to assess the quality of the evidence [10]. This systematic review has been registered in PROSPERO under number code CRD42020152677.

2.1. Search Strategy

To assess the validity, applicability, and scope of this systematic review and meta-analysis, a search strategy was carried out in the Web of Science (WOS), Scopus, Cochrane and PsycINFO databases from 29 June to 29 October 2020. The terms included in the search are shown in Table 1. This string was applied to the title + abstract + keywords fields. The electronic search was completed with a review of the bibliographic references of the included studies.

Table 1. Key Search Terms.

	Key Seach Terms
Population	(ADHD OR attention deficit OR hyperactivity disorder) AND children
Intervention	virtual reality OR virtual environment OR virtual rehabilitation OR augmented reality OR serious games
Comparation	neurorehabilitation OR cognitive training OR cognitive therapy OR neuropsychological rehabilitation OR neuropsychological training OR neuropsychological therapy OR attention training
Outcome	cognition OR attention OR sustained attention OR impulsivity OR cognitive impulsivity OR executive function

2.2. Selection of Studies

Covidence (a web-based systematic review program that aims to make evidence synthesis a more proficient process, www.covidence.org) was used for the selection of articles. Randomized controlled clinical trials (RCT) or non-randomized controlled clinical trials that conducted VR-based interventions in children with a diagnosis of ADHD and that had been published in English or Spanish were included. Studies using immersive or semi-immersive VR or AR for the improvement of cognitive functioning were also selected. Articles (1) that did not include children or adolescents with ADHD; (2) that did not include VR-based interventions or AR, with robots or simple SG; (3) that were case series; (4) that were RCT protocols or clinical-trial protocols that did not present results; or (5) that focused on the application of VR exclusively to the educational field as a method of teaching a subject, were excluded.

No restrictions were placed on the minimum sample size of the studies or on the follow-up time. Two independent reviewers selected studies and extracted relevant data (A.T.-G. and D.R.-A.). Discrepancies were resolved by a third independent reviewer (M.C.R.-M.).

2.3. Data Extraction and Analysis

Four researchers (P.A.-C., A.T.-G., M.C.R.-M., D.R.-A.) carried out the bibliographic searches, and two reviewers (A.T.-G. and D.R.-A.) subsequently reviewed the relevance of the titles and abstracts according to the inclusion and exclusion criteria. Data extraction was performed by four researchers (P.A.-C., A.T.-G., M.C.R.-M., D.R.-A.). Clinical efficacy was defined by whether study results showed that a test or a treatment improved any symptoms [11]. A data-extraction form was developed that included the following data from each study: article title, country, year, author, type of study, sample size, follow-up time, main characteristics of the participants, description of the intervention, main outcomes, and conclusions.

2.4. Summary Measures

The objective measures of effect used to assess the effect of the intervention were Conners' Continuous Performance Test (CPT) and the Virtual Classroom Task Assessment (VCTA). The CPT assesses sustained attention and vigilance for a simple task over a time interval [12]. It can be used in children aged four years to adulthood. The child must press a key when a letter appears on the computer screen, except when it is the letter "X". The test lasts approximately 14 min. There are 324 non-X stimuli interspersed with 36 X stimuli, presented in blocks of trials with interstimulus intervals of 1, 2, and 4 s, which vary between blocks. Results for CPT performance include number of hits, number of omission errors, number of commission errors, hit reaction time (RT), perceptual sensitivity (d'), and response bias (B). The omissions refer to the lack of response to the target stimuli. Therefore, omissions indicate inattention, which can be motivated by a temporary lack of response or by looking away when the stimuli are presented. Commission errors, which refer to the responses given to stimuli other than the target stimulus, are caused by the inability to inhibit motor responses as a consequence of an impulsive response trend. Perceptual sensitivity (d'), which refers to errors due to difficulties in the discrimination of perceptual characteristics, is related to selective attention. Response bias (B) represents an individual's response tendency.

The VCTA [13] is based on a continuous performance test and consists of a virtual system that uses a head-mounted display (HMD) that recreates a classroom with three rows of desks, a blackboard, and the teacher's desk. One of the sides of the classroom is a window that overlooks a playground with buildings, vehicles, and people, while the other three sides are walls. The virtual teacher instructs the children to press the mouse when they see the letter "K" preceded by the letter "A". There are auditory distractors (e.g., footsteps) visual distractors (e.g., a paper plane flying in the classroom), and mixed distractors (auditory and visual), like a car rumbling outside the window. The experiment consists of five blocks (over a period of 100 s each) with 20 targets (AK). Five hundred stimuli were presented throughout the task (500 s). The test registers the number of correct answers (number of cases in which an answer occurred together with target "AK") and commission errors (number of cases in which a joint response occurred with a non-target).

2.5. *Synthesis of Results (Statistical Analysis Plan)*

The pre and post-intervention means with their standard deviations (SD) were used, and differences between scores after and before intervention (post-pre differences) were calculated. The SD not reported for these differences were calculated by imputing a correlation coefficient that was calculated in studies with the adequate information, from the pre- and post-SD and the SD of the difference. The weighted mean of these coefficients ($r = 0.86$) was calculated and applied to the rest of the studies. The effect size was determined using the adjusted Hedges G standardized mean difference (SMD) with a 95% confidence interval. The overall effect size was weighted by the sample size of the studies using the inverse variance method and a random-effects model. The 95% confidence interval (95% CI) and statistical significance were calculated using the z test. The magnitude of the effect was interpreted using Cohen's criteria: 0.2: small effect; 0.5: medium; and 0.8: large effect. Satisfactory values ≥ 0.6 were considered [13]. The individual and the combined effect of all studies were plotted by forest plot using RevMan software [14], including assessment of risk of bias for individual studies. Due to the small sample size of the studies included in the meta-analysis, separate effects were calculated for each of the VCTA and CPT subscales: omissions, commissions, correct hits, reaction time, and perceptual sensitivity. All of these scales could not be combined into a single global estimate of the intervention effect.

2.6. *Assessment of Risk of Bias in Individual Studies*

An independent reviewer (A. S.-F.) assessed the methodological quality of the studies using the items included in RevMan: random sequence generation (selection bias), allocation concealment (selection bias), blinding of participants and personnel (performance bias), blinding of outcome assessment (detection bias), incomplete outcome data (attrition bias), and selective reporting (reporting bias). These items were categorized as 'high', 'low' or 'unclear'.

2.7. *Assessment of the Degree of Evidence of the Set of Studies*

The GRADE system was used [9] to consider eight factors to assess the possible downgrade or upgrade of the level of quality of the evidence.

The GRADE system defines four levels of quality of evidence: high, moderate, low, and very low. The meta-analysis was based on controlled trials (randomized or non-randomized), so it was based on a high-quality level of evidence. Based on this, a series of factors were considered to downgrade or upgrade the final level of evidence.

The factors that downgraded the level of evidence were: (1) risk of bias of the set of studies; (2) inconsistency (heterogeneity) between studies; (3) indirect evidence; (4) imprecision; and (5) publication bias. The factors considered that upgraded the level of evidence were: (6) large effect magnitude (SMD > 0.8); (7) dose-response gradient; and (8) control for confounding factors.

2.7.1. Risk of Bias of the Set of Studies

The studies that met the selection criteria were assessed with the items included in the review manager, according to the following characteristics: generation of the randomization sequence, concealment of the allocation sequence, blinding of participants and personnel, blinding of the outcome assessment, incomplete outcome data, and selective reporting of results. Each of these items was categorized as high, low, or unclear. Based on the joint assessment of the six items, the risk of bias of the study was categorized as follows: (1) low risk when all items were at low risk of bias; (2) unclear risk when one or more items have unclear risk; and (3) high risk when one or more items were at high risk of bias.

2.7.2. Heterogeneity

To measure the degree of variability or heterogeneity in the effects of the intervention between the different studies, the I^2 statistic (% of the variability of SMD attributable to heterogeneity and not to chance) was used, and the chi-square test was used to assess its statistical significance. It was assessed by visual examination of the forest plot and the chi-square statistic. The I^2 was interpreted as absent (0%), low (25%), moderate (50%), or high heterogeneity (≥75%) [14]. The chi-square test was used to assess whether the differences observed between the studies were compatible with simple hazard [9].

2.7.3. Indirect Evidence

Direct evidence is understood as that obtained from research that directly compares the interventions of interest, assessed in the type of patients in whom we are interested, and that measures relevant outcomes for patients. The level of evidence decreases when the population studied, the intervention, or the results measured are not adequate.

2.7.4. Imprecision

Imprecision was assessed by the calculation of the optimal information size (OIS) [15], which is a conventional calculation to detect an SMD equal to the minimum clinically important difference and the post-SD of the control group. The calculation was performed using the comparison of the post-pre means in independent groups, based on the use of ANOVA of repeated measures (group-time interaction). Accepting an alpha risk of 0.05 and a beta risk of 0.1 (90% statistical power) in a two-sided contrast, the OIS would be 28 subjects in the experimental group and 28 in the control group to detect a standardized SMD effect size = 0.2.

2.7.5. Publication Bias

Publication bias was assessed by visual examination of the funnel plot complemented with the DOI plot, both created with METAXL [16]. In addition, the Begg test and the Egger test calculated with Stata, and the Luis Furuya-Kanamori index (LFK) were used [17]. The Begg and Egger tests contrast the null hypothesis of absence of publication bias. Begg uses the rank correlation between the effect of the standardized intervention and its standard error [18]. Egger uses linear regression of the estimate of the intervention effect against its standard error, weighted by the inverse of the variance of the estimate of the intervention effect [19]. The LFK index uses a new graphical method, the DOI plot, to visualize the skew between studies. An LFK ≤ 1 was considered as no skewness = no publication bias; >1 ≤ 2 as minor skewness = low risk of publication bias; and > 2 as major skew = high risk of publication bias.

3. Results

3.1. Study Selection and Characteristics

A total of 471 studies were identified. Of these, 123 studies were duplicates and automatically discarded by Covidence. After de-duplicating, 348 manuscripts were reviewed by title and abstract, excluding 245 studies (124 included the wrong population; 75 were non-VR based interventions; 20 were case studies; 6 were protocols without results; and 20 were studies focused on the application of VR exclusively to the educational field), leaving 103 manuscripts for a complete reading. Of these 103 studies, 36 were not clinical trials; 39 included the wrong population (population with only autism spectrum disorder (ASD), ADHD with ASD comorbidity, or other neurodevelopmental disorders (NDD); 11 had a subject age > 18; and 11 used non-VR based interventions. The review of the full texts reported six studies. Of these, four were included in the meta-analysis (Figure 1; Table 2). The two studies not included in the meta-analysis were those of Tabrizi et al. [20] and Bul et al. [21]. Tabrizi et al. conducted a study in order to verify the effectiveness of virtual-reality systems to improve memory in children with ADHD. Eighteen children between seven and 12 years old participated in this study, divided into three groups: experimental, with pharmacological treatment, and control group. The type of sampling was intentional. The intervention consisted of 10 sessions. The virtual environment was a classroom in which different target stimuli appeared, and the child had to remember them at the end of the session. In addition, auditory and visual stimuli were incorporated, demanding greater inhibition of interference in the children. As the intervention advanced, the difficulty of the task also increased, increasing the number of targets and distractors. The results before and after the intervention were compared using the SNAP-4 questionnaire (a test of attention span and working memory (WISC-IV)) and the Raven Progressive Matrix test. After the intervention, the children who obtained the best results were those who followed VR. The results showed that VR-based interventions, similar to pharmacological treatment, improved memory in children with ADHD in both the post-test and follow-up stages. The study by Bul et al. [21] was the only one found that aimed to improve daily life skills, such as planning, time management, and social skills, through an SG named "Plan-It-Commander", in which the child must perform 10 different missions. The sample was composed of 170 children diagnosed with ADHD according to the DSM-IV TR between eight and 12 years old, and of these, 88 of them received the intervention. The period of the intervention was 10 weeks, and it was used as a complementary treatment to a pharmacological one. To know the changes after the intervention (post-pre differences), a time-management questionnaire, the planning subscale of the Behavior Rating Inventory of Executive Function (BRIEF) questionnaire, and the cooperation subscale of the Social Skills Rating System (SSRS) were used [21]. According to the parents' report, the children significantly improved their time-management skills ($p = 0.04$), social skills ($p = 0.04$), and working memory ($p = 0.002$), compared to the control group. The effects of the experimental group were maintained 10 weeks after the intervention.

3.2. Characteristics of the Studies Included in the Meta-Analysis

The four studies finally included in the meta-analysis are summarized in Table 2. Of these, three were RCT [22–24] and one was a non-randomized controlled trial [25]. The type of experimental intervention was immersive VR using a head-mounted display (HMD), and in some studies using a head tracker with 3 degrees of freedom (DOF) [25]. The study presented by Lee et al. [25] also performed EEG recordings, and in Cho's study [22], neurofeedback was used at the same time as VR, although the neurofeedback protocol was not reported. The total number of participants included in the meta-analysis was 125; of these, 44 were in the experimental group and 81 were in the comparison one. The mean age was 12.9 years. The vast majority were male (92%).

The clinical profile of the participants was characterized by presenting the clinical symptoms for the diagnosis of ADHD according to the DSM-IV. Three of the four studies indicated that they had no previous experience with the use of VR-based interventions, and that all the participants did so voluntarily and could withdraw at any time from the study.

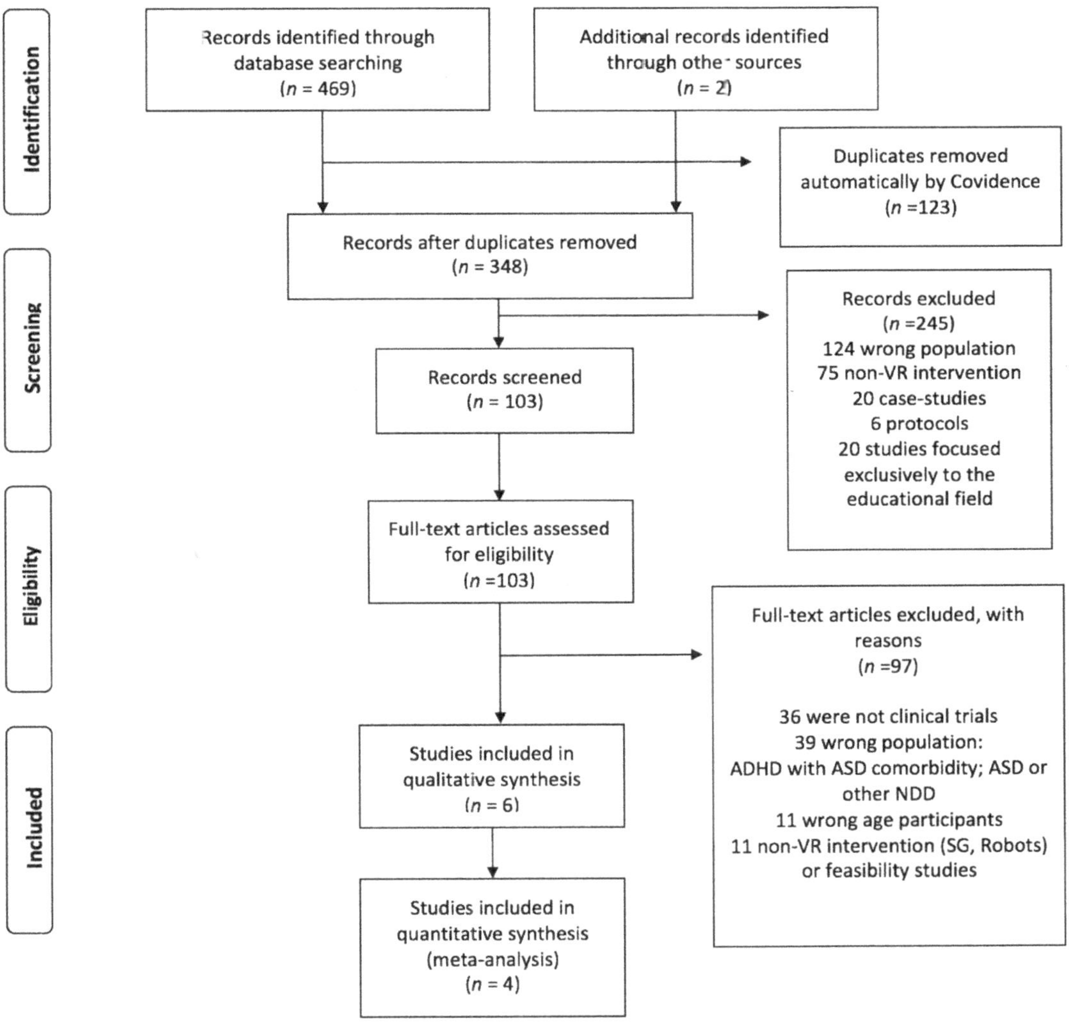

Figure 1. PRISMA flow diagram. ADHD: Attention deficit hyperactivity disorder; ASD: autism spectrum disorder; NDD: Neurodevelopmental disorder; VR: Virtual Reality; SG: Serious games.

Table 2. The studies included in the meta-analysis.

Authors and Year	Title	Measures	Intervention: Experimental Group	Intervention: Comparison Group	Outcome/Results
Bioulac, S., Micoulad-Franchi, J.A., Maire, J., Bouvard, M.P., Rizzo, A.A., Sagaspe, P. & Philip, P. 2020 [23]	Virtual Remediation versus methylphenidate to improve distractibility in children with ADHD: A controlled randomized clinical trial study	ADHD-RS Symptom Inventory according to DSM-IV Continuous Performance Test (CPT) Virtual AULA (HMD)	The experimental group received VR-based intervention. No. of participants = 16 children with ADHD, between 7 and 11 years old, with Diagnosis according to DSM-IV; with an IQ > 85 and a Score > 28 on the ADHD-RS. No. of sessions = 12 Duration of sessions = 30 min, Frequency of sessions = 2 times a week Intervention period = 6 weeks Children were asked to detect letters while inhibiting various distractors (e.g., falling pencils, footsteps, intercom announcements, etc.)	**Group with long-acting methylphenidate (QUASYM)** No. of participants = 16 A clinical interview was conducted every two weeks for 8 weeks. The maximum dosage was 1 mg/Kg. **Group with placebo psychotherapy training** No. of participants = 16 Duration of sessions = 30 min Intervention period = 6–8 weeks, No. of sessions = 12 The intervention focused on attention, support and psychoeducation.	The children who received the VR-based intervention obtained higher performance in the tasks and tests of sustained attention both in the CPT and in the virtual AULA tests. After intervention, there were no differences in the number of omissions in the CPT between the VR-based intervention group and methylphenidate group ($p = 0.03$). There were differences due to commission errors between these two groups, being lower in VR-based intervention group ($p = 0.001$); The number of hits in the virtual classroom cognitive remediation group was significantly higher than in the psychotherapy group ($p < 0.001$). There were no differences in the number of commissions between the groups with psychotherapy and pharmacological treatment. In the CPT task, there were significant differences in the number of commissions between the virtual classroom cognitive rehabilitation group and the methylphenidate group ($p = 0.05$). No child in the VR-based intervention group reported adverse effects, such as cybersickness.
Cho, et al., 2002 [24]	The Effect of Virtual Reality Cognitive Training for Attention Enhancement	Continuous Performance Test (CPT)	**VR-based intervention group (HMD)** No. of participants = 9 No. of sessions = 8 Duration of sessions = 20 min Intervention period = 2 weeks Treatment focuses on tasks of sustained, selective, divided or alternating attention, with different tasks where they have to stop an activity at a signal, as a flag, comparing objects and observe similarities, etc.	**Group Non-VR** No. of participants = 9 Cognitive rehabilitation similar to VR but using a computer **Control group** No. of participants = 9 They received no intervention	Perceptual sensitivity decreased in all groups, being higher and significant in the VR-based intervention group ($p < 0.01$). Only the response bias decreased in the VR-based intervention group ($p < 0.01$). Correct hits on the CPT was higher in the VR-based intervention group, although the differences were not statistically significant.

Table 2. *Cont.*

Authors and Year	Title	Measures	Intervention: Experimental Group	Intervention: Comparison Group	Outcome/Results
Cho et al., 2004 [22]	Neurofeedback training with VR for inattention and impulsiveness	Continuous Performance Test CPT	**VR-based intervention group (HMD)** VE was a classroom No. of participants = 10 No. of sessions = 8 Duration of sessions = 20 min Intervention period = 2 weeks	**Non-VR Group = 9** Cognitive rehabilitation similar to VR but using a computer. **Control Group = 9** They received no intervention.	The VR-based intervention group improved the number of correct responses after the intervention ($p < 0.001$), decreased its reaction time ($p < 0.001$), the perceptual sensitivity ($p < 0.01$) and commissions ($p < 0.05$) after the intervention. Response bias increased in all groups ($p < 0.001$). The group that improved the most in the impulsivity parameters was the VR-based intervention one.
Lee et al., 2001 [25]	A study on the system for treatment of ADHD using virtual reality	Continuous Performance Test (CPT)	**VR-based intervention group** HDM and tracking system with three EEG electrodes (Cz, grounded in the right and left ears). The EEG signal acquisition frequency was 256 Hz. They extracted the frequency parameters Delta (0.5–3 Hz), Theta (4–7 Hz), Alpha (8–12 Hz), SMR (12–15 Hz) and Beta (15–18 Hz). The data was updated every 0.5 s. No. of participants = 10 No. of sessions = 10 Duration of each session = 10 min Intervention period = 2 weeks When the child's Beta threshold value increased (15–18 Hz), there was a small change in the virtual environment. The virtual task was centered on dinosaurs, where information about them was presented and then the child was asked to answer a series of questions about the information presented.	**Control Group** No. of participants = 10 They received no intervention	The VR-based intervention group showed a reduction of omissions and commissions versus the control group. The perceptual sensitivity decreased after VR-based intervention

3.3. *Interventions*

All VR-based interventions used HMD systems with immersive, through cognitive tasks of attention, where the child was instructed to keep their attention focused on the activity, to select targets, and to inhibit responses to target stimuli. In all the studies, the interventions were individual. In Lee's study [25], the setting was a game with a dinosaur. In the other three studies, the virtual environment simulated a classroom. The type of control interventions in the case of the study by Lee et al. [25] received no intervention. In the study by Bioulac et al. [23], there were two comparison groups, one of which received only pharmacological treatment with QUASYM, and the other of which received only supportive psychotherapy and psychoeducation. In the two studies by Cho et al. [22,24], there were two comparison groups, one of which received cognitive rehabilitation through computerized tasks, while the control group received no treatment. The intervention period in three of the four studies was two weeks. Only the most recent study by Biolac et al. [23] lasted six weeks. The number of sessions varied from eight to 12 (Table 2).

3.4. *Effect of the VR-Based Interventions on the Different Factors of Sustained Attention and Impulsivity in Children with ADHD*

Figure 2 shows the forest plot with the results of the individual studies and the meta-analysis on omissions. In summary, the four studies with seven comparisons showed a large magnitude of the effect on omissions (SMD = −1.38; $p = 0.009$).

	Experimental			Control				Std. Mean Difference
Study or Subgroup	Mean	SD	Total	Mean	SD	Total	Weight	IV, Random, 95% CI
Bioulac 2018 CPT Omissions Vs Methyl	2.18	13.88	8	-4.93	10.93	16	16.2%	0.57 [-0.29, 1.44]
Bioulac 2018 CPT Omissions Vs Psychother	2.18	13.88	8	7.02	14.37	19	16.3%	-0.33 [-1.16, 0.50]
Cho 2002 CPT Att Omission error Vs Control	-9.38	4.66	4	-0.66	2.8	9	12.7%	-2.38 [-3.99, -0.77]
Cho 2002 CPT Att Omission error Vs Non VR	-9.38	4.66	4	-4.44	3.98	9	14.3%	-1.10 [-2.38, 0.18]
Cho 2004 CPT Att Omission error Vs Control	-11.33	3.72	5	-0.66	2.8	9	11.9%	-3.18 [-4.95, -1.41]
Cho 2004 CPT Att Omission error Vs Non VR	-11.33	3.72	5	-6.9	3.29	9	14.6%	-1.21 [-2.42, 0.01]
Lee 2001 CPT Omissions	-9.55	3.08	10	-0.66	2.8	10	14.0%	-2.89 [-4.22, -1.56]
Total (95% CI)			**44**			**81**	**100.0%**	**-1.38 [-2.42, -0.35]**

Heterogeneity: Tau² = 1.53; Chi² = 31.53, df = 6 (p < 0.001); I² = 81%

Test for overall effect: Z = 2.61 (p = 0.009)

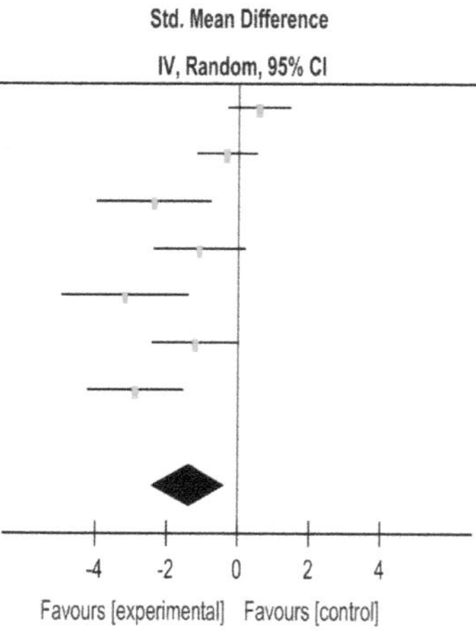

Figure 2. The results of the individual studies and meta-analysis on omissions.

The four studies with eight comparisons showed a moderate magnitude of the effect on commissions (SMD = −0.62; $p = 0.002$) (Figure 3).

The four studies with seven comparisons showed a large magnitude of the effect for correct hits (SMD = −1.50; $p = 0.004$) (Figure 4).

Finally, the four studies with five comparisons on the reaction time showed a moderate magnitude of the effect (SMD = −0.67; $p = 0.03$) (Figure 5) and a large magnitude of the effect on perceptual sensitivity (SMD = −1.21; $p < 0.001$) (Figure 6).

Study or Subgroup	Experimental Mean	Experimental SD	Experimental Total	Control Mean	Control SD	Control Total	Weight	Std. Mean Difference IV, Random, 95% CI
Bioulac 2018 CPT Commissions Vs Methyl	-3.27	4.18	6	-1.42	4.06	8	13.1%	-0.42 [-1.50, 0.65]
Bioulac 2018 CPT Commissions Vs Psychother	-3.27	4.18	5	-0.85	2.74	19	14.7%	-0.77 [-1.78, 0.25]
Bioulac 2018 VCTA Commissions Vs Methyl	-11	6.87	5	-0.5	5.56	8	8.4%	-1.61 [-2.95, -0.27]
Cho 2002 CPT Imp Commission error Vs Control	-6.13	4.25	4	-4	5.48	9	10.7%	-0.33 [-1.57, 0.81]
Cho 2002 CPT Imp Commission error Vs Non VR	-6.13	4.25	4	-5.55	3.68	9	10.9%	-0.14 [-1.32, 1.04]
Cho 2004 CPT Imp Commission error Vs Control	-6.77	5.41	5	-4	5.48	9	12.2%	-0.43 [-1.59, 0.64]
Cho 2004 CPT Imp Commission error Vs Non VR	-6.77	5.41	5	-0.8	5.69	9	10.9%	-1.00 [-2.18, 0.18]
Lee 2001 CPT Commissions	-6.77	5.41	10	-4	5.48	10	19.0%	-0.49 [-1.38, 0.41]
Total (95% CI)			**44**			**81**	**100.0%**	**-0.62 [-1.01, -0.23]**

Heterogeneity: Tau² = 0.00; Chi² = 3.64, df = 7 (p = 0.82); I² = 0%

Test for overall effect: Z = 3.12 (p = 0.002)

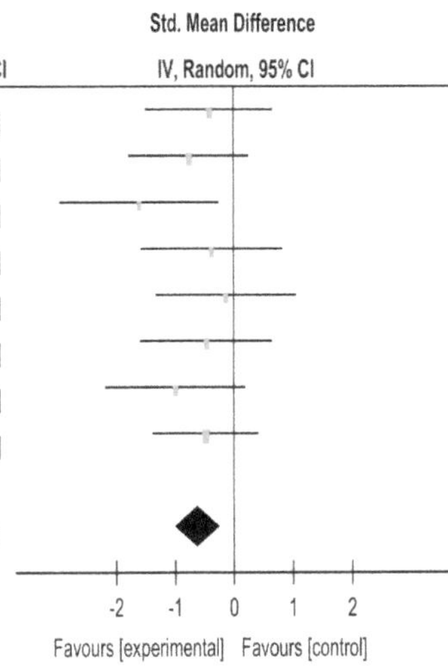

Figure 3. The results of the individual studies and meta-analysis on commissions.

Study or Subgroup	Experimental Mean	Experimental SD	Experimental Total	Control Mean	Control SD	Control Total	Weight	Std. Mean Difference IV, Random, 95% CI
Bioulac 2018 VCTA Correct hits Vs Methyl	-18.44	8.13	8	-23.81	7.81	16	16.1%	0.66 [-0.22, 1.53]
Bioulac 2018 VCTA Correct hits Vs Psychother	-18.44	8.13	8	3.4	8.2	19	15.0%	-2.59 [-3.70, -1.48]
Cho 2002 CPT Att Correct hits Vs Control	-9.37	4.66	4	-0.66	2.8	9	12.6%	-2.38 [-3.98, -0.77]
Cho 2002 CPT Att Correct hits Vs Non VR	-9.37	4.66	4	-4.44	3.98	9	14.2%	-1.10 [-2.38, 0.18]
Cho 2004 CPT Att Correct hits Vs Control	-11.44	3.76	5	-0.66	2.8	9	11.8%	-3.20 [-4.98, -1.43]
Cho 2004 CPT Att Correct hits Vs Non VR	-11.44	3.76	5	-7.9	2.28	9	14.6%	-1.16 [-2.36, 0.05]
Lee 2001 CPT Variability	-6.4	6.62	10	2.67	5.93	10	15.6%	-1.38 [-2.38, -0.38]
Total (95% CI)			**44**			**81**	**100.0%**	**-1.50 [-2.53, -0.48]**

Heterogeneity: Tau² = 1.50; Chi² = 30.42, df = 6 (p < 0.001); I² = 80%

Test for overall effect: Z = 2.87 (p = 0.004)

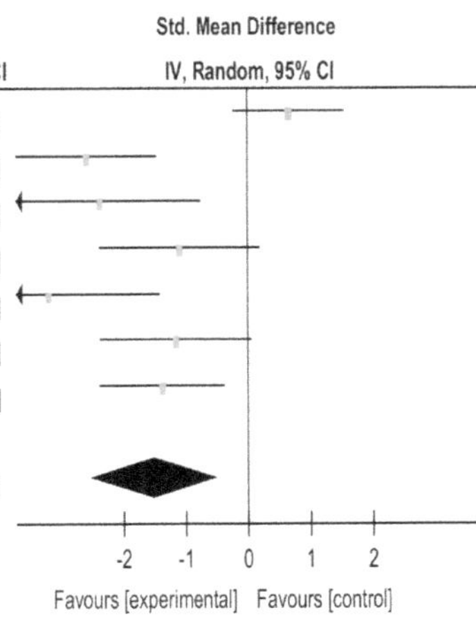

Figure 4. The results of the individual studies and meta-analysis on correct hits.

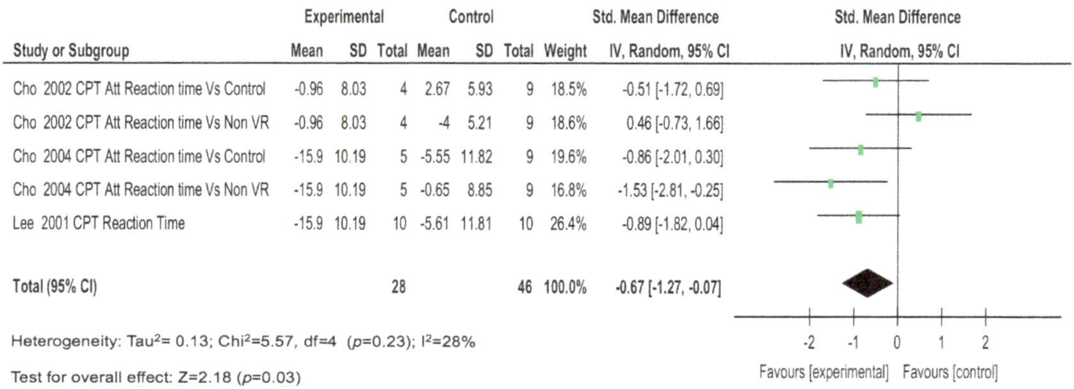

Figure 5. The results of the individual studies and meta-analysis on reaction time.

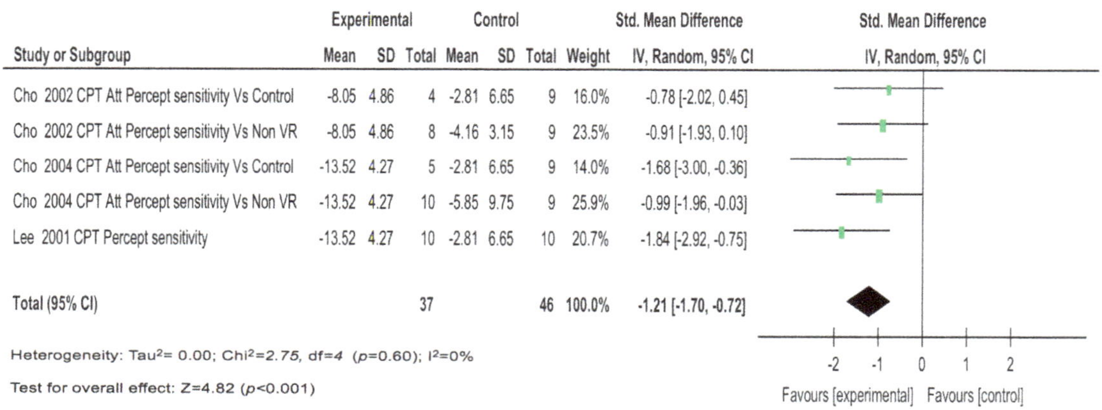

Figure 6. The results of the individual studies and meta-analysis on perceptual sensitivity.

3.5. Degree of Evidence from the Set of Studies

3.5.1. Risk of Bias of Individual Studies

Figure 7 shows the risk of bias for each study in each of the assessed criteria, using three colors: green = low risk; yellow with question mark = unclear; and red = high risk. All studies except the one by Lee et al. showed a low risk in the generation of the randomization sequence; three of the studies showed an unclear risk of bias in the allocation concealment, while in the study of Lee et al., this risk was high. All were at high risk of bias in the blinding of participants and personnel, and three of them in the blinding of outcome assessment. Only one study had a low risk of bias in incomplete outcome data and in selective reporting.

3.5.2. Heterogeneity

Total heterogeneity was high in omissions (I^2 = 81%; $p < 0.009$) and correct hits (I^2 = 80%; $p < 0.004$). It was moderate in perceptual sensitivity (I^2 = 59%; $p < 0.04$), low in reaction time (I^2 = 28%; $p < 0.23$), and null in commissions (I^2 = 0%; $p < 0.82$). This indicated inconsistency in the results for omissions, correct hits, and perceptual sensitivity.

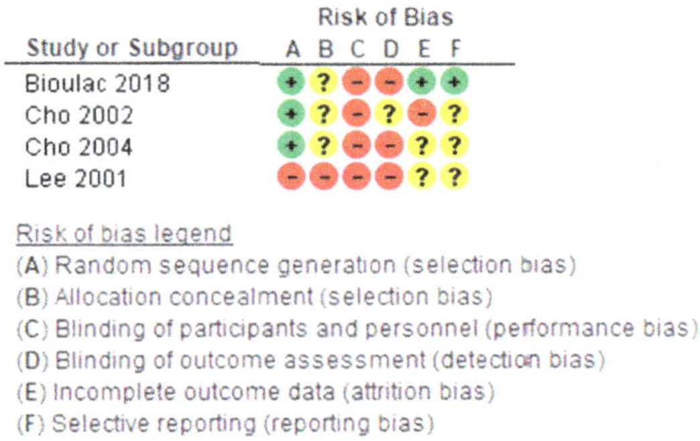

Figure 7. The risk of bias in the individual studies. green = low risk of bias; yellow with question mark = unclear risk of bias; red = high risk of bias.

3.5.3. Indirect Evidence

None of the studies found substantial differences among the study population, the intervention or the outcomes measured, and the criteria established in the meta-analysis.

3.5.4. Imprecision

The total sample size of the studies included in the meta-analysis was 125 for omissions, commissions, and correct hits (44 in the experimental group and 81 in the control group), and 74 for reaction time and perceptual sensitivity (28 in the experimental group and 46 in the control group).

3.5.5. Publication Bias

Figures 8 and 9 show the assessment of publication bias using the funnel plot and DOI plot.

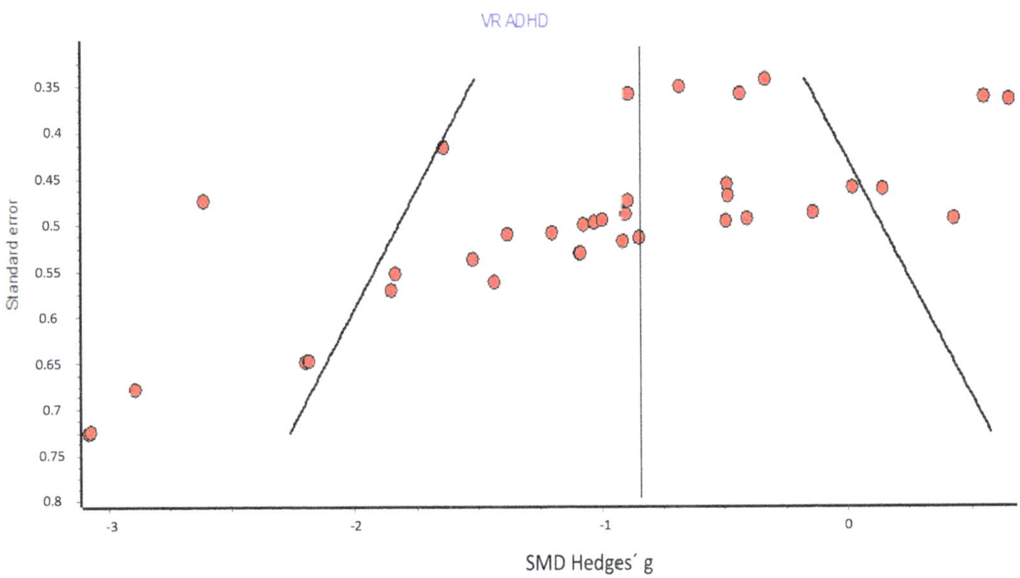

Figure 8. Publication bias: funnel plot.

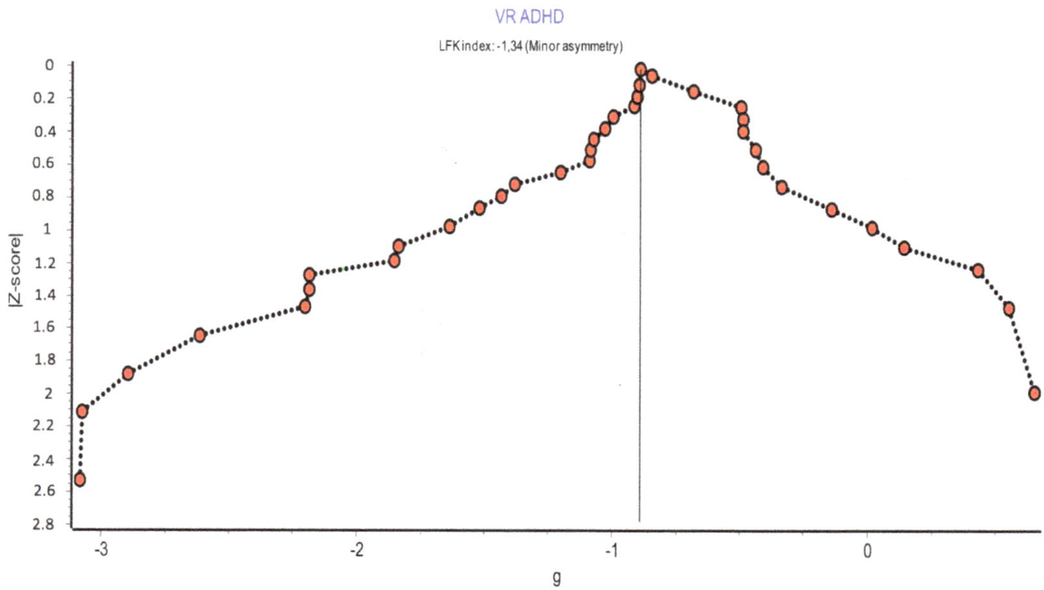

Figure 9. Publication bias: DOI plot and LFK index.

There was a certain asymmetry between the comparisons whose SMD was below or above the mean of all comparisons. Comparisons with larger effects (left of the plot) also had smaller sample sizes (larger standard errors), while those with smaller SMDs (right of the plot) had smaller standard errors and therefore larger sample sizes. It could be considered that there is a deficit of results in the lower-right quadrant of the plot. It would be a consistent bias in the non-publication of small studies with little or no effects.

There was a certain asymmetry similar to that described in the funnel plot. The LFK index showed minor asymmetry (LFK = −1.34). The statistical significance of the Begg test was $p < 0.001$, and that of the Egger test was $p < 0.001$.

4. Discussion

The aim of this meta-analysis was to know the effectiveness of VR-based interventions in ADHD children and adolescents. According to Ioannidis [26], the present study tries to overcome the drawbacks that many meta-analyses have. Therefore, our research sought to promote evidence-based practice. Our meta-analysis showed that there are few studies of VR-based interventions aimed at the cognitive rehabilitation of ADHD children. Most VR studies in ADHD populations have focused on validating the assessment of attention in a virtual classroom environment [4,13,27–29]. Furthermore, as in other NDD [30], there is a lack of consensus on the outcome measures used in the different studies, which means that there are few studies that can be compared. However, in our review, we have only included studies with the same outcome measures. In this sense, this represents a strength of our meta-analysis, since this is a consequence of establishing rigorous criteria on the type of outcome measures and type of intervention, with the aim of knowing more clearly the effectiveness of VR-based interventions, and considering the difficulties noted by other meta-analysis that have addressed the effectiveness of psychosocial treatment in ADHD [31]. Moreover, our study attempted to respond to the criticism made by another meta-analysis of meta-analysis of psychosocial treatments in ADHD, in which the authors address this issue as the problem of: *Apples and Apples or Apples and Oranges?* [31].

All the studies except for Lee's [25] used a classroom as a virtual environment and focused on cognitive tasks, similar to those required by the CPT-type sustained attention tests. In this way, there was a notable reduction in the type of demands for vigilance and sustained attention that have been raised in the studies. It is noticeable that this is so when, in addition to attention deficits, children with ADHD have significant executive deficits, such as planning, execution, and supervision of action, which requires the development of self-regulation. In addition, the deficits of these children also affect the scope of activities of daily living, social and recreational activities. Only the study by Bul et al. [21] attempted to address this type of difficulties, although it did so using SG. On the other hand, the study by Tabrizi only tried to address the deficits in working memory in these children, but again in the virtual classroom setting [20].

4.1. Effect of VR-Based Interventions on Each Type of Outcome (Omissions, Commissions, Correct Hits, Reaction Time, Perceptual Sensitivity)

In summary, although there were a limited number of studies, the results suggest that VR-based interventions help to improve the cognitive performance of children and adolescents with ADHD in vigilance and sustained-attention tasks, reducing the number of omissions, and increasing the number of correct responses to the target stimuli with large effect size. Meanwhile, a medium effect on performance was observed in the reaction time to the target stimuli and the number of errors per commission. This suggests that the effect is more notable on vigilance, and less on the improvement of impulsivity or control inhibitory. These results are of interest because they suggest that VR-based interventions could improve inattention symptoms and therefore be very useful in children with ADHD of the inattention subtype, in whom a greater number of omissions and fewer correct answers have been observed [1].

On the other hand, the results of the Bioulac study [23] showed that children who received VR-based interventions can better inhibit distractors. Moreover, they also showed less impulsivity (with a lower number of commissions). The authors of this study also indicated the good acceptability of this type of intervention. However, no improvements were observed by parents according to the results of the ADHD-RS, showing that although there was an improvement in the parameters of the attention tasks, there was no transfer to activities of daily living [32], which suggests that it is necessary to increase the ecological validity of this type of intervention, as mentioned by the authors themselves. The simple fact of modifying the environment of the task does not mean that the task has ecological validity (pressing a button when a stimulus appears). It is necessary to differentiate between tasks and environment and carefully analyze the task and adapt it so it has ecological validity in accordance with age-appropriate demands, and with significant value for the child [33].

4.2. GRADE Quality of Evidence

4.2.1. Assessment of Risk of Bias in the Individual Studies

Risk of bias is considered high, as all studies had one or more items with a high risk of bias. For this reason, it is considered to downgrade the level of evidence in omissions, commissions, correct hits, reaction time, and perceptual sensitivity.

4.2.2. Assessment of Heterogeneity

In omissions and correct hits, evidence was downgraded a level for heterogeneity because the studies presented a high heterogeneity. Downgrading was not considered for commissions, reaction time, and perceptual sensitivity.

4.2.3. Assessment of Indirect Measurement

It was not considered to downgrade the level of evidence by indirect measurements, since all measurements were direct.

4.2.4. Assessment of Imprecision

Because the sample size equaled or exceeded the OIS in all outcomes, it was not considered to downgrade one level due to imprecision.

4.2.5. Assessment of Publication Bias

Despite the fact that there was a certain degree of asymmetry and risk of publication bias, and the statistical significance of the Begg and Egger tests lead to rejecting the null hypothesis of the absence of publication bias, the LFK index showed less asymmetry (LFK = −1.34). Therefore, it was not considered to downgrade a level due to publication bias.

The criteria used to upgrade the level of evidence were: (1) Large effect size—it was considered to upgrade one level in omissions and correct hits. It was not considered to upgrade a level of evidence in commissions, reaction time, and perceptual sensitivity, since the observed effect showed a moderate or small improvement; (2) Dose-response effect—it was not considered to upgrade the level of evidence because the dose-response effect was not assessable in this meta-analysis (there was not a gradual exposure to the intervention in any of the studies included); and (3) Control of blinding factors—although it was considered that the control of blinding was relatively good in the case of the three RCTs and the non-randomized controlled trial, it was not considered to upgrade a level of evidence, since most of the studies had small sample sizes. Therefore, in summary, the GRADE level of evidence on the effects of VR-based interventions remains as seen in Table 3.

Table 3. The assessment of the quality of the studies.

	No. Studies (Comparisons)	Risk of Bias	Inconsistency Heterogeneity	Indirect Evidence	Imprecision	Publication Bias	Global Effect SMD (CI 95%)	Quality of Evidence
Omissions	4 (7)	High (−1)	High (−1)	No (-)	No (-)	Low (-)	−1.38 (−2.2, −0.35)	Low
Commissions	4 (8)	High (−1)	Null	No (-)	No (-)	Low (-)	−0.62 (−1.01, −0.23)	Moderate
Correct hits	4 (7)	High (−1)	High (−1)	No (-)	No (-)	Low (-)	−1.50 (−2.53, −0.38)	Low
Reaction time	4 (5)	High (−1)	Low	No (-)	No (-)	Low (-)	−0.67 (−1.27, −0.07)	Moderate
Perceptual sensitivity	4 (5)	High (−1)	Moderate	No (-)	No (-)	Low (-)	−1.07 (−1.92, −0.22)	Moderate

Note: RCT: randomized control trial; CI: confidence interval; SMD: standardized mean difference; (−1) = downgrade one level; (-) = same level.

This study has a number of limitations. First, it is likely that not all studies were identified, despite using extensive search strategies. Second, the variety of clinical settings, evaluation protocols, and interventions did not allow the findings to be generalized. Third, the methodological shortcomings of the studies and the absence of post-intervention follow-up did not allow us to know if the effect achieved is lasting. Fourth, the studies included have small sample sizes. Meta-analyses based on studies with small sample sizes could produce heterogeneous effect sizes. In this meta-analysis, heterogeneity was high in some results, indicating an inconsistency in the findings of the various studies, so they should be interpreted with caution.

Although the number of studies with VR-based interventions as a complementary therapy in ADHD has increased, the vast majority are intra-subject design research [17], without a comparison group [17–19] or cross-sectional studies conducted to find the specific performance in a virtual task [20,21]. The results of our study show the need for more robust RCTs with larger sample sizes and with methodological planning that includes blinding of participants and personnel, blinding of outcome assessments, and allocation concealment. As stated in a recent systematic review, there is a limited number of RCTs; studies on VR-based interventions are scarce, mostly without control groups and with small sample sizes [11], and have very different outcomes. It is necessary to encourage studies that include VR-based interventions with higher methodological quality that allow conclusions to be drawn and provide evidence of their effectiveness.

Given the advances in VR systems, which allow simulating the body and interoceptive and proprioceptive perception [34], future studies could improve self-regulation in children with ADHD in different contexts of daily life, and it is recommended that the tasks implemented through VR have ecological validity [33]. Furthermore, it is necessary to develop more studies that address the planning and supervision of the action and organizational skills, since they are symptoms that continue into adulthood and are hardly addressed in current approaches [35], being basic skills for personal autonomy in ADL [33,36]. Likewise, other studies have indicated the need for the technologies used with children with NDD to be flexible and adaptable, given the heterogeneity of the needs of each child [4,37]. Finally, we note that VR-based interventions, in children between six and 11 years old, could make it difficult to for them to distinguish between memories based on VR and real ones [13]; therefore, the use of VR-based interventions should always be supervised by a healthcare professional [9]. In the future, we consider studies in which brain activity is recorded simultaneously with the use of VR-based interventions to be of interest.

5. Conclusions

To the best of our knowledge, this is the first systematic review and meta-analysis on the effectiveness of VR-based interventions in children and adolescents with ADHD. The studies included in this meta-analysis were three RCTs and one non-randomized controlled trial that analyzed the effect of VR-based interventions to improve cognitive functioning in children with ADHD and that were published between 2001 and 2020.

The review analyzed 469 articles. We selected four studies that included immersive or semi-immersive VR-based interventions [22–25]. No RCTs or non-randomized controlled trials with augmented or semi-immersive reality were found. The total number of participants among all the studies included was 125 children and adolescents with ADHD (115 males and 10 females); the ages ranged from eight to 18 years, with a mean age of 12.9 years.

Our study provides relevant results for scientific advancement in the design and implementation of new VR-based interventions. VR-based interventions were effective in improving cognitive performance in ADHD, such as sustained vigilance, which showed a decrease in omissions.

Future RCTs of VR-based interventions should consider the following recommendations: (1) New studies should include other virtual environments alternative to the classroom, such as free-play environments (for example, a school playground, park, etc.), basic activities of daily living, environments where the main demand is social, or the use of the environment, such as that of the instrumental activities of daily living; (2) New interventions should include tasks that require the child to plan and supervise action, adherence to rules, correction of errors, and working memory, because these are core deficits in ADHD; (3) In addition, it would be convenient for the new RCTs to include different ADHD comparison groups, especially due to its prevalence in children with only inattentive subtypes and with hyperactive-impulsive predominance (to date there are none); (4) The new VR-based interventions should allow graduating these cognitive and social demands according to the age of the child and the deficits severity; and (5)new studies should include follow-up measures to determine if the improvement is maintained over time. All of these recommendations will help researchers and clinicians to design studies and tools with greater ecological validity.

Author Contributions: Conceptualization, D.R.-A., J.M.T.-J.; methodology, D.R.-A., A.S.-F., A.T.-G., M.d.C.R.-M., P.A.-C.; formal analysis, A.S.-F., D.R.-A.; writing—original draft preparation, D.R.-A., A.S.-F.; writing—review and editing P.G., J.M.T.-J., M.d.C.R.-M., A.T.-G., P.A.-V., A.D.P.G.; funding acquisition, D.R.-A., P.G. All authors have read and agreed to the published version of the manuscript.

Funding: This research was funded by Ayudas para el Apoyo y Fomento a la Investigación en Materia de Igualdad e Inclusión del programa 50 del Plan Propio de Investigación y Transferencia de la Universidad de Granada. Convocatoria 2020 INV-INC83-2020. In addition, it was also funded by the Spanish Ministry of Economy and Competitiveness and by EU FEDER funds under project grant PID2019-108915RB-I00.

Institutional Review Board Statement: Not applicable.

Informed Consent Statement: Not applicable.

Data Availability Statement: The data presented in this study are available on request from the corresponding author.

Conflicts of Interest: The authors declare no conflict of interest.

References

1. Alqithami, S.; Alzahrani, M.; Alzahrani, A.; Mustafa, A. AR-Therapist: Design and Simulation of an AR-Game Environment as a CBT for Patients with ADHD. *Healthcare* **2019**, *7*, 146. [CrossRef] [PubMed]
2. APA. *Diagnostic and Statistical Manual of Mental Disorders: DSM-5*, 5th ed.; American Psychiatric Association: Arlington, VA, USA, 2013; p. 947.
3. Barkley, R.A. Behavioral inhibition, sustained attention, and executive functions: Constructing a unifying theory of ADHD. *Psychol. Bull.* **1997**, *121*, 65–94. [CrossRef] [PubMed]
4. Areces, D.; Dockrell, J.; García, T.; González-Castro, P.; Rodríguez, C. Analysis of cognitive and attentional profiles in children with and without ADHD using an innovative virtual reality tool. *PLoS ONE* **2018**, *13*, e0201039. [CrossRef] [PubMed]
5. Keshav, N.U.; Vogt-Lowell, K.; Vahabzadeh, A.; Sahin, N.T. Digital Attention-Related Augmented-Reality Game: Significant Correlation between Student Game Performance and Validated Clinical Measures of Attention-Deficit/Hyperactivity Disorder (ADHD). *Children* **2019**, *6*, 72. [CrossRef] [PubMed]
6. Kokol, P.; Vošner, H.B.; Završnik, J.; Vermeulen, J.; Shohieb, S.; Peinemann, F. Serious Game-based Intervention for Children with Developmental Disabilities. *Curr. Pediatr. Rev.* **2020**, *16*, 26–32. [CrossRef] [PubMed]
7. Hall, J.; Kellett, S.; Berrios, R.; Bains, M.K.; Scott, S. Efficacy of Cognitive Behavioral Therapy for Generalized Anxiety Disorder in Older Adults: Systematic Review, Meta-Analysis, and Meta-Regression. *Am. J. Geriatr. Psychiatry* **2016**, *24*, 1063–1073. [CrossRef]
8. Cochrane. Cochrane Handbook for Systematic Reviews of Interventions. Available online: https://handbook-5-1.cochrane.org/ 2020 (accessed on 8 December 2020).
9. Guyatt, G.H.; Oxman, A.D.; Akl, E.A.; Kunz, R.; Vist, G.; Brozek, J.; Norris, S.; Falck-Ytter, Y.; Glasziou, P.; Debeer, H. GRADE guidelines: 1. Introduction—GRADE evidence profiles and summary of findings tables. *J. Clin. Epidemiol.* **2011**, *64*, 383–394. [CrossRef]
10. Shamseer, L.; Sampson, M.; Bukutu, C.; Schmid, C.H.; Nikles, J.; Tate, R.; Johnston, B.C.; Zucker, D.; Shadish, W.R.; Kravitz, R.; et al. CONSORT extension for reporting N-of-1 trials (CENT) 2015: Explanation and elaboration. *BMJ* **2015**, *350*, h1793. [CrossRef]
11. Valentine, A.Z.; Brown, B.J.; Groom, M.J.; Young, E.; Hollis, C.; Hall, C.L. A systematic review evaluating the implementation of technologies to assess, monitor and treat neurodevelopmental disorders: A map of the current evidence. *Clin. Psychol. Rev.* **2020**, *80*, 101870. [CrossRef]
12. Baron, I.S. *Neuropsychological Evaluation of the Child*; Oxford University Press: Oxford, UK, 2004.
13. Rizzo, A.A.; Bowerly, T.; Buckwalter, J.G.; Klimchuk, D.; Mitura, R.; Parsons, T.D. A Virtual Reality Scenario for All Seasons: The Virtual Classroom. *CNS Spectr.* **2006**, *11*, 35–44. [CrossRef]
14. Shiroma, E.J.; Ferguson, P.L.; Pickelsimer, E.E. Prevalence of Traumatic Brain Injury in an Offender Population: A Meta-Analysis. *J Head Trauma Rehabil.* **2012**, *27*, E1–E10. [CrossRef] [PubMed]
15. Guyatt, G.H.; Oxman, A.D.; Kunz, R.; Brozek, J.; Alonso-Coello, P.; Rind, D.; Devereaux, P.J.; Montori, V.M.; Freyschuss, B.; Vist, G.; et al. GRADE guidelines 6. Rating the quality of evidence—Imprecision. *J. Clin. Epidemiol.* **2011**, *64*, 1283–1293. [CrossRef] [PubMed]
16. MetaXL. Available online: https://www.epigear.com/index_files/metaxl.html (accessed on 8 December 2020).
17. Furuya-Kanamori, L.; Barendregt, J.J.; Doi, S.A. A new improved graphical and quantitative method for detecting bias in meta-analysis. *Int. J. Evid. Based Healthc.* **2018**, *16*, 195–203. [CrossRef] [PubMed]
18. Begg, C.B.; Mazumdar, M. Operating Characteristics of a Rank Correlation Test for Publication Bias. *Biometrics* **1994**, *50*, 1088. [CrossRef]
19. Egger, M.; Smith, G.D.; Schneider, M.; Minder, C. Bias in meta-analysis detected by a simple, graphical test. *BMJ* **1997**, *315*, 629–634. [CrossRef]
20. Manshaee, G.; Tabrizi, M.; Ghamarani, A.; Rasti, J. Comparison of the effectiveness of virtual reality with medication on the memory of attention deficit hyperactivity disorder students. *Int. Arch. Heal. Sci.* **2020**, *7*, 37–42. [CrossRef]
21. Bul, K.; Kato, P.M.; Van Der Oord, S.; Danckaerts, M.; Vreeke, L.J.; Willems, A.; Van Oers, H.J.; Heuvel, R.V.D.; Birnie, D.; Amelsvoort, T.A.M.J.V.; et al. Behavioral Outcome Effects of Serious Gaming as an Adjunct to Treatment for Children With Attention-Deficit/Hyperactivity Disorder: A Randomized Controlled Trial. *J. Med. Internet. Res.* **2016**, *18*, e26. [CrossRef]
22. Cho, B.H.; Kim, S.; Shin, D.I.; Lee, J.H.; Min Lee, S.; Young Kim, I.; Kim, S.I. Neurofeedback training with virtual reality for inattention and impulsiveness. *Cyberpsychol. Behav.* **2004**, *7*, 519–526. [CrossRef]
23. Bioulac, S.; Micoulaud-Franchi, J.-A.; Maire, J.; Bouvard, M.P.; Rizzo, A.A.; Sagaspe, P.; Philip, P. Virtual Remediation Versus Methylphenidate to Improve Distractibility in Children With ADHD: A Controlled Randomized Clinical Trial Study. *J. Atten. Disord.* **2020**, *24*, 326–335. [CrossRef]

24. Cho, B.H.; Ku, J.; Jang, D.P.; Kim, S.; Lee, Y.H.; Kim, I.Y.; Lee, J.H.; I Kim, S. The Effect of Virtual Reality Cognitive Training for Attention Enhancement. *CyberPsychol. Behav.* **2002**, *5*, 129–137. [CrossRef]
25. Lee, J.M.; Cho, B.H.; Ku, J.H.; Kim, J.S.; Lee, J.H.; Kim, I.Y.; Kim, S.I. A study on the system for treatment of ADHD using virtual reality. In Proceedings of the 23rd Annual EMBS International Conference, Istanbul, Turkey, 25–28 October 2001.
26. Ioannidis, J. The Mass Production of Redundant, Misleading, and Conflicted Systematic Reviews and Meta-analyses. *Milbank Q.* **2016**, *94*, 485–514. [CrossRef] [PubMed]
27. Parsons, T.; Bowerly, T.; Buckwalter, J.G.; Rizzo, A.A. A Controlled Clinical Comparison of Attention Performance in Children with ADHD in a Virtual Reality Classroom Compared to Standard Neuropsychological Methods. *Child Neuropsychol.* **2007**, *13*, 363–381. [CrossRef] [PubMed]
28. Coleman, B.; Marion, S.; Rizzo, A.; Turnbull, J.; Nolty, A. Virtual Reality Assessment of Classroom—Related Attention: An Ecologically Relevant Approach to Evaluating the Effectiveness of Working Memory Training. *Front. Psychol.* **2019**, *10*, 1851. [CrossRef]
29. Pollak, Y.; Weiss, P.L.; Rizzo, A.A.; Weizer, M.; Shriki, L.; Shalev, R.S.; Gross-Tsur, V. The Utility of a Continuous Performance Test Embedded in Virtual Reality in Measuring ADHD-Related Deficits. *J. Dev. Behav. Pediatr.* **2009**, *30*, 2–6. [CrossRef] [PubMed]
30. Mesa-Gresa, P.; Gil-Gómez, H.; Lozano, J.A.; Gil-Gómez, J.-A. Effectiveness of Virtual Reality for Children and Adolescents with Autism Spectrum Disorder: An Evidence-Based Systematic Review. *Sensors* **2018**, *18*, 2486. [CrossRef] [PubMed]
31. Fabiano, G.A.; Schatz, N.K.; Aloe, A.M.; Chacko, A.; Chronis-Tuscano, A. A Systematic Review of Meta-Analyses of Psychosocial Treatment for Attention-Deficit/Hyperactivity Disorder. *Clin. Child Fam. Psychol. Rev.* **2015**, *18*, 77–97. [CrossRef] [PubMed]
32. Ayuso, D.M.R. Activities of daily living. *An. Psicol.* **2007**, *23*, 264–271.
33. Romero-Ayuso, D.; Castillero-Perea, Á.; González, P.; Navarro, E.; Molina-Massó, J.P.; Funes, M.J.; Ariza-Vega, P.; Toledano-González, A.; Triviño-Juárez, J.M. Assessment of cognitive instrumental activities of daily living: A systematic review. *Disabil. Rehabil.* **2019**, *2019*, 1–17. [CrossRef]
34. Riva, G.; Mancuso, V.; Cavedoni, S.; Stramba-Badiale, C. Virtual reality in neurorehabilitation: A review of its effects on multiple cognitive domains. *Expert Rev. Med. Devices* **2020**, *17*, 1035–1061. [CrossRef]
35. Bikic, A.; Reichow, B.; McCauley, S.A.; Ibrahim, K.; Sukhodolsky, D.G. Meta-analysis of organizational skills interventions for children and adolescents with Attention-Deficit/Hyperactivity Disorder. *Clin. Psychol. Rev.* **2017**, *52*, 108–123. [CrossRef]
36. Pfiffner, L.J.; Hinshaw, S.P.; Owens, E.; Zalecki, C.; Kaiser, N.M.; Villodas, M.; McBurnett, K. A two-site randomized clinical trial of integrated psychosocial treatment for ADHD-inattentive type. *J. Consult. Clin. Psychol.* **2014**, *82*, 1115–1127. [CrossRef] [PubMed]
37. Navarro, E.; González, P.; López-Jaquero, V.; Montero, F.; Molina, J.P.; Romero-Ayuso, D. Adaptive, Multisensorial, Physiological and Social: The Next Generation of Telerehabilitation Systems. *Front. Aging Neurosci.* **2018**, *12*, 43. [CrossRef] [PubMed]

children

MDPI

Review

The Effectiveness of Hippotherapy to Recover Gross Motor Function in Children with Cerebral Palsy: A Systematic Review and Meta-Analysis

Laura De Guindos-Sanchez [1,2], David Lucena-Anton [3,*], Jose A. Moral-Munoz [3,4,5] and Alejandro Salazar [4,5,6], Ines Carmona-Barrientos [3]

1 Department of Physiotherapy, Upacesur Medical and Functional Rehabilitation Center, 41710 Utrera, Spain; lauraguindos@gmail.com
2 Department of Physiotherapy, Macrosad Early Childhood Care, 41620 Marchena, Spain
3 Department of Nursing and Physiotherapy, University of Cadiz, 11009 Cadiz, Spain; ines.carmona@uca.es (I.C.-B.); joseantonio.moral@uca.es (J.A.M.-M.)
4 Institute of Research and Innovation in Biomedical Sciences of the Province of Cadiz (INiBICA), University of Cadiz, 11009 Cadiz, Spain; alejandro.salazar@uca.es
5 The Observatory of Pain, University of Cadiz, 11009 Cadiz, Spain
6 Department of Statistics and Operational Research, University of Cadiz, 11009 Cadiz, Spain
* Correspondence: david.lucena@uca.es

Received: 27 July 2020; Accepted: 17 August 2020; Published: 19 August 2020

Abstract: Cerebral palsy (CP) is a permanent disorder of the posture and movement, which can result in impairments of gross motor function, among others. Hippotherapy (HPT) is an emerging intervention to promote motor recovery in patients with neurological disorders, providing a smooth, precise, rhythmic, and repetitive pattern of movement to the patient. The main objective of this systematic review and meta-analysis of randomized controlled clinical trials was to analyze the effectiveness of HPT interventions on gross motor function in subjects with CP. The following databases were searched in May 2019: PubMed, Scopus, Embase, and Web of Science. The methodological quality of the randomized controlled trials was assessed using the Physiotherapy Evidence Database (PEDro) scale. A total of 10 studies were analyzed in this review, involving 452 participants. Favorable effects were obtained on the gross motor function (Gross Motor Function Measure-66, standardized mean difference (SMD) = 0.81, 95% confidence interval (CI) = 0.47–1.15, Gross Motor Function Measure-88 dimension A SMD = 0.64, 95% CI = 0.30–0.97, dimension B SMD = 0.42, 95% CI = 0.09–0.75, and dimension E SMD = 0.40, 95% CI = 0.06–0.73). The results obtained in the present review show the potential benefit of HPT intervention in improving gross motor function in children with CP.

Keywords: hippotherapy; cerebral palsy; equine-assisted therapy; physical therapy; gross motor function

1. Introduction

Cerebral palsy (CP) is the main source of physical disability in children [1]. The prevalence of CP is 2.11/1000 live births since 1985 in high-income developed countries. Children with CP usually present several limitations in terms of postural control, balance, walking, and gross motor function, as well as sensory and perceptual disturbances, spasticity, visual impairment, mental retardation, epilepsy, etc. [2]. These disorders are responsible for inefficient and ineffective movements and activities and it often leads to limitations in carrying out activities of daily living [2]. The neurodevelopmental therapies are usually used in the neurological rehabilitation of children with CP. These therapies are focused on decreasing excessive tone, giving the patient a sense of normal position and movement, and easing normal movement patterns [3].

Hippotherapy (HPT) is an equine-assisted therapy that applies the specific movement of horses in the rehabilitation of patients with neurological disorders [4], improving the neurological functions and sensory processes [5,6]. The research in HPT has increased in recent years as a complementary therapy to traditional treatments [6]. HPT is based on two main action mechanisms: (i) the transmission of the warmth and (ii) the transmission of three-dimensional movements with rhythmic impulses from the horse to the patient's body. The pelvis of the patient is moved in a repetitive, rhythmic, and soft pattern, which is similar to the movement carried out during human gait. This three-dimensional movement stimulates balance reactions, improves postural balance and the trunk straightening [4]. This therapy provides movements in all the movement planes, coming from the alternating elevation of the horse's back that originate anteversion/retroversion, elevation/decrease, and lateral movement with rotation [5]. In addition, HPT provides sensory input and induces greater postural control and motor responses [6]. Several favorable physical effects of HPT were found in muscle coordination, muscle tone, balance, posture, strength, endurance, and flexibility, improving gait and patterns of abnormal movement. In addition, it also showed positive improvements at the social, cognitive, and psychological levels [6]. Furthermore, several recent reviews suggested that HPT could be effective for the neurological rehabilitation of subjects with CP: Novak et al. stated that HPT was a successful allied health therapy to improve muscle symmetry in subjects with CP [7]; Mendizábal Alonso [8] suggested that HPT was effective to improve postural alignment in subjects with CP; Martin-Valero et al. [9] also reported benefits in the performance of the activities of daily living and quality of life; and Zadnikar and Kastrin [10] also obtained favorable results on postural balance in subjects with CP.

Regarding the motor function of children with CP, the main aim of therapeutic interventions is to increase the performance of the gross motor skills that are key components of the functional mobility [11]. To the best of our knowledge, only a systematic review carried out in 2012 by Whalen and Case-Smith [12] suggested that HPT could produce benefits on gross motor function in subjects with CP. Therefore, the current evidence through meta-analysis analyzing the use of HPT to recover gross motor function in patients with CP is limited. Consequently, the aim of this systematic review and meta-analysis is to evaluate the effectiveness of HPT for improving gross motor function in children with CP.

2. Materials and Methods

2.1. Search Strategy

The present review was carried out following the preferred reporting items for systematic reviews and meta-analyses (PRISMA) [13] recommendations for systematic reviews. The literature search was carried out using the databases: PubMed, Web of Science (WoS), Scopus, and Embase. The search covered up to May 2019, without a limit in the starting date. It was performed by combining the following keywords: "hippotherapy" and "cerebral palsy". No filters were applied in relation to the publication dates or language, but the results were filtered to obtain only studies that corresponded to randomized clinical trials (RCTs).

2.2. Selection Criteria

The articles included in this review met the following inclusion criteria based on the PICOS model: (P) population: subjects diagnosed with CP; (I) intervention: HPT; (C) comparison: with conventional physical therapy intervention or placebo; (O) outcomes: gross motor function; and (S) study design: RCTs. The exclusion criteria were: (I) studies that involved healthy participants; (II) more than one intervention compared in the study; and (III) an intervention performed using HPT simulators.

In addition, we excluded articles in which the intervention was based on therapeutic riding because the instructors may not always be medical professionals using an interdisciplinary team approach [10].

2.3. Study Selection Process and Data Extraction

First, a literature search was conducted in the scientific databases by combining keywords. Afterwards, we identified and excluded the duplicated articles. After this first selection, the titles and abstracts of the articles found were reviewed. Next, a second exclusion process was made of those studies that did not fulfill the inclusion criteria. These articles obtained after this last selection were evaluated in depth to fulfill the specific inclusion criteria. Finally, the studies that form part of this review were included. Two reviewers (L.D.-G.S. and D.L.A.) independently selected, reviewed, and extracted data form the studies. An additional reviewer (I.C.B.) participated in the consensus of the decisions. We extracted the following information from each study: author, year of publication, number of participants from both groups, average age, gender, levels of the gross motor function classification system (GMFCS), type of CP, intervention carried out, frequency, duration, outcomes, measuring instruments, and results.

2.4. Assessment of the Methodological Quality of the Studies

The PEDro [14] was used to assess the methodological quality of the studies. This scale comprises different items in terms of the following domains: performance, selection, information, detection, and attribution bases. A higher score shows a higher methodological quality. A study with a PEDro score of 6 or higher is considered as evidence level 1 (6–8 is good; 9–10 is excellent), and a study with a score of 5 or less is considered as evidence level 2 (4–5 is acceptable; <4 is poor) [15].

3. Results

Once the database searches were completed, using the different keywords, a total of 276 documents were obtained, as shown in Figure 1. Finally, 10 studies met the inclusion criteria for review.

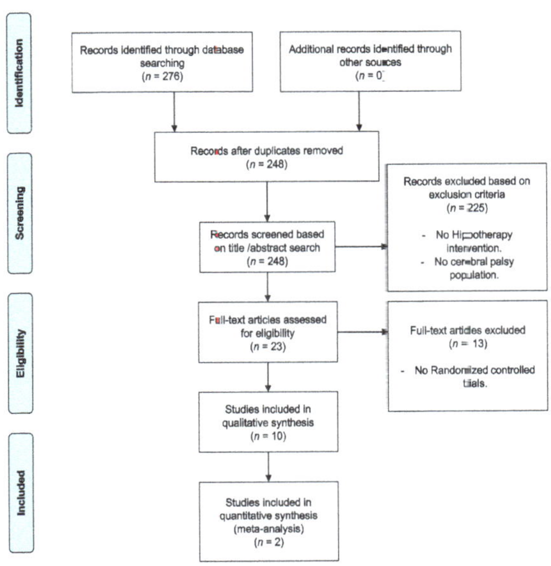

Figure 1. Flow diagram of included articles.

3.1. Methodological Quality of the Studies

Table 1 shows the PEDro scores achieved by the articles reviewed in this study. Three of ten articles were considered to have a high methodological quality: McGibbon et al. [16]; Kwon et al. [17], and Lucena-Antón et al. [5]. Matusiak-Wieczorek et al. [18] achieved the lowest score. The overall methodological quality was acceptable (average total score = 5.1, range 3–7).

Table 1. Analysis of the methodological quality of the studies (PEDro scores).

Study	1	2	3	4	5	6	7	8	9	10	11	Total
Benda et al., 2003 [19]	-	Yes	Yes	No	No	No	No	Yes	No	Yes	Yes	5
McGibbon et al., 2009 [16]	-	Yes	Yes	Yes	No	No	Yes	Yes	No	Yes	Yes	7
Kang et al., 2012 [20]	-	Yes	No	Yes	No	No	No	Yes	No	Yes	Yes	5
El-Meniawy and Thabet 2012 [21]	-	Yes	No	Yes	No	No	No	No	No	Yes	Yes	4
Park et al., 2014 [22]	-	Yes	No	Yes	No	No	No	Yes	No	Yes	Yes	5
Kwon et al., 2015 [17]	-	Yes	No	Yes	Yes	No	Yes	Yes	No	Yes	Yes	7
Matusiak-Wieczorek et al., 2016 [18]	-	Yes	No	No	No	No	No	No	No	Yes	Yes	3
Alemdaroglu et al., 2016 [23]	-	Yes	No	Yes	No	No	No	No	No	Yes	Yes	4
Deutz et al., 2017 [24]	-	Yes	No	Yes	No	No	Yes	No	No	Yes	No	4
Lucena-Antón et al., 2018 [5]	-	Yes	No	Yes	No	No	Yes	Yes	Yes	Yes	Yes	7

Range: 0–10. Item 1 is not included in the total score. Item 1: Eligibility criteria; Item 2: Random allocation; Item 3: Concealed allocation; Item 4: Baseline similarity; Item 5: Subject blinding; Item 6: Therapist blinding; Item 7: Assessor blinding; Item 8: >85% follow up; Item 9: Intention-to-treat analysis; Item 10: Between-group statistical comparison; Item 11: Point and variability measures.

3.2. Main Characteristics of the Studies Included in the Systematic Review

Regarding the age of the participants, the highest average age among the control groups was found in the study by McGibbon et al. [16] (8.8 years), while among the intervention groups, it was found in the study by Lucena-Antón et al. [5] (9.6 years). The lowest average age in both groups was presented in the study by Kwon et al. [17] (5.9 and 5.7 years, respectively). In terms of the sample size, the study by Kwon et al. [17] achieved the highest sample size with a total of 91 participants. The overall sample size ranged from 15 to 73 subjects. Table 2 shows the main clinical and demographic characteristics of the participants.

Concerning the different effects analyzed in the different studies, three studies [17,22,23] analyzed the effects of HPT interventions on gross motor function, four studies [17,18,20,23] analyzed the effects on balance, two studies [5,23] analyzed the spasticity, and two studies [16,19] analyzed the muscle activity through electromyography. The main intervention characteristics of the studies included in the systematic review are shown in Table 3.

Table 2. Main clinical and demographic characteristics of the participants.

Study	Participants (n)	Age (Years) ± SD	Female/Male	GMFCS Levels	Type: Diplegia/Hemiplegia (n)	Diagnosis
Benda et al., 2003 [19]	IG: ($n = 7$) CG: ($n = 8$) $N = 15$	4–12	ND	ND	ND	Spastic ($n = 15$)
McGibbon et al., 2009 [16]	Phase 1: IG: ($n = 25$) CG: ($n = 19$) $N = 44$ Phase 2: IG: ($n = 6$)	IG: 8.5 CG: 8.8	IG: 9/16 CG: 11/11	I: ($n = 27$) II: ($n = 9$) III: ($n = 5$) IV: ($n = 6$)	IG: 12/4 CG: 13/3 Quadriplegia: 9	Spastic ($n = 38$) Mixed ($n = 6$)
Kang et al., 2012 [20]	IG1:($n = 14$) IG2: ($n = 15$) CG: ($n = 15$) $N = 44$	IG1: 8.2 ± 1.1 IG2: 8.2 ± 1.2 CG: 7.8 ± 1.5	IG1: 7/7 IG2: 7/8 CG: 7/7	ND	IG1: 5/9 IG2: 5/10 CG: 5/9	ND
El-Meniawy and Thabet 2012 [21]	IG: ($n = 15$) CG: ($n = 15$) $N = 30$	7.02 ± 0.5	ND	ND	ND	Spastic ($n = 30$)
Park et al., 2014 [22]	IC: ($n - 34$) CG: ($n = 21$) $N = 55$	IG: 6.68 ± 2.6 CG: 7.76 ± 3.7	IG: 19/15 CG: 11/10	I: ($n = 14$) II: ($n = 15$) III: ($n = 11$) IV: ($n - 15$)	IG: 32/2 CG: 19/2	Spastic ($n = 55$)
Kwon et al., 2015 [17]	IG: ($n = 45$) CG: ($n = 46$) $N = 91$	IG: 5.7 ± 1.9 CG: 5.9 ± 1.8	IG: 25/20 CG: 17/29	I: ($n = 24$) II: ($n = 24$) III: ($n = 23$) IV: ($n = 20$)	IG: 41/4 CG: 40/6	Spastic ($n = 84$) Dyskinetic ($n = 4$) Ataxic ($n = 3$)
Matusiak-Wieczorek et al., 2016 [18]	IG: ($n = 19$) CG: ($n = 20$) $N = 39$	IG: 8.42 ± 2.2 CG: 8.3 ± 2.6	IG: 9/10 CG: 9/11	I: ($n = 23$) II: ($n = 16$)	IG: 6/13 CG: 5/15	Spastic ($n = 39$)

Table 2. *Cont.*

Study	Participants (n)	Age (Years) ± SD	Female/Male	GMFCS Levels	Type: Diplegia/Hemiplegia (n)	Diagnosis
Alemdaroğlu et al., 2016 [23]	IG: (n = 9) CG: (n = 7) N = 16	7.5 ± 1.7	7/9	IG: I–IV CG: I–V	ND	Spastic (n = 16)
Deutz et al., 2017 [24]	IG: (n = 35) CG: (n = 38) N = 73	IG: 9.29 ± 3.7 CG: 8.87 ± 2.9	IG: 12/23 CG: 17/21	II: (n = 27) III: (n = 17) IV: (n = 29)	IG: 35/0 CG: 38/0	Spastic (n = 73)
Lucena-Antón et al., 2018 [5]	IG: (n = 22) CG: (n = 22) N = 44	IG: 9.5 ± 2.7 CG: 8.2 ± 2.4	IG: 9/13 CG: 7/15	IV–V	ND	Spastic (n = 44)

CG: control group; GMFCS: Gross Motor Function Classification System; IG: Intervention group; ND: Not described.

Table 3. Summary of interventions carried out by the different studies included in the systematic review.

Study	Participants	Intervention	Frequency	Session Duration	Total Duration	Outcomes	Measuring Instruments	Results
Benda et al., 2003 [19]	IG: (n = 7) CG: (n = 8)	IG: HPT CG: Exercises on a barrel	One session	8 min	One session	Muscle activity in the paravertebral, hip abductors/adductors when sitting, standing, and walking	EMG	IG got better results than CG. Mean change improvements: IG = 64.6% (SD = 28.3) vs. CG = −12.8% (SD = 88.8); (p = 0.051)
McGibbon et al., 2009 [16]	Phase 1: IG: (n = 25) CG: (n = 19) Phase 2: IG: (n = 6)	IG: HPT CG: Exercises on a barrel	Phase 1: One session Phase 2: Once a week	Phase 1: 10 min Phase 2: 40 min	Phase 1: One session Phase 2: 36 weeks	Hip adductors muscle activity	SEMG	Phase 1: The IG significantly improved the muscle asymmetry of hip adductors (p < 001; d = 1.32) Phase 2: After 12 weeks, 4 of 6 children improved the muscle symmetry of hip adductors

Table 3. *Cont.*

Study	Participants	Intervention	Frequency	Session Duration	Total Duration	Outcomes	Measuring Instruments	Results
Kang et al., 2012 [20]	IG1:(n = 15) IG2: (n = 15) CG: (n = 15)	IG1: HPT IG2: PT CG: Non treatment	Once a week	30 min	8 weeks	Sitting balance	Force plate	The results showed that pathway and velocity significantly decreased in the HPT group ($p < 0.05$) compared to the PT and CON groups
El-Meniawy and Thabet 2012 [21]	IG: (n = 15) CG: (n = 15)	IG: HPT CG: Exercise	IG: Once a week CG: 3 times/week	IG: 30 min CG: 1 h	12 weeks	Back geometry parameters: lateral deviation, trunk imbalance, pelvic tilt, rotation	Formetric instrument system	The results showed improvements in favor of the IG in all the outcomes ($p < 0.05$)
Park et al., 2014 [22]	IG: (n = 34) CG: (n = 21)	IG: HPT CG: Non treatment	2 times/week	45 min	8 weeks	Gross motor function Functional performance	GMFM-66 GMFM-88 PEDI-FSS	Significant results were obtained in IG after the intervention compared to the CG: GMFM-66 (all dimensions); GMFM-88 (B and C dimensions); and 3 domains of the PEDI-FSS: ($p < 0.05$)
Kwon et al., 2015 [17]	IG: (n = 45) CG: (n = 46)	IG: HPT CG: Aerobic exercise	2 times/week	30 min	8 weeks	Gross motor function. Balance	GMFM-66 GMFM-88 PBS	Significant results were found between groups ($p < 0.05$): GMFM- 66, GMFM-88 (total score and dimensions B, C, D, and E). Moreover, significant results were found in balance ($p < 0.05$)
Matusiak-Wieczorek et al., 2016 [18]	IG: (n = 19) CG: (n = 20)	IG: HPT CG: NI	Once a week	30 min	12 weeks	Body balance in sitting position	SAS	Significant results were obtained in IG for arm function and control of trunk position: ($p = 0.018$)
Alemdaroğlu et al., 2016 [23]	IG: (n = 9) CG: (n = 7)	IG: HPT CG: PT	IG: 2 times/week CG: 5 times/week	30 min	5 weeks	Gross motor function, hip adductors spasticity, balance, hip abduction angle, knee distance	GMFMCS MAS MFRT Goniometer	Significant improvements were observed between groups in spasticity ($p = 0.016$). Not significant results were found in other outcomes
Deutz et al., 2017 [24]	IG: (n = 35) CG: (n = 38)	IG: HPT CG: PT	1–2 times/week	ND	16–20 weeks	Gross motor function and quality of life	GMFM-66 KIDSCREEN-27 questionnaire CHQ	Improvements were observed in GMFM-66 dimension E for IG ($p = 0.02$) compared to CG. Not significant results were found in quality of life
Lucena-Antón et al., 2018 [5]	IG: (n = 22) CG: (n = 22)	IG: HPT CG: PT	IG: Once a week CG: 2 times/week	45 min	12 weeks	Hip adductors spasticity	MAS	Significant results were obtained between groups for IG in spasticity ($p = 0.04$ for left adductors and $p = 0.047$ for right adductors)

CG: control group; CHQ: Child Health Questionnaire; EMG: Electromyography; GMFM: Gross Motor Function Measure; HPT: Hippotherapy; IG: Intervention group; MAS: Modified Ashworth Scale; MFRT Modified Functional Reach Test; Min: Minutes; ND: not described; PBS Pediatric Balance Scale; PEDI-FSS: Pediatric Evaluation of Disability Inventory-Functional Skills Scale; PT: Physical therapy. SAS Sitting Assessment Scale; PDM Multifunction Force Measure Plate; SD: Standard deviation; SEMG: Surface Electromyography.

3.3. Meta-Analysis of the Study Groups

The groups were created according to the measuring instrument used to assess the gross motor function. Accordingly, seven groups were set up: (i) GMFM-66 total scores; (ii) GMFM-88 total scores; and (iii–vii) GMFM-88 dimensions A–E.

The gross motor function measure (GMFM) is commonly used in neurological rehabilitation to assess the gross motor function in subjects with CP. The GMFM-66 scale is an updated version of GMFM-88. It includes 66 of the original 88 items providing more information to encourage the goal setting process [11]. Both scales include different items that assess how much of an activity can be carried out rather than the quality of performing the activities [25]. Both versions have been validated to evaluate changes in children with CP. A higher score is an indicator of better gross motor function [26].

Two studies analyzed the differences in gross motor function using the GMFM-66. The overall result of this study group was favorable (Figure 2).

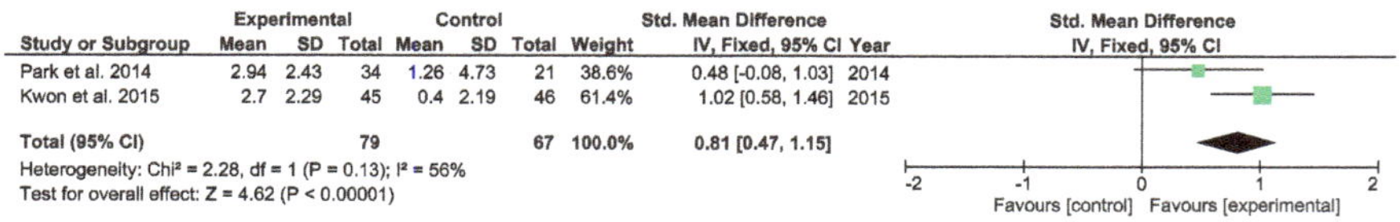

Figure 2. Forest plot for gross motor function measured by the GMFM-66 scale.

Regarding the GMFM-88 scale, it is divided into five dimensions (A: lying and rolling, B: sitting, C: crawling and kneeling, D: standing, and E: walking, running, and jumping). The total score ranges from 0 to 100. For the GMFM-88 total score, the overall result of the meta-analysis was not conclusive (Figure 3).

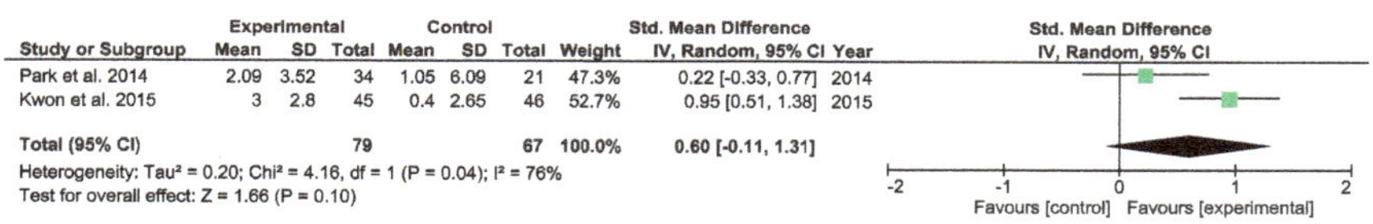

Figure 3. Forest plot for gross motor function measured by the GMFM-88 total scores.

Regarding the different dimensions included in the GMFM-88 scale, the overall result of the meta-analysis was favorable in GMFM-88 dimensions A, B, and E, while the overall result of the meta-analysis was inconclusive for GMFM-88 dimensions C and D. The results are shown in Figures 4–8.

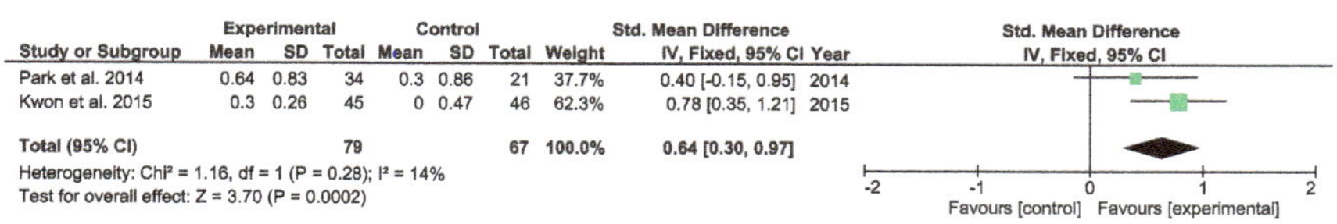

Figure 4. Forest plot for GMFM-88 Dimension A.

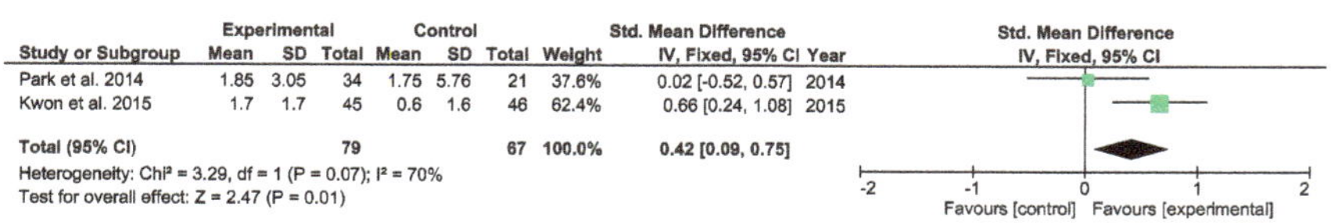

Figure 5. Forest plot for GMFM-88 Dimension B.

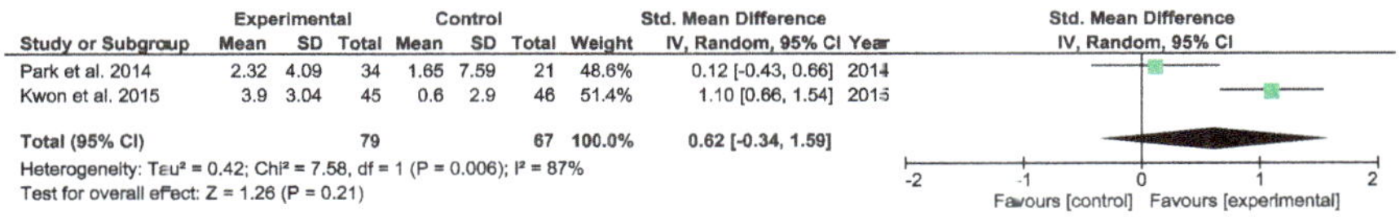

Figure 6. Forest plot for GMFM-88 Dimension C.

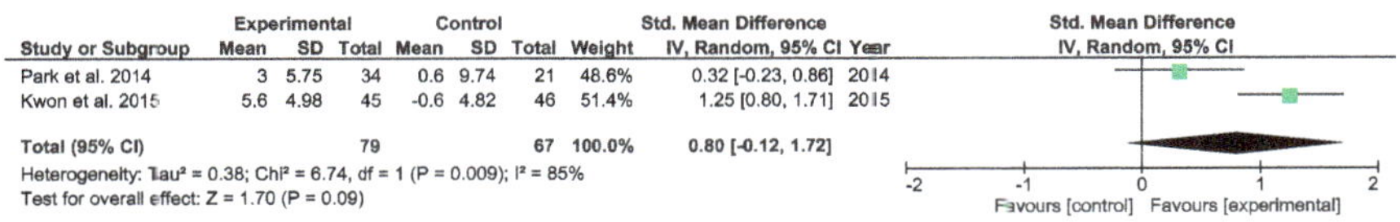

Figure 7. Forest plot for GMFM-88 Dimension D.

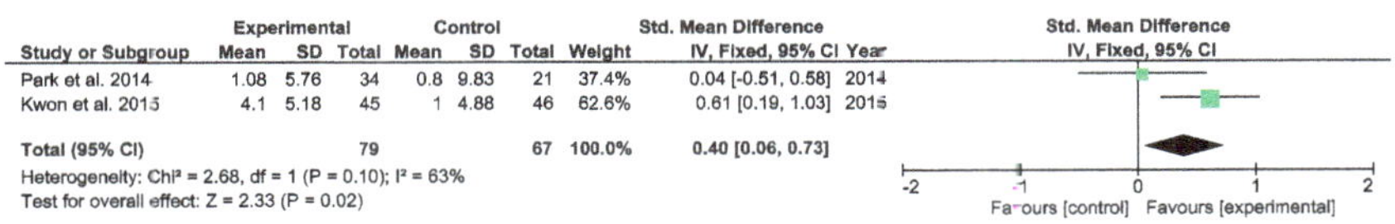

Figure 8. Forest plot for GMFM-88 Dimension E.

4. Discussion

The objective of this systematic review and meta-analysis of RCTs was to analyze the effectiveness of HPT interventions on improving gross motor function in subjects with CP. A total of ten RCTs were analyzed in the systematic review, involving 452 participants. In view of our results, we could conclude that HPT could be an effective intervention to improve gross motor function in children with CP.

From a clinical perspective, the findings obtained in the present review suggest that HPT stands for an emerging intervention in neurological rehabilitation, which could be used in addition to neurodevelopmental based methods. The findings on the GMFM-66 scale and GMFM-88 dimensions A, B, and E showed that HPT interventions had significant improvements on gross motor function and, more specifically, on the ability to perform lying and rolling, sitting, and walking. We can hypothesize that the rhythmic and symmetrical movement of the horse could stimulate the proprioception and balance reactions. Furthermore, according to Casady and Nichols-Larsen [27], HPT could stimulate the motor learning and subjects could be able to transfer the movement patterns learned from HPT to other usual environments. According to Bertoti [28], and considering that three of four studies [17,18,20,23] did obtain significant effects on balance and two studies [5,23] reported significant effects on the spasticity of hip adductors, we can suggest that the positive effects obtained on balance and muscle spasticity contributed to improvements in the functional outcomes and, thus, to the significant results obtained in the GMFM-66 and GMFM-88 dimensions.

Regarding the intervention characteristics, most studies included more than 30 participants, a high number considering the difficulty to recruit patients with CP. All intervention groups received HPT in addition to physical therapy, and all of them carried out their HPT interventions through a walking pace, except for Alemdaroğlu et al. [23] and Deutz et al. [24] that did not specify it. Most studies used protocols with 8–12 weeks as the total duration and two times/week as the frequency. The session duration used in the studies was around 30 min, with unusual interventions of more than 45 min. The effects found were similar and several authors suggested that longer durations could cause fatigue in children, which was not positive for achieving the intended improvements. Therefore, we can suggest that HPT interventions based on 8–12 week programs with sessions of 30–45 min two times a week could be proper for children with CP to recover motor function.

Concerning the methodological quality of the studies included in the present review, the main limitation was found in the application of double-blind. Blinding of the participants and therapists was not possible in most studies due to the unconcealable nature of the intervention. In addition, the concealed allocation was only possible in two studies [16,19] and the assessor blinding was carried out by four studies [5,16,17,24]. Nevertheless, the overall quality of the studies was acceptable.

Our results matched with the findings of the systematic review conducted by Whalen and Case-Smith [12] in 2012, in which they stated that HPT could produce benefits on gross motor function in children with CP, but the authors highlighted that the evidence was limited. Other findings were found in different pathologies, such as Down syndrome and autism disorder. De Miguel Rubio et al. [29] suggested that HPT could not be effective to improve gross motor function in subjects with Down syndrome, and Srinivasan et al. [30] analyzed the effects of HPT interventions in subjects with autism disorder, obtaining positive effects on motor skills.

The present systematic review presented some limitations. Potential useful articles that were indexed in other scientific databases could not be included. In addition, the lack of long-term follow-up and the heterogeneity of the protocols suggests the need to unify the HPT intervention programs, specifically, in subjects with CP. Moreover, despite assessing the same outcomes between the different studies included in the review, the statistical comparison was not always possible due to studies used different scales and measuring instruments to assess the clinical differences. Thus, only two studies were included in the meta-analysis. Therefore, the results obtained should be taken with caution since a limited number of studies was analyzed.

5. Conclusions

In conclusion, we could state that HPT interventions were effective to improve gross motor function in subjects with CP. Specifically, favorable results were obtained in the GMFM-66 total scores and GMFM-88 dimensions A, B, and E. Furthermore, positive effects have been showed on balance recovery and muscle spasticity reduction.

Despite the different HPT protocols used, evidence shows that 30–45 min sessions, twice weekly for 8–12 weeks, could produce significant effects on gross motor function in children with CP.

This study can be helpful in neurological rehabilitation of children with CP using HPT interventions, as well as by providing key factors to determine which specific factors of the HPT protocols have a greater weight to achieve the desired effects in future interventions. Nevertheless, it will be necessary to carry out more randomized controlled trials with larger sample sizes and specified protocols.

Author Contributions: Conceptualization and methodology: L.D.G.-S., I.C.-B., J.A.M.-M. and D.L.-A.; statistical analysis: A.S.; writing—original draft preparation: L.D.G.-S., D.L.A., A.S. and J.A.M.-M.; writing—review and editing: D.L.-A., J.A.M.-M. and I.C.-B. All authors have read and agreed to the published version of the manuscript.

Funding: This research was funded by the Department of Nursing and Physiotherapy (University of Cadiz).

Acknowledgments: The authors are grateful for the funding from the Department of Nursing and Physiotherapy (University of Cadiz).

Conflicts of Interest: The authors declare no conflict of interest.

References

1. Petersen, R.; Procter, C.; Donald, K.A. Assessment and Management of the Child with Cerebral Palsy. In *Clinical Child Neurology*; Springer International Publishing: Cham, Switzerland, 2020; pp. 175–203.
2. Longo, E.; Regalado, I.C.R.; Galvão, E.R.V.P.; Ferreira, H.N.C.; Badia, M.; Baz, B.O. I Want to Play: Children With Cerebral Palsy Talk About Their Experiences on Barriers and Facilitators to Participation in Leisure Activities. *Pediatr. Phys. Ther.* **2020**, *32*, 190–200. [PubMed]
3. Novak, I.; Morgan, C.; Adde, L.; Blackman, J.; Boyd, R.N.; Brunstrom-Hernandez, J.; Cioni, G.; Damiano, D.; Darrah, J.; Eliasson, A.-C.; et al. Early, Accurate Diagnosis and Early Intervention in Cerebral Palsy. *JAMA Pediatr.* **2017**, *171*, 897. [CrossRef] [PubMed]
4. Dominguez-Romero, J.G.; Molina-Aroca, A.; Moral-Munoz, J.A.; Luque-Moreno, C.; Lucena-Anton, D. Effectiveness of mechanical horse-riding simulators on postural balance in neurological rehabilitation: Systematic review and meta-analysis. *Int. J. Environ. Res. Public Health* **2020**, *17*, 165. [CrossRef] [PubMed]

5. Lucena-Anton, D.; Rosety-Rodríguez, I.; Moral-Munoz, J.A. Effects of a hippotherapy intervention on muscle spasticity in children with cerebral palsy: A randomized controlled trial. *Complement Ther. Clin Pract.* **2018**, *31*, 188–192. [CrossRef]
6. Koca, T.T. What is hippotherapy? The indications and effectiveness of hippotherapy. *North Clin. Istanbul.* **2016**, *2*, 247–252. [CrossRef]
7. Novak, I.; Morgan, C.; Fahey, M.; Finch-Edmondson, M.; Galea, C.; Hines, A.; Langdon, K.; Mc Namara, M.; Paton, M.C.B.; Popat, H.; et al. State of the Evidence Traffic Lights 2019: Systematic Review of Interventions for Preventing and Treating Children with Cerebral Palsy. *Curr. Neurol. Neurosci. Rep.* **2020**, *20*, 3. [CrossRef]
8. Alonso, P.M. Physiotherapy interventions through hippotherapy in the treatment of cerebral palsy. A literature review. *Rehabilitación* **2020**, *54*, 96–106.
9. Martín-Valero, R.; Vega-Ballón, J.; Perez-Cabezas, V. Benefits of hippotherapy in children with cerebral palsy: A narrative review. *Eur. J. Paediatr. Neurol.* **2018**, *22*, 1150–1160 [CrossRef]
10. Zadnikar, M.; Kastrin, A. Effects of hippotherapy and therapeutic horseback riding on postural control or balance in childrenwith cerebral palsy: A meta-analysis. *Dev. Med. Child Neurol.* **2011**, *53*, 684–691. [CrossRef]
11. Alotaibi, M.; Long, T.; Kennedy, E.; Bavishi, S. The efficacy of GMFM-88 and GMFM-66 to detect changes in gross motor function in children with cerebral palsy (CP): A literature review. *Disabil. Rehabil.* **2014**, *36*, 617–627. [CrossRef]
12. Whalen, N.C.; Case-Smith, J. Therapeutic effects of horseback riding therapy on gross motor function in children with cerebral palsy: A Systematic Review. *Phys. Occup. Ther. Pediatr.* **2012**, *32*, 229–242. [CrossRef] [PubMed]
13. Hutton, B.; Catalá-López, F.; Moher, D. The PRISMA statement extension for systematic reviews incorporating network meta-analysis: PRISMA-NMA. *Med. Clin.* **2016**, *147*, 262–266. [CrossRef]
14. Maher, C.G.; Sherrington, C.; Herbert, R.D.; Moseley, A.M.; Elkins, M. Reliability of the PEDro Scale for Rating Quality of Randomized Controlled Trials. *Phys. Ther.* **2003**, *83*, 713–721. [CrossRef] [PubMed]
15. Moseley, A.M.; Herbert, R.D.; Sherrington, C.; Maher, C.G. Evidence for physiotherapy practice: A survey of the Physiotherapy Evidence Database (PEDro). *Aust. J. Physiother.* **2002**, *48*, 43–49. [CrossRef]
16. McGibbon, N.H.; Benda, W.; Duncan, B.R.; Silkwood-Sherer, D. Immediate and long-term effects of Hippotherapy on symmetry of adductor muscle activity and functional ability in children with spastic cerebral palsy. *Arch Phys. Med. Rehabil.* **2009**, *90*, 966–974. [CrossRef]
17. Kwon, J.-Y.; Chang, H.J.; Yi, S.-H.; Lee, J.Y.; Shin, H.-Y.; Kim, Y.-H. Effect of hippotherapy on gross motor function in children with cerebral palsy: A randomized controlled trial. *J. Altern Complement Med.* **2015**, *21*, 15–21. [CrossRef]
18. Matusiak-Wieczorek, E.; Małachowska-Sobieska, M.; Synder, M. Influence of Hippotherapy on Body Balance in the Sitting Position Among Children with Cerebral Palsy. *Ortop. Traumatol. Rehabil.* **2016**, *18*, 165–175. [CrossRef]
19. Benda, W.; McGibbon, N.H.; Grant, K.L. Improvements in muscle symmetry in children with cerebral palsy after equine-assisted therapy (Hippotherapy). *J. Altern Complement Med* **2003**, *9*, 817–825. [CrossRef]
20. Kang, H.; Jung, J.; Yu, J. Effects of Hippotherapy on the Sitting Balance of Children with Cerebral Palsy: A Randomized Control Trial. *J. Phys. Ther. Sci.* **2012**, *24*, 833–836. [CrossRef]
21. El-Meniawy, G.H.; Thabet, N.S. Modulation of back geometry in children with spastic diplegic cerebral palsy via hippotherapy training. *Egypt J. Med. Hum. Genet.* **2012**, *13*, 63–71. [CrossRef]
22. Park, E.S.; Rha, D.-W.; Shin, J.S.; Kim, S.; Jung, S. Effects of Hippotherapy on gross motor function and functional performance of children with cerebral palsy. *Yonsei Med. J.* **2014**, *55*, 1736–1742. [CrossRef] [PubMed]
23. Alemdaroğlu, E.; Oken, O.; Ucan, H.; Ersöz, M.; Köseoğlu, B.F.; Kapıcıoğlu, M. İsmail S.; Yanıkoğlu, I. Horseback riding therapy in addition to conventional rehabilitation program decreases spasticity in children with cerebral palsy: A small sample study. *Complement Ther. Clin. Pract.* **2016**, *23*, 26–29. [CrossRef]
24. Deutz, U.; Heussen, N.; Weigt-Usinger, K.; Leiz, S.; Raabe, C.; Polster, T.; Steinbüchel, D.; Moll, C.; Lücke, T.; Krägeloh-Mann, I.; et al. Impact of Hippotherapy on Gross Motor Function and Quality of Life in Children with Bilateral Cerebral Palsy: A Randomized Open-Label Crossover Study. *Neuropediatrics* **2018**, *49*, 185–192. [CrossRef] [PubMed]

25. Russell, D.; Rosenbaum, P.; Avery, L.; Lane, M. *Gross Motor Function Measure (GMFM-66 and GMFM-88) User's Manual: Clinics in Development Medicine*; Mac Keith Press: London, UK, 2002.
26. Wei, S.; Wang, S.J.; Liao, Y.G.; Hong, Y.; Xu, X.J.; Shao, X.M. Reliability and validity of the GMFM-66 in 0- to 3-year-old children with cerebral palsy. *Am. J. Phys. Med. Rehabil.* **2006**, *85*, 141–147. [CrossRef] [PubMed]
27. Casady, R.L.; Nichols-Larsen, D.S. The effect of hippotherapy on ten children with cerebral palsy. *Pediatr. Phys. Ther.* **2004**, *16*, 165–172. [CrossRef]
28. Bertoti, D.B. Effect of therapeutic horseback riding on posture in children with cerebral palsy. *Phys. Ther.* **1988**, *68*, 1505–1512. [PubMed]
29. De Miguel, A.; De Miguel, M.D.; Lucena-Anton, D.; Rubio, M.D. Effects of hypotherapy on the motor function of persons with Down's syndrome: A systematic review. *Rev. Neurol.* **2018**, *67*, 233–241.
30. Srinivasan, S.M.; Cavagnino, D.T.; Bhat, A.N. Effects of Equine Therapy on Individuals with Autism Spectrum Disorder: A Systematic Review. *Rev. J. Autism Dev. Disord.* **2018**, *5*, 156–175. [CrossRef]

children

MDPI

Article

Pain and Communication in Children with Cerebral Palsy: Influence on Parents' Perception of Family Impact and Healthcare Satisfaction

Inmaculada Riquelme [1,2,*], Álvaro Sabater-Gárriz [1,2,3] and Pedro Montoya [1]

1 Research Institute of Health Sciences (IUNICS-IdISBa), University of the Balearic Islands, 07122 Palma, Spain; alvaro.sabater@uib.es (Á.S.-G.); pedro.montoya@uib.es (P.M.)
2 Department of Nursing and Physiotherapy, University of the Balearic Islands, 07122 Palma, Spain
3 Fundación Aspace Baleares, Ctra. Vieja de Bunyola, Km 8.2, 07141 Marratxí, Spain
* Correspondence: inma.riquelme@uib.es; Tel.: +34-971-171-310; Fax: +34-971-172-309

Abstract: Cerebral palsy (CP) is an impacting chronic condition. Concomitant comorbidities such as pain and speech inability may further affect parents' perception of the pathology impact in the family quality of life and the provided care. The objective of this cross-sectional descriptive correlational study was to compare parental reports on family impact and healthcare satisfaction in children with CP with and without chronic pain and with and without speech ability. Parents of 59 children with CP (age range = 4–18 years) completed several questions about pain and speech ability and two modules of the Pediatric Quality of Life Measurement Model: The PedsQLTM 2.0 Family Impact Module and the PedsQLTM Healthcare Satisfaction Generic Module. Our findings revealed that children's pain slightly impacted family physical health, social health and worry. In children without pain, speech inability increased the perceived health impact. Parents' healthcare satisfaction was barely affected by pain or speech inability, both increasing parents' satisfaction in the *professional technical skills* and *inclusion of family* domains on the care plan. In conclusion, pain and speech inability in children with CP can impact family health but not healthcare satisfaction. Regular assessment and intervention in family health is essential for the design of family-centred programs for children with CP.

Keywords: cerebral palsy; pain; speech; family impact; healthcare satisfaction

Citation: Riquelme, I.; Sabater-Gárriz, Á.; Montoya, P. Pain and Communication in Children with Cerebral Palsy: Influence on Parents' Perception of Family Impact and Healthcare Satisfaction. *Children* **2021**, *8*, 87. https://doi.org/10.3390/children8020087

Academic Editor: Dulce María Romero-Ayuso

Received: 11 December 2020
Accepted: 22 January 2021
Published: 27 January 2021

1. Introduction

Children with cerebral palsy (CP) have unique demands, causing significant impact to the quality of life of their families. The care that people with cerebral palsy require throughout their lives involves a great financial burden, a significant investment of time and significant repercussions on work and social activities [1–3]. Undoubtedly, all this can generate chronic stress in the family and caregivers who take care of these persons [4,5], thus compromising their health and well-being [5,6,7]. Thus, parents of children with CP have reported poorer physical and mental health than the general population, with higher levels of depression, musculoskeletal pain and fatigue [7–12]. Furthermore, the family impact does not appear to be associated with the dependency level, age, type or severity of CP [4,10,11,13]. Even improvements in the child's motor function do not produce changes in the quality of life of the parents [14]. Rather, parents develop negative feelings due to reductions or difficulties in the health, social skills, behaviours or emotions experienced by their children [4,15,16]. In this context, pain may be an important factor influencing family well-being, as concern for the child's pain is one of the most reported causes of emotional stress in parents of children with CP [13,17].

More than half of children with CP experience frequent moderate to severe pain at multiple body locations [18,19]. Recurrent pain produces an increase of behavioural and emotional problems in children with CP, reducing their quality of life and negatively affecting their participation in daily and social activities and the satisfaction of parents with performing these activities [20–22]. Pain constitutes an additional burden for the health system, producing more demand for health services than the severity of the pathology [23], with more frequent visits to the family physician, more prescription of analgesics [18] and more recurrent use of conventional and alternative therapies [24]. Furthermore, pain is one of the main concerns of parents when their children are faced with a health intervention [25] and one of the main factors influencing parents' evaluation of the intervention success [26]. Therefore, frequent pain reduces satisfaction with motor rehabilitation, while a low level of post-operative pain increases satisfaction after recovery and effective pain management is considered to improve the quality of healthcare [27,28].

The child's inability to speak is an important risk factor for parental stress and depression [17,29], increasing the vulnerability perceived by parents in interventions that affect health, such as surgery [30], and poor perception of the child's health-related quality of life [31]. Although parents are able to detect pain in their children in spite of their speech impairments [32,33], parent report increased frequency, duration and intensity of musculoskeletal pain in more severely affected children who are unable to self-report [34]. Moreover, discrepancies between parents and health professionals in pain detection are greater in children with speech problems [32].

Although pain and speech are important factors affecting parents' quality of life and satisfaction with health services, little research has focused on their specific associations. This study aims to compare parental reports on family impact and healthcare satisfaction in children with cerebral palsy with and without chronic pain, as well as with and without speech ability.

2. Materials and Methods

2.1. Participants

This is a cross-sectional descriptive correlational study, with purposive sampling and a survey method for data collection. The staff, which is responsible for 11 specialized centres dedicated to education, care or leisure for individuals with disabilities in Majorca (Spain), identified the participants with cerebral palsy. The inclusion criterion was a diagnosis of CP and age between 4 and 18 years. Most of the participants were identified in care centres for children with cerebral palsy (80% of families), while a smaller percentage were identified in educational or leisure centres that support different developmental conditions. The parents of 70 children with CP were initially contacted through a letter explaining the objectives and protocol of the study. Moreover, informative meetings were held with the families at the centres to explain the objectives and methods of the study throughout the last quarter of 2016. Parents of 59 children with CP (age range = 4–18, mean age = 11.58 (4.61), 34 girls) agreed to participate in the study and provided written informed consent. In addition, children with CP with a sufficient cognitive level expressed verbal or gestural willingness to participate. The study was approved by the Ethics Committee of the Regional Government of the Balearic Islands (Reference code: IB3156/16 PI).

2.2. Interview and Questionnaires

The week following the signing of the informed consent, each family was assigned an anonymous code for data collection. Parents completed a semi-structured interview, and two 2-report questionnaires were delivered to be completed at home. The semi-structured interview (Supplementary Table S1) consisted of several questions about demographic data (Table 1), as well as about the pain and communication characteristics of their children. A member of the research team was in permanent telephone contact with the families to resolve possible doubts while the questionnaires were being completed. Parents were asked to return the completed questionnaires to the centre in a sealed envelope, and a member of the research team collected them each week. The type of CP, the cognitive level and the level of motor impairment, determined by the Gross Motor Function Classification System (GMFCS-R) [35], were obtained from the children's medical history. Table 2 displays the clinical characteristics of children with CP.

Table 1. Families' sociodemographic characteristics.

Mother's age (years; mean, SD)	41.54 (5.71)
Father's age (years; mean, SD)	42.93 (6.46)
Number of siblings (*n*, %)	
One	7, 11.86%
Two	42, 71.19%
More than two	10, 16.95%
Marital status (*n*, %)	
Single	5, 8.48%
Married	45, 76.27%
Divorced	9, 15.25%
Education (*n*, %)	
Primary education	36, 61.02%
Secondary education	16, 27.12%
Higher education	7, 11.86%
Socioeconomic status (*n*, %)	
Low	11, 18.64%
Middle-low	27, 45.76%
Middle-high	20, 33.89%
High	1, 1.70%
Employment (*n*, %)	
Both parents full time employed	37, 62.71%
One parent half-time employed	13, 22.03%
Unemployed	9, 15.25%
Residence (*n*, %)	
Urban	14, 23.73%
Country	45, 76.27%

Table 2. Clinical characteristics of children with cerebral palsy. GMFCS = Gross motor function classification system (1 = walks without limitations, 5 = transported in a manual wheelchair) [35].

	n, %
Type of cerebral palsy	
Bilateral spastic	40, 67.80%
Unilateral spastic	4, 6.78%
Diskinetic	11, 18.64%
Ataxic	4, 6.78%
Cognitive impairment	
None	19, 32.20%
Mild	7, 11.86%
Moderate	3, 5.09%
Severe	30, 50.85%
Motor impairment (GMFCS)	
Level 1	7, 11.86%
Level 2	7, 11.86%
Level 3	12, 20.34%
Level 4	6, 10.17%
Level 5	27, 45.76%
Type of education	
Ordinary centre	47, 79.66%
Special centre	12, 20.34%

Children's pain was measured using the following information from the interview: (1) Whether they were experiencing chronic pain (pain lasting more than 3 months) or not (yes/no response); (2) ratings of current and worst pain in the last week using a 11-point numerical rating scale (0 = no pain, 10 = unbearable pain); and (3) location of painful body regions using a human figure drawing (QL07/00 Pediatric Pain Questionnaire) [36]. Speech ability was assessed with a yes/no question.

Parents completed two questionnaires included in the Pediatric Quality of Life Measurement Model (PedsQL^{TM}, Lyon, France) [37] to assess family impact and healthcare satisfaction. The PedsQL^{TM} 2.0 Family Impact Module consists of 36 items comprising 8 dimensions: *Physical functioning, emotional functioning, social functioning, cognitive functioning, communication, worry, daily activities* and *family relationships*. Items are rated on a Likert scale from 0 (never) to 4 (almost always) and are transformed into a score from 0 to 100, with higher scores indicating better functioning (less impact). The 8 dimensions are combined into 3 total scores: The *Total impact score, Parent health-related quality of life summary score* and *Family functioning summary score*. The PedsQL^{TM} Healthcare Satisfaction Generic Module consists of 24 items comprising 6 dimensions: *Information, inclusion of family, communication, technical skills, emotional needs* and *overall satisfaction*. Items are rated on a Likert scale from 0 (never) to 4 (always) and are transformed into a score from 0 to 100, with higher scores indicating greater satisfaction. The PedsQL^{TM} model and its different questionnaires have proven to be valid and reliable for assessing different aspects of paediatric health-related quality of life [36].

2.3. Statistical Analyses

Multivariate analyses of variance (MANOVA) were performed on family impact and healthcare satisfaction separately. The factors PAIN (children with pain vs. children without pain) and SPEECH (children with speech ability vs. children without speech ability) were used as between-subject factors in the statistical design. In addition, the factor DIMENSION was used as within-subjects to assess effects on the different subscales of each module. In case of significant effects due to DIMENSION, separate ANOVAs on the scores of each subscale were planned to further explore the differences due to PAIN and SPEECH. All results were adjusted using Bonferroni corrections for post-hoc comparisons. In addition, Pearson and Spearman correlations were performed to establish associations among the different dimensions of the family impact and healthcare satisfaction questionnaires with pain characteristics. The missing data were not replaced or completed by statistical methods and were discarded from the analyses. Significance levels were set at $p < 0.05$.

3. Results

Once the recruitment performed, the sample size was estimated at 30 children. Pain was reported in 51% of the children ($n = 30$), and 40.7% had speech problems ($n = 24$). Parents reported moderate impact (mean = 69.14 (17.03), range = 26.39–96.53) and healthcare satisfaction (mean = 64.96 (21.94), range = 2–100). The descriptive data of the different dimensions for each of the four groups are displayed in Table 3.

In the Family Impact Module questionnaire, the MANOVA revealed only a main effect due to DIMENSION (F (7,27) = 17.77, $p < 0.001$), indicating that scores in the different subscales were significantly different. To further explore this effect, separate ANOVAs were performed on each dimension to examine the effects due to PAIN and SPEECH (Table 4). For the *physical functioning* dimension, a significant effect due to PAIN × SPEECH (F (1,39) = 5.04, $p = 0.031$) was yielded, indicating that parents of children without speech ability reported lower scores (higher negative impact) than those of children with verbal speech when children have no chronic pain ($p = 0.044$) (Figure 1). By contrast, no differences due to speech ability were observed on physical impact when children have chronic pain ($p = 0.268$). For the *social functioning* dimension, a significant interaction PAIN × SPEECH (F (1,39) = 4.38, $p = 0.044$) was also found, revealing that parents of children without speech ability reported lower scores (higher impact) than those of children with verbal speech when children report no chronic pain ($p = 0.087$) (Figure 1). No differences due to speech ability were observed on social functioning when children report chronic pain ($p = 0.260$). No other significant effects were found in the rest of the domains.

Table 3. Mean (standard deviation) and range of the different domains of the PedsQL^{TM} 2.0 Family Impact Module and the PedsQL^{TM} Healthcare Satisfaction Generic Module in every group of children.

	No Pain, Speech (N = 18)	No Pain, No Speech (N = 11)	Pain, Speech (N = 17)	Pain, No Speech (N = 13)
Family Impact Module				
Global scores				
Total impact	69.71 (20.91), 26.39–94.44	61.46 (12.52), 38.89–72.22	70.49 (13.44), 46.53–88.89	74.90 (14.21), 50.69–96.53
Parent health-related quality of life summary	79.11 (20.83), 37.50–100	62.71 (14.80), 42.50–75.00	73.91 (15.68), 48.75–96.25	78.57 (15.56), 50.00–100
Family functioning summary	75.00 (27.56), 0–100	72.45 (14.83), 53.57–92.86	73.81 (14.83), 46.43–92.86	83.67 (15.82), 57.14–100
Dimensions				
Physical functioning	79.72 (22.82), 25.00–100	58.33 (20.27), 33.33–83.33	64.38 (16.62), 37.50–95.83	76.79 (29.74), 16.67–100
Emotional functioning	76.67 (25.96), 10.00–100	56.43 (22.12), 20.00–80.00	61.50 (30.65), 0–100	63.57 (23.58), 30.00–100
Social functioning	80.42 (16.00), 43.75–100	65.48 (16.31), 37.50–87.50	71.25 (20.24), 43.75–100	83.93 (27.68), 37.50–100
Cognitive functioning	79.64 (25.53), 15.00–100	77.86 (20.59), 50.00–100	83.33 (11.99), 70–100	91.43 (20.56), 45.00–100
Communication	83.93 (22.38), 33.33–100	70.24 (30.89), 41.67–100	82.41 (17.40), 50.00–100	85.71 (11.50), 66.67–100
Worry	41.43 (35.91), 0–100	50.00 (26.93), 0–75.00	58.33 (13.23), 40–80	56.43 (22.86), 30.00–95.00
Daily activities	61.61 (34.13), 0–100	37.50 (27.00), 0–87.50	55.56 (25.09), 0–75.00	60.71 (34.93), 0–100
Family relationships	80.36 (29.32), 0–100	86.43 (16.26), 65.00–100	81.11 (15.77), 50.00–100	92.86 (9.51), 80.00–100
Healthcare Satisfaction Generic Module				
Global score	94.13 (25.50), 2.22–94.13	58.97 (15.14), 40.07–82.00	59.27 (24.63), 16.50–59.27	76.89 (15.49), 50.00–100
Information	54.60 (32.99), 0–95.00	55.00 (27.02), 25.00–90.00	60.83 (18.29), 40.00–100	70.29 (31.68), 25.00–100
Inclusion of family	66.00 (31.60), 0–100	45.83 (28.96), 0–75.00	54.44 (38.75), 0–100	85.71 (20.32), 43.75–100
Communication	63.27 (29.60), 0–100	49.00 (11.24), 35.00–60.00	63.04 (31.27), 5.00–100	63.97 (22.47), 40.00–100
Technical skills	57.51 (28.74), 8.33–100	75.00 (13.94), 66.67–100	54.38 (38.75), 0–100	88.33 (17.45), 60.00–100
Emotional needs	50.83 (29.47), 0–93.75	41.46 (31.05), 0–87.50	51.56 (40.35), 0–100	63.75 (21.07), 40.00–100
Overall satisfaction	79.22 (33.09), 0–100	87.50 (26.46), 58.33–100	83.33 (27.22), 25.00–100	89.29 (10.67), 60.49–100

Table 4. Statistical values of group comparisons in all the different dimensions of the Family Impact and Healthcare Satisfaction modules. Two-way ANOVAs, with PAIN (children with pain vs. children without pain) and SPEECH (children with speech ability vs. children without speech ability) as between-subject factors. * $p < 0.05$, ** $p < 0.01$.

	Main Effect PAIN	Main Effect SPEECH	Interaction PAIN × SPEECH
Family Impact Module			
Global scores			
Total impact	F = 1.39, p = 0.247	F = 0.10, p = 0.752	F = 1.107, p = 0.301
Parent health-related quality of life summary	F = 0.70, p = 0.408	F = 0.85, p = 0.363	F = 2.75, p = 0.108
Family functioning summary	F = 0.49, p = 0.488	F = 0.26, p = 0.613	F = 0.75, p = 0.392
Dimensions			
Physical functioning	F = 0.04, p = 0.838	F = 0.36, p = 0.555	F = 5.04, p = 0.031 *
Emotional functioning	F = 0.21, p = 0.653	F = 1.06, p = 0.311	F = 1.59, p = 0.215
Social functioning	F = 0.50, p = 0.486	F = 0.29, p = 0.865	F = 4.38, p = 0.044 *
Cognitive functioning	F = 1.43, p = 0.241	F = 0.19, p = 0.665	F = 0.47, p = 0.499
Communication	F = 1.12, p = 0.298	F = 0.62, p = 0.437	F = 1.66, p = 0.207
Worry	F = 0.24, p = 0.629	F = 0.89, p = 0.768	F = 0.89, p = 0.768
Daily activities	F = 0.65, p = 0.425	F = 0.79, p = 0.379	F = 1.89, p = 0.178
Family relationships	F = 0.24, p = 0.629	F = 1.46, p = 0.235	F = 0.15, p = 0.703
Healthcare Satisfaction Generic Module			
Global score	F = 0.96, p = 0.335	F = 0.88, p = 0.354	F = 1.73, p = 0.197
Information	F = 1.14, p = 0.294	F = 0.24, p = 0.629	F = 0.20, p = 0.657
Inclusion of family	F = 2.50, p = 0.123	F = 0.38, p = 0.540	F = 8.24, p = 0.007 **
Communication	F = 0.62, p = 0.437	F = 0.31, p = 0.482	F = 0.66, p = 0.423
Technical skills	F = 0.27, p = 0.609	F = 6.80, p = 0.014 *	F = 0.70, p = 0.410
Emotional needs	F = 1.06, p = 0.312	F = 0.16, p = 0.901	F = 0.93, p = 0.343
Overall satisfaction	F = 0.89, p = 0.768	F = 0.32, p = 0.478	F = 0.14, p = 0.907

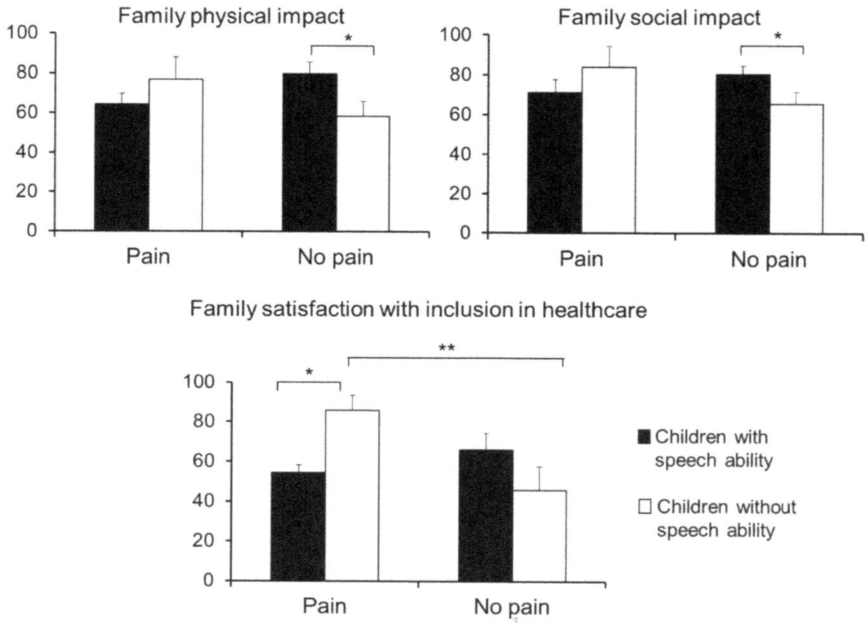

Figure 1. Mean and standard errors of the four groups of children in the significant dimensions of the Family Impact and Healthcare Satisfaction modules. * $p < 0.05$, ** $p < 0.01$.

In addition, the number of pain locations correlated negatively with scores in the *worry* dimension of the family impact (r = −0.37, $p = 0.033$), indicating increased parents' worry (lower functioning) when the number of painful body locations increased. The worst pain during the week correlated with the *communication* dimension (r = 0.515, $p = 0.029$), revealing lower impact in family communication with higher intensity of the child's pain.

In the Healthcare Satisfaction Module questionnaire, the MANOVA revealed a main effect due to DIMENSION (F (5,27) = 6.17, $p < 0.001$), indicating that scores in the different subscales were significantly different. In order to further explore differences due to PAIN and SPEECH, separate ANOVAs were performed on the scores of these subscales (Table 4). In the *technical skills* dimension, a significant main effect due to SPEECH (F (1,36) = 6.80, $p = 0.014$) revealed higher satisfaction in parents of children without speech ability compared with parents of children with verbal speech. In the *inclusion of family* dimension, a significant interaction PAIN × SPEECH (F (1,37) = 8.24, $p = 0.007$) indicated that (1) parents of children without speech ability reported higher satisfaction when children report chronic pain than when they report no pain ($p = 0.009$), whereas no differences were observed in children with verbal speech ability ($p = 0.293$); and (2) parents of children with pain reported higher satisfaction when children did not have speech ability than when they have speech ability ($p = 0.021$), whereas no differences were found in children without chronic pain ($p = 0.113$) (Figure 1). There were no other significant ANOVA effects or significant correlations regarding parents' healthcare satisfaction.

4. Discussion

The objective of the present study was to explore the mutual influence of children's pain and speech ability on parental perception about the family impact and healthcare satisfaction in children with cerebral palsy. Our findings point to a slight impact of pain on family functioning. Only a few dimensions, such as *physical functioning, social functioning* and *worry,* seem to be affected by the presence of pain, which modulates the least perceived impact when the child has verbal speech. Parental satisfaction with healthcare was barely affected by pain or the lack of speech, increasing both the parental satisfaction with professional technical skills and inclusion in the plan of care.

Pain affected physical and social family functioning and the number of pain locations impacted on parental worrying. Pain has been reported to be a factor that increases the demand for care also in other chronic paediatric pathologies such as osteogenesis imperfecta [38]. Other studies have reported a good parental understanding of children's expressions of pain, even when they cannot communicate verbally [32,39]. In the present study, we observed that families of children with chronic pain (with and without speech abilities) reported equal impact on physical and social health. A periodic evaluation of the physical, social and psychological status of the parents should be included in the protocols of the family-centred care models for children with CP in order to detect the specific areas (e.g., worry about child's pain) that deserve specific attention [10,16,23]. In this sense, some experiences, such as web-based intervention programs that provide training in daily care to mothers of children with CP or home-based programs that use augmentative and alternative communication, have proven to improve the experience of care and quality of life of the caregiver [40,41]. Interestingly, the greater intensity of the children's pain produced a lesser impact on family communication. Other studies with challenging situations, such as chronic life-threatening illnesses, have shown that parents concentrate on solution-focused communication, deferring potentially distressing discussions [42]. Thus, it seems that the presence of pain can help to promote pragmatic communication among family members to solve critical problems.

Inclusion in healthcare decisions, encompassing all phases of assessment, intervention and evaluation, is a critical determinant of high-quality care for parents and chronically ill children [43,44]. Families understand inclusion as the ability to communicate, understand the care plan and participate with the health team in decision-making [45]. Another factor that promotes family satisfaction with healthcare is professional competence [46], which is defined in a complex way and encompasses the attributes of emotional and communication skills (providing empathy for child/family, explaining procedures, answering questions) [47–49]. By contrast, misunderstanding of the problem or differences in intervention priorities negatively affect the parent-professional relationship [25,50]. Challenging situations, such as a lack of verbal speech or pain, require focusing on the problem, and require health professionals to improve their competences, reinforcing parental satisfaction with healthcare.

Limitations. The questionnaires were answered by one of the parents (mostly the mother), even in divorced families. Therefore, the perception of the other partner may differ. Our sample was small and biased toward participants with high motor difficulties (76.3% of the sample had GMFCS levels from 3 to 5), since most of the participants were identified at specialized centres for children with cerebral palsy (80% of the families). Similarly, our prevalence of pain and speech disability was slightly higher than that reported by other studies [51,52], probably due to the overrepresentation of children with greater impairments. These facts do not reflect the general distribution in the CP population, and the generalizability of the findings should be limited to children with the most severe impairments.

In conclusion, pain and, to a lesser extent, the ability to speak in children with CP can have an impact on the physical, social and psychological health of their families, although it does not seem to affect healthcare satisfaction. Periodic assessment and intervention of the family's health and needs should be considered in the design of family-centred programs for children with CP.

Supplementary Materials: The following are available online at https://www.mdpi.com/2227-9067/8/2/87/s1, Table S1: Interview questions.

Author Contributions: Conceptualization, I.R. and P.M.; methodology, I.R.; formal analysis, I.R.; investigation, I.R.; resources, P.M.; writing—original draft preparation, I.R.; writing—review and editing, I.R., Á.S.-G. and P.M.; visualization, I.R. and Á.S.-G.; supervision, P.M.; project administration, P.M.; funding acquisition, P.M. All authors have read and agreed to the published version of the manuscript.

Funding: This research was funded by Spanish Ministry of Economy and Competitiveness and European Regional Development Funds, grant number #PSI2017-88388-C4-1-R.

Institutional Review Board Statement: The study was conducted according to the guidelines of the Declaration of Helsinki, and approved by the Ethics Committee of the Regional Government of the Balearic Islands (protocole code: IB3156/16 PI, approved on 24 February 2016).

Informed Consent Statement: Informed consent was obtained from all subjects involved in the study.

Data Availability Statement: The data presented in this study are available on request from the corresponding author.

Conflicts of Interest: The authors declare no conflict of interest. The funders had no role in the design of the study; in the collection, analyses, or interpretation of data; in the writing of the manuscript, or in the decision to publish the results.

References

1. Schaible, B.; Colquitt, G.; Caciula, M.C.; Carnes, A.; Li, L.; Moreau, N. Comparing impact on the family and insurance coverage in children with cerebral palsy and children with another special healthcare need. *Child Care Health Dev.* **2018**, *44*, 370–377. [CrossRef] [PubMed]
2. Tonmukayakul, U.; Shih, S.T.F.; Bourke-Taylor, H.; Imms, C.; Reddihough, D.; Cox, L.; Carter, R. Systematic review of the economic impact of cerebral palsy. *Res. Dev. Disabil.* **2018**, *80*, 93–101. [CrossRef] [PubMed]
3. Guyard, A.; Fauconnier, J.; Mermet, M.A.; Cans, C. Impact on parents of cerebral palsy in children: A literature review. *Arch. Pediatr.* **2011**, *18*, 204–214. [CrossRef] [PubMed]
4. Majnemer, A.; Shevell, M.; Law, M.; Poulin, C.; Rosenbaum, P. Indicators of distress in families of children with cerebral palsy. *Disabil. Rehabil.* **2012**, *34*, 1202–1207. [CrossRef] [PubMed]
5. Tsibidaki, A.; Tsibidakis, H.; Tsamparli, A.; Kotzia, D.; Panou, A. Impact of orthopedic surgery on parents of children affected by cerebral palsy: A preliminary study in Greece. *Folia Med.* **2019**, *61*, 384–388. [CrossRef] [PubMed]
6. Irwin, L.; Jesmont, C.; Basu, A. A systematic review and meta-analysis of the effectiveness of interventions to improve psychological wellbeing in the parents of children with cerebral palsy. *Res. Dev. Disabil.* **2019**, *95*, 103511. [CrossRef]
7. Song, J.; Mailick, M.R.; Greenberg, J.S. Health of parents of individuals with developmental disorders or mental health problems: Impacts of stigma. *Soc. Sci. Med.* **2018**, *217*, 152–158. [CrossRef]
8. Albayrak, I.; Biber, A.; Çalışkan, A.; Levendoglu, F. Assessment of pain, care burden, depression level, sleep quality, fatigue and quality of life in the mothers of children with cerebral palsy. *J. Child Health Care* **2019**, *23*, 483–494. [CrossRef]
9. Wu, J.; Zhang, J.; Hong, Y. Quality of life of primary caregivers of children with cerebral palsy: A comparison between mother and grandmother caregivers in Anhui province of China. *Child Care Health Dev.* **2017**, *43*, 718–724. [CrossRef]
10. Garip, Y.; Ozel, S.; Tuncer, O.B.; Kilinc, G.; Seckin, F.; Arasil, T. Fatigue in the mothers of children with cerebral palsy. *Disabil. Rehabil.* **2017**, *39*, 757–762. [CrossRef]
11. Byrne, M.B.; Hurley, D.A.; Daly, L.; Cunningham, C.G. Health status of caregivers of children with cerebral palsy. *Child Care Health Dev.* **2010**, *36*, 696–702. [CrossRef] [PubMed]
12. Kaya, K.; Unsal-Delialioglu, S.; Ordu-Gokkaya, N.K.; Ozisler, Z.; Ergun, N.; Ozel, S.; Ucan, H. Musculo-skeletal pain, quality of life and depression in mothers of children with cerebral palsy. *Disabil. Rehabil.* **2010**, *32*, 1666–1672. [CrossRef] [PubMed]
13. Lowes, L.; Clark, T.S.; Noritz, G. Factors associated with caregiver experience in families with a child with cerebral palsy. *J. Pediatr. Rehabil. Med.* **2016**, *9*, 65–72. [CrossRef] [PubMed]
14. Prudente, C.O.; Barbosa, M.A.; Porto, C.C. Relation between quality of life of mothers of children with cerebral palsy and the children's motor functioning, after ten months of rehabilitation. *Rev. Lat. Am. Enfermagem.* **2010**, *18*, 149–155. [CrossRef]
15. Gardiner, E.; Miller, A.R.; Lach, L.M. Family impact of childhood neurodevelopmental disability: Considering adaptive and maladaptive behaviour. *J. Intellect. Disabil. Res.* **2018**, *62*, 888–899. [CrossRef]
16. Svedberg, L.E.; Englund, E.; Malker, H.; Stener-Victorin, E. Comparison of impact on mood, health, and daily living experiences of primary caregivers of walking and non-walking children with cerebral palsy and provided community services support. *Eur. J. Paediatr. Neurol.* **2010**, *14*, 239–246. [CrossRef]
17. Parkes, J.; Caravale, B.; Marcelli, M.; Franco, F.; Colver, A. Parenting stress and children with cerebral palsy: A European cross-sectional survey. *Dev. Med. Child Neurol.* **2011**, *53*, 815–821. [CrossRef] [PubMed]
18. Tedroff, K.; Gyllensvärd, M.; Löwing, K. Prevalence, identification, and interference of pain in young children with cerebral palsy: A population-based study. *Disabil. Rehabil.* **2019**, *17*, 1–7. [CrossRef] [PubMed]
19. Riquelme, I.; Cifre, I.; Montoya, P. Age-related changes of pain experience in cerebral palsy and healthy individuals. *Pain Med.* **2011**, *12*, 535–545. [CrossRef]
20. Rapp, M.; Eisemann, N.; Arnaud, C.; Ehlinger, V.; Fauconnier, J.; Marcelli, M.; Michelsen, S.I.; Nystrand, M.; Colver, A.; Thyen, U. Predictors of parent-reported quality of life of adolescents with cerebral palsy: A longitudinal study. *Res. Dev. Disabil.* **2017**, *62*, 259–270. [CrossRef]

21. Yamaguchi, R.; Nicholson Perry, K.; Hines, M. Pain, pain anxiety and emotional and behavioural problems in children with cerebral palsy. *Disabil. Rehabil.* **2014**, *36*, 125–130. [CrossRef] [PubMed]
22. Ramstad, K.; Jahnsen, R.; Skjeldal, O.H.; Diseth, T.H. Parent-reported participation in children with cerebral palsy: The contribution of recurrent musculoskeletal pain and child mental health problems. *Dev. Med. Child Neurol.* **2012**, *54*, 829–835. [CrossRef] [PubMed]
23. Davis, E.; Mackinnon, A.; Waters, E. Parent proxy-reported quality of life for children with cerebral palsy: Is it related to parental psychosocial distress? *Child Care Health Dev.* **2012**, *38*, 553–560. [CrossRef]
24. Wray, J.; Edwards, V.; Wyatt, K.; Maddick, A.; Logan, S.; Franck, L. Parents' attitudes toward the use of complementary therapy by their children with moderate or severe cerebral palsy. *J. Altern. Complement. Med.* **2014**, *20*, 130–135. [CrossRef] [PubMed]
25. Park, M.S.; Chung, C.Y.; Lee, K.M.; Lee, S.H.; Choi, I.H.; Cho, T.J.; Yoo, W.J.; Kim, K.H. Issues of concern before single event multilevel surgery in patients with cerebral palsy. *J. Pediatr. Orthop.* **2010**, *30*, 489–495. [CrossRef] [PubMed]
26. Vargus-Adams, J.N.; Martin, L.K. Domains of importance for parents, medical professionals and youth with cerebral palsy considering treatment outcomes. *Child Care Health Dev.* **2011**, *37*, 276–281. [CrossRef] [PubMed]
27. Capjon, H.; Bjørk, I.T Rehabilitation after multilevel surgery in ambulant spastic children with cerebral palsy: Children and parent experiences. *Dev. Neurorehabil.* **2010**, *13*, 182–191. [CrossRef] [PubMed]
28. Cornec, G.; Drewnowski, G.; Desguerre, I.; Toullet, P.; Boivin, J.; Bodoria, M.; De La Cruz, J.; Brochard, S.; ESPaCe Group. Determinants of satisfaction with motor rehabilitation in people with cerebral palsy: A national survey in France (ESPaCe). *Ann. Phys. Rehabil. Med.* **2019**, *S1877-0657*, 30143–30145. [CrossRef]
29. Yilmaz, H.; Erkin, G.; Nalbant, L. Depression and anxiety levels in mothers of children with cerebral palsy: A controlled study. *Eur. J. Phys. Rehabil. Med.* **2013**, *49*, 823–827.
30. Iversen, A.S.; Graue, M.; Råheim, M. At the edge of vulnerability—Lived experience of parents of children with cerebral palsy going through surgery. *Int. J. Qual. Stud. Health Wellbeing* **2013**, *8*, 1–10. [CrossRef] [PubMed]
31. Elema, A.; Zalmstra, T.A.; Boonstra, A.M.; Narayanan, U.G.; Reinders-Messelink, H.A.; Putten, A.A. Pain and hospital admissions are important factors associated with quality of life in nonambulatory children. *Acta Paediatr.* **2016**, *105*, e419–e425. [CrossRef]
32. Riquelme, I.; Pades Jiménez, A.; Montoya, P. Parents and physiotherapists recognition of non-verbal communication of pain in individuals with cerebral palsy. *Health Commun.* **2018**, *33*, 1448–1453. [CrossRef] [PubMed]
33. Hadden, K.L.; Von Baeyer, C.L. Pain in children with cerebral palsy: Common triggers and expressive behaviors. *Pain* **2002**, *99*, 281–288. [CrossRef]
34. Barney, C.C.; Krach, L.E.; Rivard, P.F.; Belew, J.L.; Symons, F.J. Motor function predicts parent-reported musculoskeletal pain in children with cerebral palsy. *Pain Res. Manag.* **2013**, *18*, 323–327. [CrossRef] [PubMed]
35. Palisano, R.J.; Rosenbaum, P.; Bartlett, D.; Livingston, M.H. Content validity of the expanded and revised Gross Motor Function Classification System. *Dev. Med. Child Neurol.* **2008**, *50*, 744–750. [CrossRef] [PubMed]
36. Varni, J.W.; Burwinkle, T.M.; Seid, M. The PedsQL as a pediatric patient-reported outcome: Reliability and validity of the PedsQL measurement model in 25,000 children. *Expert Rev. Pharma. Outcomes Res.* **2005**, *5*, 705–719. [CrossRef]
37. Varni, J.W.; Seid, M.; Rode, C.A. The PedsQL (TM): Measurement model for the pediatric quality of life inventory. *Med. Care* **1999**, *37*, 126–139. [CrossRef]
38. Castro, A.R.; Marinello, J.; Chougui, K.; Morand, M.; Bilodeau, C.; Tsimicalis, A. The day-to-day experiences of caring for children with Osteogenesis Imperfecta: A qualitative descriptive study. *J. Clin. Nurs.* **2020**, *29*, 2999–3011. [CrossRef]
39. Carter, B.; Arnott, J.; Simons, J.; Bray, L. Developing a sense of knowing and acquiring the skills to manage pain in children with profound cognitive impairments: Mothers' perspectives. *Pain Res. Manag.* **2017**, *2017*, 2514920. [CrossRef]
40. Nobakht, Z.; Rassafiani, M.; Hosseini, S.A.; Hosseinzadeh, S. A web-based daily care training to improve the quality of life of mothers of children with cerebral palsy: A randomized controlled trial. *Res. Dev. Disabil.* **2020**, *105*, 103731. [CrossRef]
41. Gona, J.K.; Newton, C.R.; Hartley, S.; Bunning, K. A home-based intervention using augmentative and alternative communication (AAC) techniques in rural Kenya: What are the caregivers' experiences? *Child Care Health Dev.* **2014**, *40*, 29–41. [CrossRef] [PubMed]
42. Ho, A.H.Y.; Dutta, O.; Tan-Ho, G.; Choo, P.Y.; Low, X.C.; Chong, P.H.; Ng, C.; Ganapathy, S. Thematic analysis of spousal interaction patterns among Asian parents of children with chronic life-threatening illness. *BMJ Open* **2019**, *9*, e032582. [CrossRef] [PubMed]
43. Wood, D.; Geoghegan, S.; Ramnarayan, P.; Davis, P.J.; Pappachan, J.V.; Goodwin, S.; Wray, J. Eliciting the experiences of the adolescent-parent dyad following critical care admission: A pilot study. *Eur. J. Pediatr.* **2018**, *177*, 747–752. [CrossRef] [PubMed]
44. Hendriks, A.H.; De Moor, J.M.; Savelberg, M.M.; Oud, J.H. The rehabilitation process of children with motor disabilities in the Dutch therapeutic toddler class: Main phases and parent involvement. *Int J. Rehabil. Res.* **2001**, *24*, 115–122. [CrossRef] [PubMed]
45. Latta, L.C.; Dick, R.; Parry, C.; Tamura, G.S. Parental responses to involvement in rounds on a pediatric inpatient unit at a teaching hospital: A qualitative study. *Acad. Med.* **2008**, *83*, 292–297. [CrossRef] [PubMed]
46. Peeler, A.; Fulbrook, P.; Edward, K.L.; Kinnear, F.B. Parents' experiences of care in a paediatric emergency department: A phenomenological inquiry. *Australas. Emerg. Care* **2019**, *22*, 113–118. [CrossRef]
47. Rezaie, L.; Kendi, S. Exploration of the influential factors on adherence to occupational therapy in parents of children with cerebral palsy: A qualitative study. *Patient Prefer. Adherence* **2020**, *14*, 63–72. [CrossRef]

48. Taghizadeh, N.; Heard, G.; Davidson, A.; Williams, K.; Story, D. The experiences of children with autism spectrum disorder, their caregivers and health care providers during day procedure: A mixed methods study. *Paediatr. Anaesth.* **2019**, *29*, 927–937. [CrossRef]
49. Espinel, A.G.; Shah, R.K.; Beach, M.C.; Boss, E.F. What parents say about their child's surgeon: Parent-reported experiences with pediatric surgical physicians. *JAMA Otolaryngol. Head Neck Surg.* **2014**, *140*, 397–402. [CrossRef]
50. Morrow, A.M.; Quine, S.; Loughlin, E.V.; Craig, J.C. Different priorities: A comparison of parents' and health professionals' perceptions of quality of life in quadriplegic cerebral palsy. *Arch. Dis. Child* **2008**, *93*, 119–125. [CrossRef]
51. Ostojic, K.; Paget, S.; Kyriagis, M.; Morrow, A. Acute and chronic pain in children and adolescents with cerebral palsy: Prevalence, interference, and management. *Arch. Phys. Med. Rehabil.* **2020**, *101*, 213–219. [CrossRef] [PubMed]
52. Kristoffersson, E.; Dahlgren Sandberg, A.; Holck, P. Communication ability and communication methods in children with cerebral palsy. *Dev. Med. Child Neurol.* **2020**, *62*, 933–938. [CrossRef] [PubMed]

MDPI
St. Alban-Anlage 66
4052 Basel
Switzerland
Tel. +41 61 683 77 34
Fax +41 61 302 89 18
www.mdpi.com

Children Editorial Office
E-mail: children@mdpi.com
www.mdpi.com/journal/children

www.ingramcontent.com/pod-product-compliance
Lightning Source LLC
Chambersburg PA
CBHW040750250926
51850CB00007BB/1459
9783036543925